Cactus's Secret

2 Nana Haruta

Contents

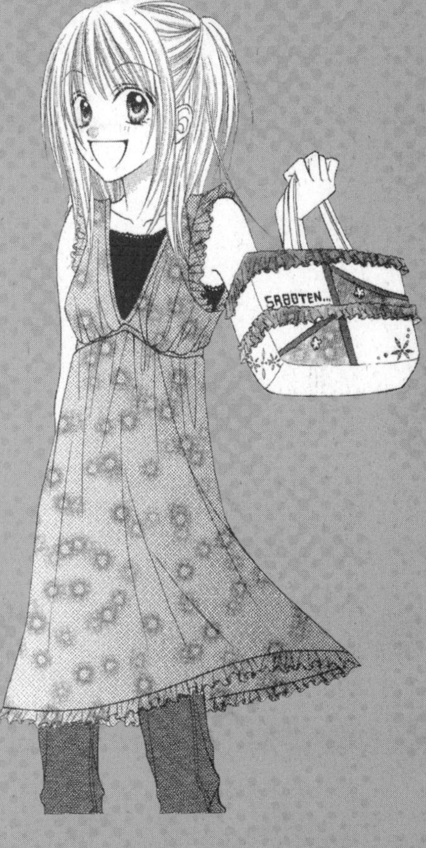
SABOTEN...

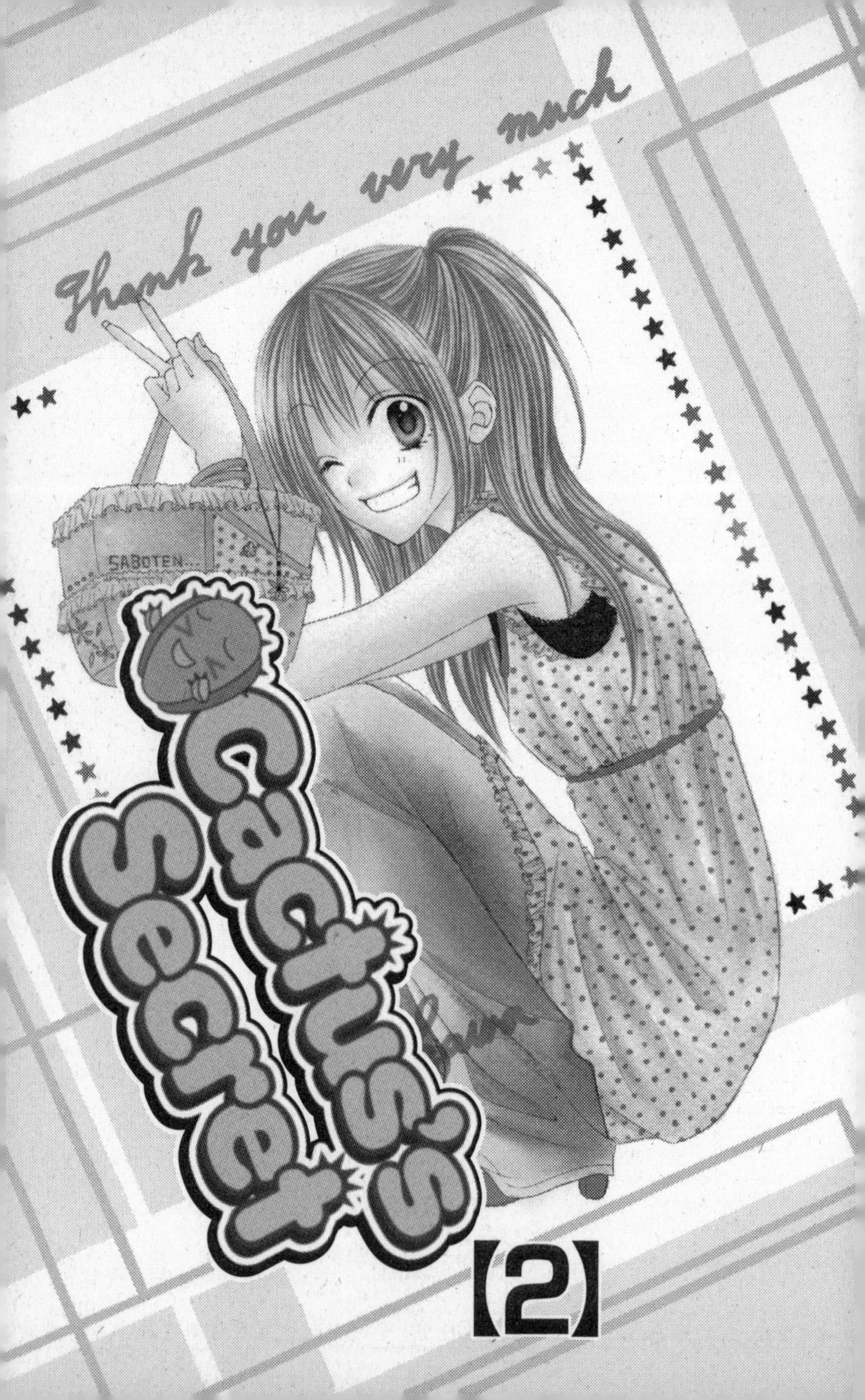
Thank you very much
SABOTEN
Cactus's Secret
2

CAST OF CHARACTERS

Plain Middle Schooler Miku

Nami Minase
Fujioka's childhood friend. She used to be in love with Fujioka.

Miku Yamada (high schooler, 2nd-year)
She's had a one-sided crush on Fujioka since middle school. She gets annoyed pretty easily, which makes her a "cactus alien"!

Kyohei Fujioka (high schooler, 2nd-year)
Miku's classmate. A former delinquent and completely clueless about love.

Itsuki Natsukawa
The son of the school chairman and the top-ranked student. He's incredibly popular with the girls.

Delinquent (?!) Middle Schooler Fujioka

Cactus's Secret

Miku has had a one-sided crush on Fujioka since middle school. In order to win his affection, Miku strives to improve her appearance and even works up the courage to confess her love. However, just before Miku can confess, the oblivious-about-love Fujioka makes fun of her makeup!

Fed up with Fujioka's ignorance, Miku decides to give him up. But when Miku is about to get yelled at by a teacher, Fujioka steps in and defends her, showing a more dashing side of himself... Reaffirmed that she really does like him, Miku doubles her resolve to win him over.

On Valentine's Day, Miku fails again to make him understand. Mistakenly thinking Miku is in love with someone else, Fujioka won't take her confession to him seriously. Then, when Miku gets upset, Fujioka suddenly turns and leaves without a word... It turns out the cause of his odd reaction lies in a love triangle involving Fujioka, his childhood friend Minase-san and another girl in their class back in middle school.

Miku worries that Fujioka and Minase-san might have feelings for each other. However, Minase-san is now with a different boyfriend and considers the fallout with Fujioka a thing of the past. Relieved at the news, Miku accidentally blurts out to Fujioka that she likes him! Though Fujioka ends up turning her down, she tells him that she's willing to keep trying and won't give up on him yet.

Now, having started a new school year, Miku and Fujioka find themselves in the same class yet again. However, it seems that the school heartthrob, Natsukawa, is interested in Miku...

STORY THUS FAR

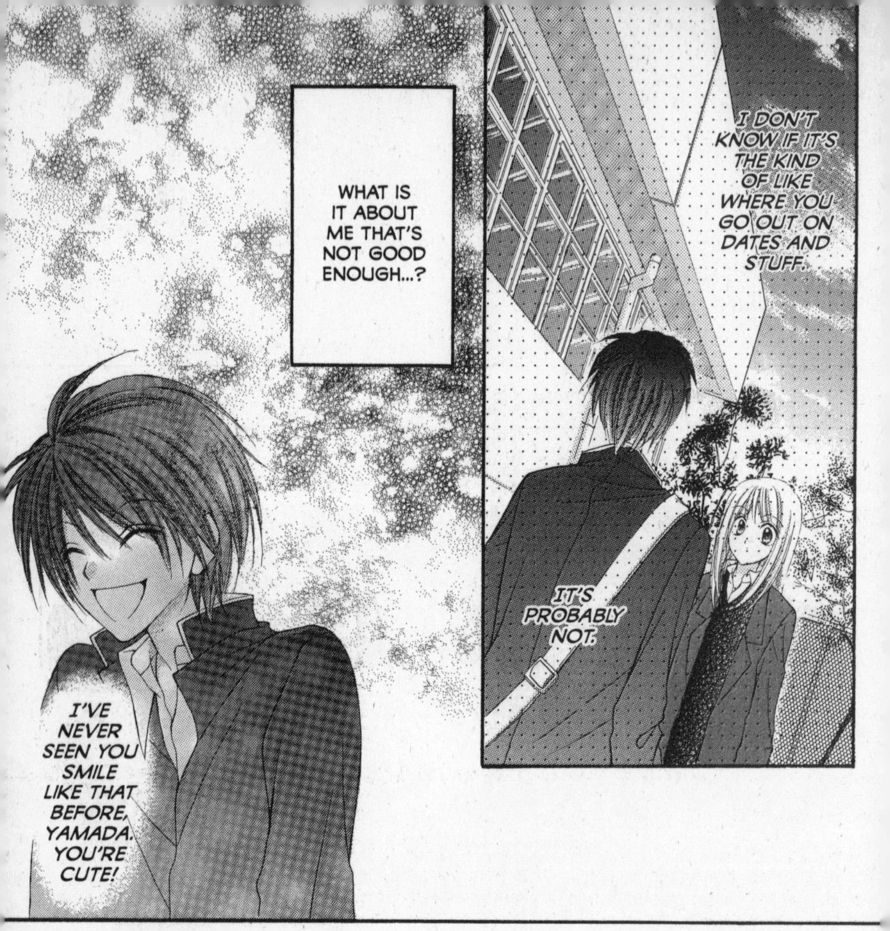
I DON'T KNOW IF IT'S THE KIND OF LIKE WHERE YOU GO OUT ON DATES AND STUFF.
IT'S PROBABLY NOT.
WHAT IS IT ABOUT ME THAT'S NOT GOOD ENOUGH...?
I'VE NEVER SEEN YOU SMILE LIKE THAT BEFORE, YAMADA. YOU'RE CUTE!

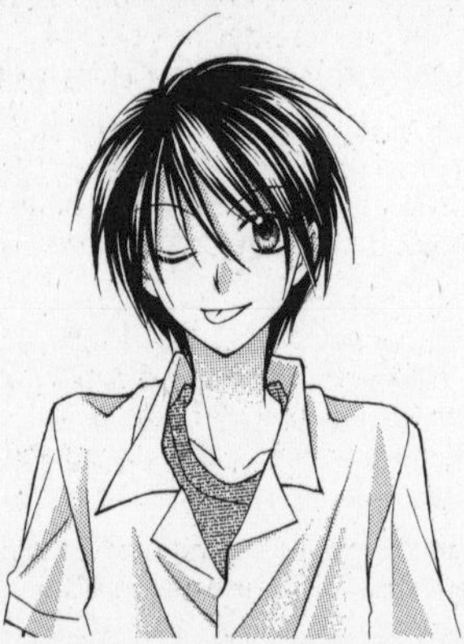

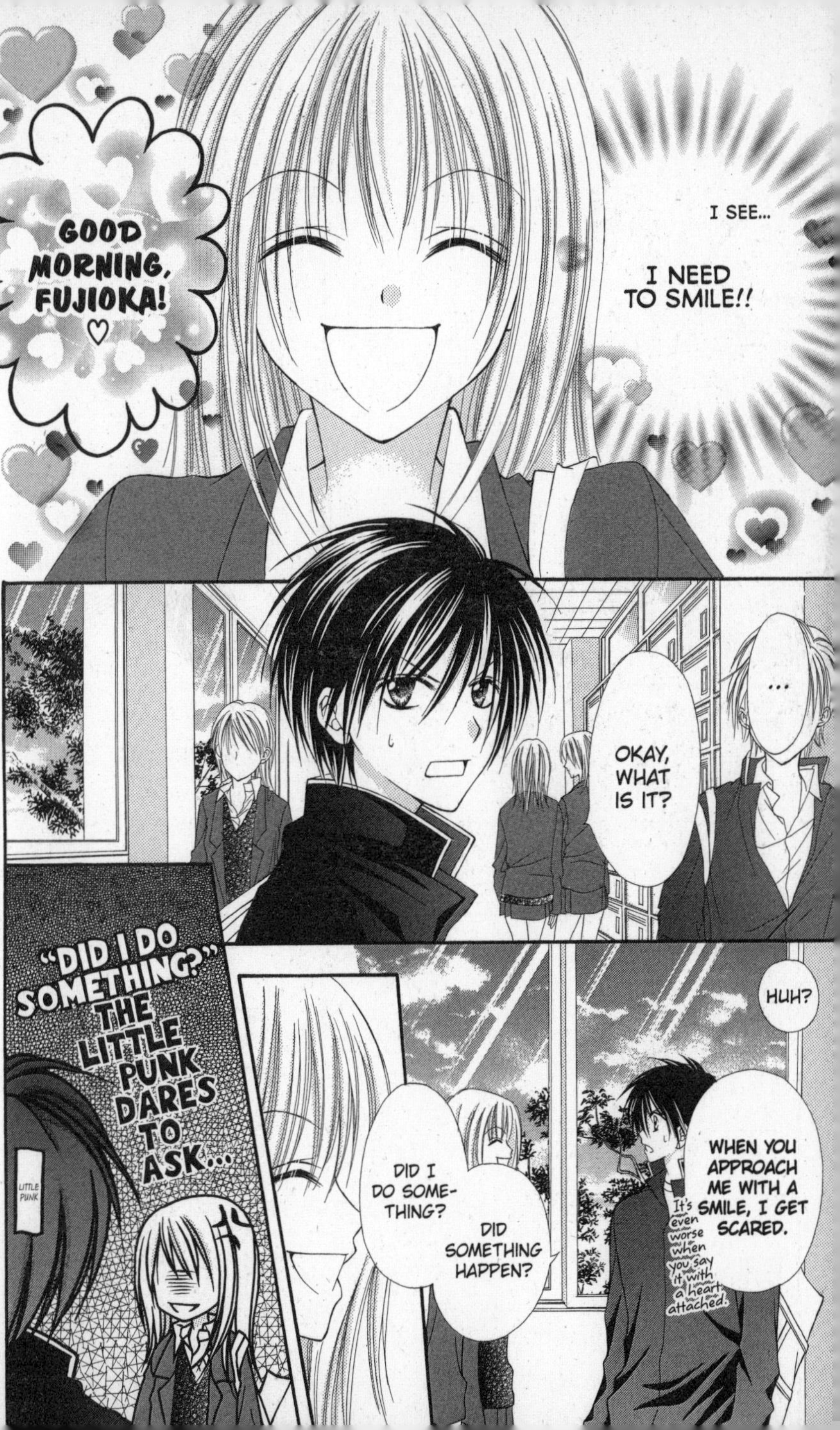
I SEE...
I NEED TO SMILE!!
GOOD MORNING, FUJIOKA! ♡
...
OKAY, WHAT IS IT?
HUH?
WHEN YOU APPROACH ME WITH A SMILE, I GET SCARED.
It's even worse when you say it with a heart attached.
DID I DO SOME-THING?
DID SOMETHING HAPPEN?
"DID I DO SOMETHING?" THE LITTLE PUNK DARES TO ASK...
LITTLE PUNK

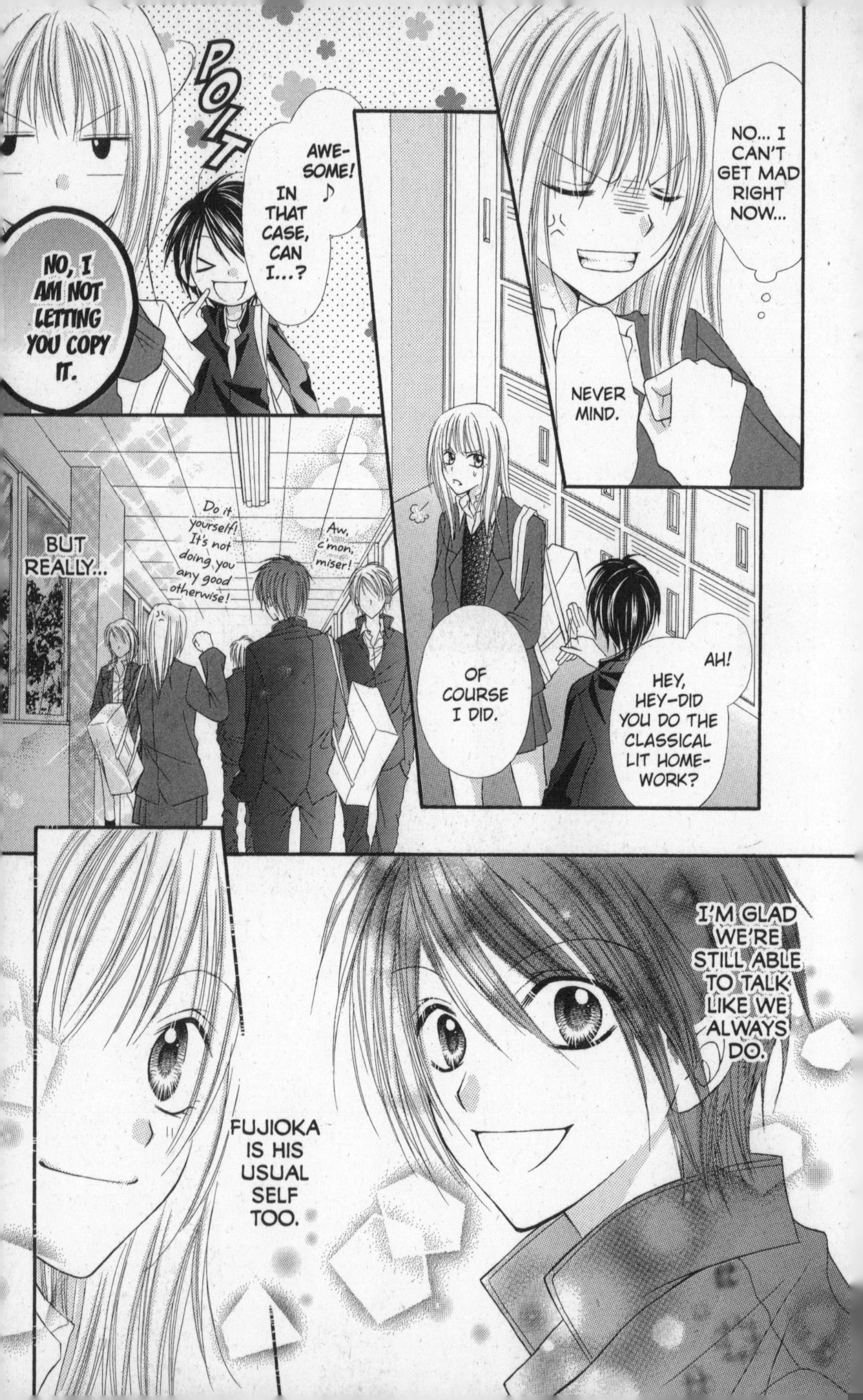
AH!
HEY, HEY—DID YOU DO THE CLASSICAL LIT HOME-WORK?
OF COURSE I DID.
AWE-SOME! ♪
IN THAT CASE, CAN I...?
POIT
NO, I AM NOT LETTING YOU COPY IT.
NO... I CAN'T GET MAD RIGHT NOW...
NEVER MIND.
BUT REALLY...
Aw, c'mon, miser!
Do it yourself! It's not doing you any good otherwise!
I'M GLAD WE'RE STILL ABLE TO TALK LIKE WE ALWAYS DO.
FUJIOKA IS HIS USUAL SELF TOO.

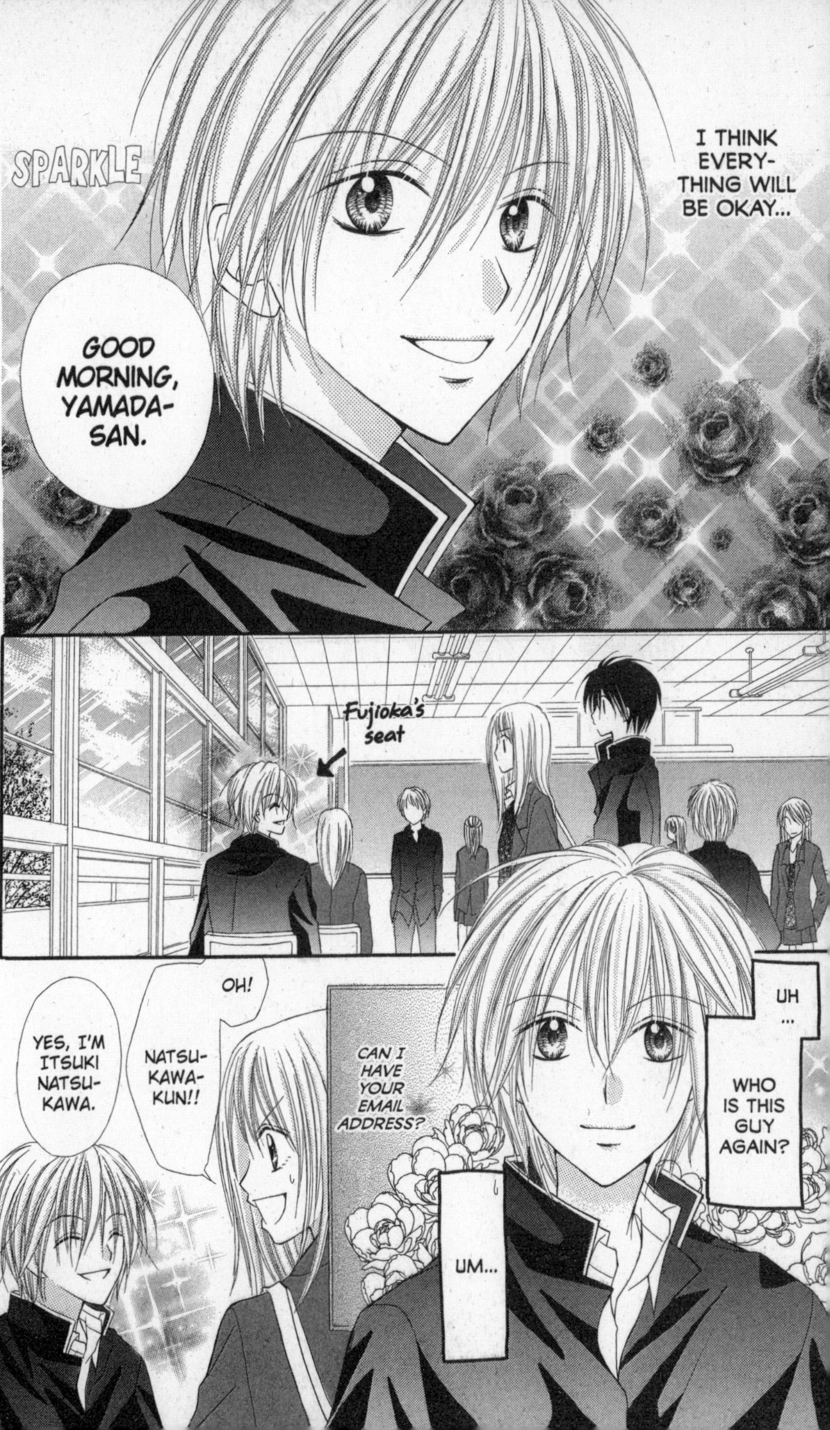
I THINK EVERY-THING WILL BE OKAY...
SPARKLE
GOOD MORNING, YAMADA-SAN.
Fujioka's seat
UH ...
WHO IS THIS GUY AGAIN?
UM...
CAN I HAVE YOUR EMAIL ADDRESS?
OH!
NATSU-KAWA-KUN!!
YES, I'M ITSUKI NATSU-KAWA.

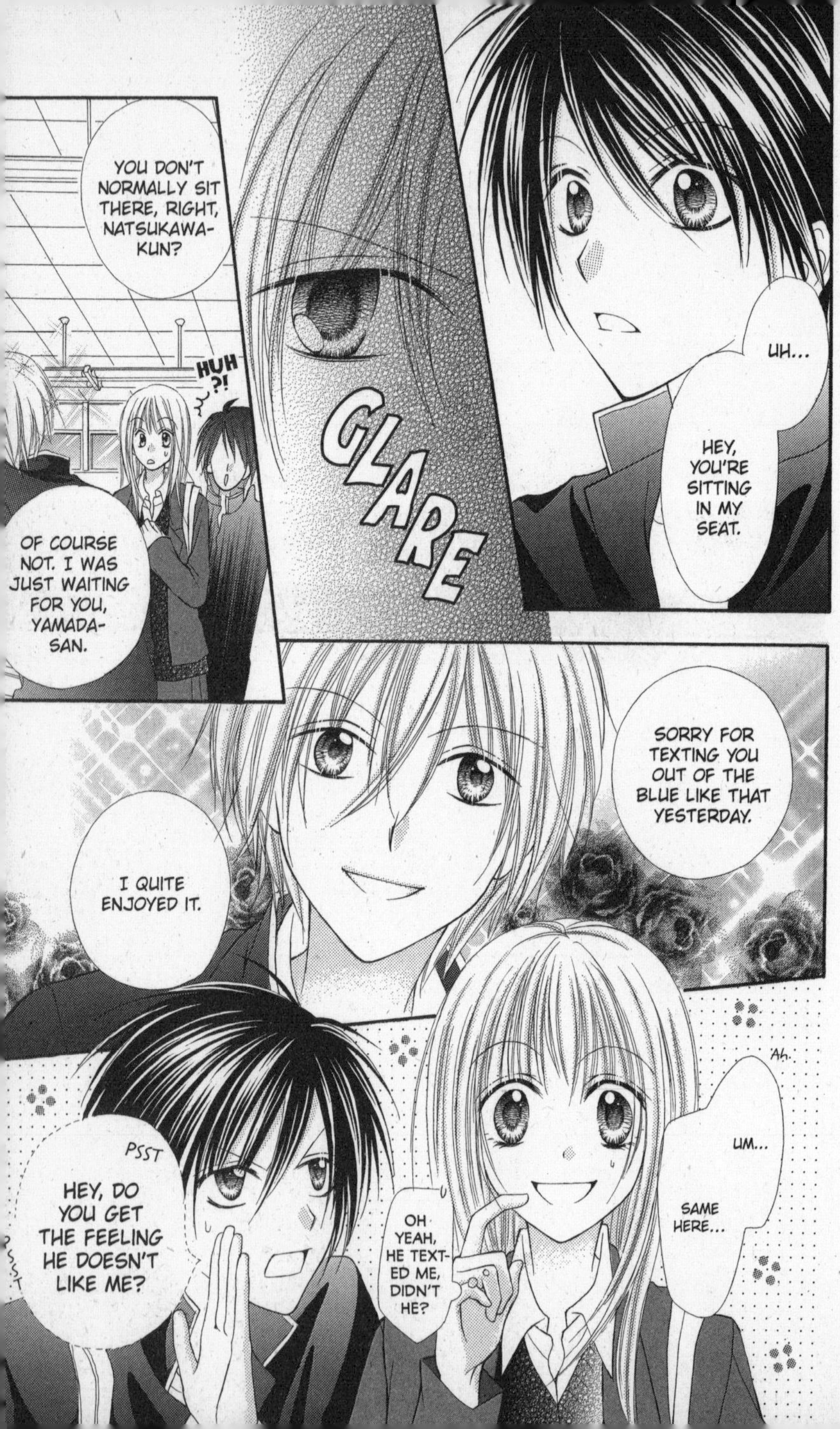
UH...
HEY, YOU'RE SITTING IN MY SEAT.
GLARE
YOU DON'T NORMALLY SIT THERE, RIGHT, NATSUKAWA-KUN?
HUH ?!
OF COURSE NOT. I WAS JUST WAITING FOR YOU, YAMADA-SAN.
SORRY FOR TEXTING YOU OUT OF THE BLUE LIKE THAT YESTERDAY.
I QUITE ENJOYED IT.
Ah.
UM... SAME HERE...
OH YEAH, HE TEXT-ED ME, DIDN'T HE?
PSST
HEY, DO YOU GET THE FEELING HE DOESN'T LIKE ME?
PSST

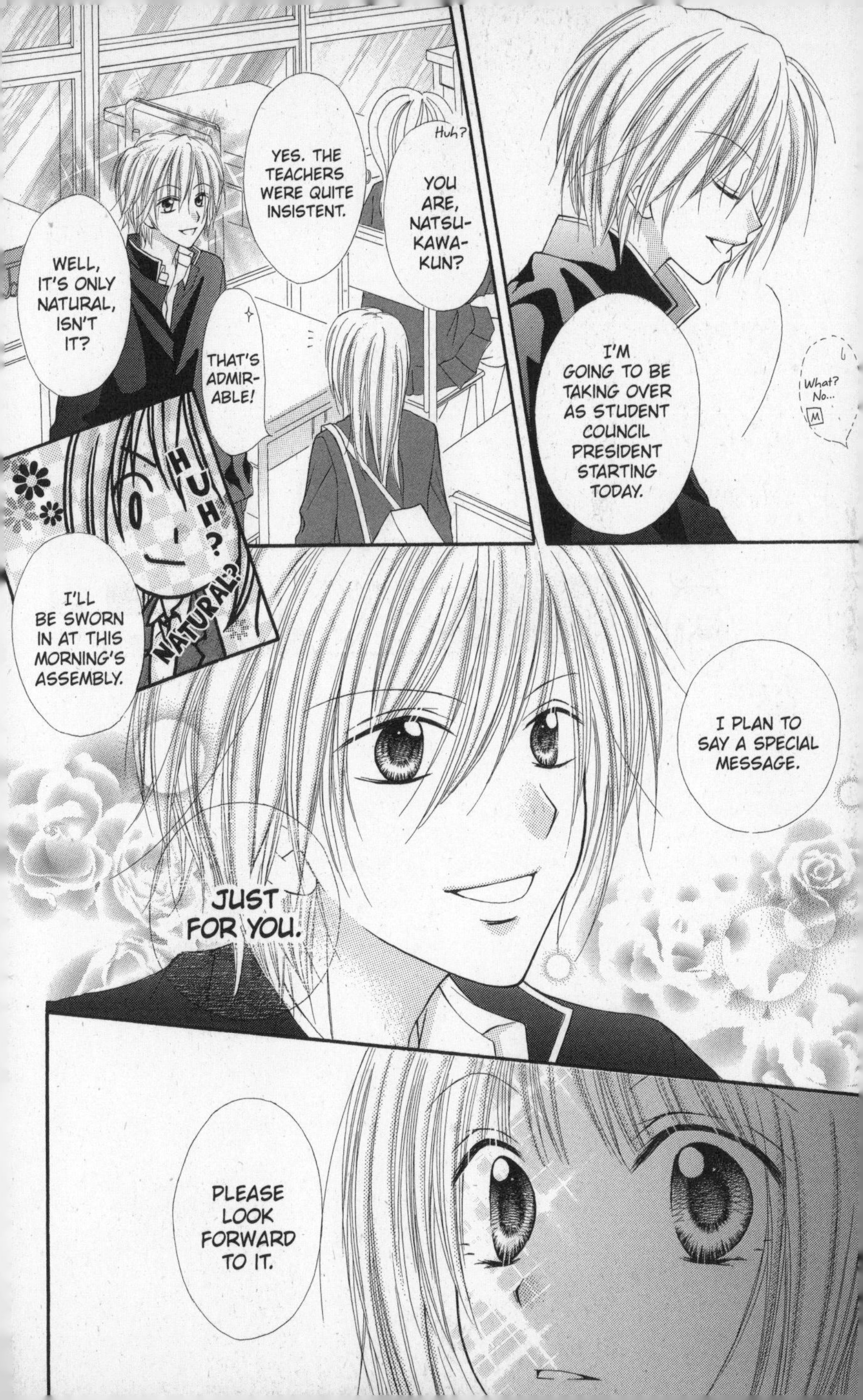
I'M GOING TO BE TAKING OVER AS STUDENT COUNCIL PRESIDENT STARTING TODAY.
What? No...
Huh?
YOU ARE, NATSU-KAWA-KUN?
YES. THE TEACHERS WERE QUITE INSISTENT.
THAT'S ADMIR-ABLE!
WELL, IT'S ONLY NATURAL, ISN'T IT?
HUH? NATURAL?
I'LL BE SWORN IN AT THIS MORNING'S ASSEMBLY.
I PLAN TO SAY A SPECIAL MESSAGE.
JUST FOR YOU.
PLEASE LOOK FORWARD TO IT.

1

Good afternoon!

IT'S CACTUS'S SECRET, VOLUME 2!

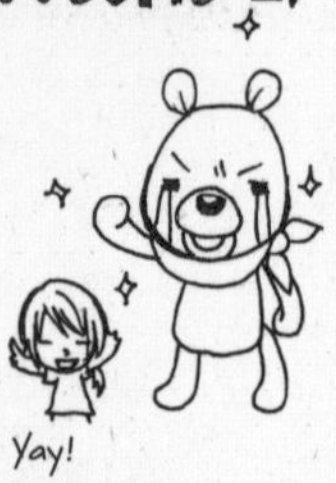
Yay!

Hello. I am Nana Haruta. In a very short time, we already have *Cactus* volume 2 out. It's amazing, isn't it? I nearly didn't make it in time with the last manga. I even ended up drawing some of it while I was on the move, so some of the writing was really messy. My goal this time is to write everything neatly! And without any mistakes! I will give it my all.

Now if despite all that, I still end up with mistakes—what then? I really, really don't have any faith in myself right now!!

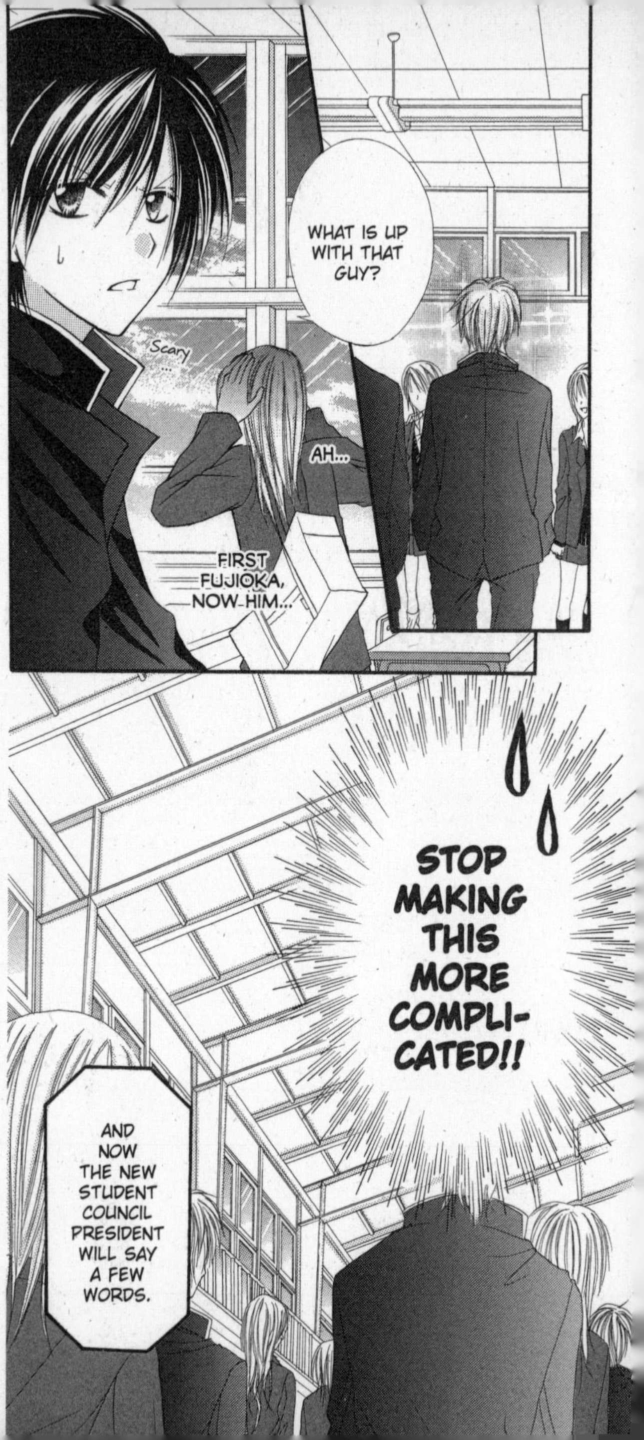
WHAT IS UP WITH THAT GUY?
Scary...
AH...
FIRST FUJIOKA, NOW HIM...
STOP MAKING THIS MORE COMPLICATED!!
AND NOW THE NEW STUDENT COUNCIL PRESIDENT WILL SAY A FEW WORDS.

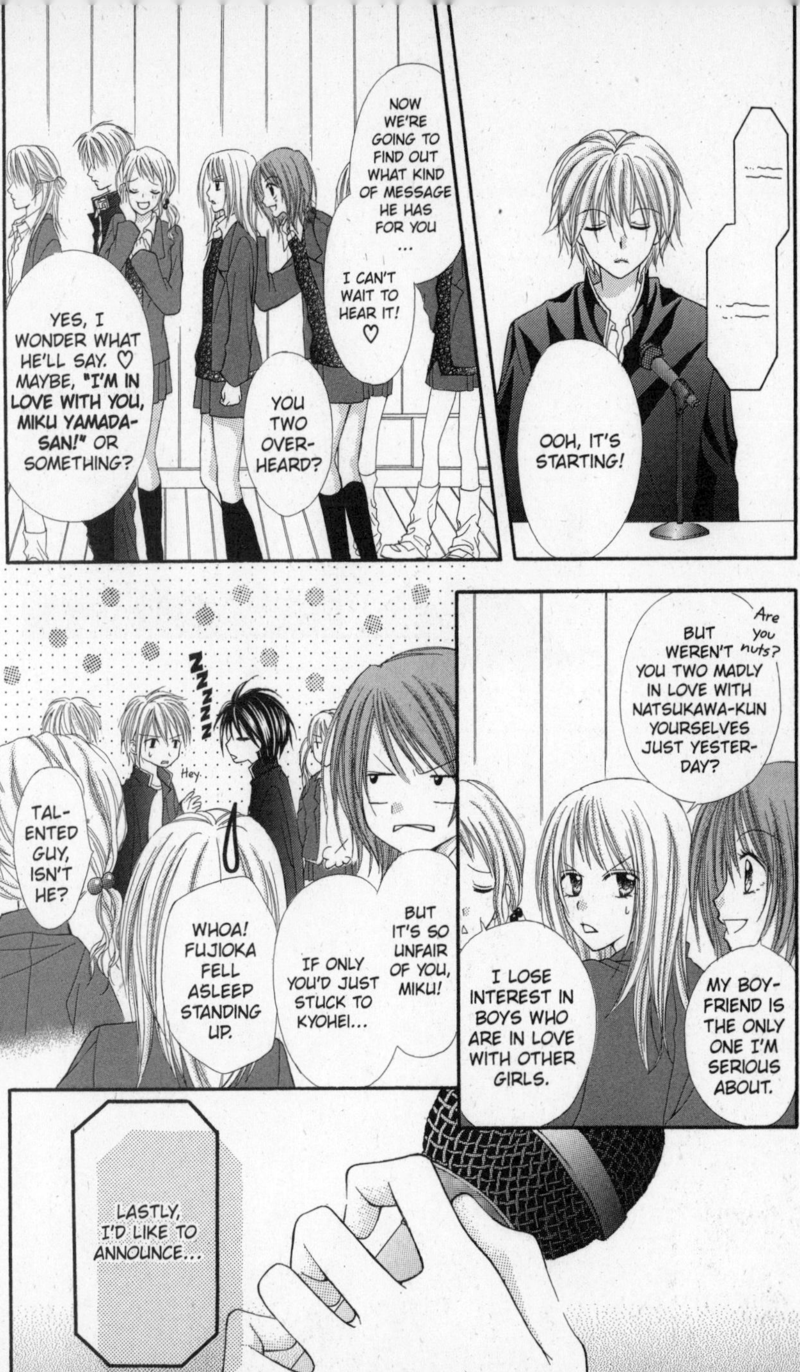
OOH, IT'S STARTING!
NOW WE'RE GOING TO FIND OUT WHAT KIND OF MESSAGE HE HAS FOR YOU... I CAN'T WAIT TO HEAR IT! ♡
YOU TWO OVER-HEARD?
YES, I WONDER WHAT HE'LL SAY. ♡ MAYBE, "I'M IN LOVE WITH YOU, MIKU YAMADA-SAN!" OR SOMETHING?
Are you nuts?
BUT WEREN'T YOU TWO MADLY IN LOVE WITH NATSUKAWA-KUN YOURSELVES JUST YESTER-DAY?
MY BOY-FRIEND IS THE ONLY ONE I'M SERIOUS ABOUT.
I LOSE INTEREST IN BOYS WHO ARE IN LOVE WITH OTHER GIRLS.
BUT IT'S SO UNFAIR OF YOU, MIKU!
IF ONLY YOU'D JUST STUCK TO KYOHEI...
ZZZZZ
Hey.
TAL-ENTED GUY, ISN'T HE?
WHOA! FUJIOKA FELL ASLEEP STANDING UP.
LASTLY, I'D LIKE TO ANNOUNCE...

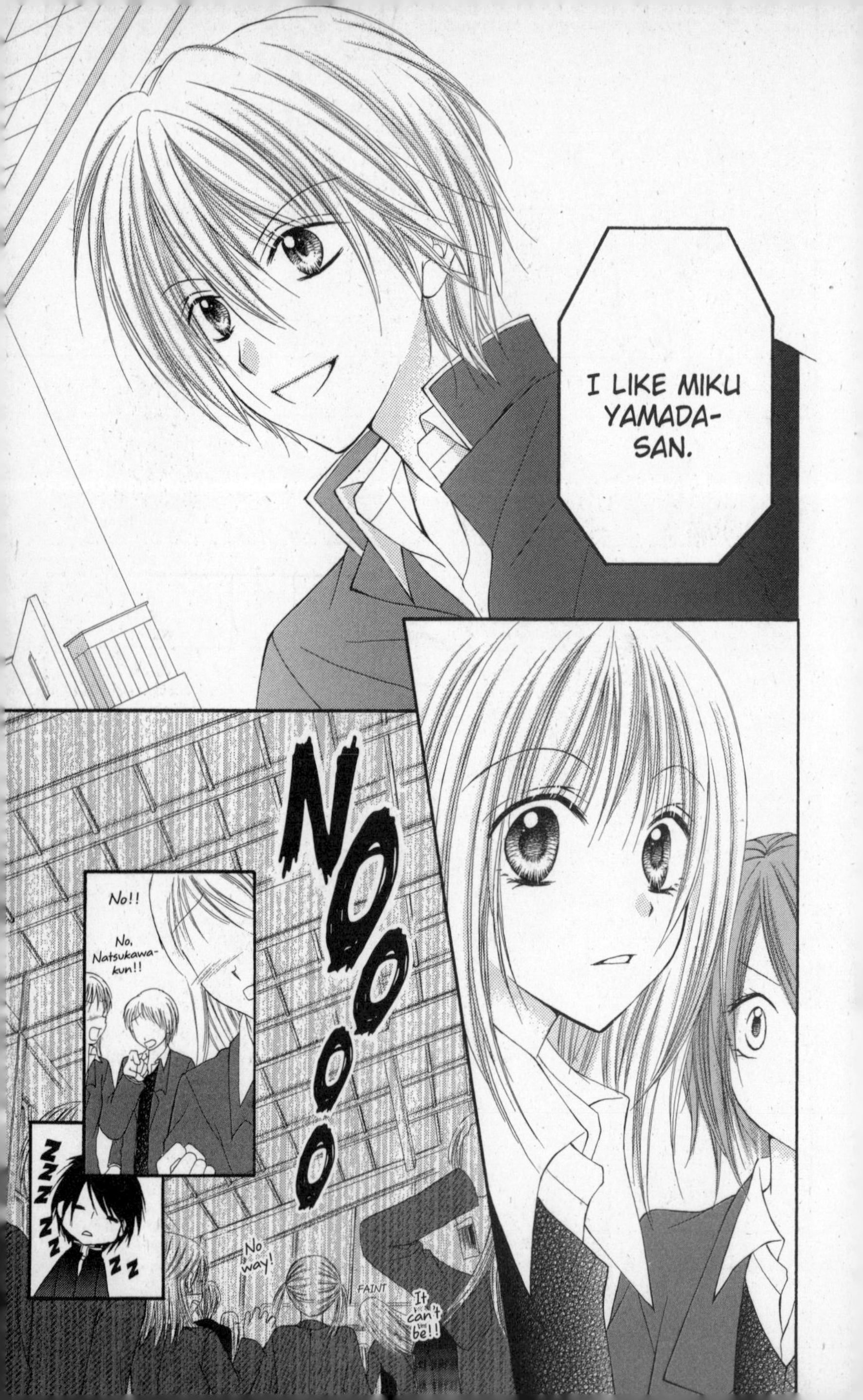
I LIKE MIKU YAMADA-SAN.
NOOOOOO
No!!
No, Natsukawa-kun!!
ZZZZZ
No way!
FAINT
It can't be!!

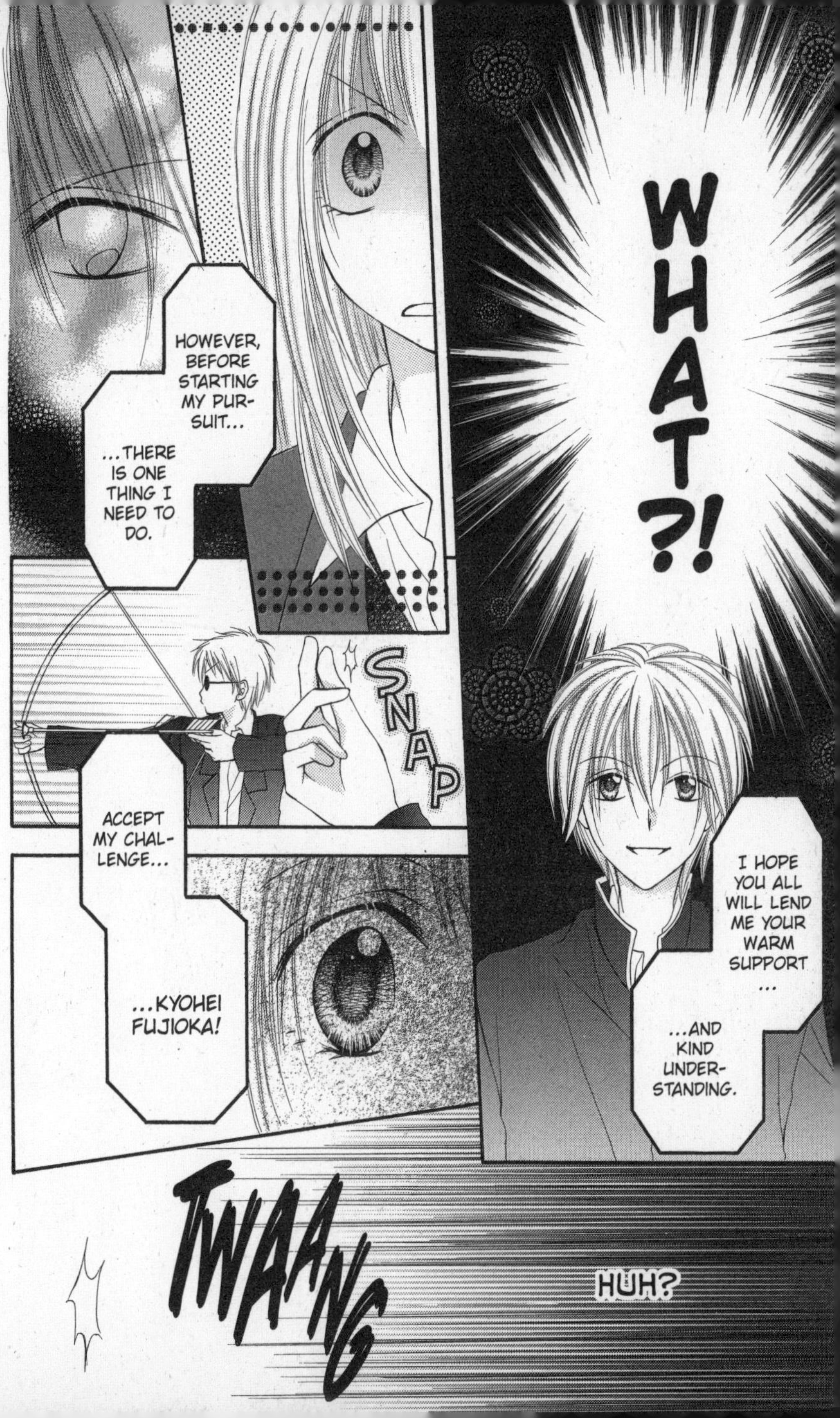
WHAT?!
I HOPE YOU ALL WILL LEND ME YOUR WARM SUPPORT...
...AND KIND UNDER-STANDING.
HOWEVER, BEFORE STARTING MY PUR-SUIT...
...THERE IS ONE THING I NEED TO DO.
SNAP
ACCEPT MY CHAL-LENGE...
...KYOHEI FUJIOKA!
TWAANG
HUH?

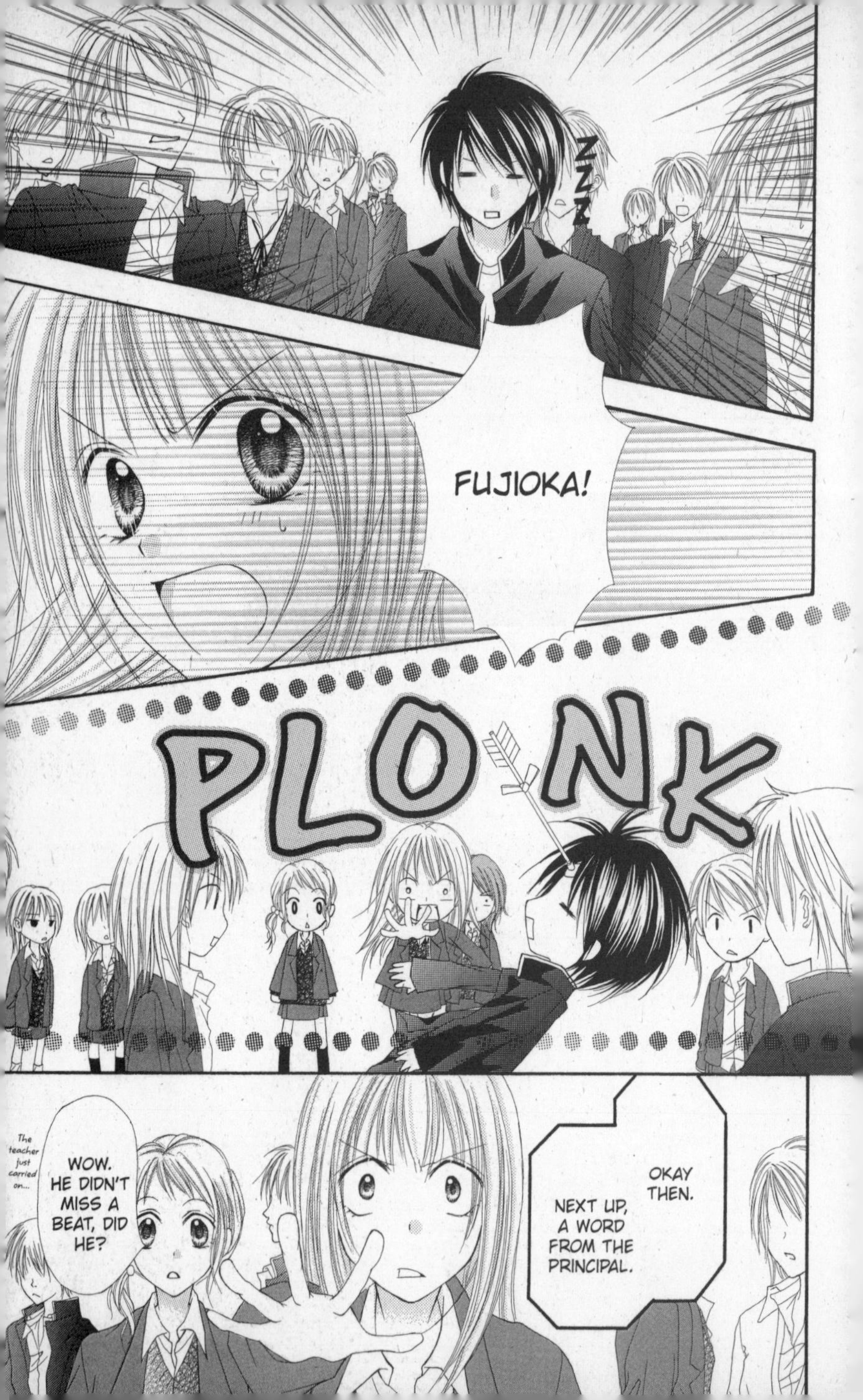
ZZZ
FUJIOKA!
PLONK
OKAY THEN.
NEXT UP, A WORD FROM THE PRINCIPAL.
WOW. HE DIDN'T MISS A BEAT, DID HE?
The teacher just carried on...

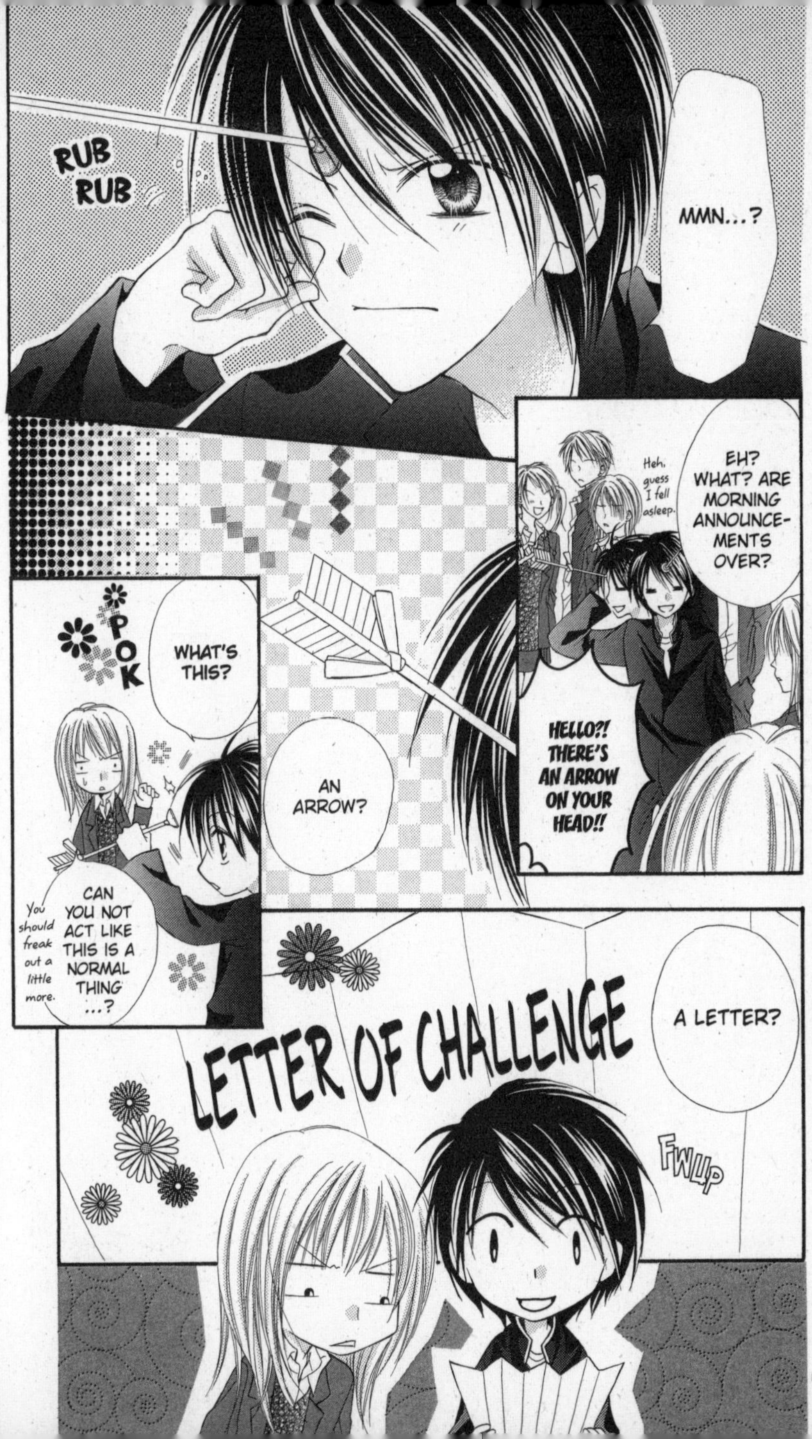
RUB RUB
MMN...?
Heh, guess I fell asleep.
EH? WHAT? ARE MORNING ANNOUNCEMENTS OVER?
HELLO?! THERE'S AN ARROW ON YOUR HEAD!!
POK
WHAT'S THIS?
AN ARROW?
CAN YOU NOT ACT LIKE THIS IS A NORMAL THING ...?
You should freak out a little more.
A LETTER?
FWLIP
LETTER OF CHALLENGE

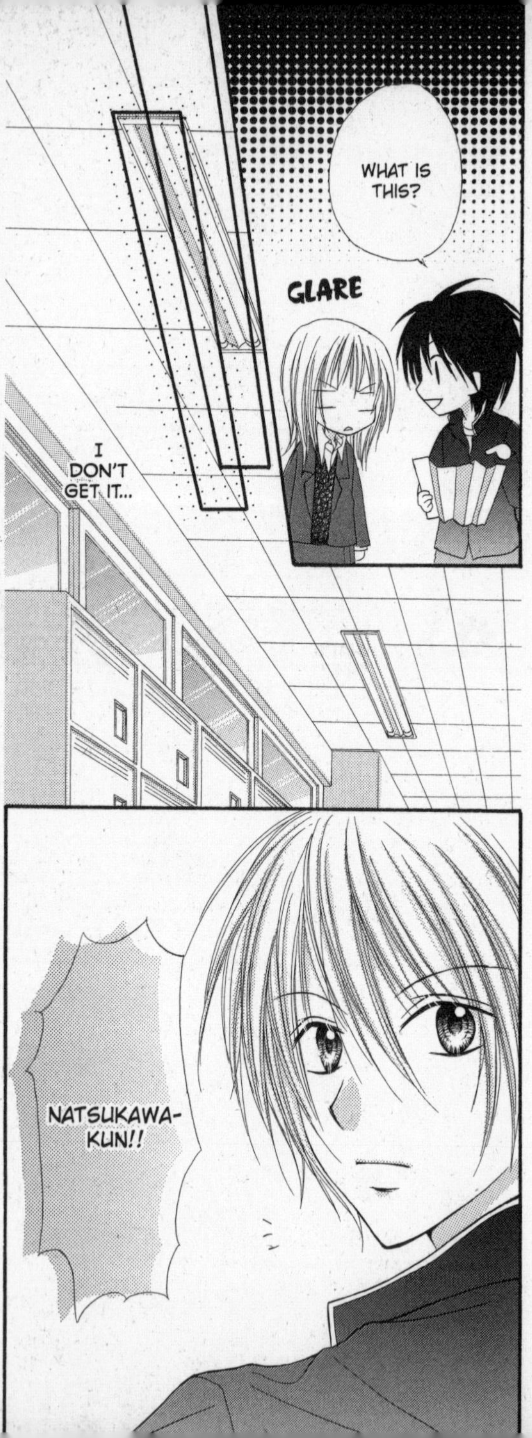
WHAT IS THIS?
GLARE
I DON'T GET IT...
NATSUKAWA-KUN!!

2

It's been a while since I've put so much genuine effort into the act of writing... I'm trying even harder than I did on my essays in high school. Though come to think of it, my many errors were often pointed out to me on those too. Hmm, I wonder why I'm even announcing to the world what an airhead I am.

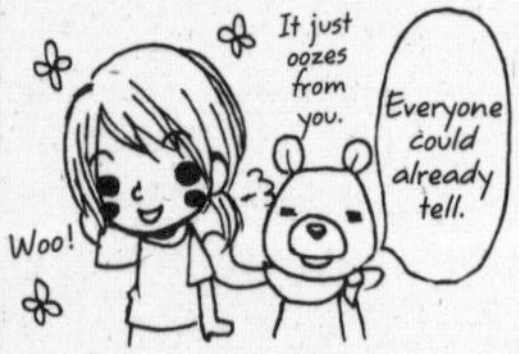
Everyone could already tell.
It just oozes from you.
Woo!

But even if I write neatly, it doesn't look all that different, does it? Once, a while back, my editor tried to encourage me by saying, "Well, your handwriting really isn't very well formed to begin with, so I'm not going to tell you to write well. Just write a little neater." (Translation: "Your handwriting is so messy it's hardly legible, moron.") Actually, does that really count as encouragement?

Well, that's enough about handwriting. But I've still got half a sidebar to fill. Umm... Oh yeah! I don't remember which promo piece this was in, but I once had Miku wear a shirt on which the w-inds logo appeared and, unexpectedly, a lot of readers really responded to it. It's actually a concert T-shirt for the boy band w-inds. I couldn't copy it outright, so I altered it at the bottom (which isn't visible in the printing). I ended up drawing it after going to the concert. Fans of w-inds, I'm so sorry!!

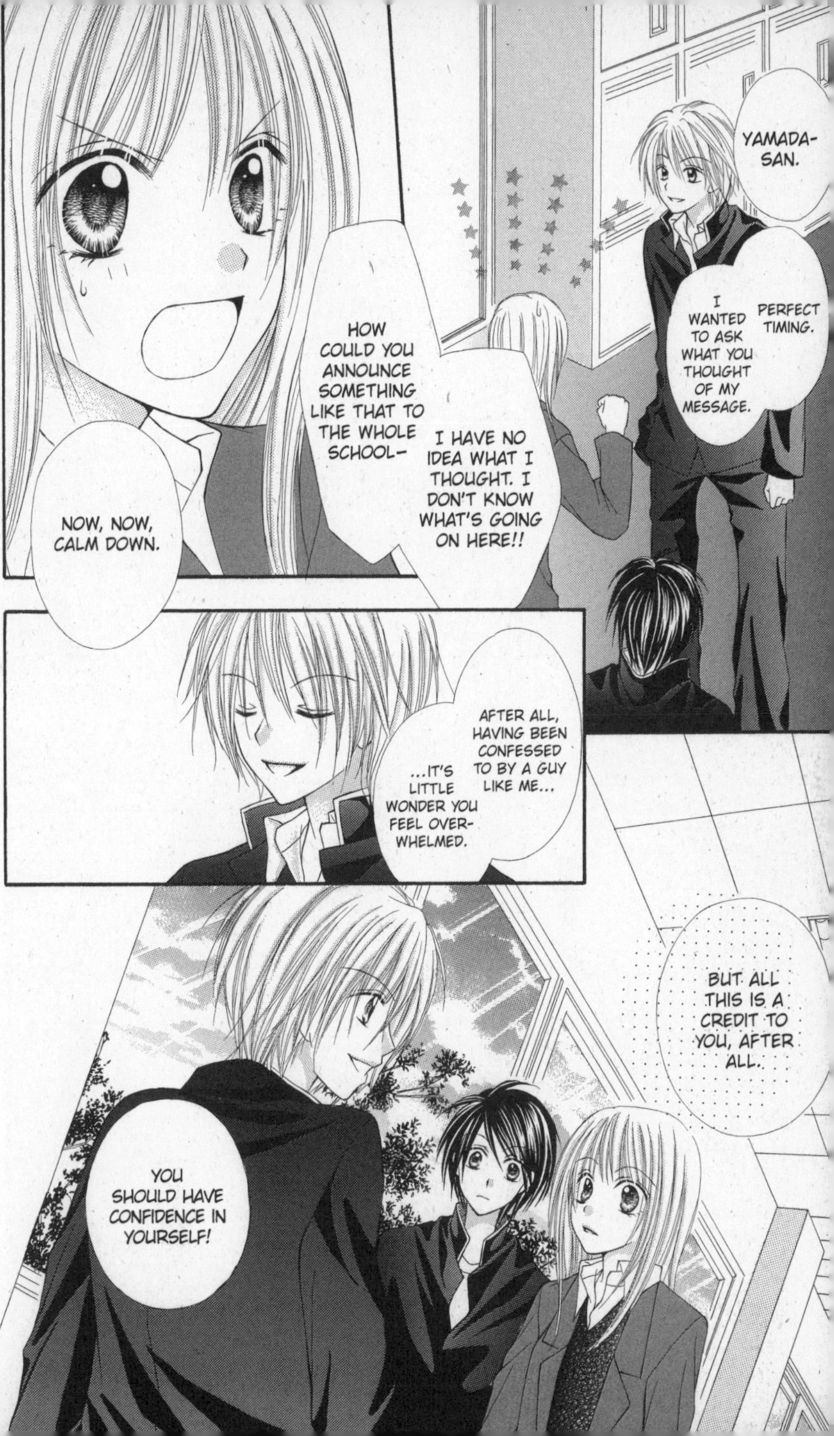
YAMADA-SAN.
PERFECT TIMING.
I WANTED TO ASK WHAT YOU THOUGHT OF MY MESSAGE.
HOW COULD YOU ANNOUNCE SOMETHING LIKE THAT TO THE WHOLE SCHOOL–
I HAVE NO IDEA WHAT I THOUGHT. I DON'T KNOW WHAT'S GOING ON HERE!!
NOW, NOW, CALM DOWN.
AFTER ALL, HAVING BEEN CONFESSED TO BY A GUY LIKE ME...
...IT'S LITTLE WONDER YOU FEEL OVER-WHELMED.
BUT ALL THIS IS A CREDIT TO YOU, AFTER ALL.
YOU SHOULD HAVE CONFIDENCE IN YOURSELF!

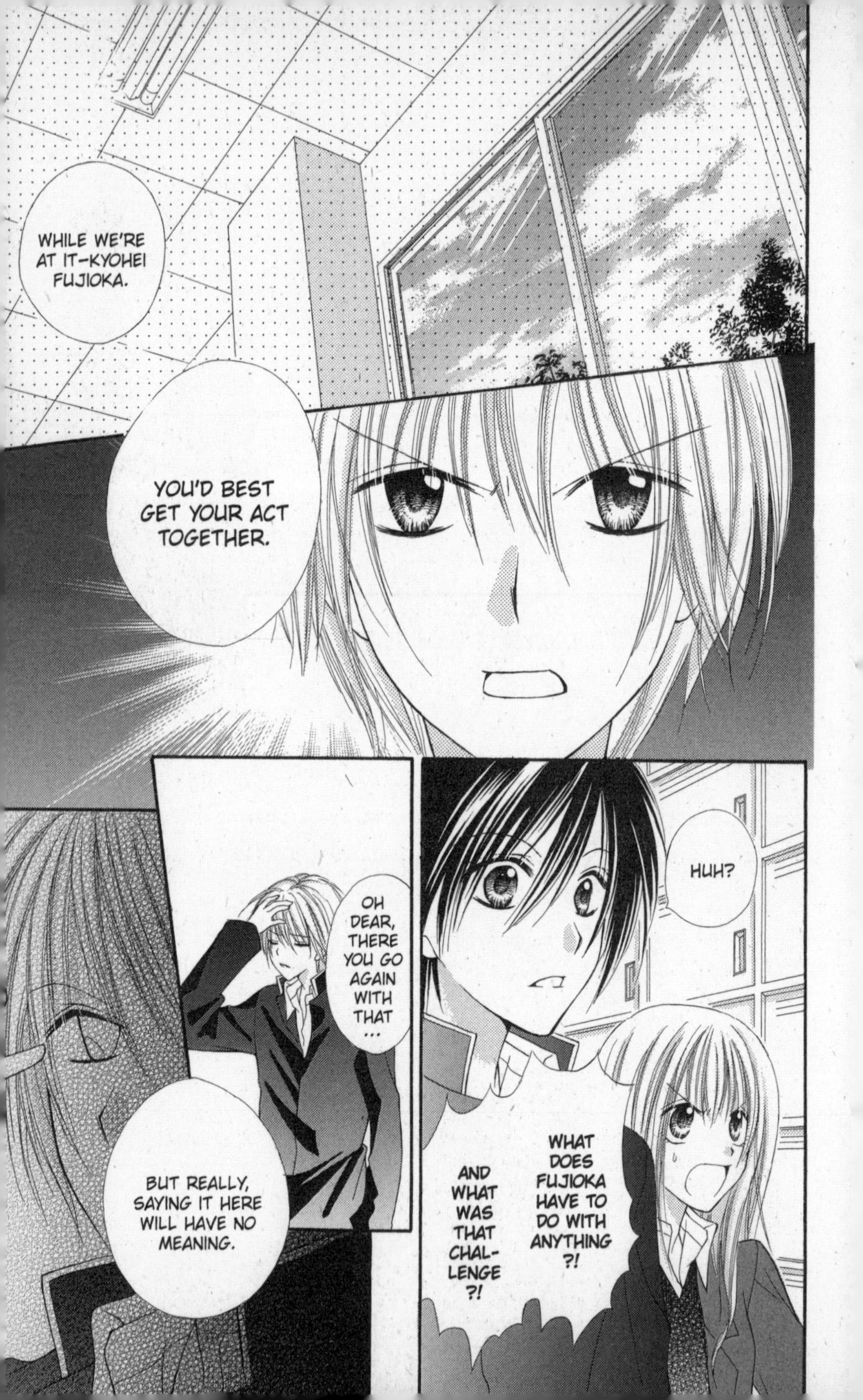
WHILE WE'RE AT IT-KYOHEI FUJIOKA.
YOU'D BEST GET YOUR ACT TOGETHER.
HUH?
WHAT DOES FUJIOKA HAVE TO DO WITH ANYTHING ?!
AND WHAT WAS THAT CHAL-LENGE ?!
OH DEAR, THERE YOU GO AGAIN WITH THAT ...
BUT REALLY, SAYING IT HERE WILL HAVE NO MEANING.

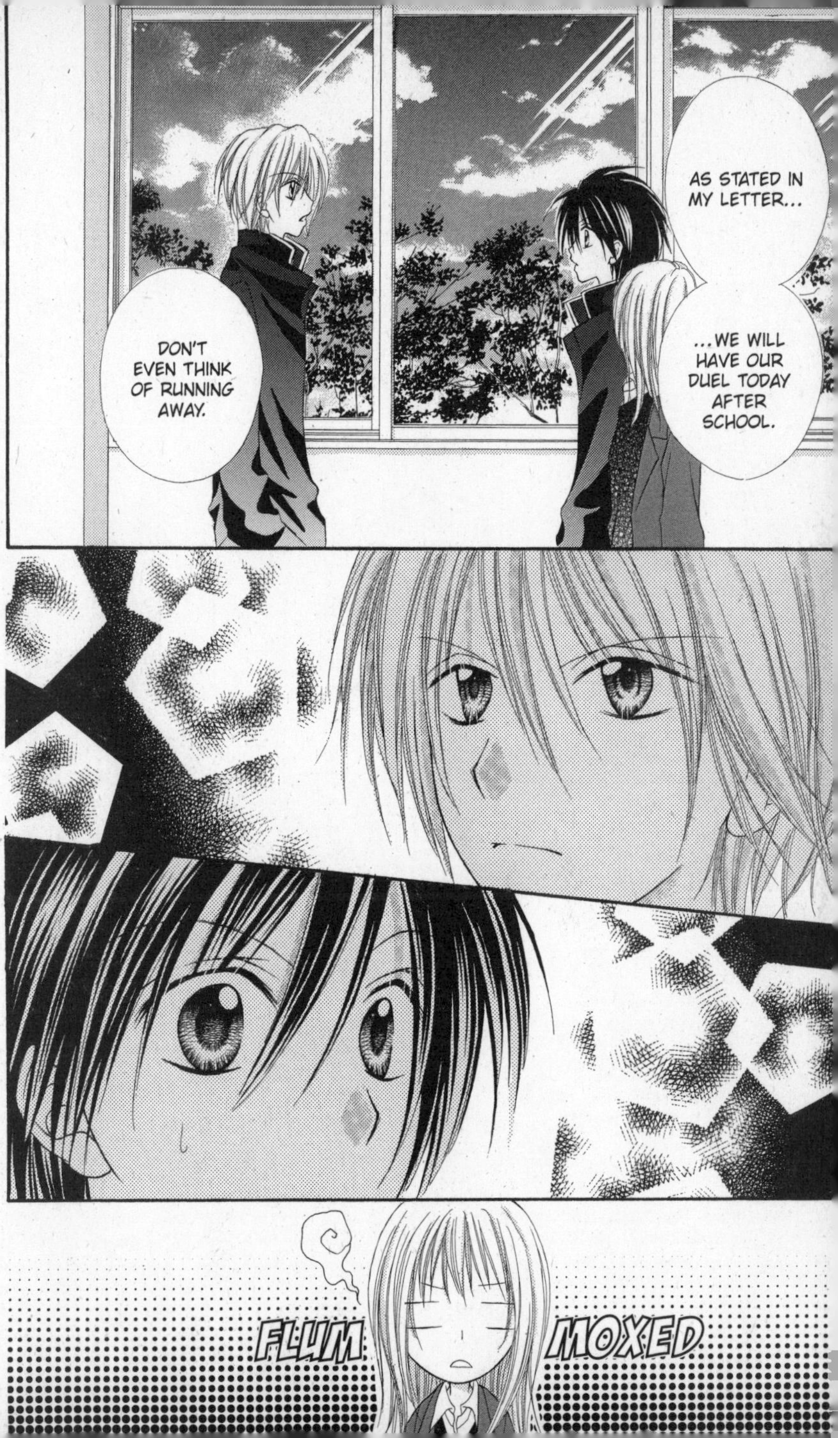
AS STATED IN MY LETTER...
...WE WILL HAVE OUR DUEL TODAY AFTER SCHOOL.
DON'T EVEN THINK OF RUNNING AWAY.
FLUM MOXED

3

The Niigata earthquake. More than anything, I just have to address this. The readers who knew I was from Niigata were so sweet and worried about me. I received tons of emails and letters asking how I was. Thank you so much.

But actually, I wasn't in Niigata when the earthquake hit. And even if I had been, my parents' house is in the city center, where there wasn't much damage, so I would've been okay. I really want to thank everyone who thought about me. Please don't worry—I'm fine. Sorry to have caused trouble for everybody. To everyone who was affected by the quake, I pray for your swift recovery.

After the quake, my very first editor got worried and gave me a call. I was incredibly touched because it had been over three years since he'd worked with me! Even though I'd already moved, he still worried about my parents too! Thank you so much for that!

This is completely off topic, but I just got a call from the *Ribon* office. They pointed out a typo I made in a promo piece I'd just sent them the other day. "It was so like you, Haruta-san, that we had a laugh about it," they said. Yikes!

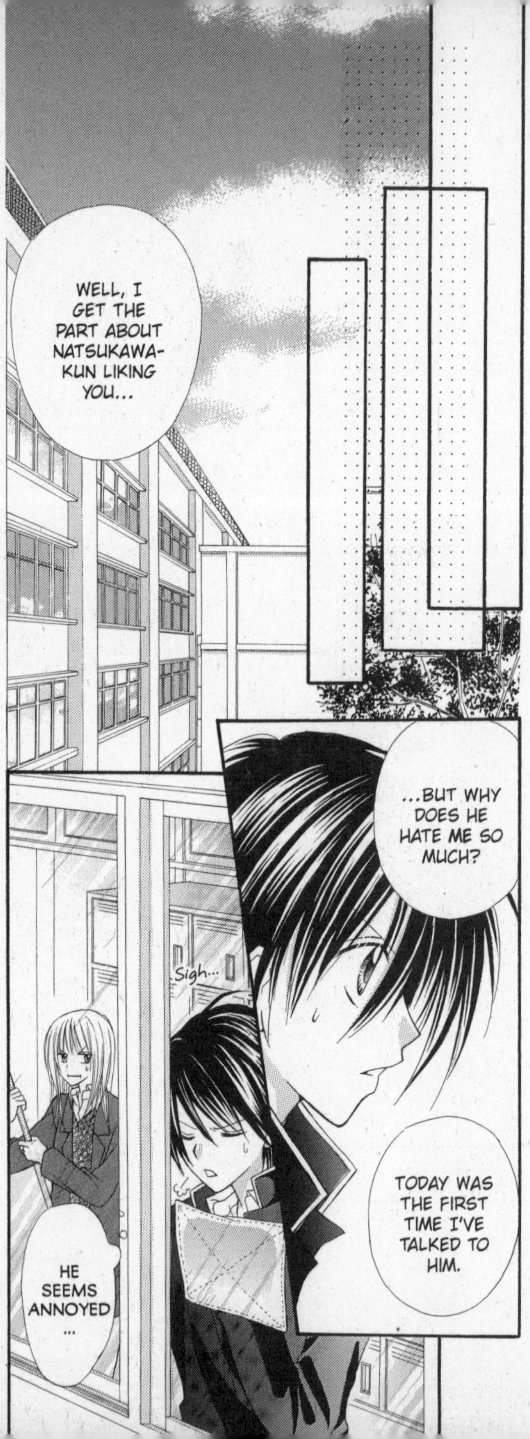
WELL, I GET THE PART ABOUT NATSUKAWA-KUN LIKING YOU...
...BUT WHY DOES HE HATE ME SO MUCH?
TODAY WAS THE FIRST TIME I'VE TALKED TO HIM.
Sigh...
HE SEEMS ANNOYED ...

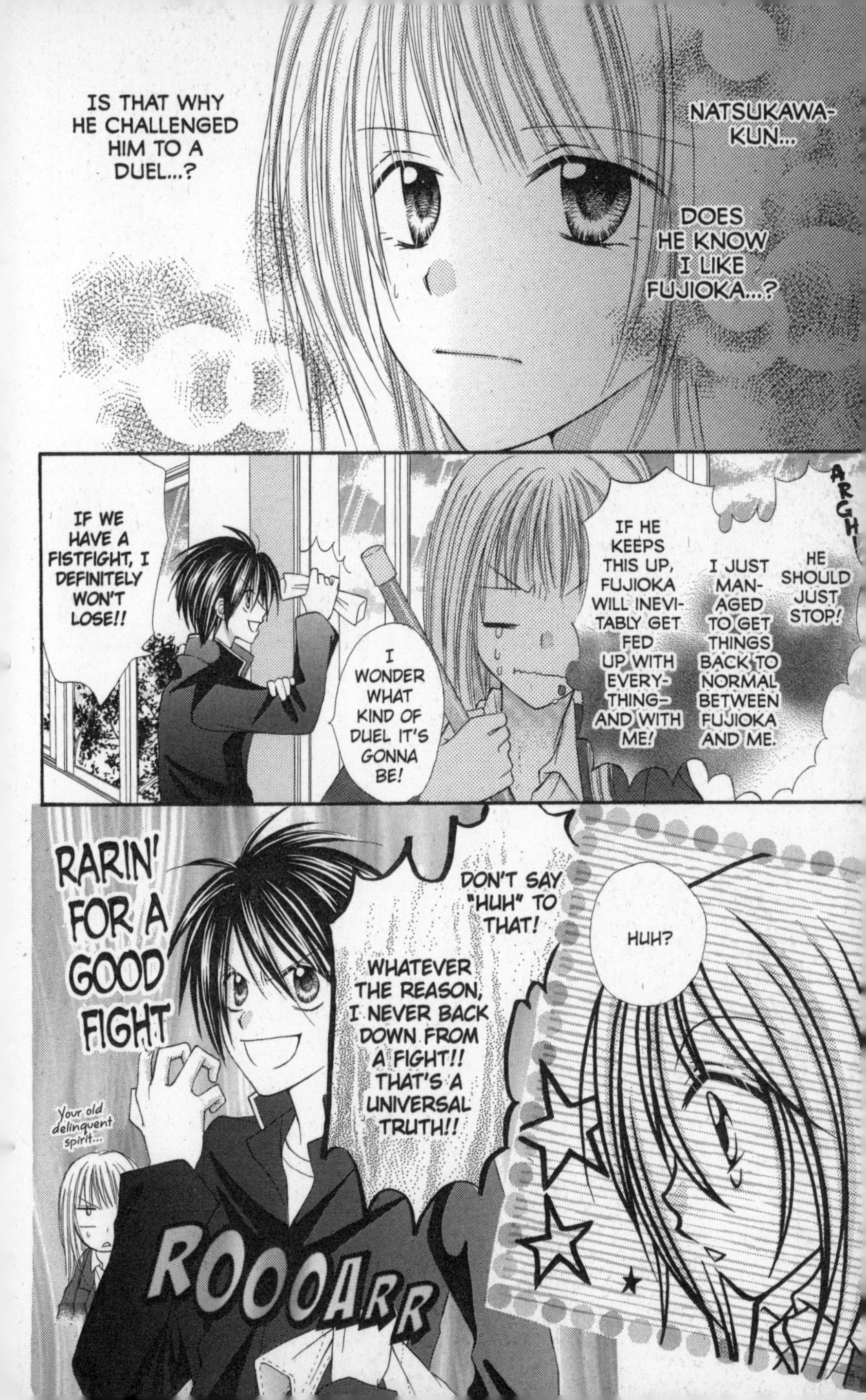
NATSUKAWA-KUN...
DOES HE KNOW I LIKE FUJIOKA...?
IS THAT WHY HE CHALLENGED HIM TO A DUEL...?
ARGH
HE SHOULD JUST STOP!
I JUST MAN-AGED TO GET THINGS BACK TO NORMAL BETWEEN FUJIOKA AND ME.
IF HE KEEPS THIS UP, FUJIOKA WILL INEVI-TABLY GET FED UP WITH EVERY-THING— AND WITH ME!
I WONDER WHAT KIND OF DUEL IT'S GONNA BE!
IF WE HAVE A FISTFIGHT, I DEFINITELY WON'T LOSE!!
HUH?
DON'T SAY "HUH" TO THAT!
WHATEVER THE REASON, I NEVER BACK DOWN FROM A FIGHT!! THAT'S A UNIVERSAL TRUTH!!
RARIN' FOR A GOOD FIGHT
Your old delinquent spirit...
ROOOARR

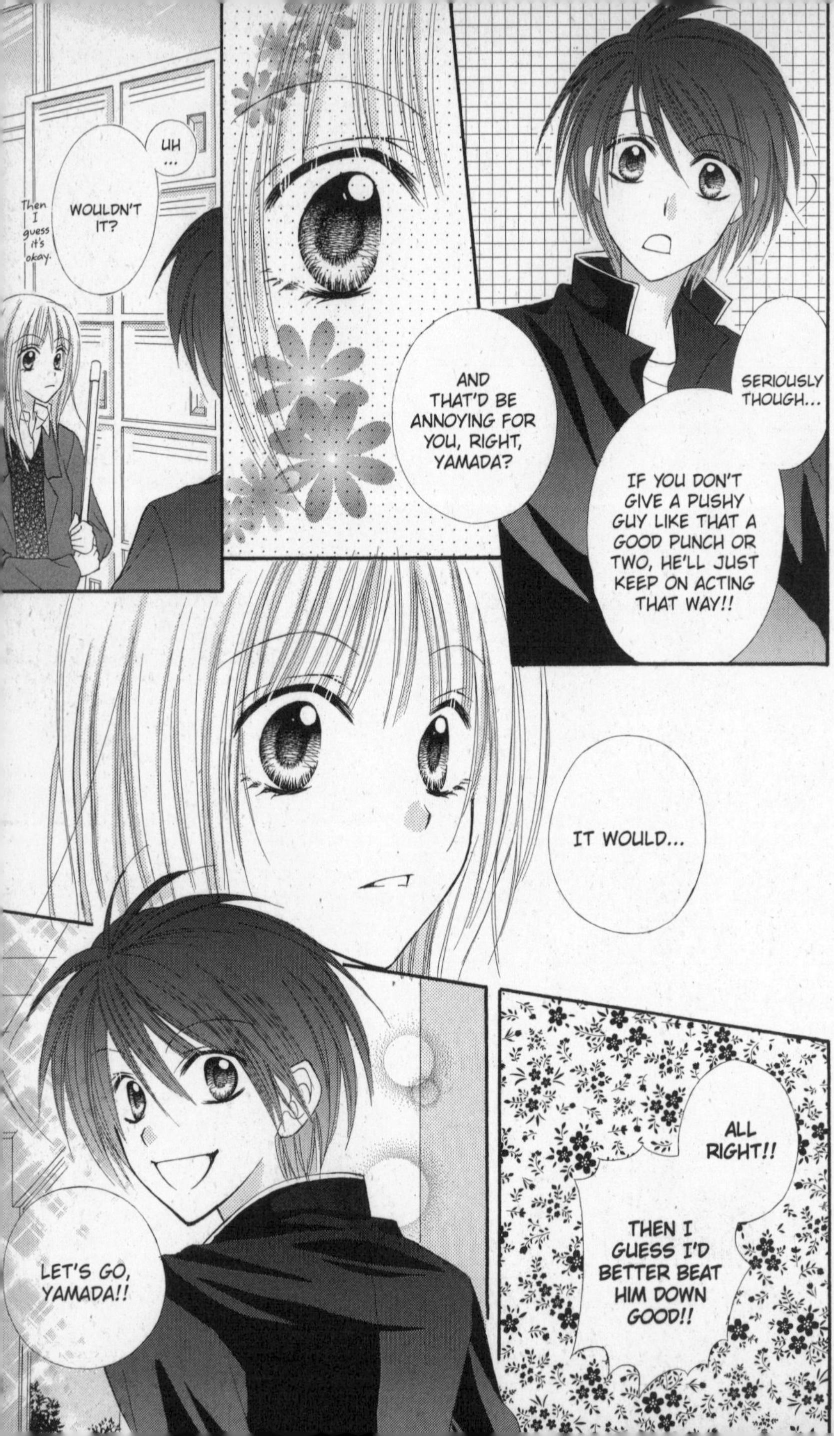
SERIOUSLY THOUGH...
IF YOU DON'T GIVE A PUSHY GUY LIKE THAT A GOOD PUNCH OR TWO, HE'LL JUST KEEP ON ACTING THAT WAY!!
AND THAT'D BE ANNOYING FOR YOU, RIGHT, YAMADA?
UH...
WOULDN'T IT?
Then I guess it's okay.
IT WOULD...
ALL RIGHT!!
THEN I GUESS I'D BETTER BEAT HIM DOWN GOOD!!
LET'S GO, YAMADA!!

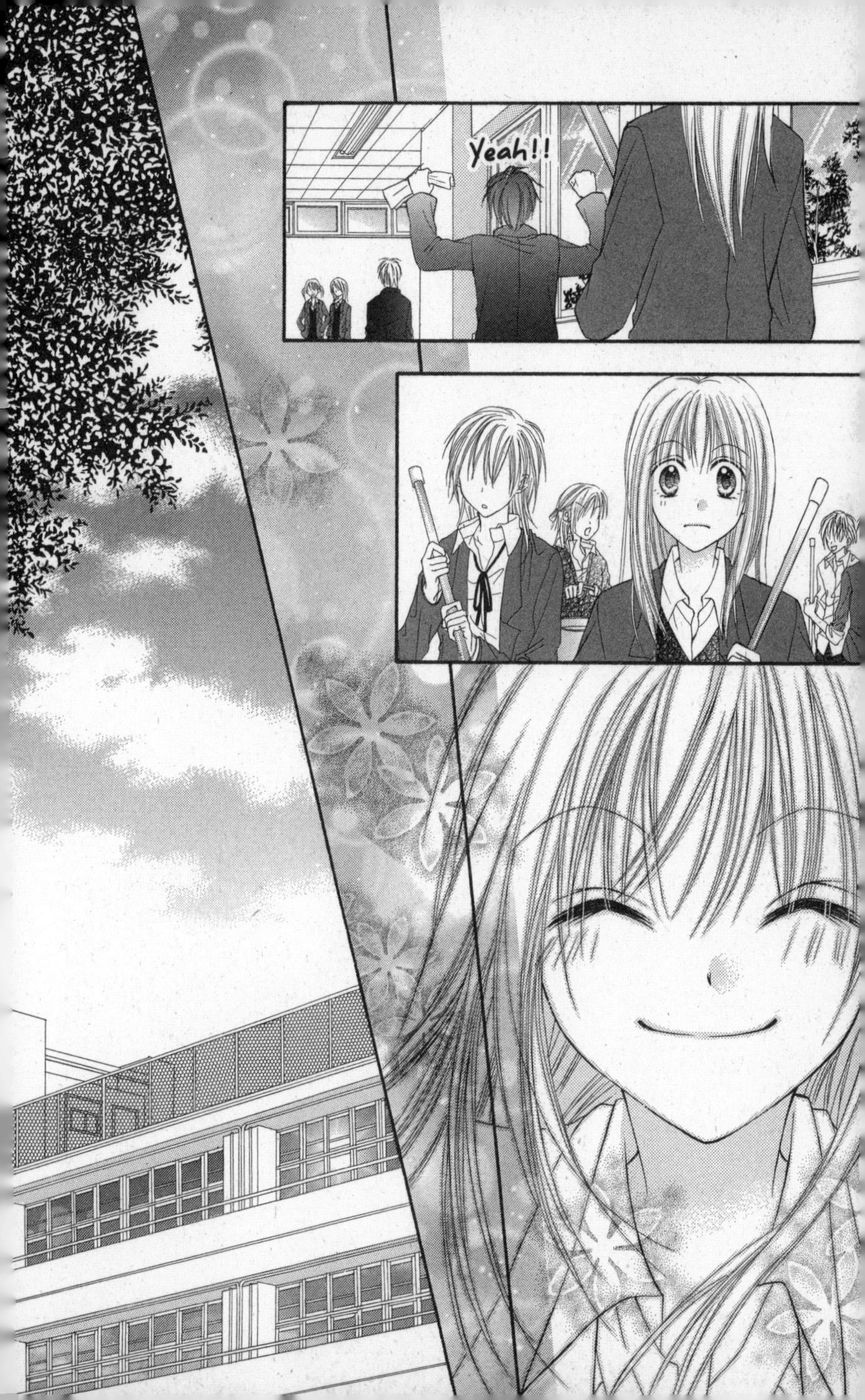
Yeah!!

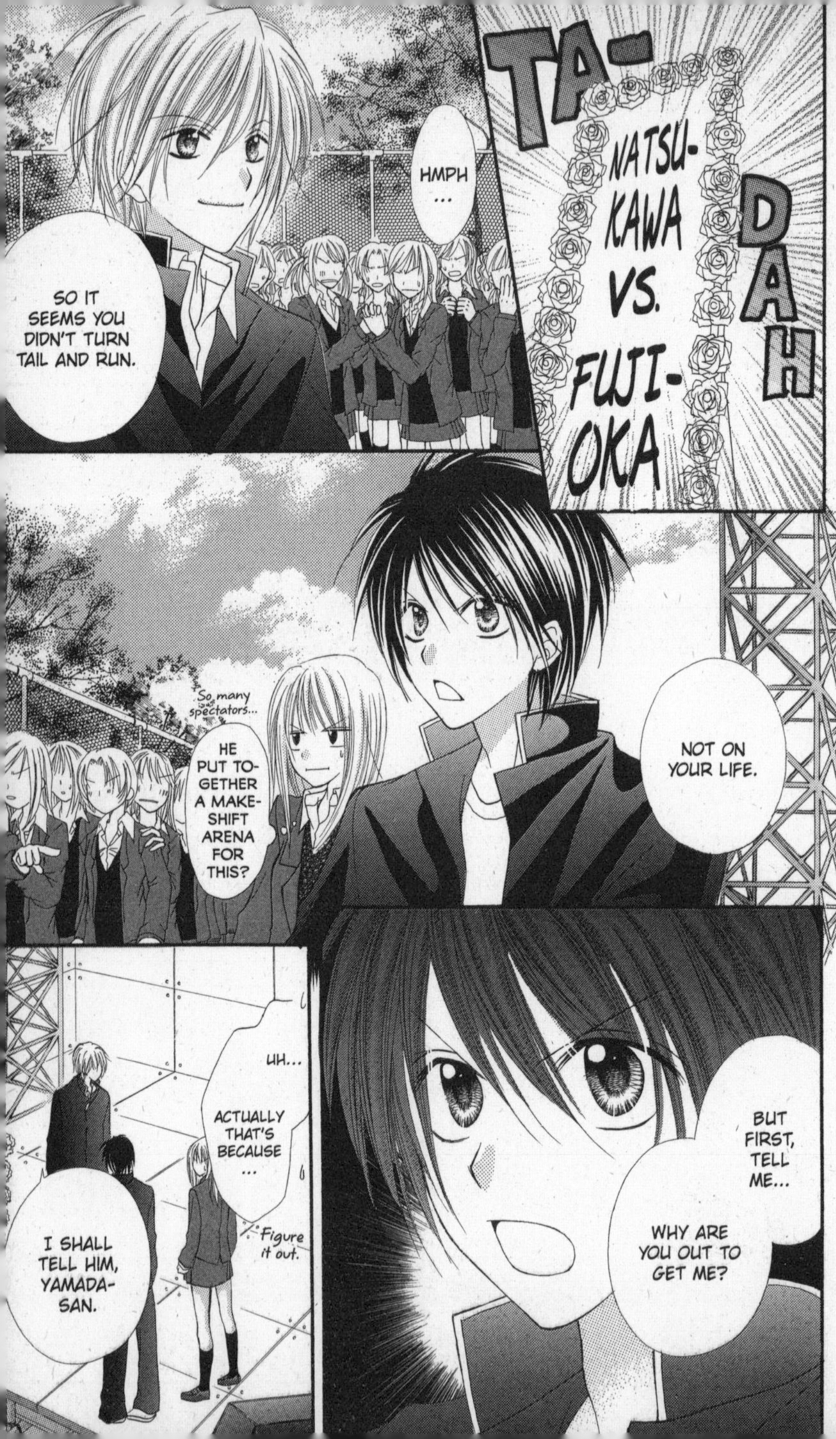
TA-DAH
NATSUKAWA VS. FUJIOKA
HMPH...
SO IT SEEMS YOU DIDN'T TURN TAIL AND RUN.
NOT ON YOUR LIFE.
So many spectators...
HE PUT TOGETHER A MAKESHIFT ARENA FOR THIS?
BUT FIRST, TELL ME...
WHY ARE YOU OUT TO GET ME?
UH...
ACTUALLY THAT'S BECAUSE...
Figure it out.
I SHALL TELL HIM, YAMADA-SAN.

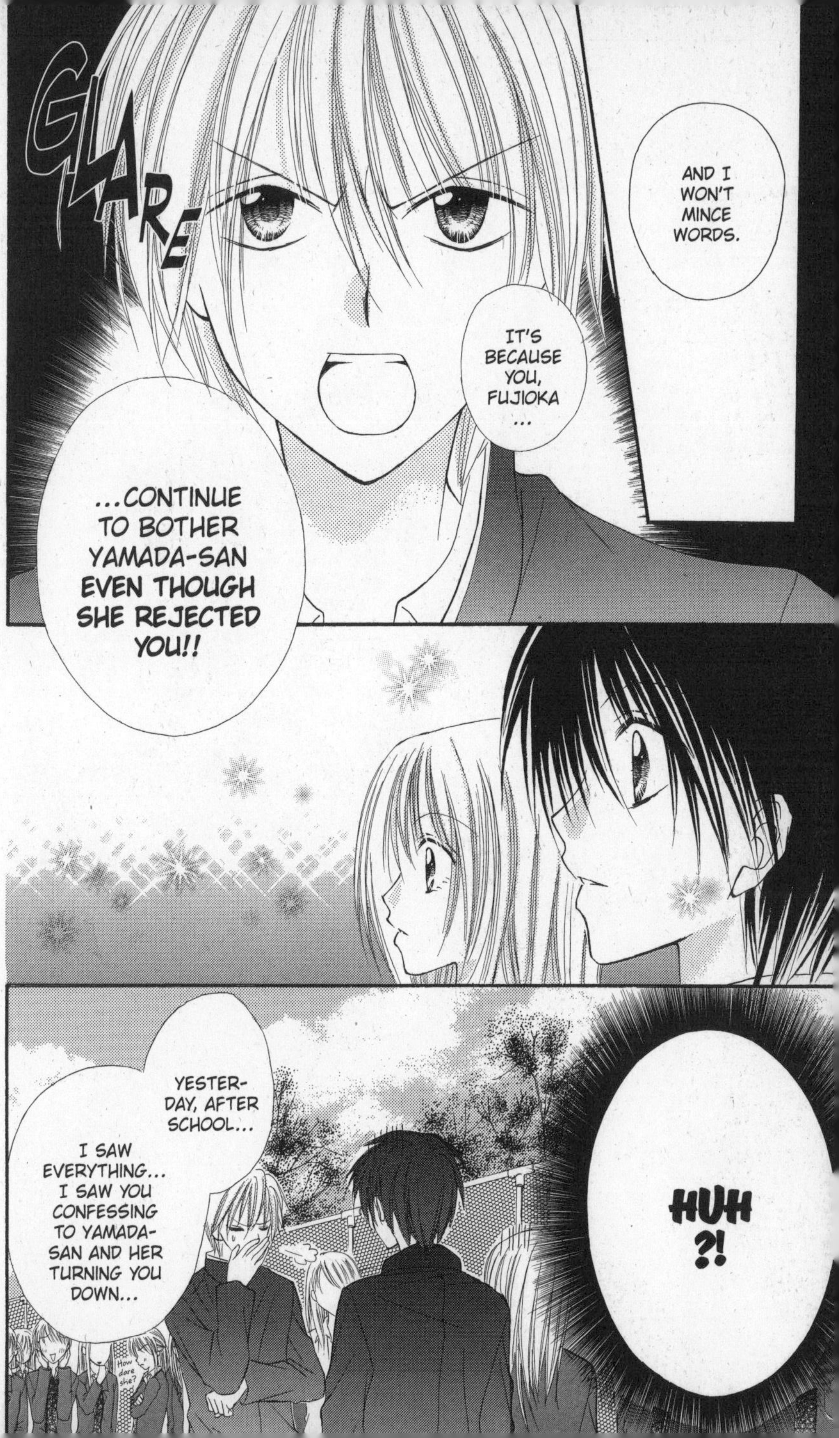
GLARE
AND I WON'T MINCE WORDS.
IT'S BECAUSE YOU, FUJIOKA...
...CONTINUE TO BOTHER YAMADA-SAN EVEN THOUGH SHE REJECTED YOU!!
HUH?!
YESTER-DAY, AFTER SCHOOL...
I SAW EVERYTHING... I SAW YOU CONFESSING TO YAMADA-SAN AND HER TURNING YOU DOWN...
How dare she?

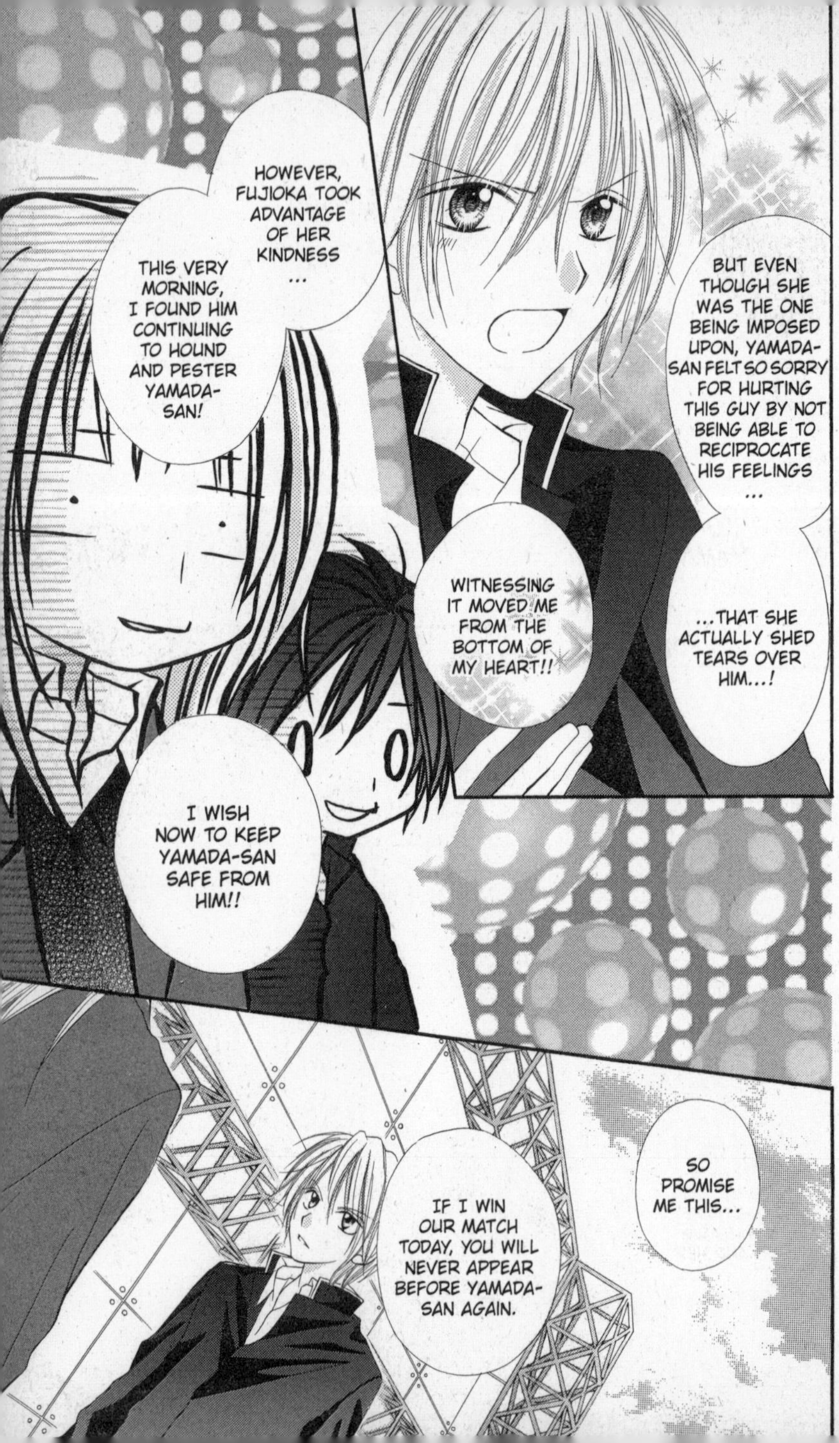
BUT EVEN THOUGH SHE WAS THE ONE BEING IMPOSED UPON, YAMADA-SAN FELT SO SORRY FOR HURTING THIS GUY BY NOT BEING ABLE TO RECIPROCATE HIS FEELINGS ...
...THAT SHE ACTUALLY SHED TEARS OVER HIM...!
WITNESSING IT MOVED ME FROM THE BOTTOM OF MY HEART!!
HOWEVER, FUJIOKA TOOK ADVANTAGE OF HER KINDNESS ...
THIS VERY MORNING, I FOUND HIM CONTINUING TO HOUND AND PESTER YAMADA-SAN!
I WISH NOW TO KEEP YAMADA-SAN SAFE FROM HIM!!
SO PROMISE ME THIS...
IF I WIN OUR MATCH TODAY, YOU WILL NEVER APPEAR BEFORE YAMADA-SAN AGAIN.

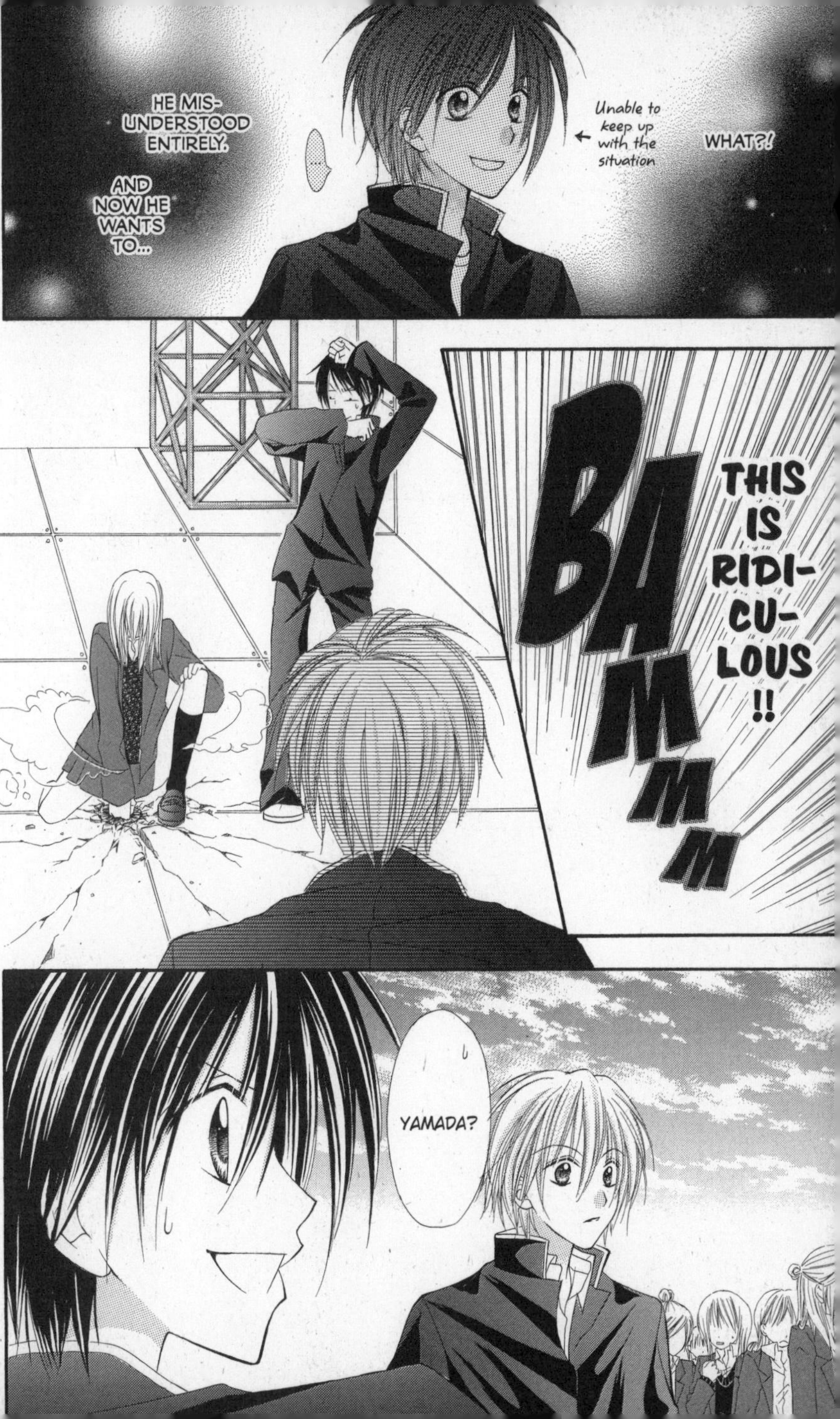
WHAT?!
Unable to keep up with the situation
...
HE MIS-UNDERSTOOD ENTIRELY.
AND NOW HE WANTS TO...
THIS IS RIDI-CU-LOUS!!
BAMMM
YAMADA?

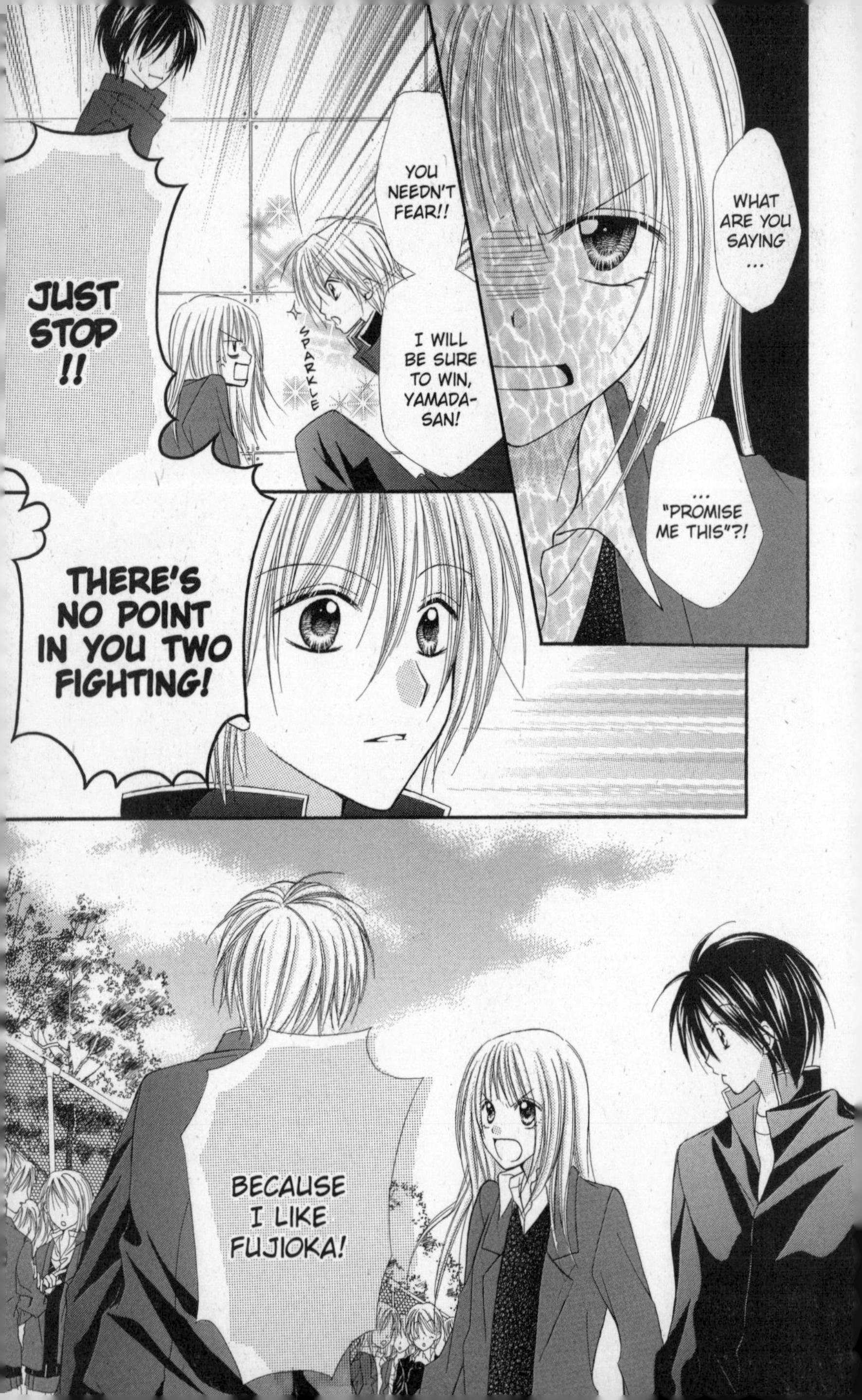
WHAT ARE YOU SAYING ...
... "PROMISE ME THIS"?!
YOU NEEDN'T FEAR!!
I WILL BE SURE TO WIN, YAMADA-SAN!
SPARKLE
JUST STOP !!
THERE'S NO POINT IN YOU TWO FIGHTING!
BECAUSE I LIKE FUJIOKA!

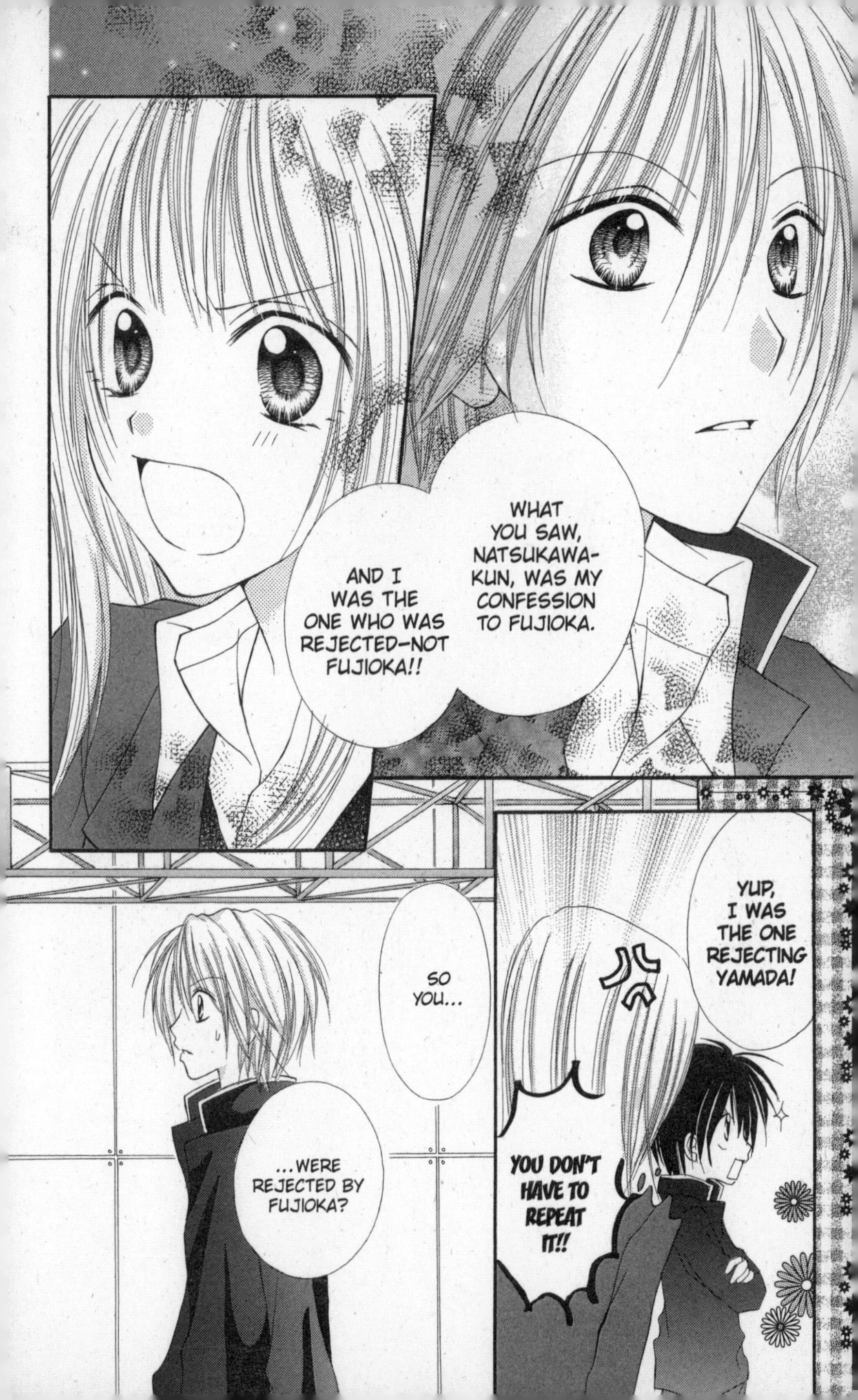
WHAT YOU SAW, NATSUKAWA-KUN, WAS MY CONFESSION TO FUJIOKA.
AND I WAS THE ONE WHO WAS REJECTED—NOT FUJIOKA!!
SO YOU...
...WERE REJECTED BY FUJIOKA?
YUP, I WAS THE ONE REJECTING YAMADA!
YOU DON'T HAVE TO REPEAT IT!!

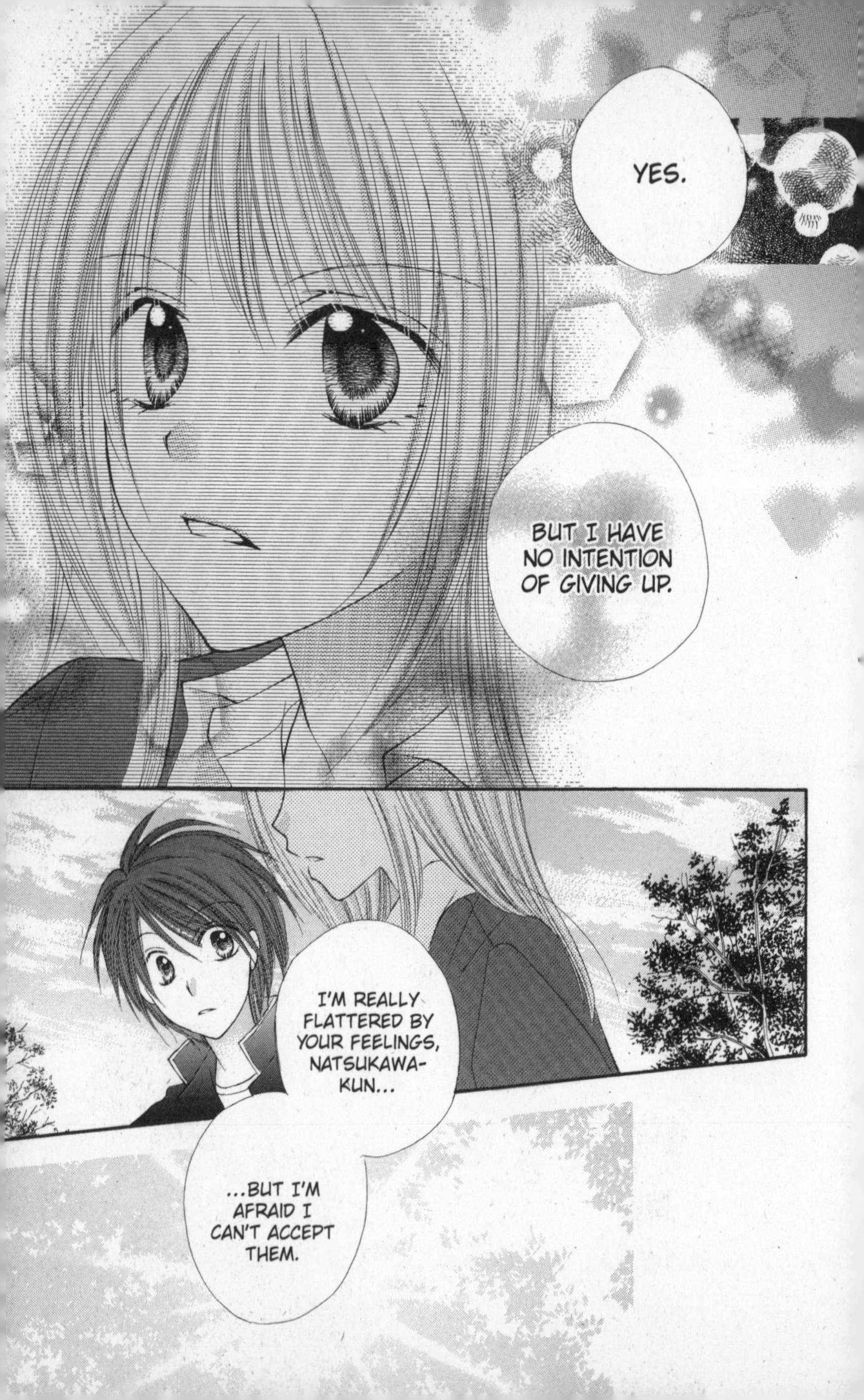
YES.
BUT I HAVE NO INTENTION OF GIVING UP.
I'M REALLY FLATTERED BY YOUR FEELINGS, NATSUKAWA-KUN...
...BUT I'M AFRAID I CAN'T ACCEPT THEM.

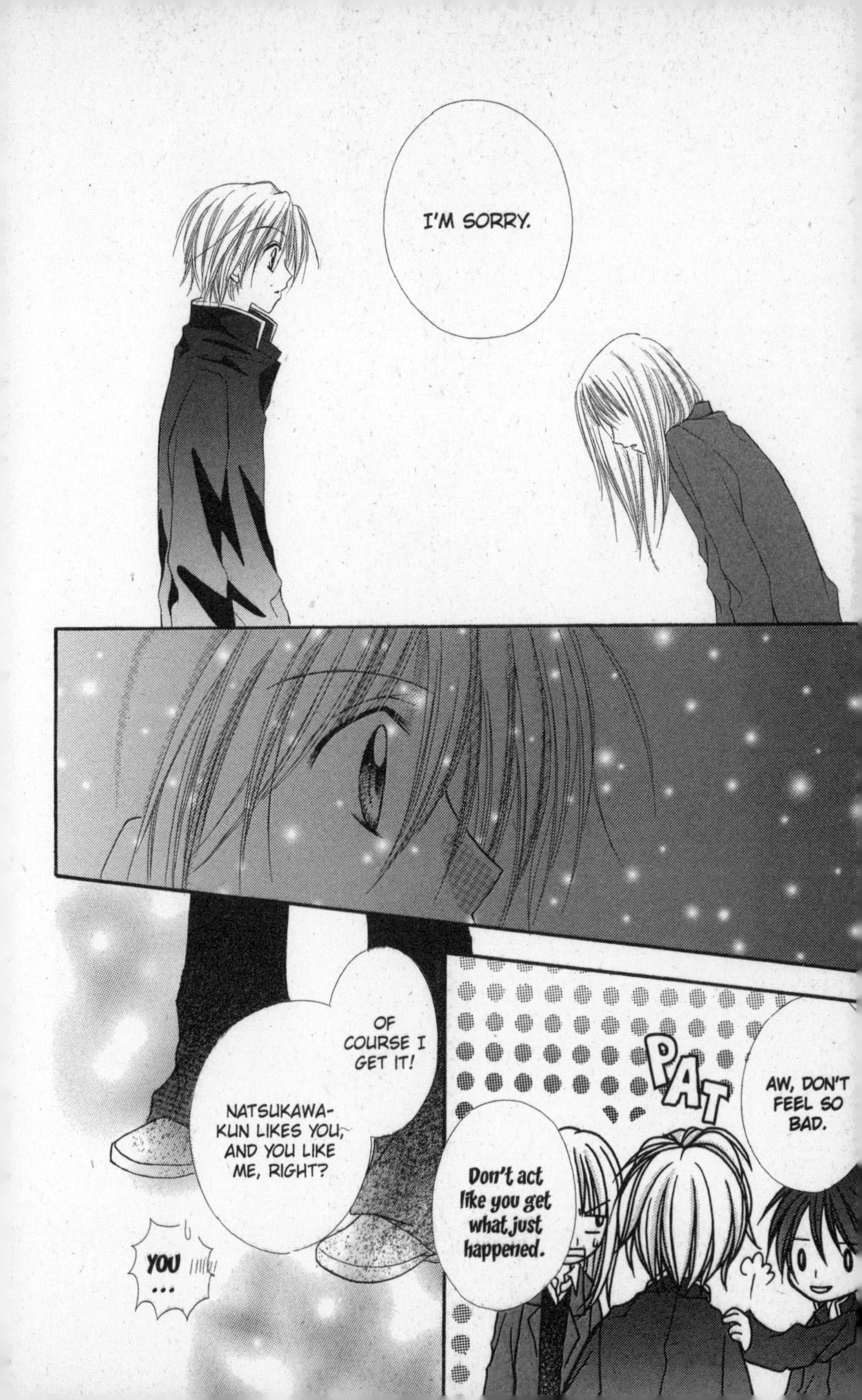
I'M SORRY.
OF COURSE I GET IT!
NATSUKAWA-KUN LIKES YOU, AND YOU LIKE ME, RIGHT?
YOU ...
AW, DON'T FEEL SO BAD.
PAT
Don't act like you get what just happened.

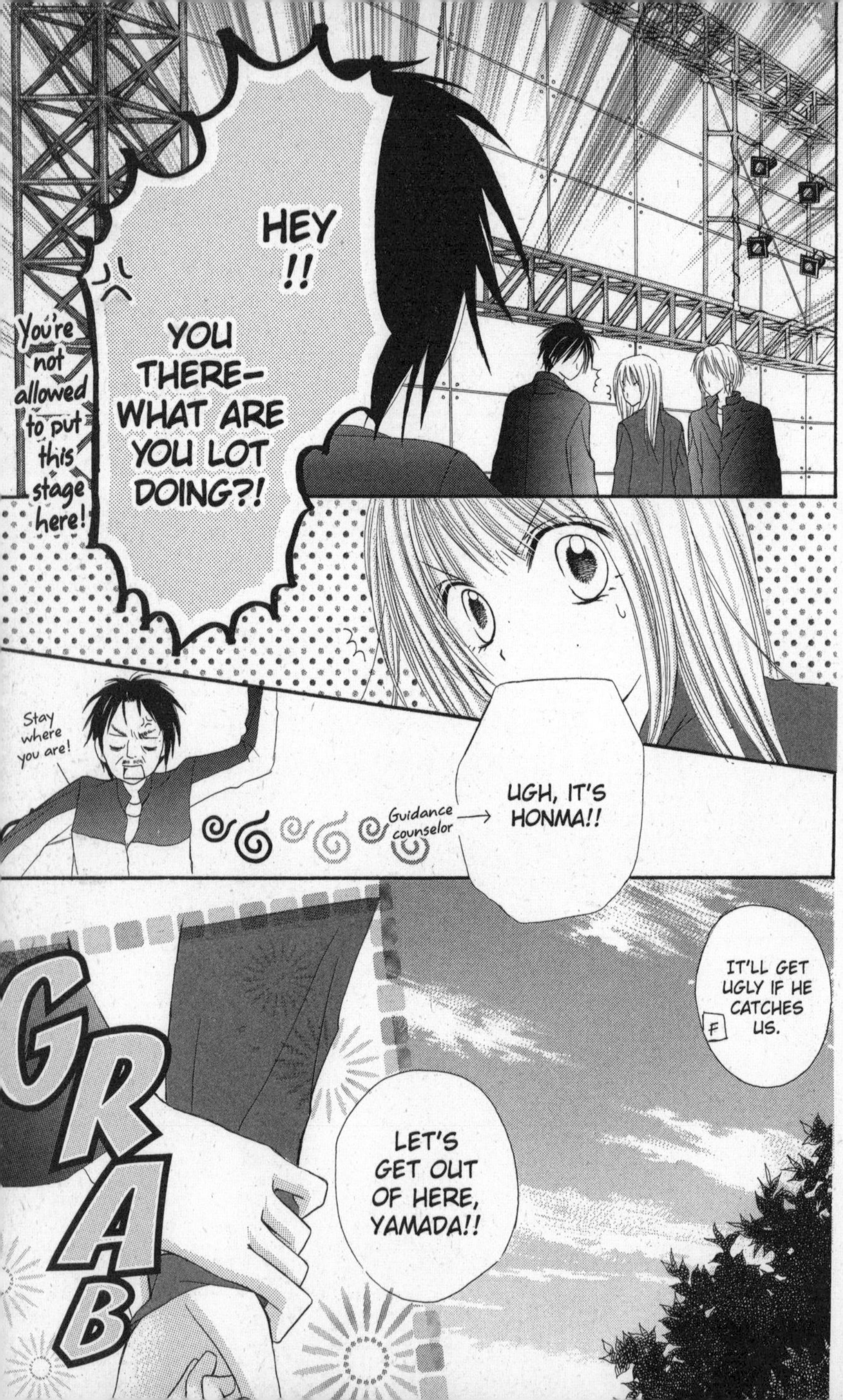
HEY!! YOU THERE- WHAT ARE YOU LOT DOING?!
You're not allowed to put this stage here!
UGH, IT'S HONMA!!
Guidance counselor
Stay where you are!
IT'LL GET UGLY IF HE CATCHES US.
F
LET'S GET OUT OF HERE, YAMADA!!
GRAB

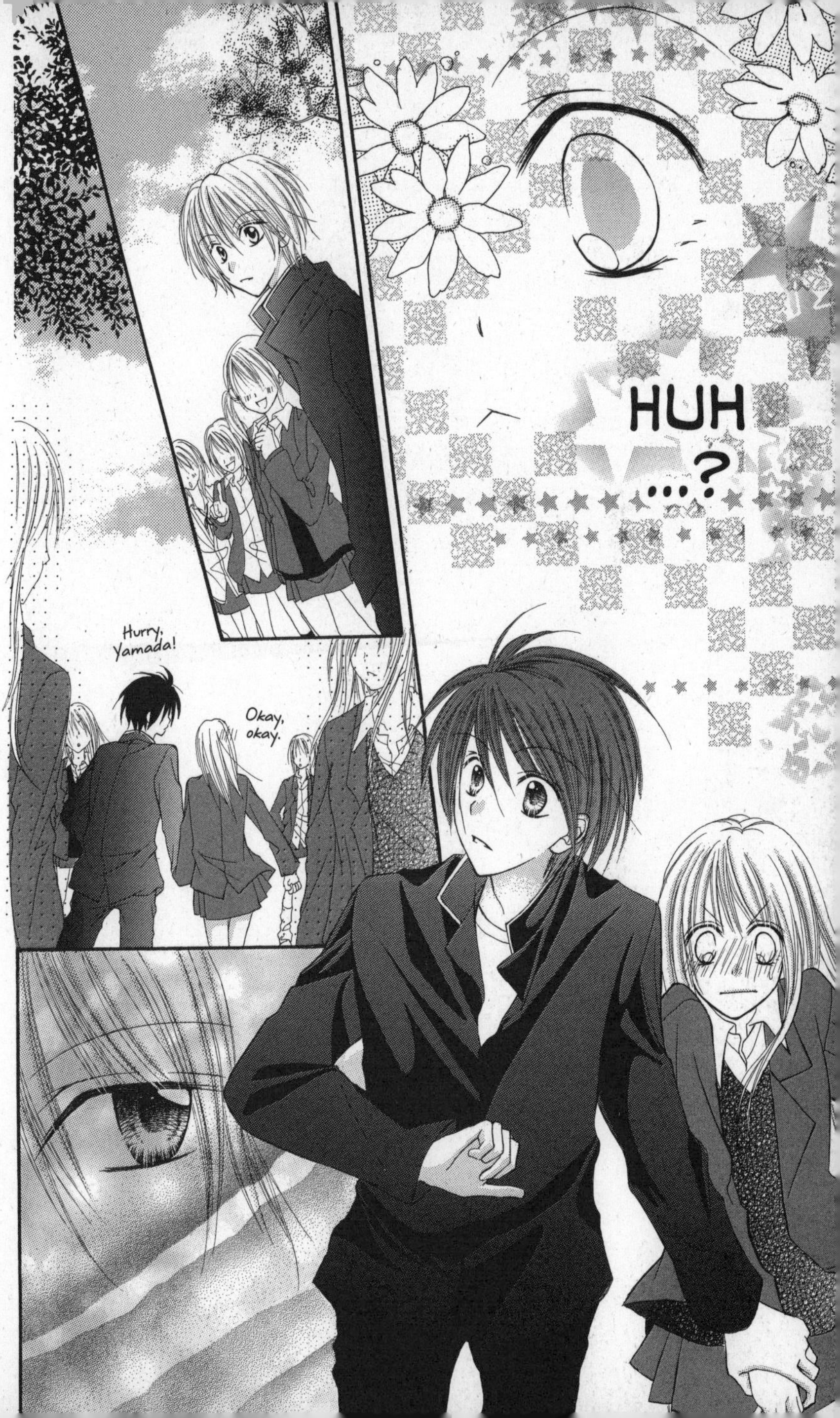
HUH ...?
Hurry, Yamada!
Okay, okay.

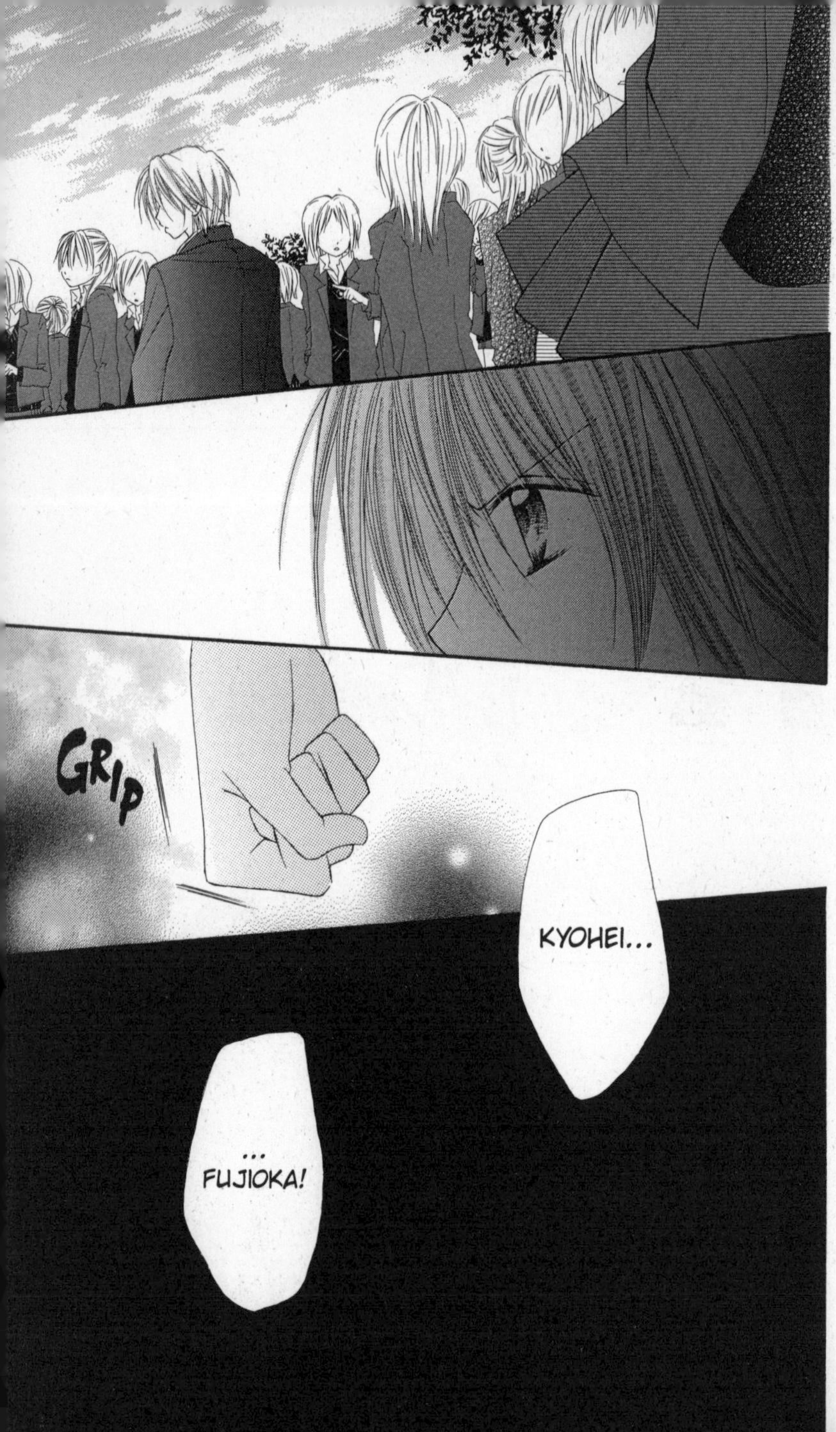
GRIP
KYOHEI...
...FUJIOKA!

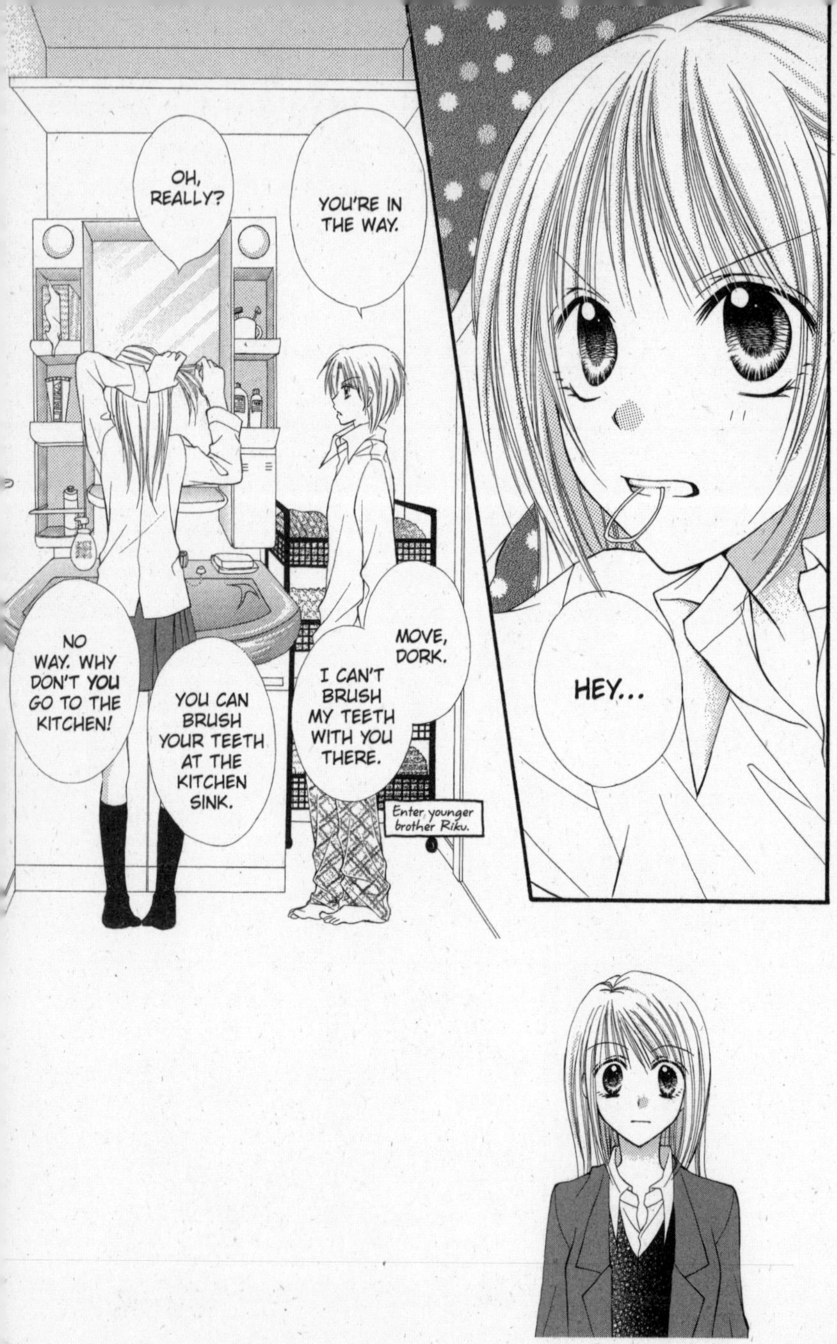
HEY...
YOU'RE IN THE WAY.
OH, REALLY?
MOVE, DORK.
I CAN'T BRUSH MY TEETH WITH YOU THERE.
Enter younger brother Riku.
YOU CAN BRUSH YOUR TEETH AT THE KITCHEN SINK.
NO WAY. WHY DON'T YOU GO TO THE KITCHEN!

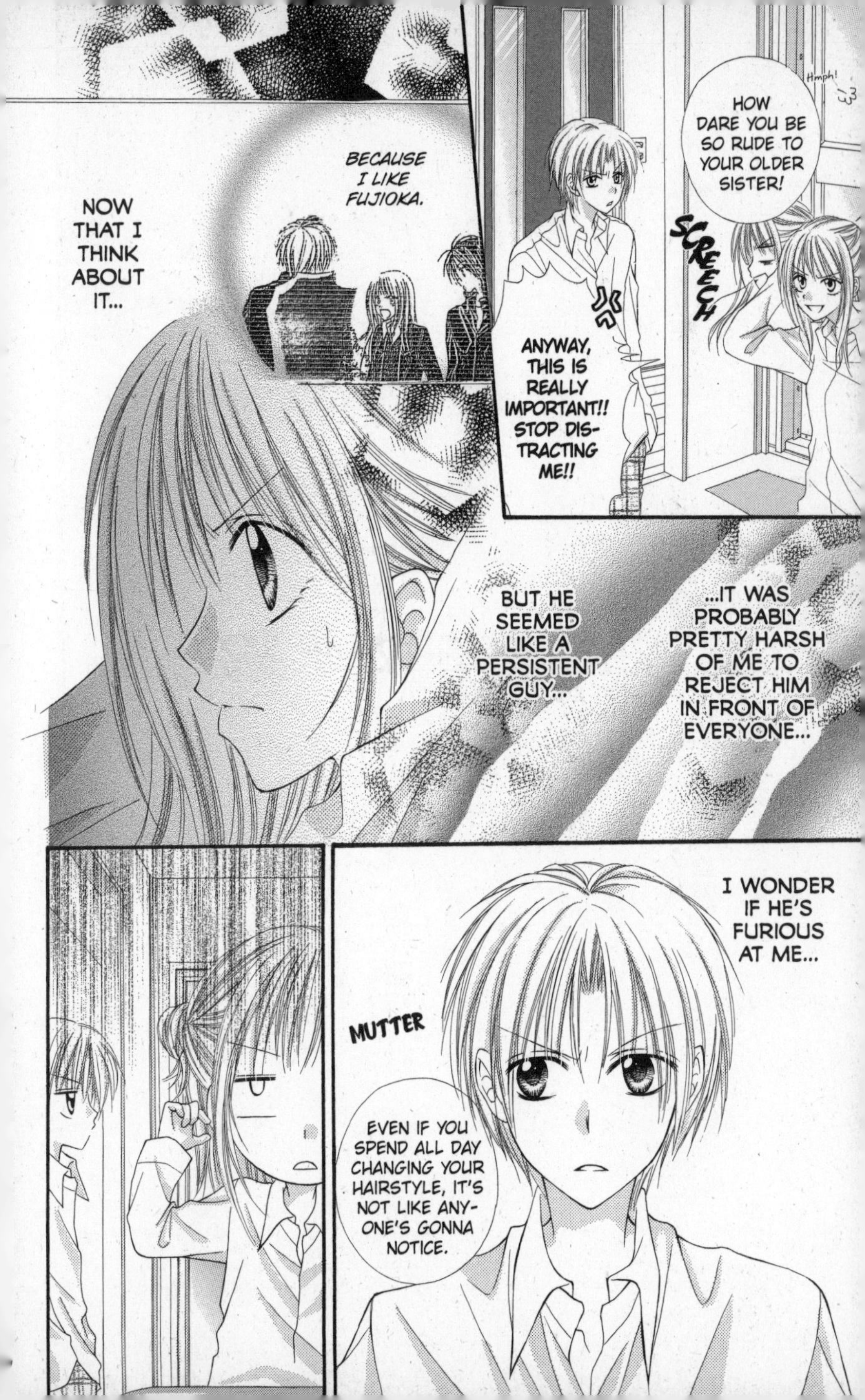
Hmph!
HOW DARE YOU BE SO RUDE TO YOUR OLDER SISTER!
SCREECH
ANYWAY, THIS IS REALLY IMPORTANT!! STOP DIS-TRACTING ME!!
BECAUSE I LIKE FUJIOKA.
NOW THAT I THINK ABOUT IT...
...IT WAS PROBABLY PRETTY HARSH OF ME TO REJECT HIM IN FRONT OF EVERYONE...
BUT HE SEEMED LIKE A PERSISTENT GUY...
I WONDER IF HE'S FURIOUS AT ME...
MUTTER
EVEN IF YOU SPEND ALL DAY CHANGING YOUR HAIRSTYLE, IT'S NOT LIKE ANY-ONE'S GONNA NOTICE.

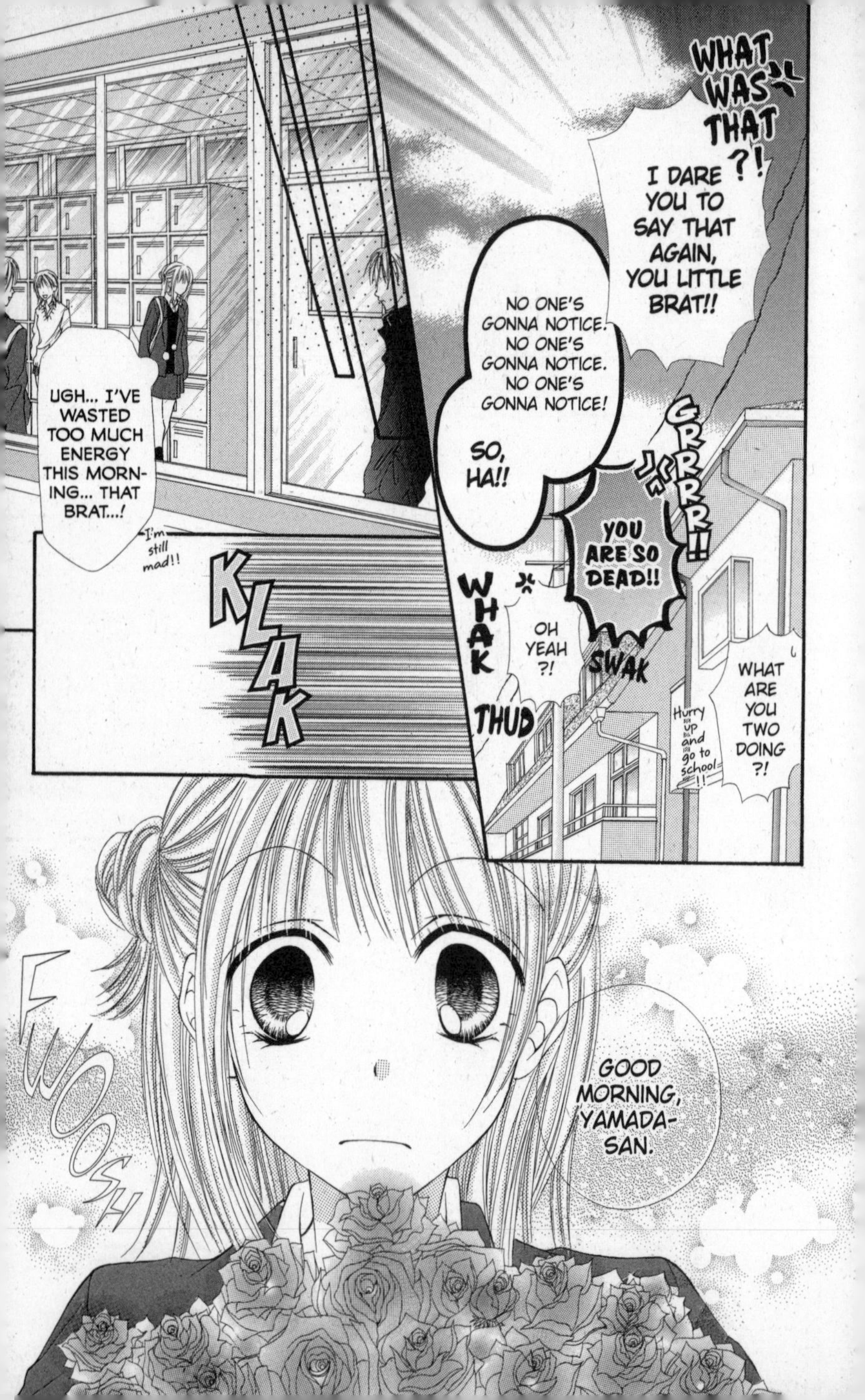
WHAT WAS THAT?!
I DARE YOU TO SAY THAT AGAIN, YOU LITTLE BRAT!!
NO ONE'S GONNA NOTICE. NO ONE'S GONNA NOTICE. NO ONE'S GONNA NOTICE!
SO, HA!!
GRRRR!!
YOU ARE SO DEAD!!
WHAK
OH YEAH?!
SWAK
THUD
WHAT ARE YOU TWO DOING?!
Hurry up and go to school!!
UGH... I'VE WASTED TOO MUCH ENERGY THIS MORNING... THAT BRAT...!
I'm still mad!!
KLAK
FWOOSH
GOOD MORNING, YAMADA-SAN.

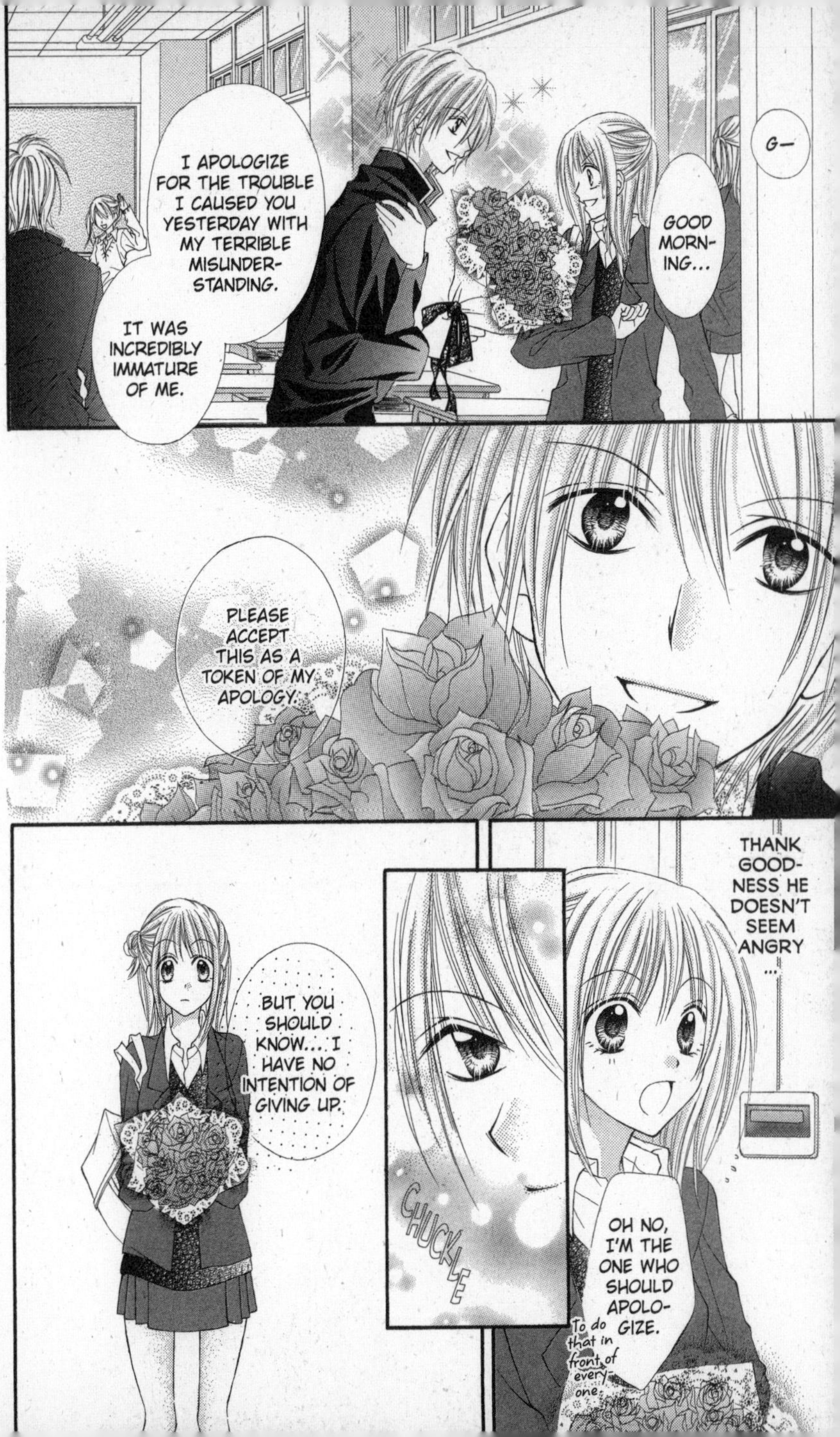
G—
GOOD MORNING...
I APOLOGIZE FOR THE TROUBLE I CAUSED YOU YESTERDAY WITH MY TERRIBLE MISUNDERSTANDING.
IT WAS INCREDIBLY IMMATURE OF ME.
PLEASE ACCEPT THIS AS A TOKEN OF MY APOLOGY.
THANK GOODNESS HE DOESN'T SEEM ANGRY...
OH NO, I'M THE ONE WHO SHOULD APOLOGIZE.
To do that in front of everyone
CHUCKLE
BUT YOU SHOULD KNOW... I HAVE NO INTENTION OF GIVING UP.

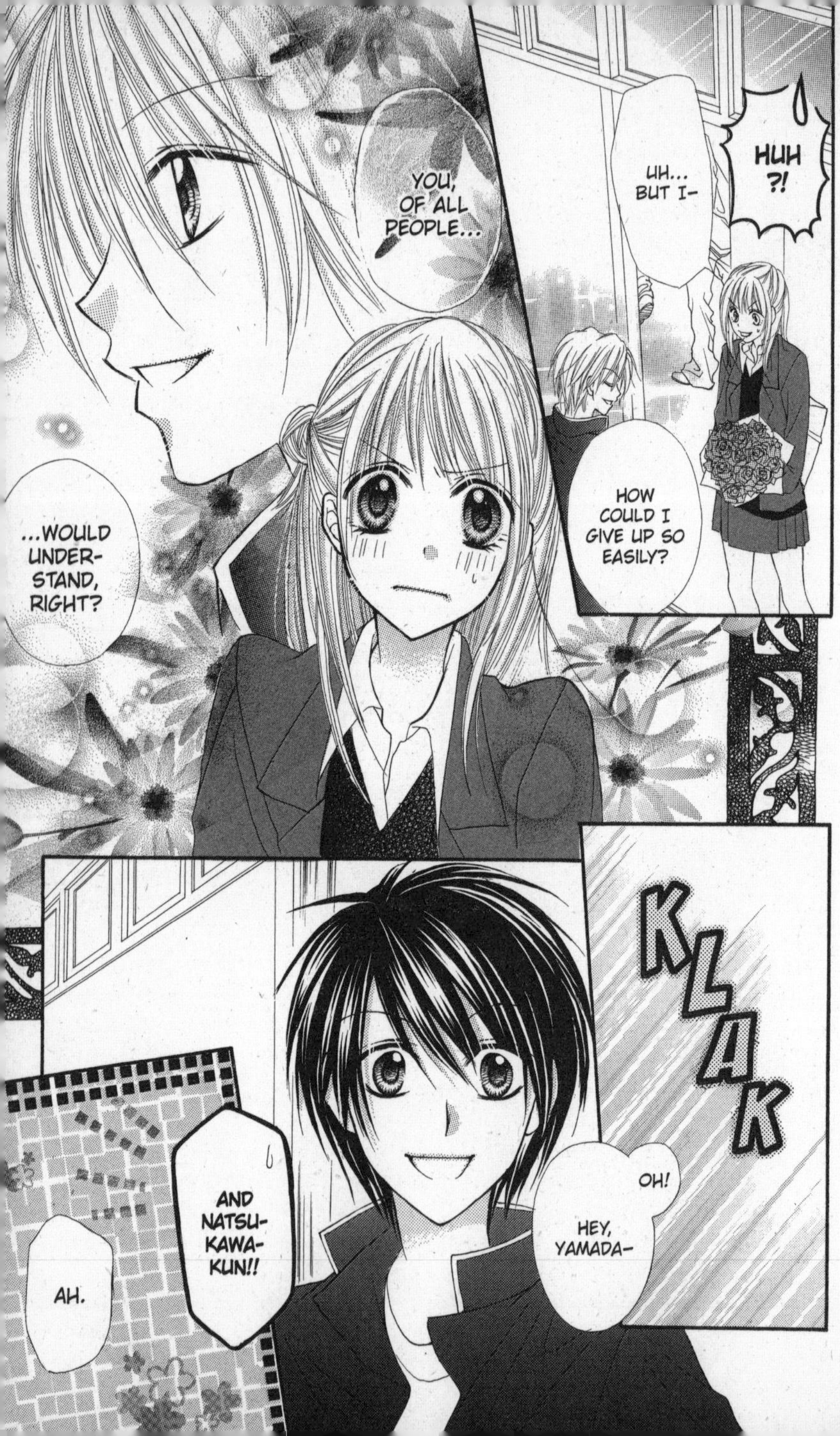
HUH ?!
UH... BUT I-
HOW COULD I GIVE UP SO EASILY?
YOU, OF ALL PEOPLE...
...WOULD UNDER-STAND, RIGHT?
KLAK
OH!
HEY, YAMADA-
AND NATSU-KAWA-KUN!!
AH.

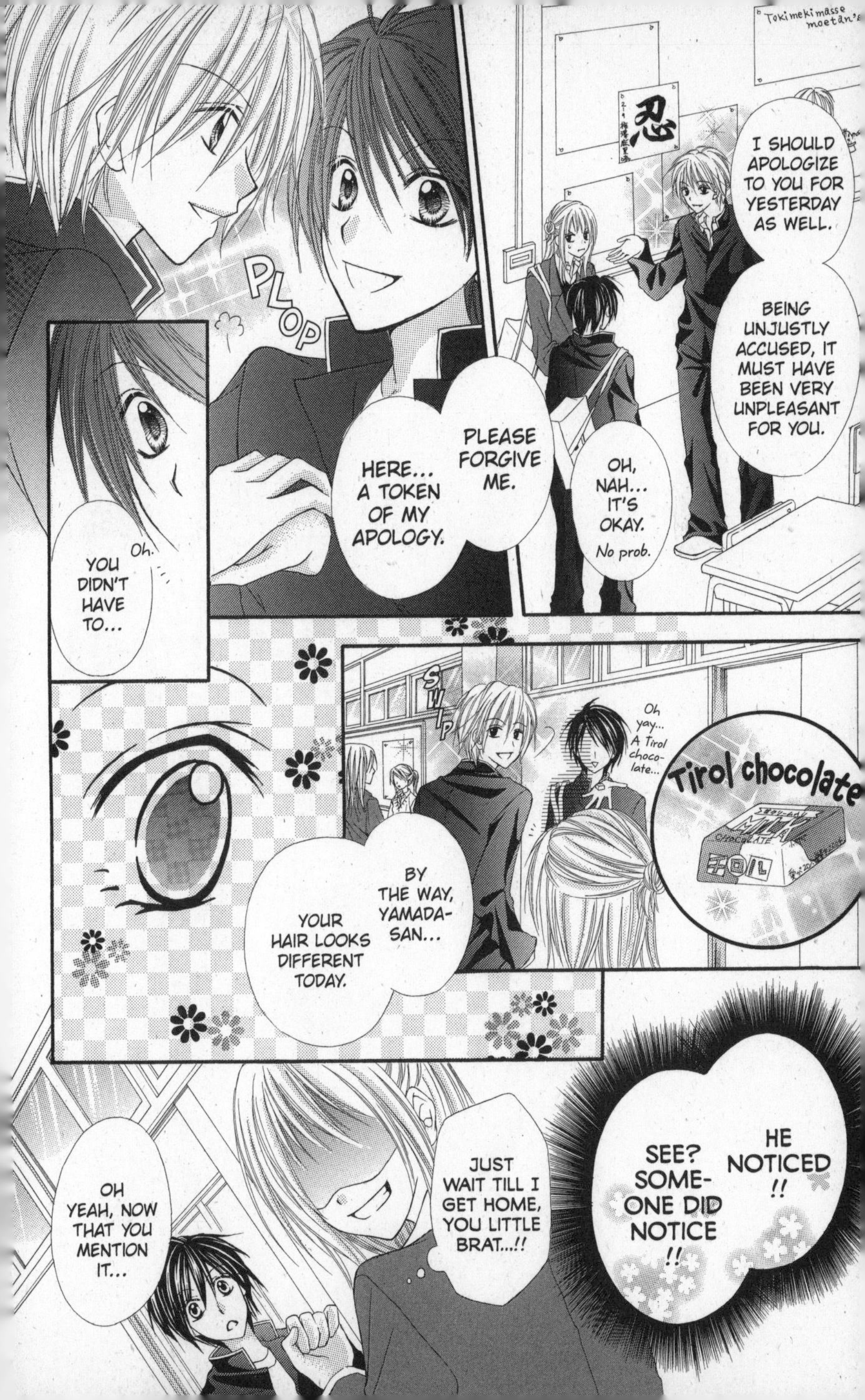
Tokimekimasse moetan's
I SHOULD APOLOGIZE TO YOU FOR YESTERDAY AS WELL.
BEING UNJUSTLY ACCUSED, IT MUST HAVE BEEN VERY UNPLEASANT FOR YOU.
OH, NAH... IT'S OKAY.
No prob.
PLOP
PLEASE FORGIVE ME.
HERE... A TOKEN OF MY APOLOGY.
Oh.
YOU DIDN'T HAVE TO...
SLIP
Oh yay... A Tirol chocolate...
Tirol chocolate
BY THE WAY, YAMADA-SAN...
YOUR HAIR LOOKS DIFFERENT TODAY.
HE NOTICED!!
SEE? SOME-ONE DID NOTICE!!
JUST WAIT TILL I GET HOME, YOU LITTLE BRAT...!!
OH YEAH, NOW THAT YOU MENTION IT...

4

Real-time news!! ...Or rather, a shameless plug!

In the current February issue of *Ribon* magazine (January 2005) that's on sale, there's an insert featuring a one-shot story by me! It's been two years since I've drawn one of these, so for anyone who only buys *Cactus* books, please check out the current *Ribon* issue. It'll be a while before you can see it published in a book, so you should use this opportunity to read it now. I thought it'd be impossible for me to draw an extra story while in the middle of *Cactus*'s serialization, but I jumped at the chance when my editor asked me if I could do it. I've always wanted to draw one! I really didn't have the time to do it, but I had SOOOOOOOO much fun doing it. I ended up really liking the story's love interest, Chihiro-kun. If you liked Setsu from my story "Samurai Darling," you'll probably like him too. The main character's name is Mao. It might be a nice surprise if you haven't read any of my work outside of *Cactus*. Or maybe I'm the only one who thinks so.

Please pick up a copy of the February issue of *Ribon* so you can read my one-shot, plus (of course) the latest chapter of *Cactus*! If you can, please buy it!

And that ends my plug...

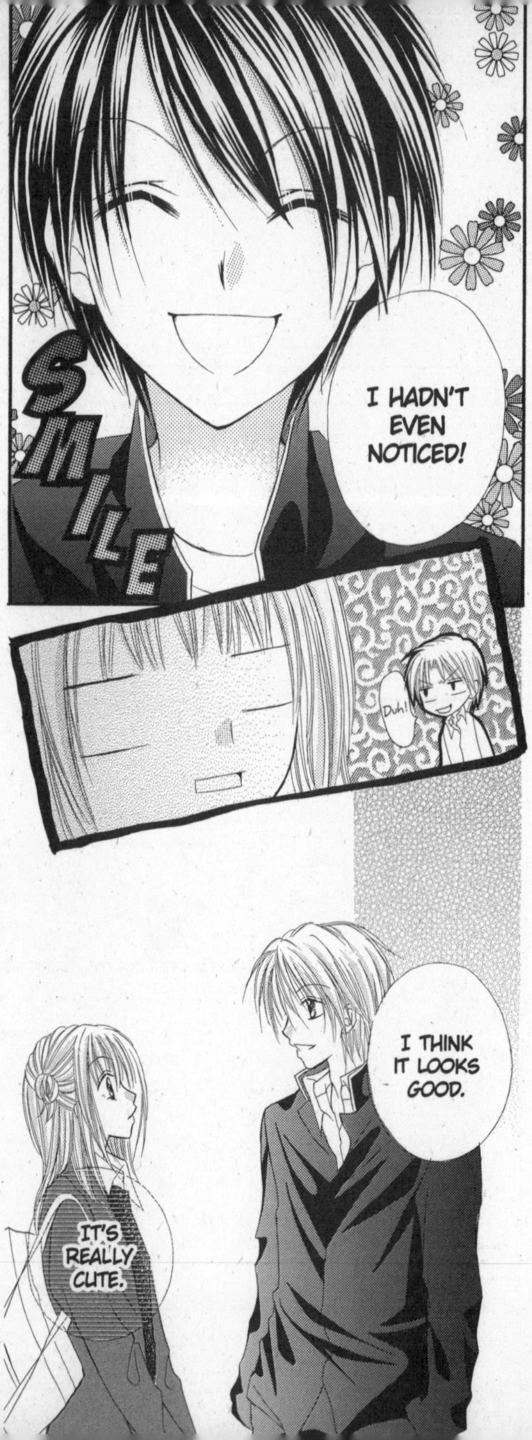
I HADN'T EVEN NOTICED!
SMILE
Duh!
I THINK IT LOOKS GOOD.
IT'S REALLY CUTE.

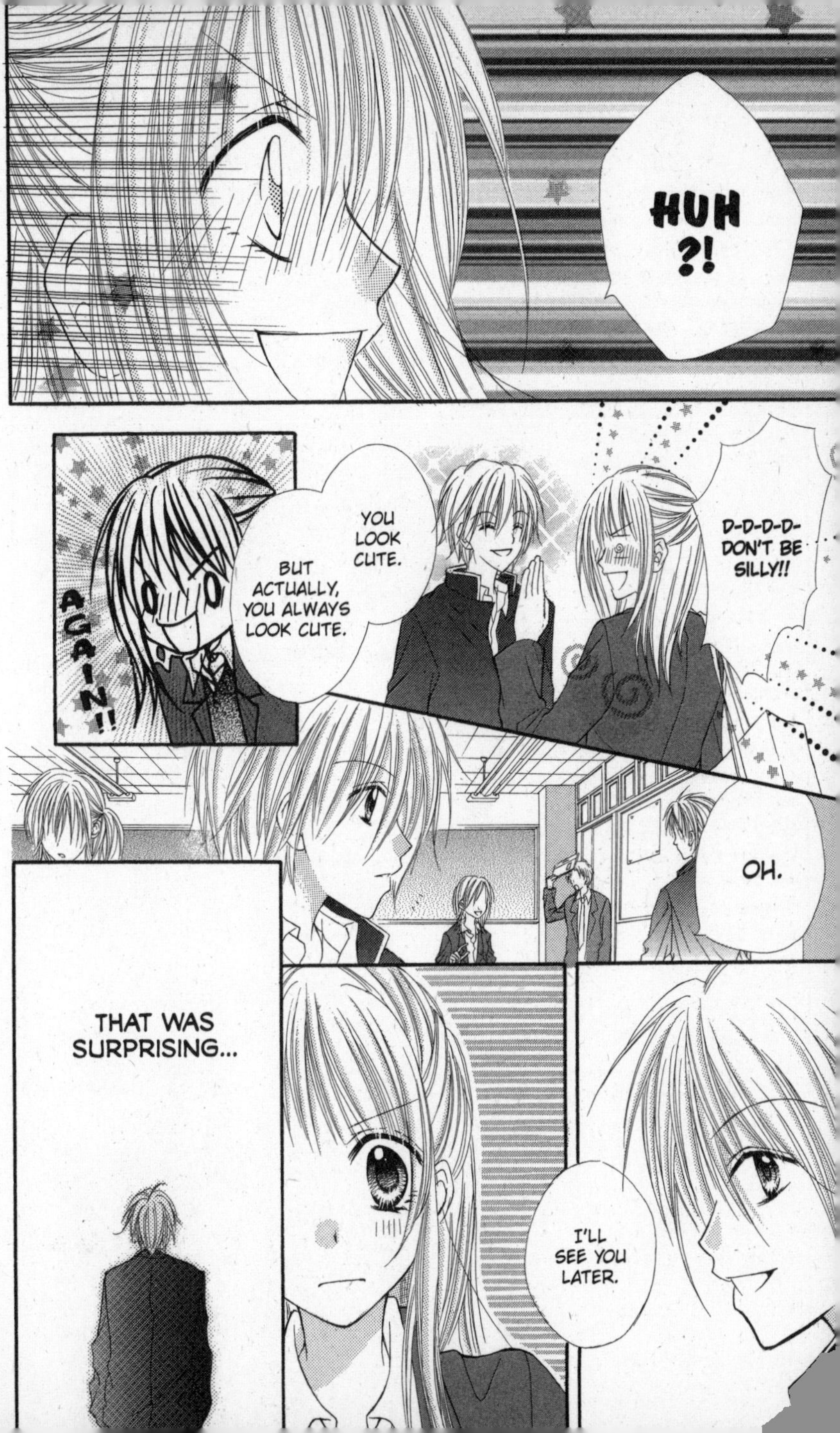
HUH ?!
YOU LOOK CUTE. BUT ACTUALLY, YOU ALWAYS LOOK CUTE.
D-D-D-D-DON'T BE SILLY!!
AGAIN!!
OH.
I'LL SEE YOU LATER.
THAT WAS SURPRISING...

5

Those of you who buy *Ribon* magazine probably already know this, but anyone who sends in an order can receive a free *Cactus's Secret* drama CD! (This was for December 2004's issue, so unfortunately you can't order it anymore.) Never in my wildest dreams did I imagine I would get to hear my characters speaking, so it came as quite a surprise. "Are you sure it's okay to make my manga into a drama CD?" I would ask hesitantly, but honestly, I'm super excited.

The CD is 20 minutes long and ends just before Natsukawa-kun makes his first appearance, so the main characters are Miku, Fujioka and Minase-san. The voice actors have very busy schedules, so I apologize greatly if I was too demanding. I'm just brimming with gratitude to them. (babbling)

Being allowed to watch the post-recording chat was also a good experience. Though I felt really out of place. Well, our worlds are totally different after all, so I guess that was only natural.

So is everyone who ordered a copy of the CD still waiting for theirs to arrive too? Hope you look forward to it!

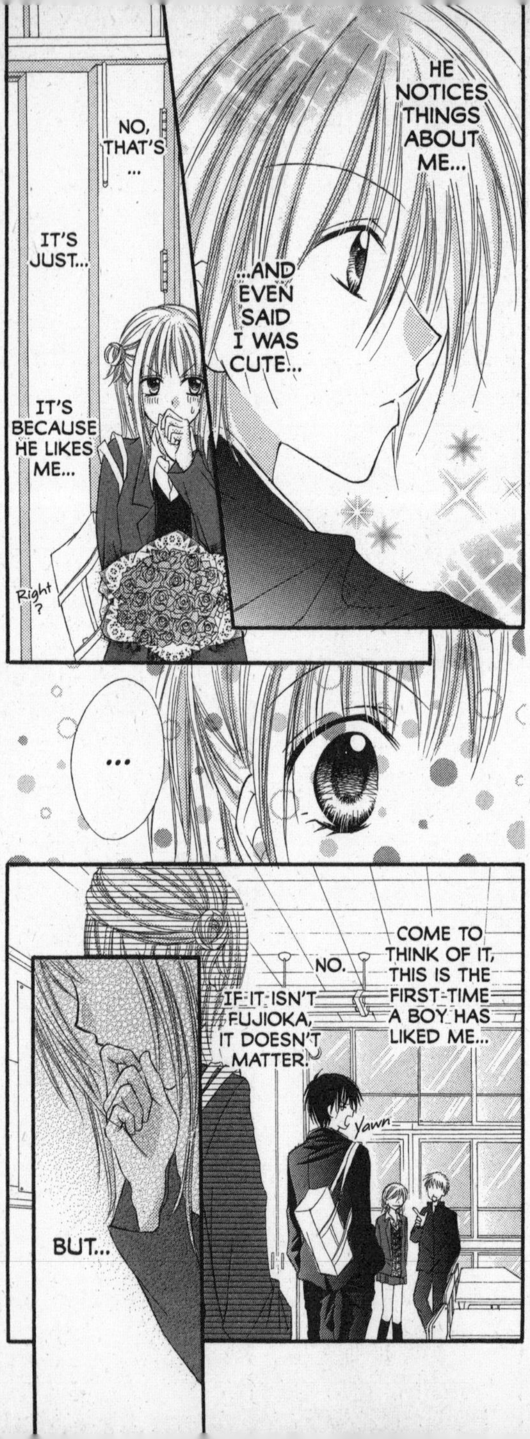
HE NOTICES THINGS ABOUT ME...
...AND EVEN SAID I WAS CUTE...
NO, THAT'S...
IT'S JUST...
IT'S BECAUSE HE LIKES ME...
Right?
...
COME TO THINK OF IT, THIS IS THE FIRST TIME A BOY HAS LIKED ME...
NO.
IF IT ISN'T FUJIOKA, IT DOESN'T MATTER.
Yawn
BUT...

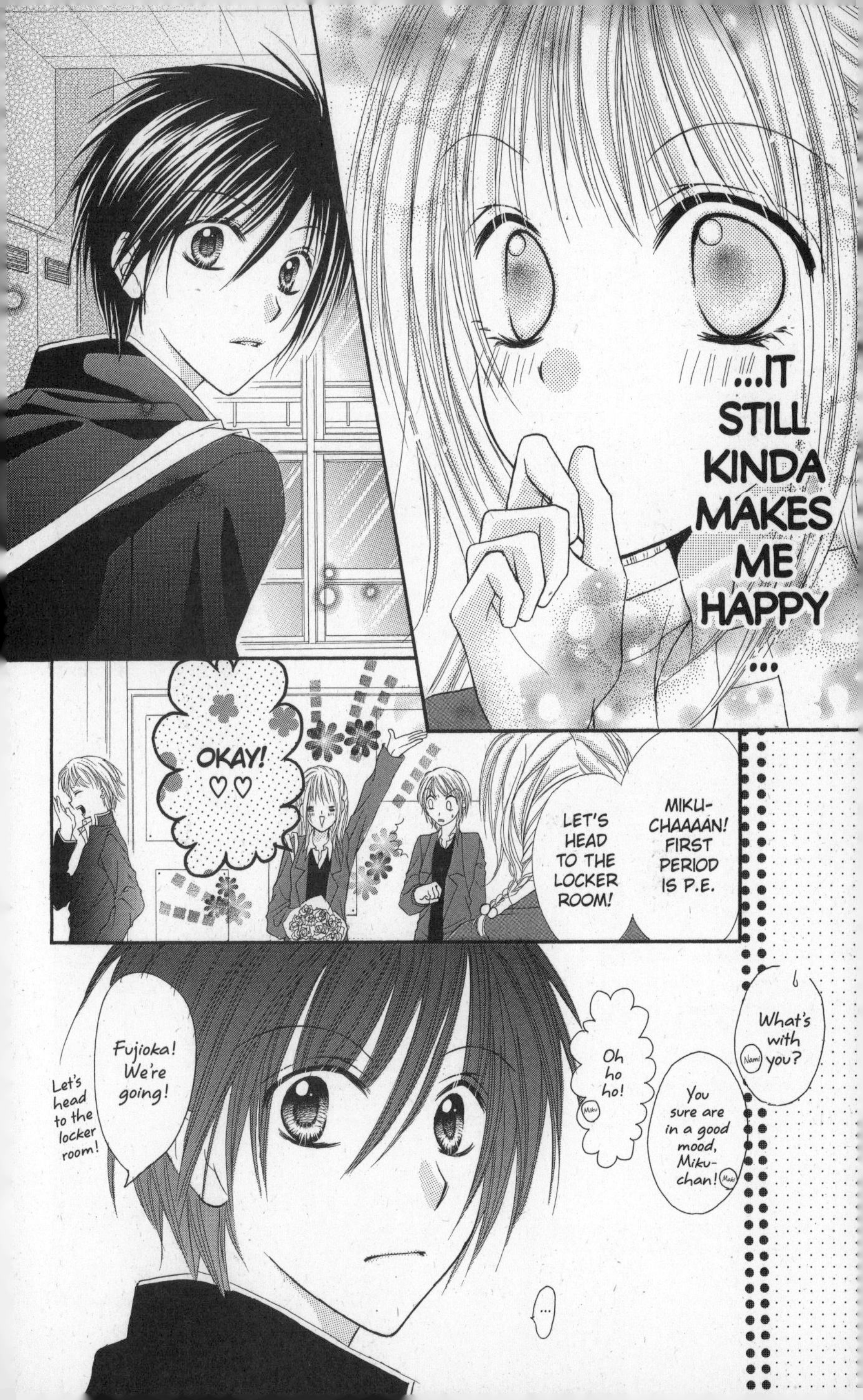
...IT STILL KINDA MAKES ME HAPPY ...
MIKU-CHAAAAN! FIRST PERIOD IS P.E.
LET'S HEAD TO THE LOCKER ROOM!
OKAY! ♡♡
What's with you?
Nami
You sure are in a good mood, Miku-chan!
Maki
Oh ho ho!
Miku
Fujioka! We're going!
Let's head to the locker room!
...

6

Waah! What a shocker!! Something just happened (in real time), and I'm totally in shock!!

Oh, sorry. Just now a courier came by to pick up my latest manuscript (yep, they have that kind of service these days), and the deliveryman suddenly asked, "This is being serialized right now, right?" This is what I was thinking at that moment: ↓

Serialized? Does he mean a manga serialization? Yes, he must!! Does he know I'm using a pen name for my manga?! Oh no, what should I do?! My real name is on the door—how embarrassing!! Who is this Haruta person? Hey! Heeeey!!

In shock. 11/28 at 9 P.M.

Despite thinking all that in my head, I answered calmly, "Oh yes." Acting all cool... Heh heh.

It turns out his daughter reads my manga and buys the books... Thank you so much! I was caught off guard, but I'm really happy about this! It made me want to work harder.

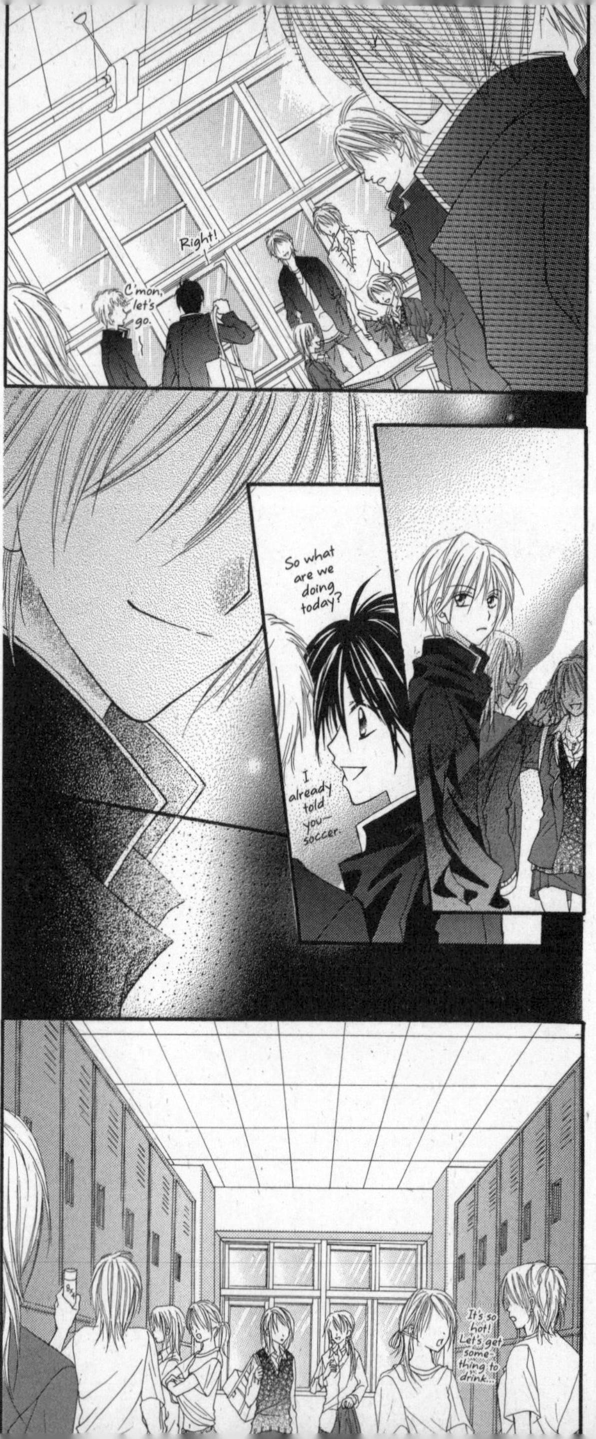
C'mon, let's go.
Right!
So what are we doing today?
I already told you—soccer.
It's so hot! Let's get something to drink...

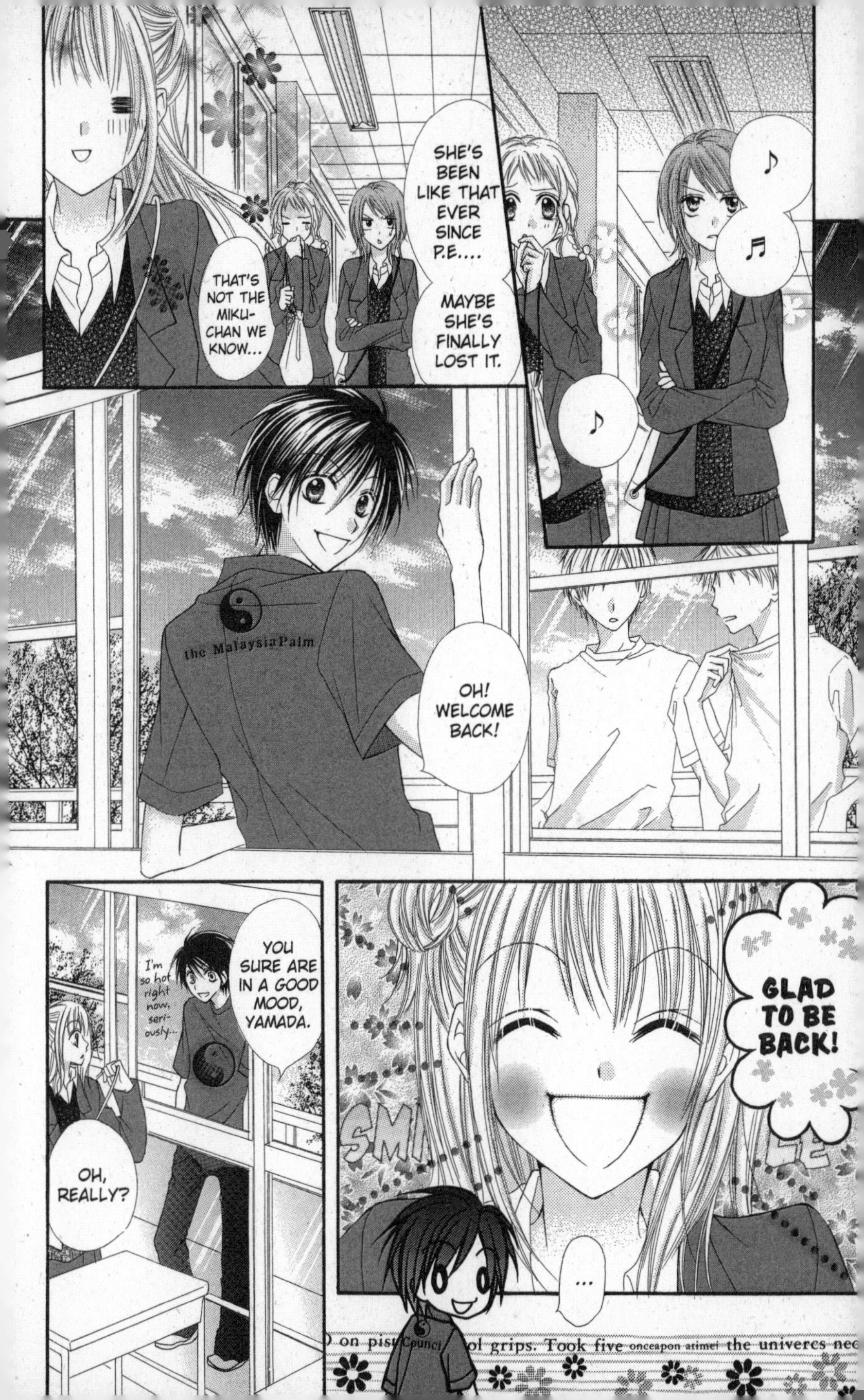
♪
♬
♪
SHE'S BEEN LIKE THAT EVER SINCE P.E....
MAYBE SHE'S FINALLY LOST IT.
THAT'S NOT THE MIKU-CHAN WE KNOW...
the MalaysiaPalm
OH! WELCOME BACK!
GLAD TO BE BACK!
...
YOU SURE ARE IN A GOOD MOOD, YAMADA.
I'm so hot right now, seriously...
OH, REALLY?

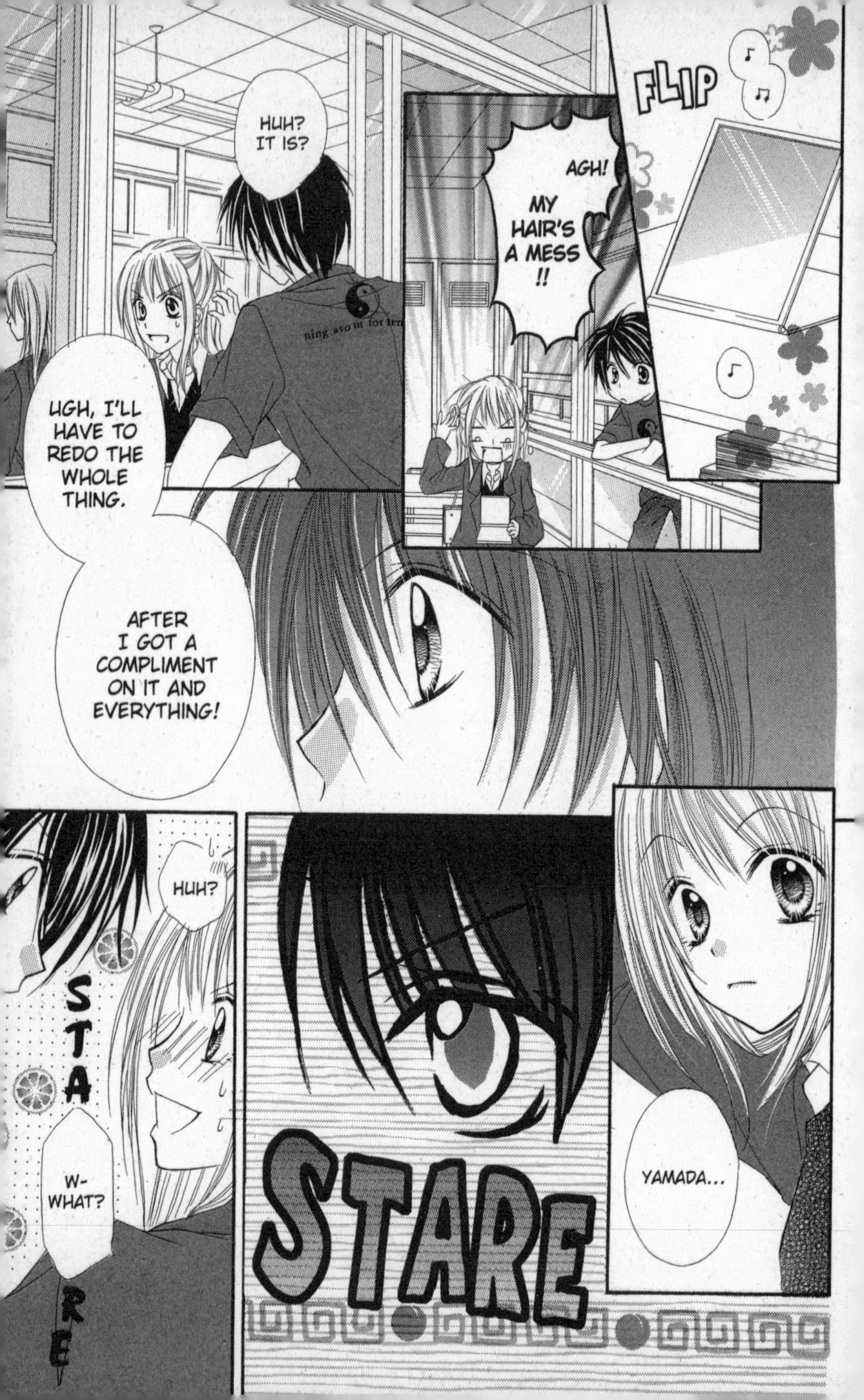
FLIP
AGH! MY HAIR'S A MESS !!
HUH? IT IS?
UGH, I'LL HAVE TO REDO THE WHOLE THING.
AFTER I GOT A COMPLIMENT ON IT AND EVERYTHING!
YAMADA...
STARE
HUH?
STA
W- WHAT?
RE

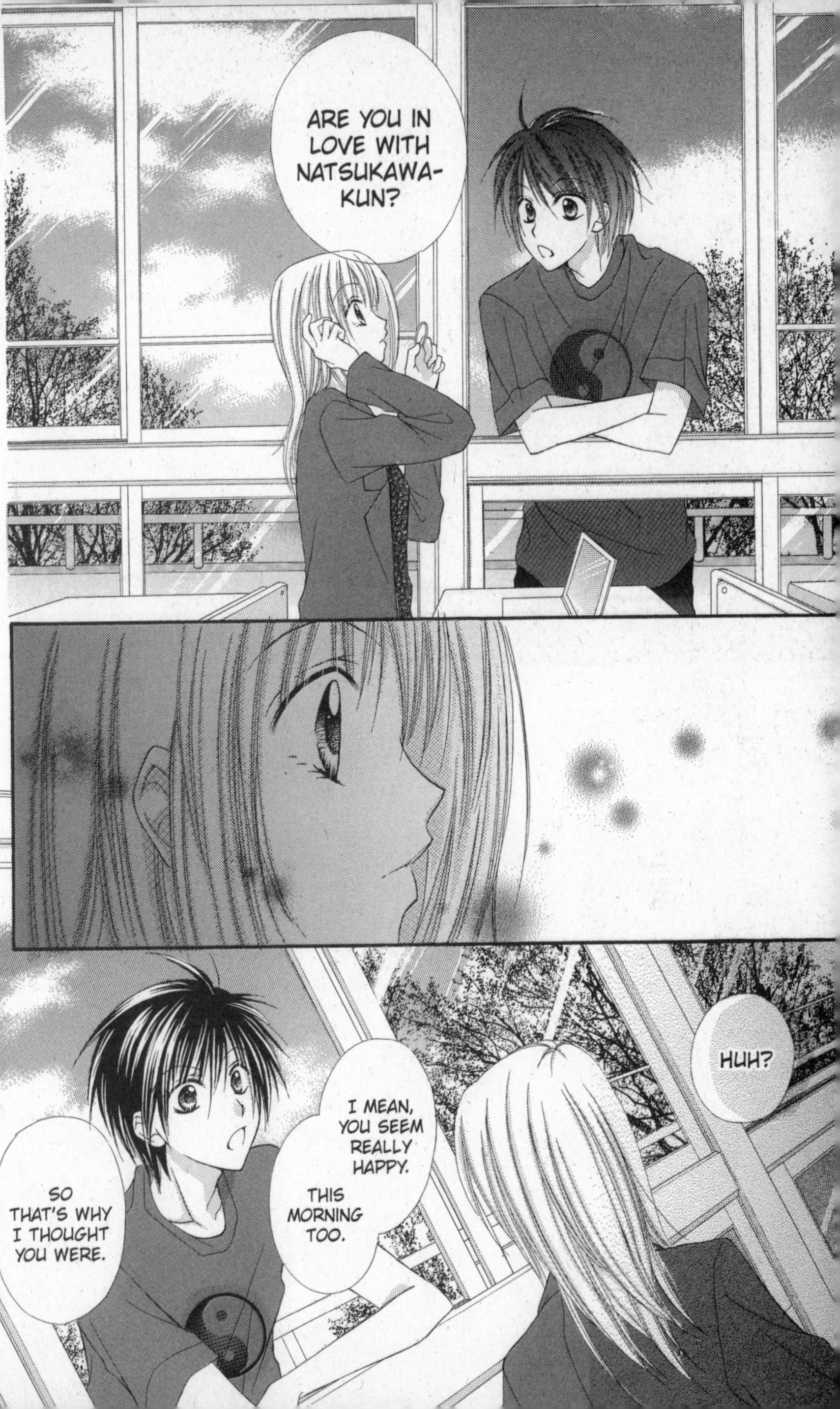
ARE YOU IN LOVE WITH NATSUKAWA-KUN?
HUH?
I MEAN, YOU SEEM REALLY HAPPY.
THIS MORNING TOO.
SO THAT'S WHY I THOUGHT YOU WERE.

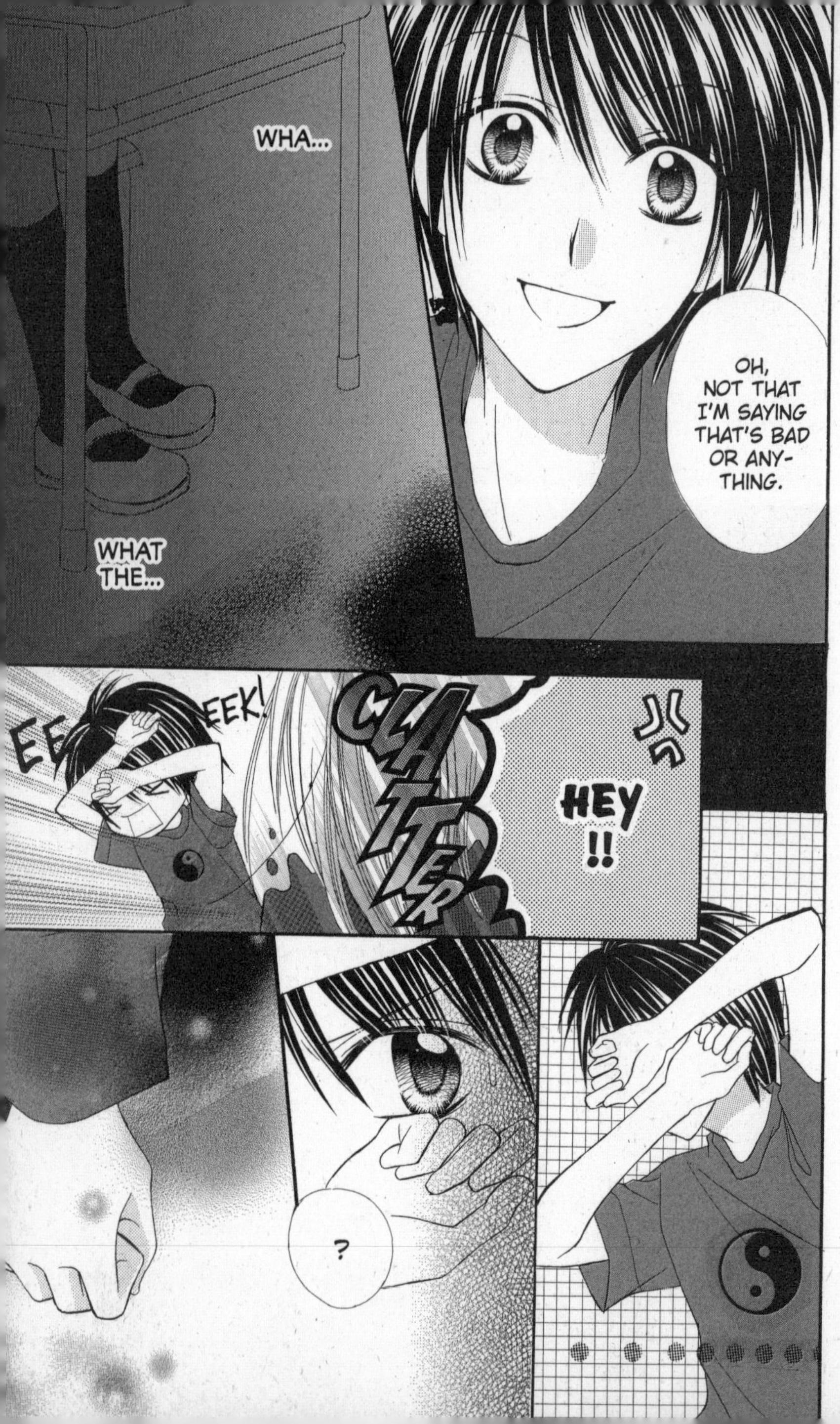
OH, NOT THAT I'M SAYING THAT'S BAD OR ANY-THING.
WHA...
WHAT THE...
HEY !!
CLATTER
EEEEK!
?

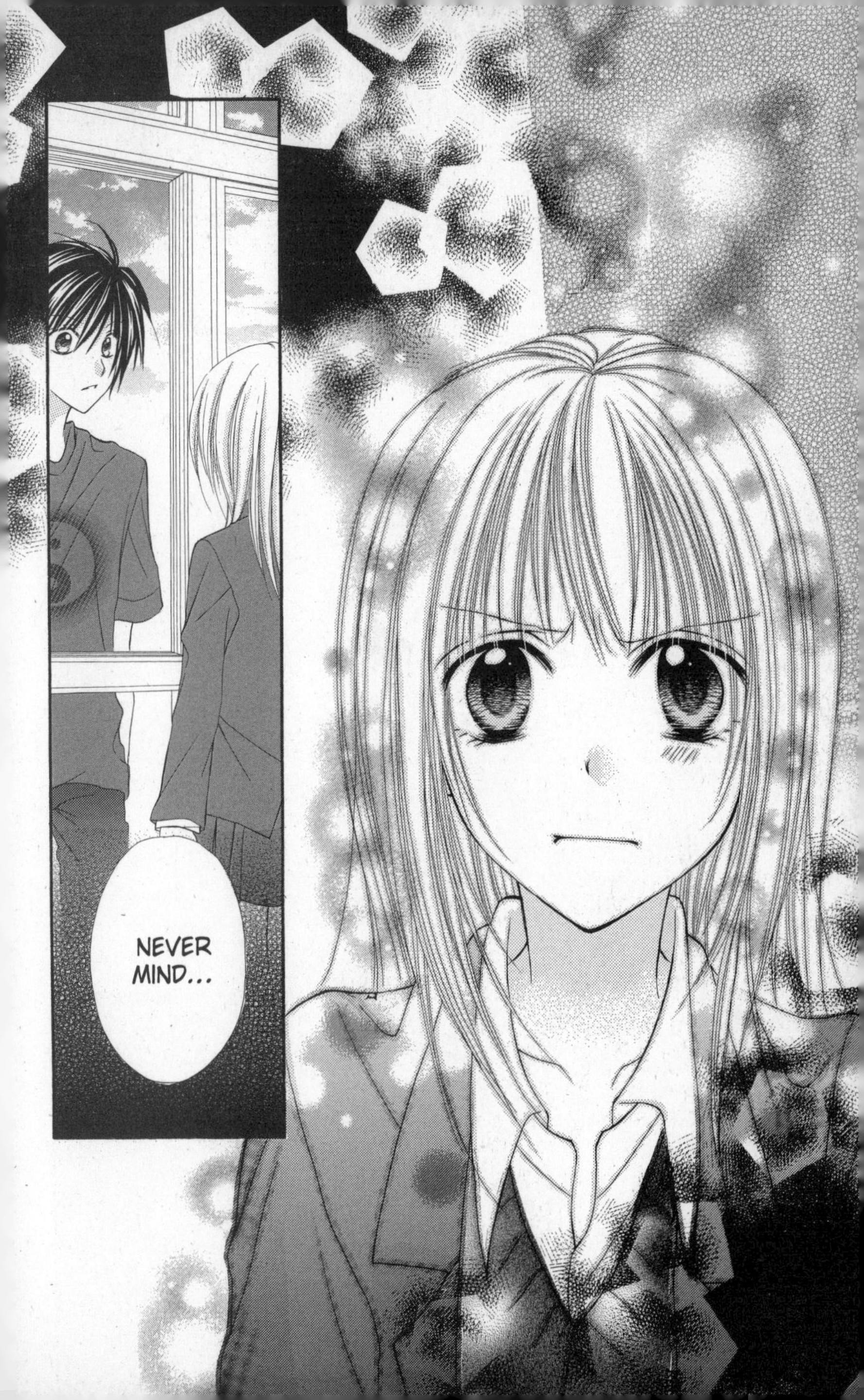
NEVER MIND...

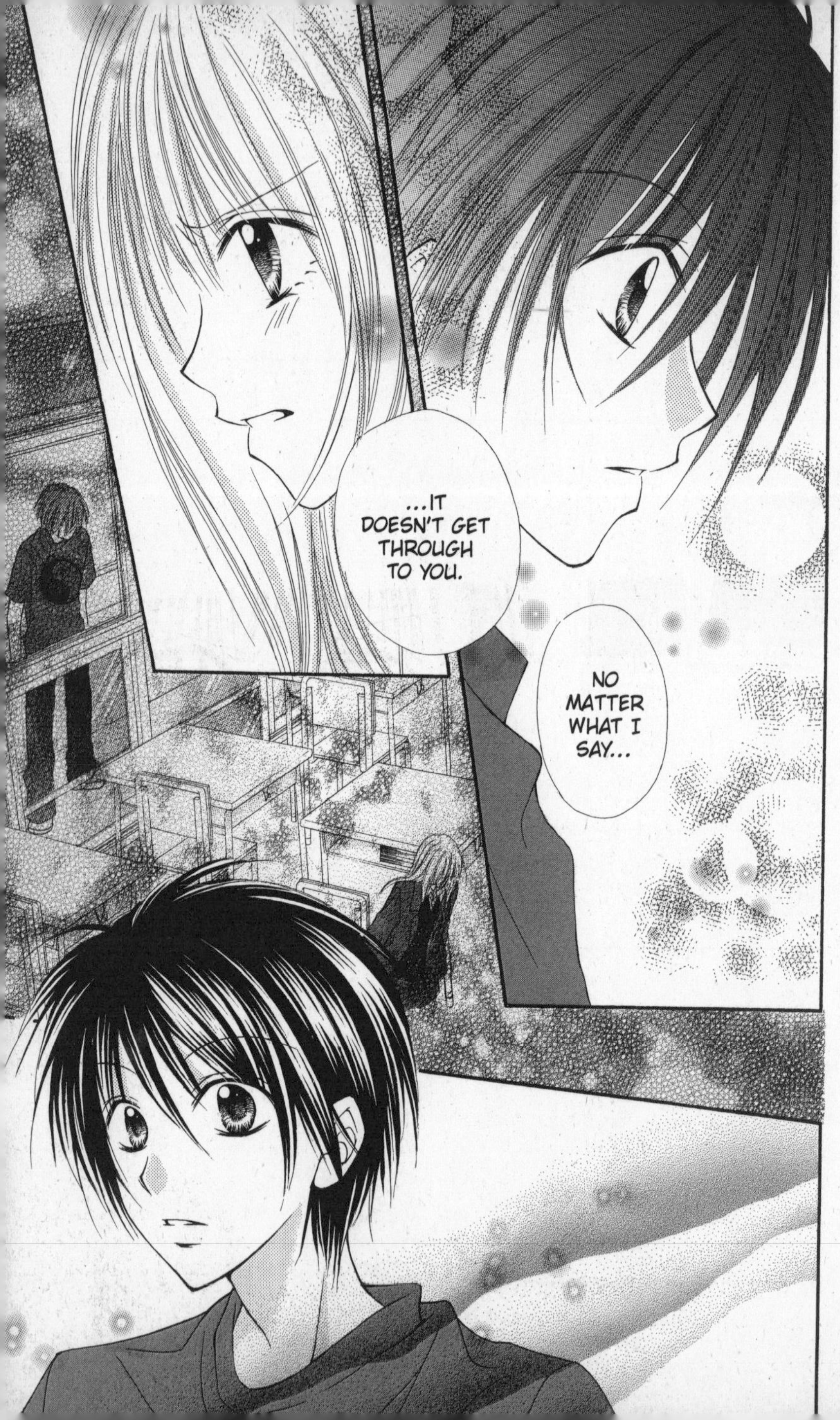
NO MATTER WHAT I SAY...
...IT DOESN'T GET THROUGH TO YOU.

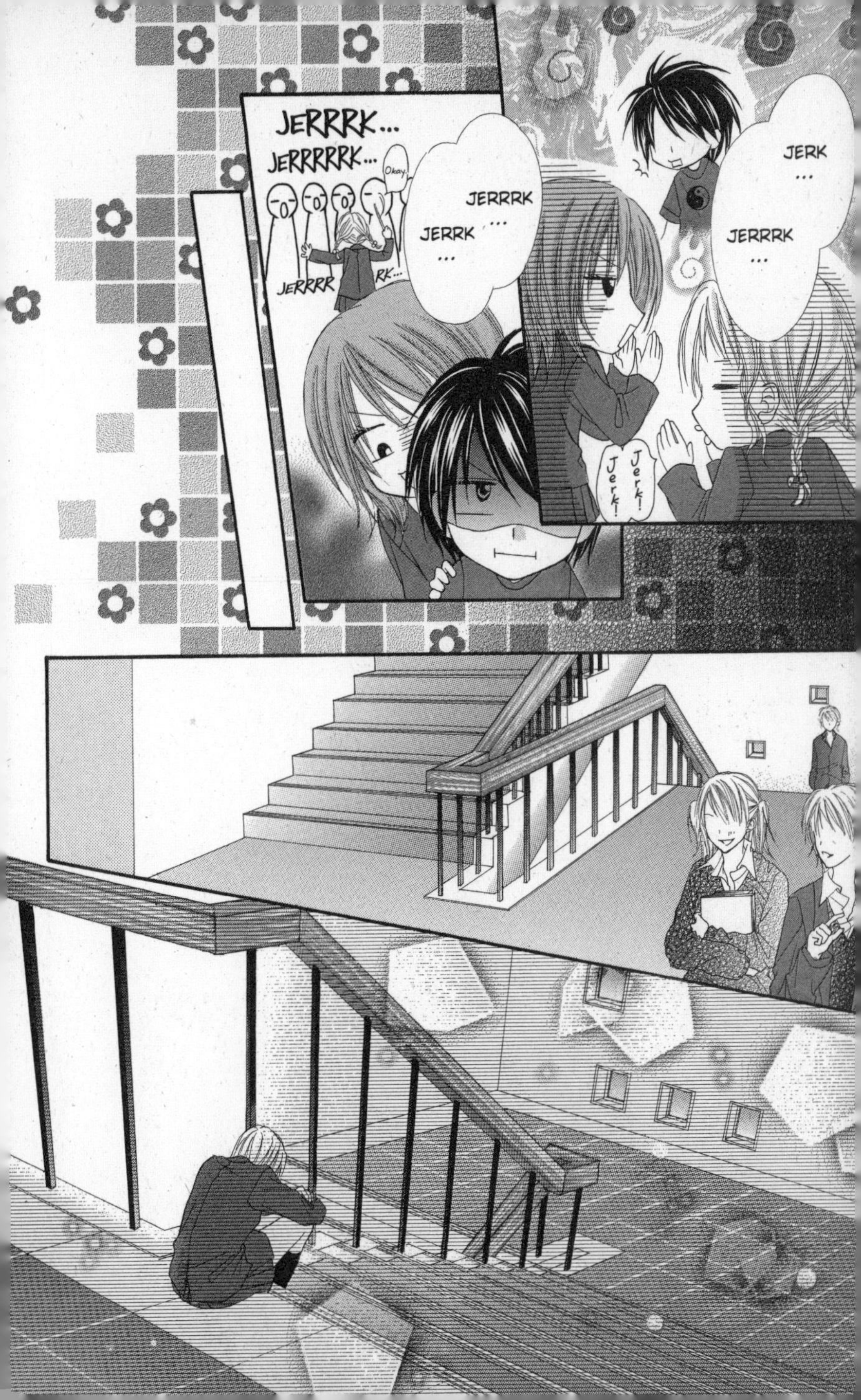
JERK ... JERRRK ...
Jerk! Jerk!
JERRRK ... JERRK ...
JERRRK...
JERRRRRK...
Okay.
JERRRR
RK...

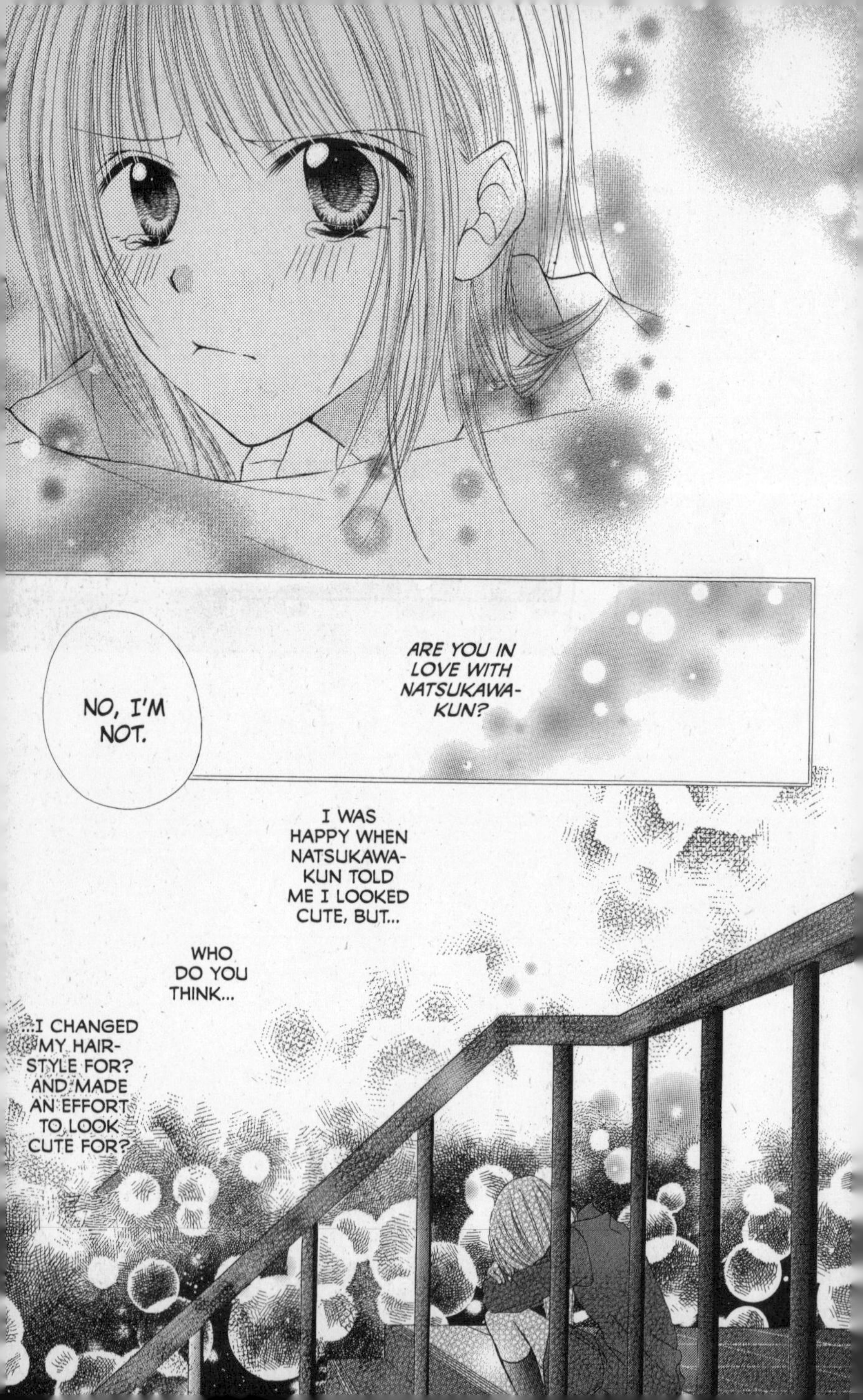
ARE YOU IN LOVE WITH NATSUKAWA-KUN?
NO, I'M NOT.
I WAS HAPPY WHEN NATSUKAWA-KUN TOLD ME I LOOKED CUTE, BUT...
WHO DO YOU THINK...
...I CHANGED MY HAIR-STYLE FOR? AND MADE AN EFFORT TO LOOK CUTE FOR?

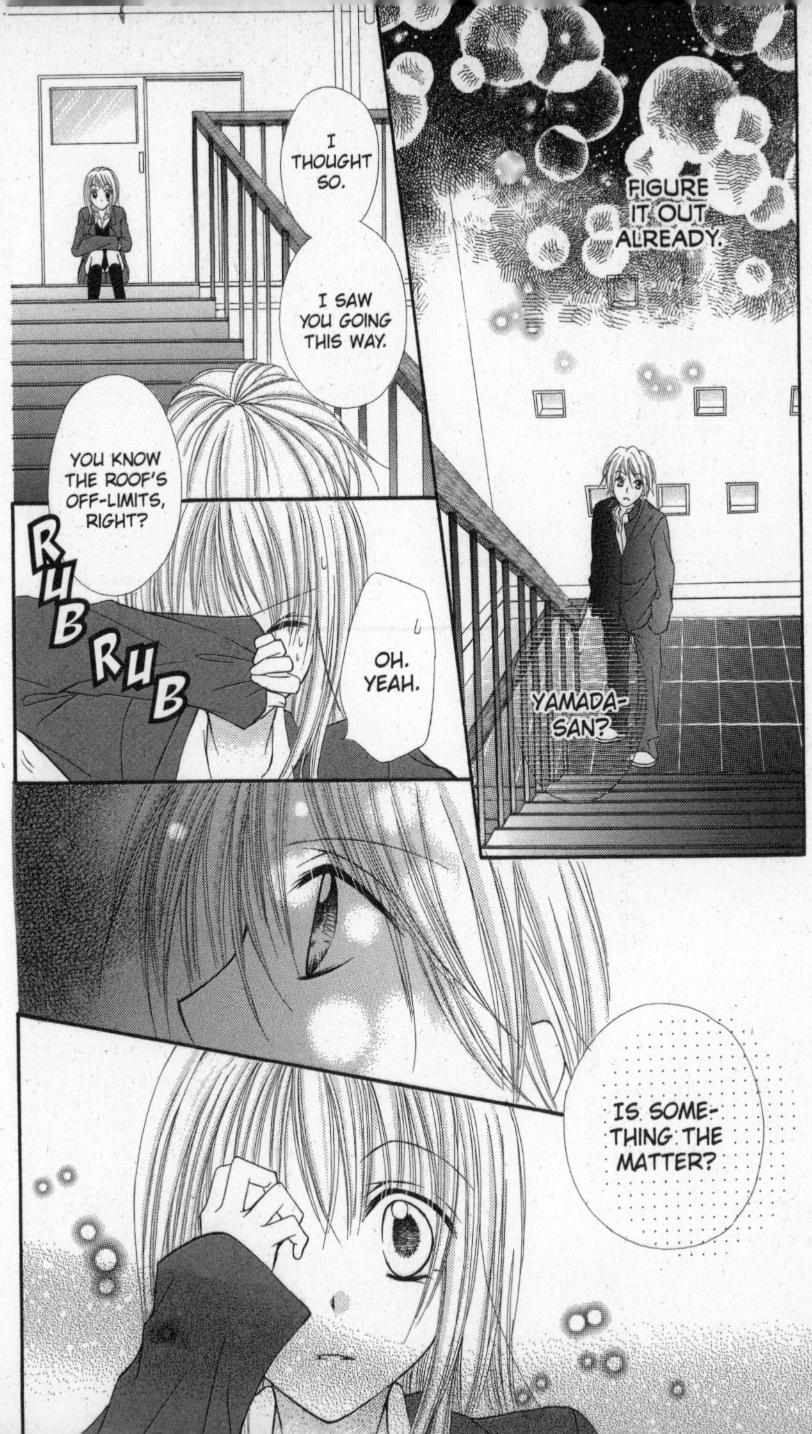
FIGURE IT OUT ALREADY.
YAMADA-SAN?
I THOUGHT SO.
I SAW YOU GOING THIS WAY.
YOU KNOW THE ROOF'S OFF-LIMITS, RIGHT?
RUB RUB RUB
OH. YEAH.
IS SOMETHING THE MATTER?

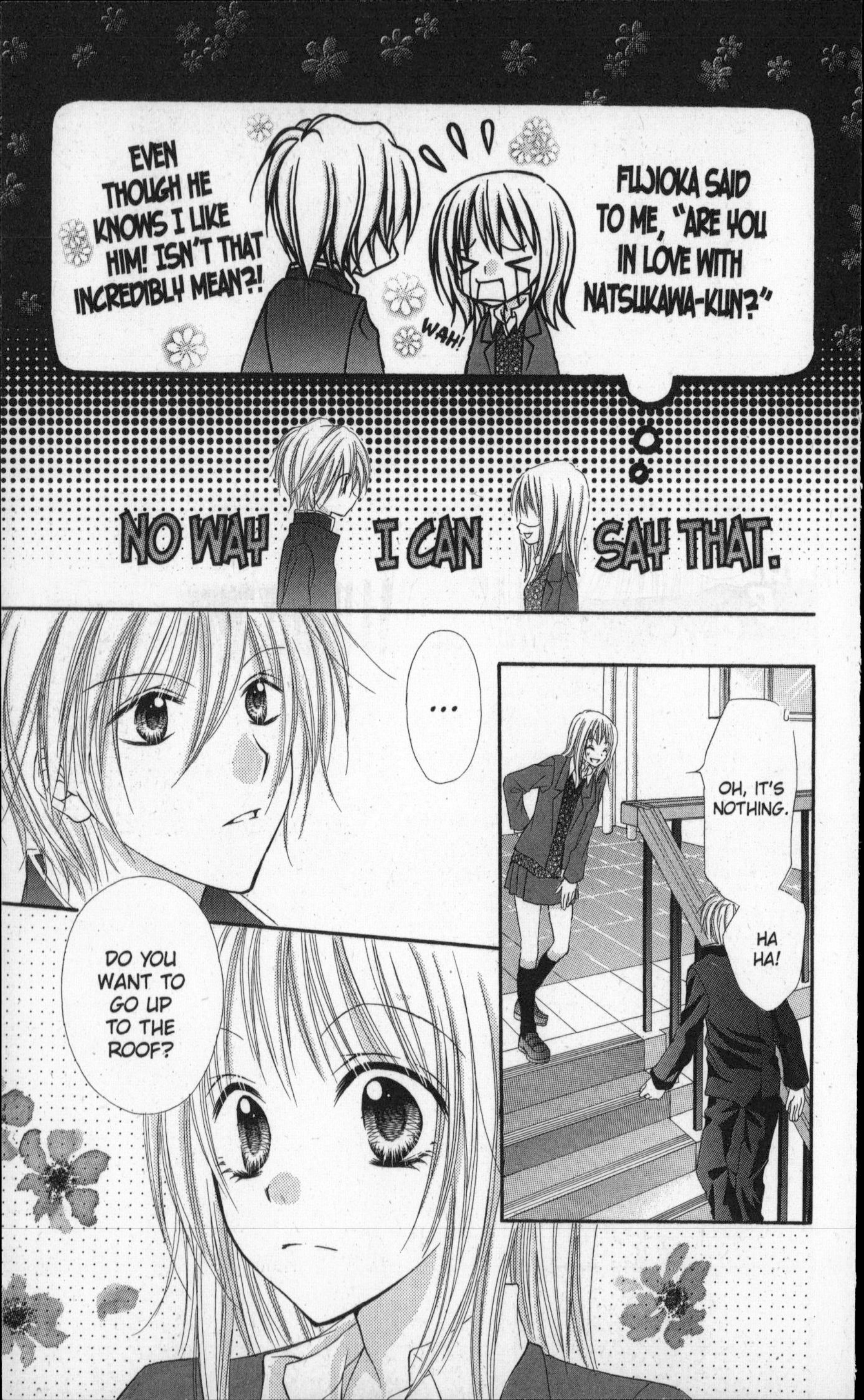
FUJIOKA SAID TO ME, "ARE YOU IN LOVE WITH NATSUKAWA-KUN?"
EVEN THOUGH HE KNOWS I LIKE HIM! ISN'T THAT INCREDIBLY MEAN?!
WAH!
NO WAY I CAN SAY THAT.
OH, IT'S NOTHING.
HA HA!
...
DO YOU WANT TO GO UP TO THE ROOF?

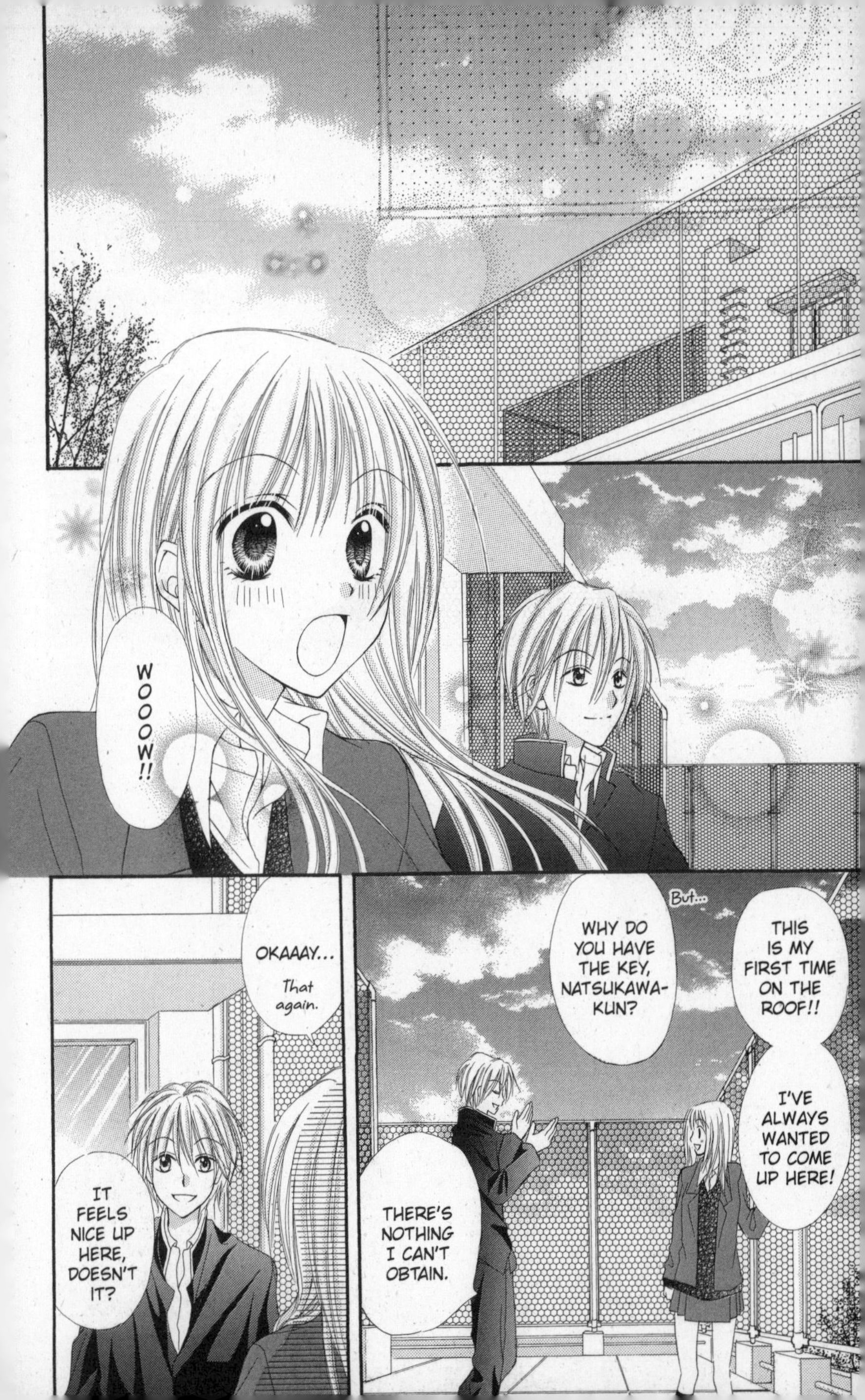
WOOOW!!
THIS IS MY FIRST TIME ON THE ROOF!!
I'VE ALWAYS WANTED TO COME UP HERE!
But...
WHY DO YOU HAVE THE KEY, NATSUKAWA-KUN?
THERE'S NOTHING I CAN'T OBTAIN.
OKAAAY... That again.
IT FEELS NICE UP HERE, DOESN'T IT?

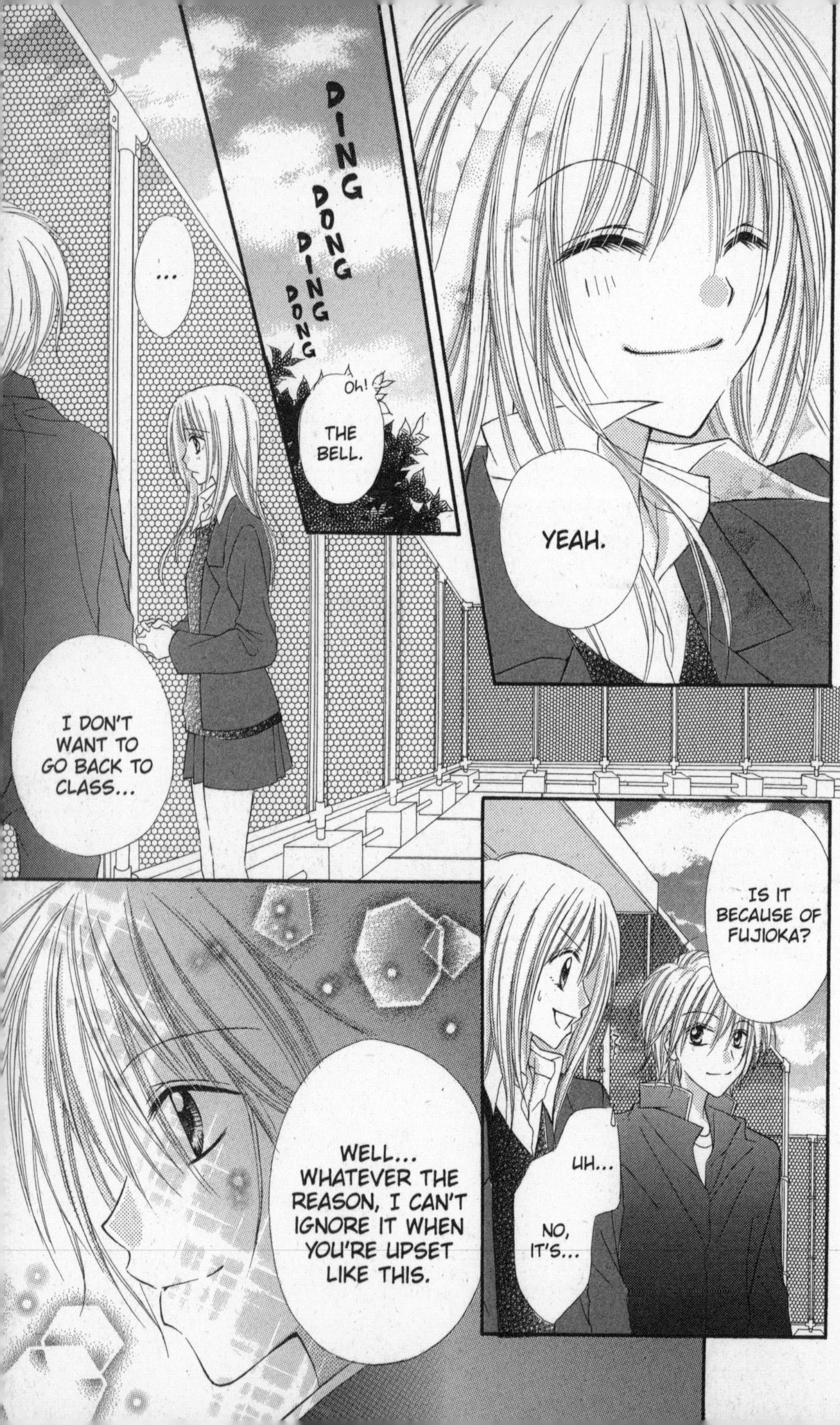
DING DONG DING DONG
Oh!
THE BELL.
YEAH.
...
I DON'T WANT TO GO BACK TO CLASS...
IS IT BECAUSE OF FUJIOKA?
UH...
NO, IT'S...
WELL... WHATEVER THE REASON, I CAN'T IGNORE IT WHEN YOU'RE UPSET LIKE THIS.

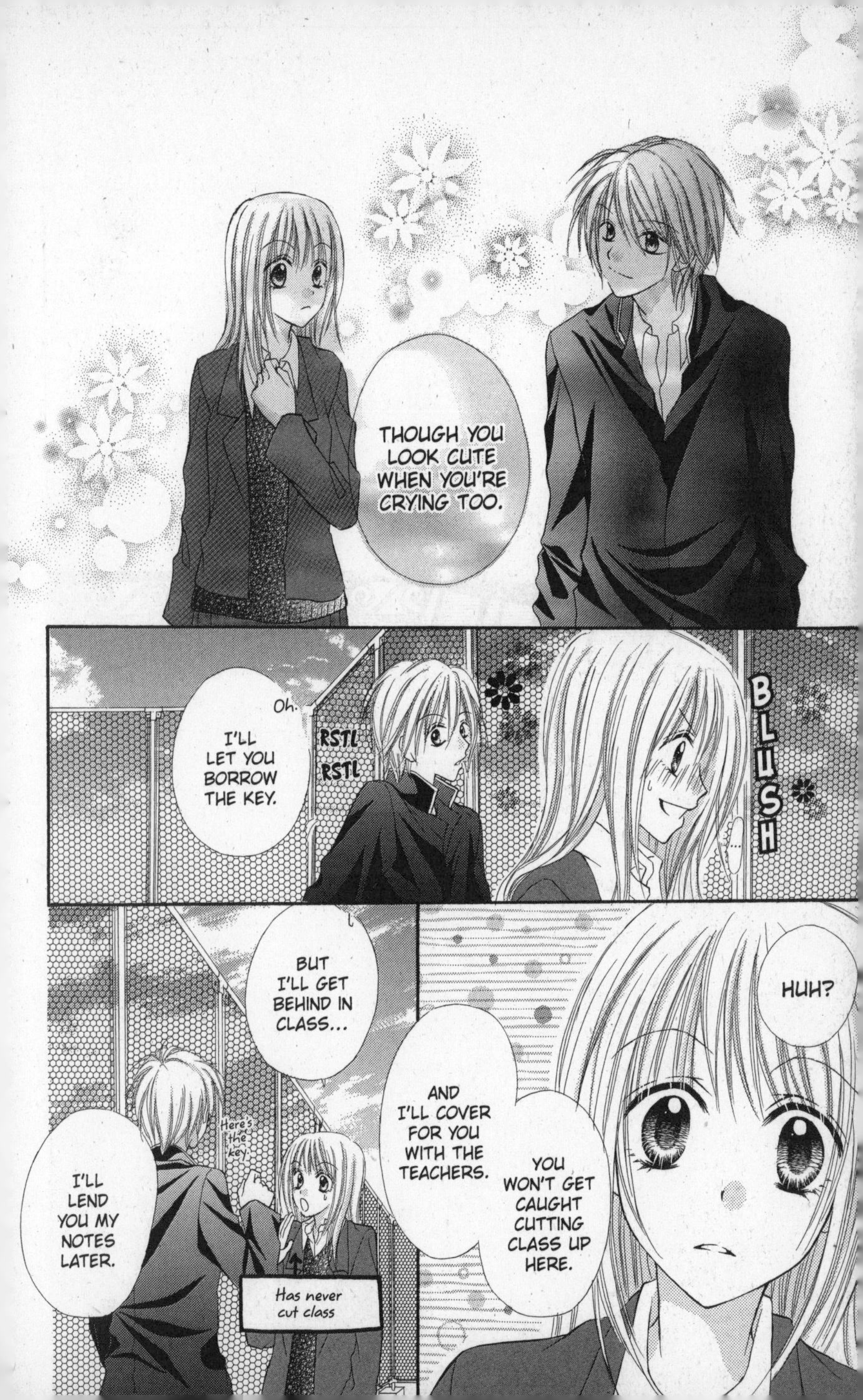
THOUGH YOU LOOK CUTE WHEN YOU'RE CRYING TOO.
BLUSH
...
Oh.
RSTL
RSTL
I'LL LET YOU BORROW THE KEY.
HUH?
YOU WON'T GET CAUGHT CUTTING CLASS UP HERE.
BUT I'LL GET BEHIND IN CLASS...
AND I'LL COVER FOR YOU WITH THE TEACHERS.
Here's the key.
I'LL LEND YOU MY NOTES LATER.
Has never cut class

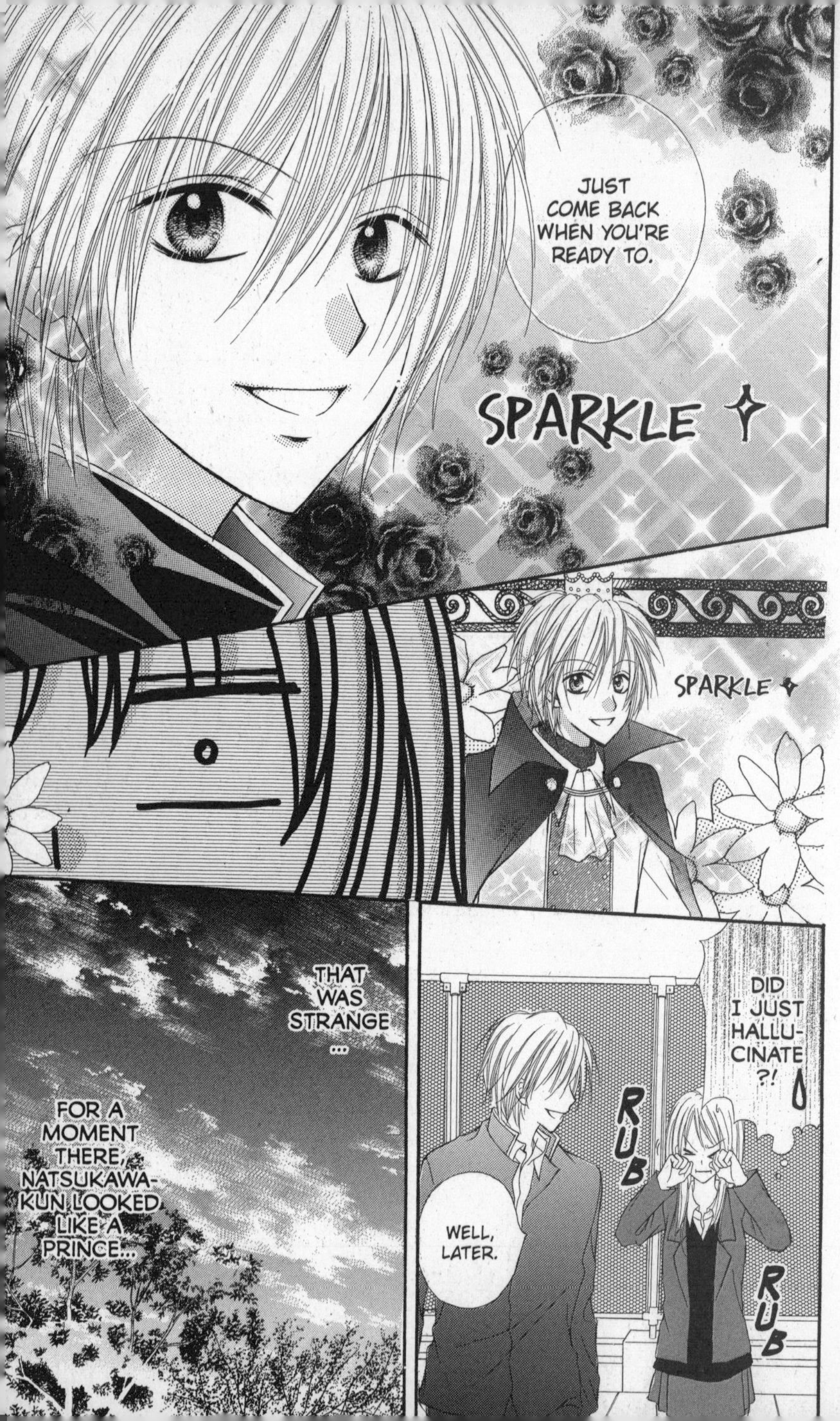
JUST COME BACK WHEN YOU'RE READY TO.
SPARKLE
SPARKLE
DID I JUST HALLUCINATE?!
RUB
RUB
WELL, LATER.
THAT WAS STRANGE...
FOR A MOMENT THERE, NATSUKAWA-KUN LOOKED LIKE A PRINCE...

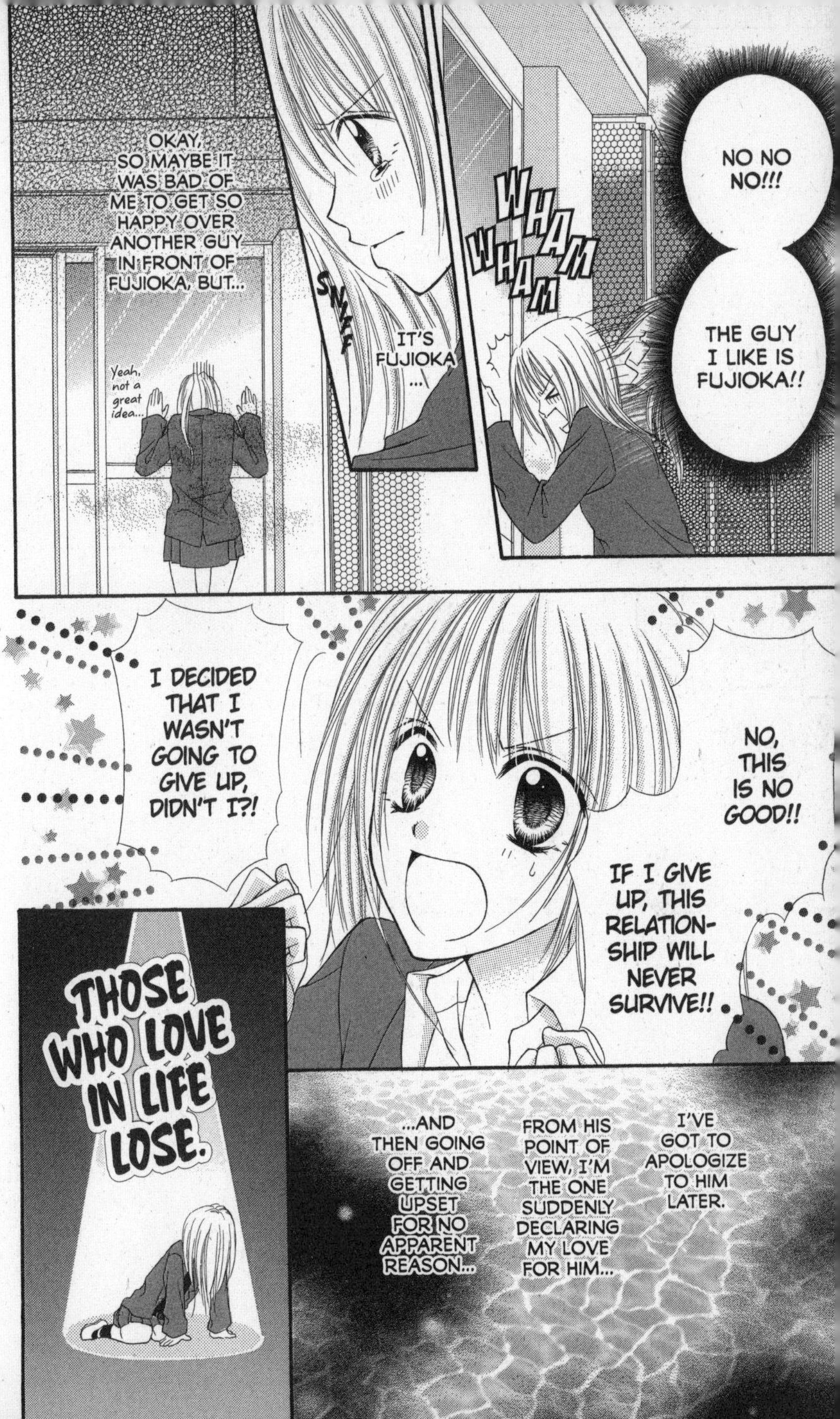
NO NO NO!!!
THE GUY I LIKE IS FUJIOKA!!
WHAM WHAM
SNIFF
IT'S FUJIOKA ...
OKAY, SO MAYBE IT WAS BAD OF ME TO GET SO HAPPY OVER ANOTHER GUY IN FRONT OF FUJIOKA, BUT...
Yeah, not a great idea...
NO, THIS IS NO GOOD!!
IF I GIVE UP, THIS RELATION-SHIP WILL NEVER SURVIVE!!
I DECIDED THAT I WASN'T GOING TO GIVE UP, DIDN'T I?!
I'VE GOT TO APOLOGIZE TO HIM LATER.
FROM HIS POINT OF VIEW, I'M THE ONE SUDDENLY DECLARING MY LOVE FOR HIM...
...AND THEN GOING OFF AND GETTING UPSET FOR NO APPARENT REASON...
THOSE WHO LOVE IN LIFE LOSE.

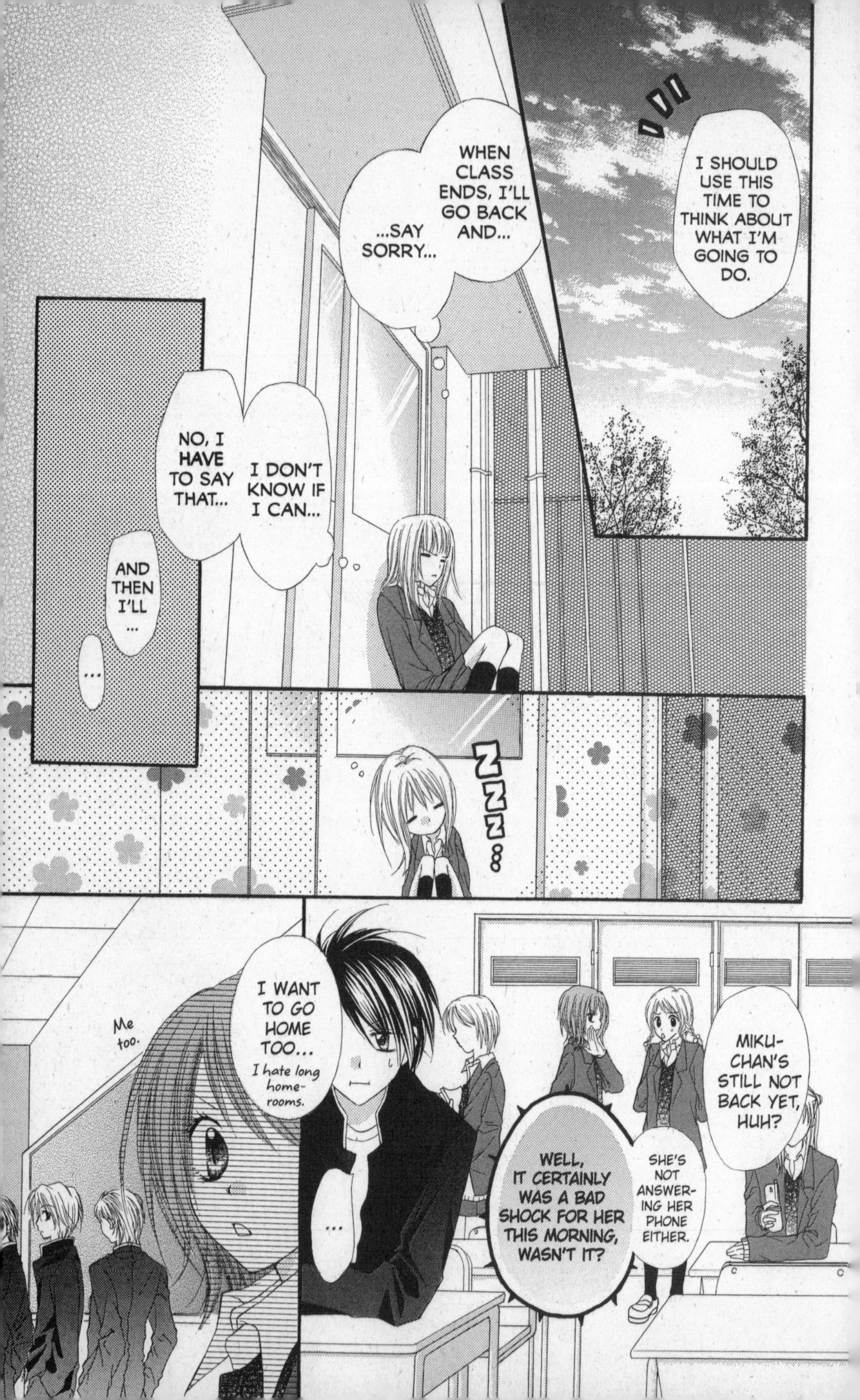
I SHOULD USE THIS TIME TO THINK ABOUT WHAT I'M GOING TO DO.
WHEN CLASS ENDS, I'LL GO BACK AND...
...SAY SORRY...
I DON'T KNOW IF I CAN...
NO, I **HAVE** TO SAY THAT...
AND THEN I'LL ...
...
ZZZ..
MIKU-CHAN'S STILL NOT BACK YET, HUH?
SHE'S NOT ANSWERING HER PHONE EITHER.
WELL, IT CERTAINLY WAS A BAD SHOCK FOR HER THIS MORNING, WASN'T IT?
I WANT TO GO HOME TOO...
I hate long homerooms.
...
Me too.

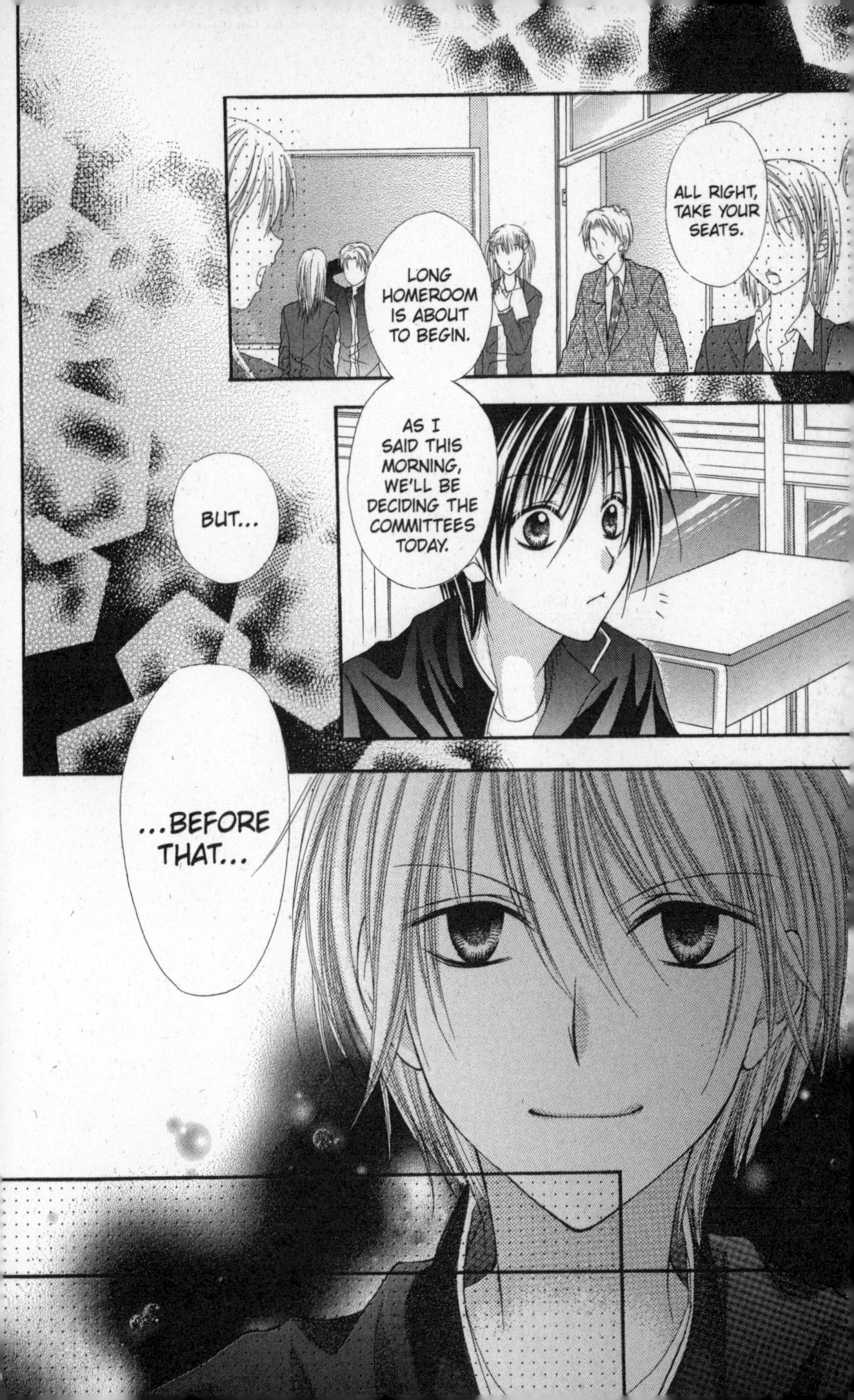
ALL RIGHT, TAKE YOUR SEATS.
LONG HOMEROOM IS ABOUT TO BEGIN.
AS I SAID THIS MORNING, WE'LL BE DECIDING THE COMMITTEES TODAY.
BUT...
...BEFORE THAT...

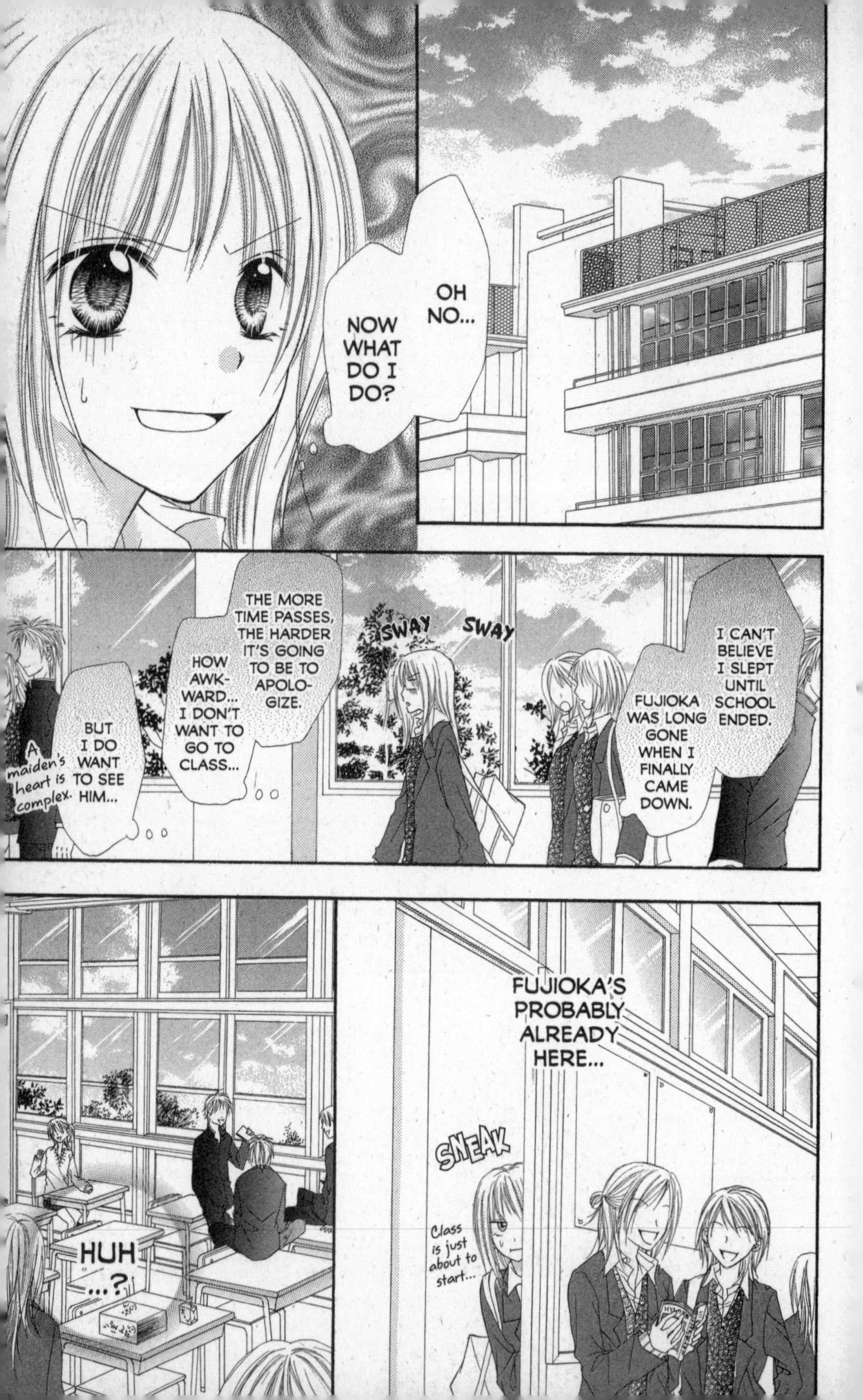
OH NO... NOW WHAT DO I DO?
I CAN'T BELIEVE I SLEPT UNTIL SCHOOL ENDED.
FUJIOKA WAS LONG GONE WHEN I FINALLY CAME DOWN.
SWAY
SWAY
THE MORE TIME PASSES, THE HARDER IT'S GOING TO BE TO APOLOGIZE.
HOW AWK-WARD... I DON'T WANT TO GO TO CLASS...
BUT I DO WANT TO SEE HIM...
A maiden's heart is complex.
FUJIOKA'S PROBABLY ALREADY HERE...
SNEAK
Class is just about to start...
HUH ...?

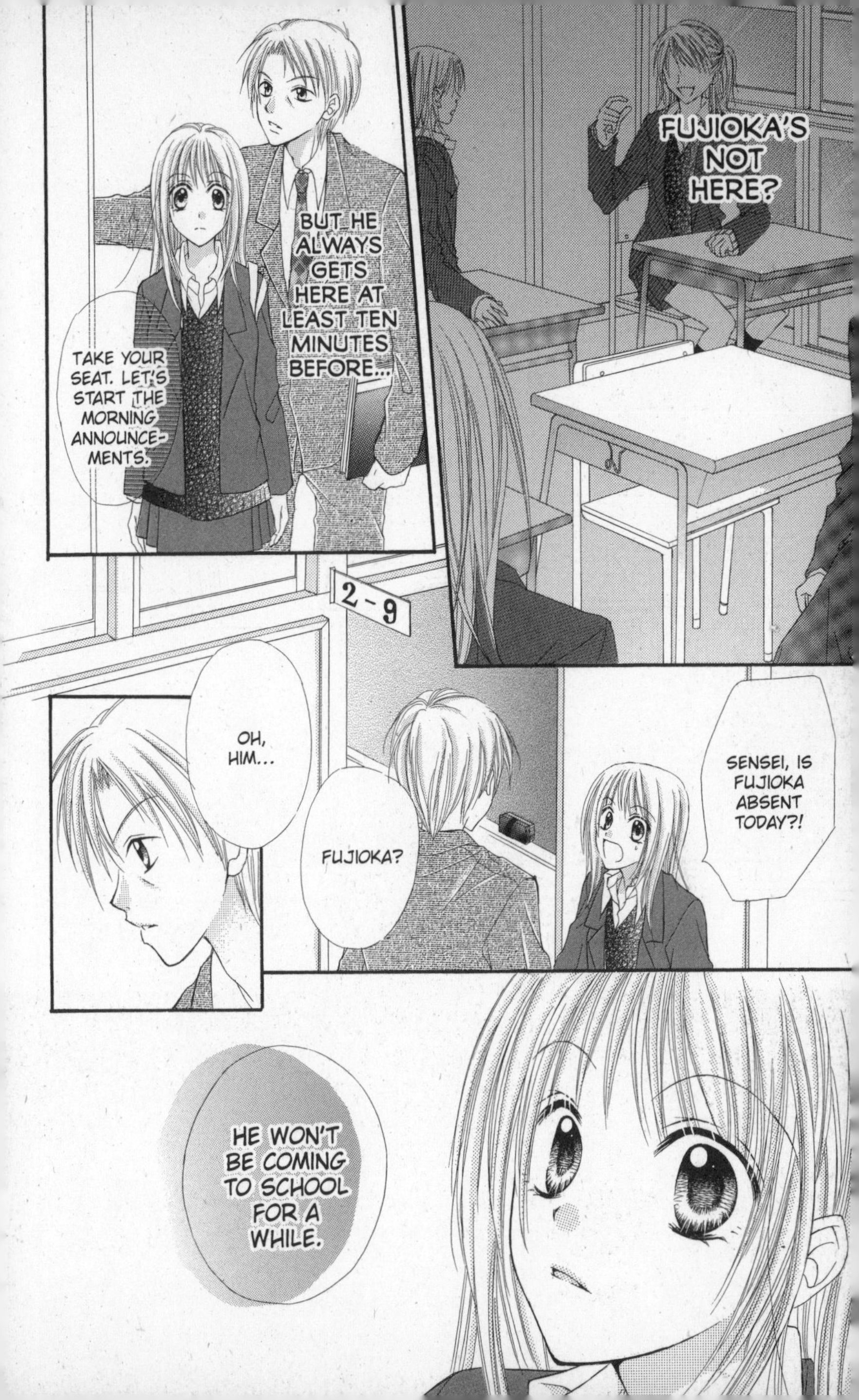
FUJIOKA'S NOT HERE?
BUT HE ALWAYS GETS HERE AT LEAST TEN MINUTES BEFORE...
TAKE YOUR SEAT. LET'S START THE MORNING ANNOUNCEMENTS.
2-9
SENSEI, IS FUJIOKA ABSENT TODAY?!
FUJIOKA?
OH, HIM...
HE WON'T BE COMING TO SCHOOL FOR A WHILE.

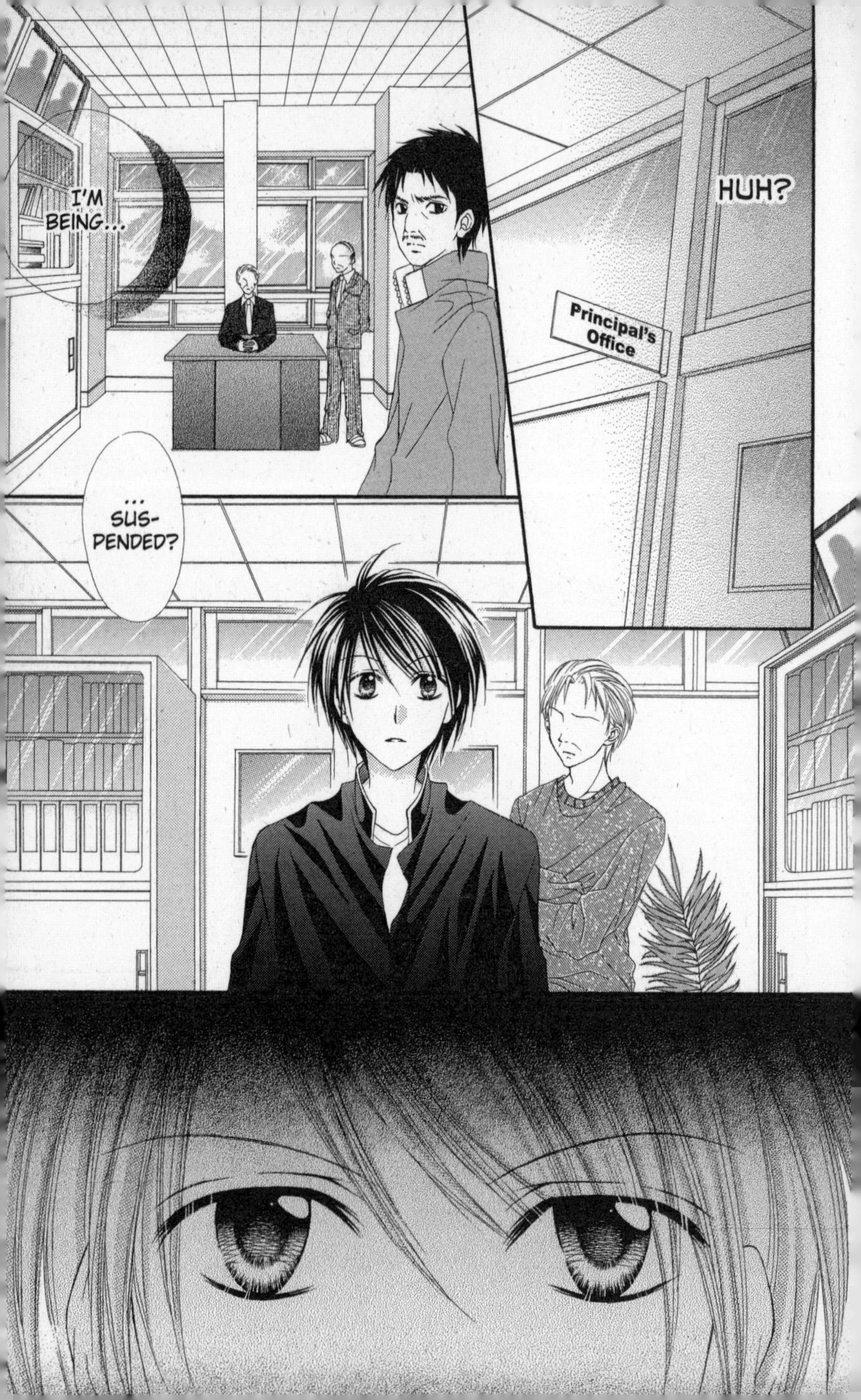
HUH?
Principal's Office
I'M BEING...
... SUS-PENDED?

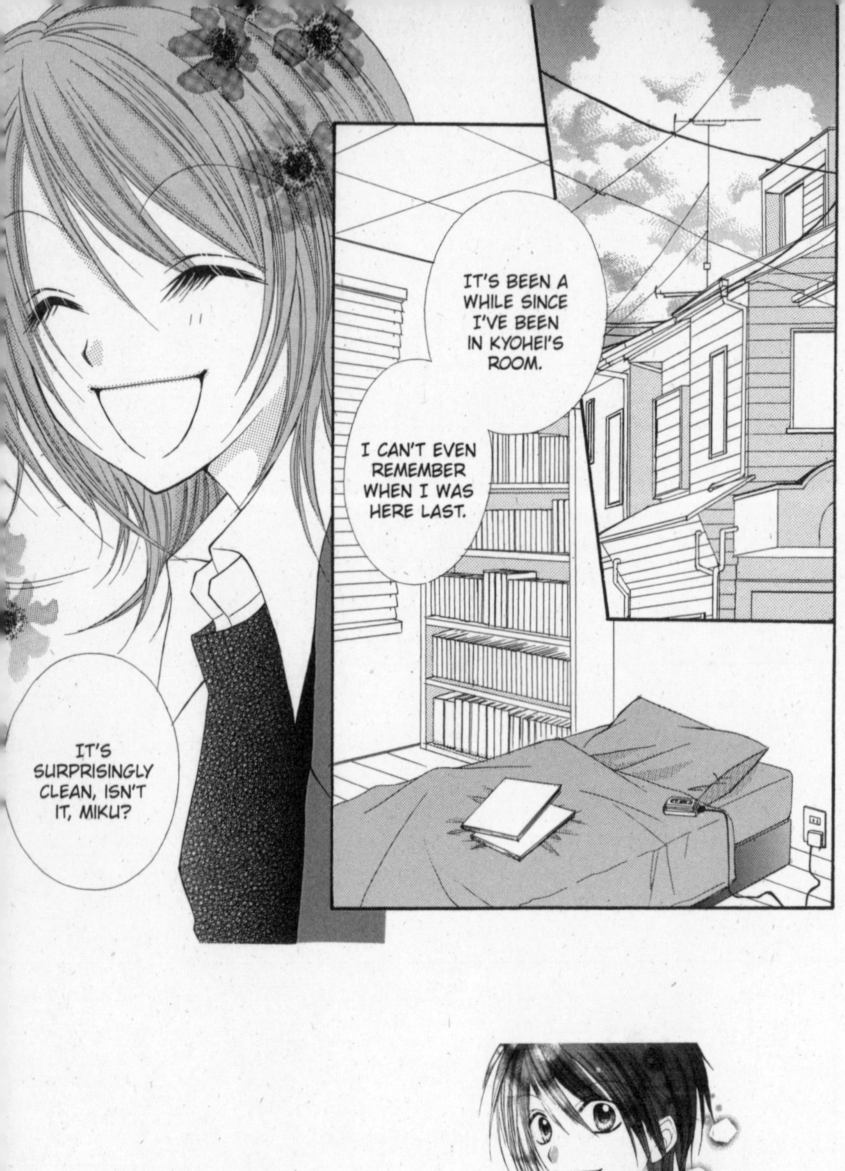
IT'S BEEN A WHILE SINCE I'VE BEEN IN KYOHEI'S ROOM.
I CAN'T EVEN REMEMBER WHEN I WAS HERE LAST.
IT'S SURPRISINGLY CLEAN, ISN'T IT, MIKU?

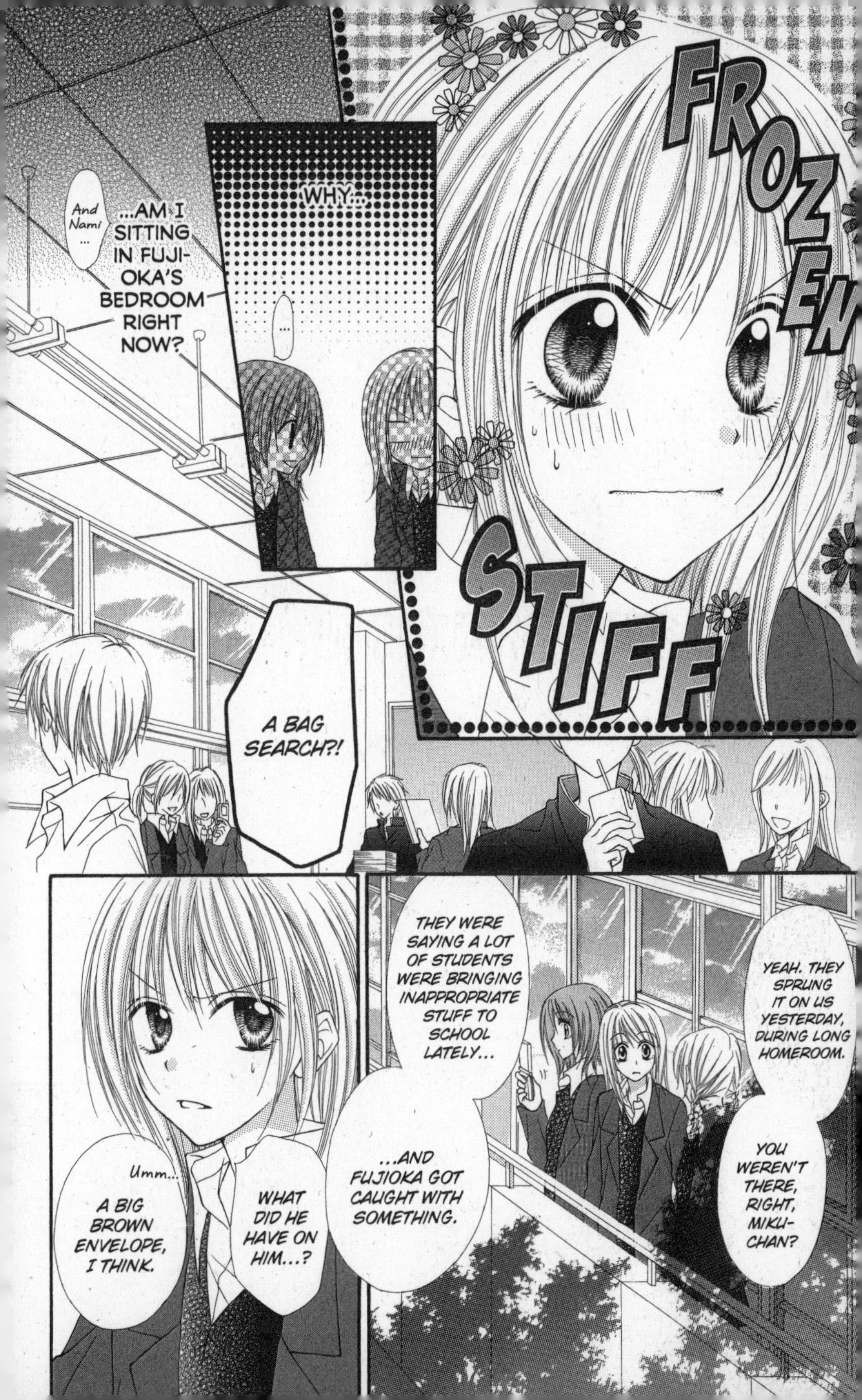
FROZEN
STIFF
WHY...
...
And Nami...
...AM I SITTING IN FUJI-OKA'S BEDROOM RIGHT NOW?
A BAG SEARCH?!
YEAH. THEY SPRUNG IT ON US YESTERDAY, DURING LONG HOMEROOM.
THEY WERE SAYING A LOT OF STUDENTS WERE BRINGING INAPPROPRIATE STUFF TO SCHOOL LATELY...
YOU WEREN'T THERE, RIGHT, MIKU-CHAN?
...AND FUJIOKA GOT CAUGHT WITH SOMETHING.
WHAT DID HE HAVE ON HIM...?
Umm...
A BIG BROWN ENVELOPE, I THINK.

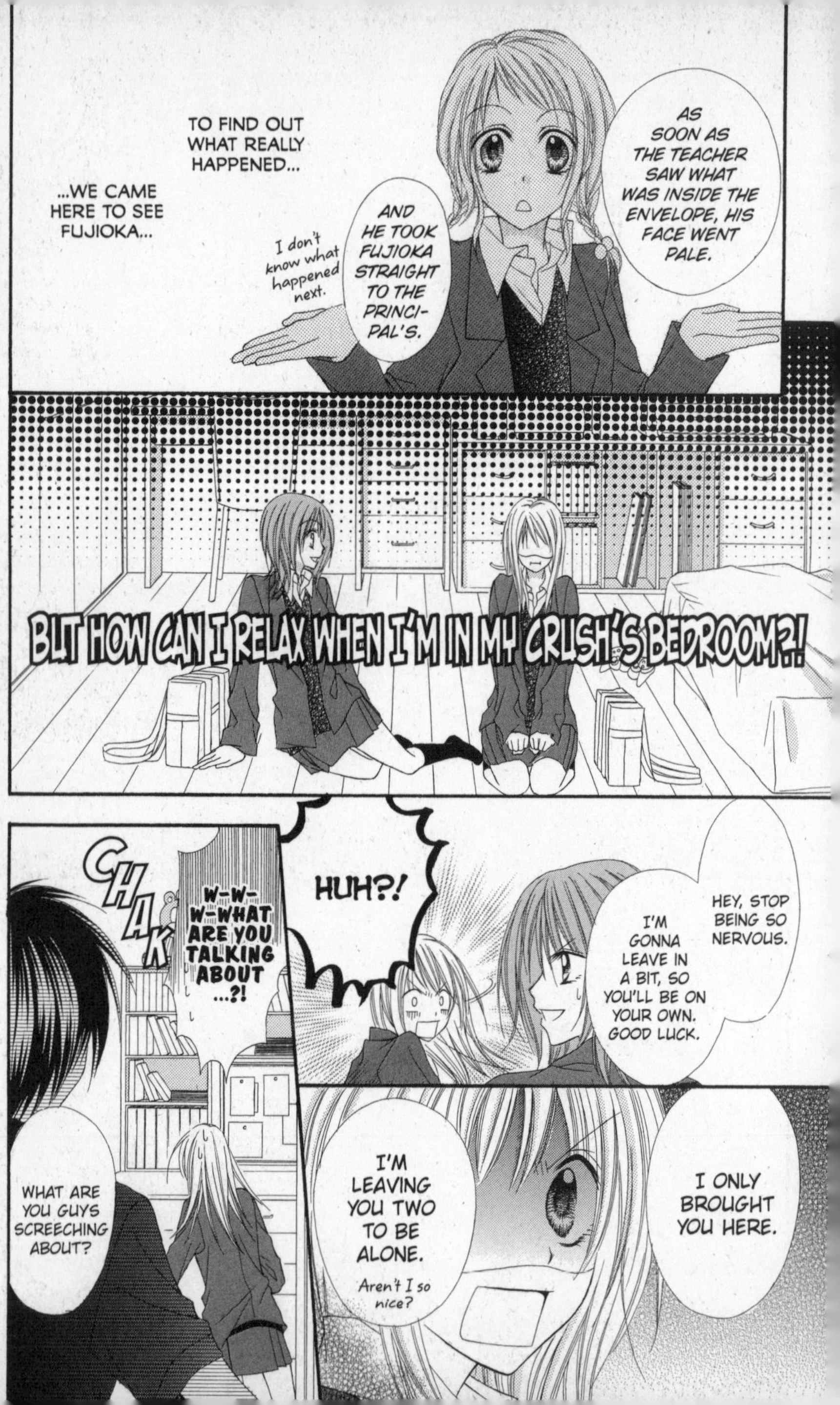
AS SOON AS THE TEACHER SAW WHAT WAS INSIDE THE ENVELOPE, HIS FACE WENT PALE.
AND HE TOOK FUJIOKA STRAIGHT TO THE PRINCIPAL'S.
I don't know what happened next.
TO FIND OUT WHAT REALLY HAPPENED...
...WE CAME HERE TO SEE FUJIOKA...
BUT HOW CAN I RELAX WHEN I'M IN MY CRUSH'S BEDROOM?!
HEY, STOP BEING SO NERVOUS.
I'M GONNA LEAVE IN A BIT, SO YOU'LL BE ON YOUR OWN. GOOD LUCK.
HUH?!
I ONLY BROUGHT YOU HERE.
I'M LEAVING YOU TWO TO BE ALONE.
Aren't I so nice?
CHAK
W-W-W-WHAT ARE YOU TALKING ABOUT...?!
WHAT ARE YOU GUYS SCREECHING ABOUT?

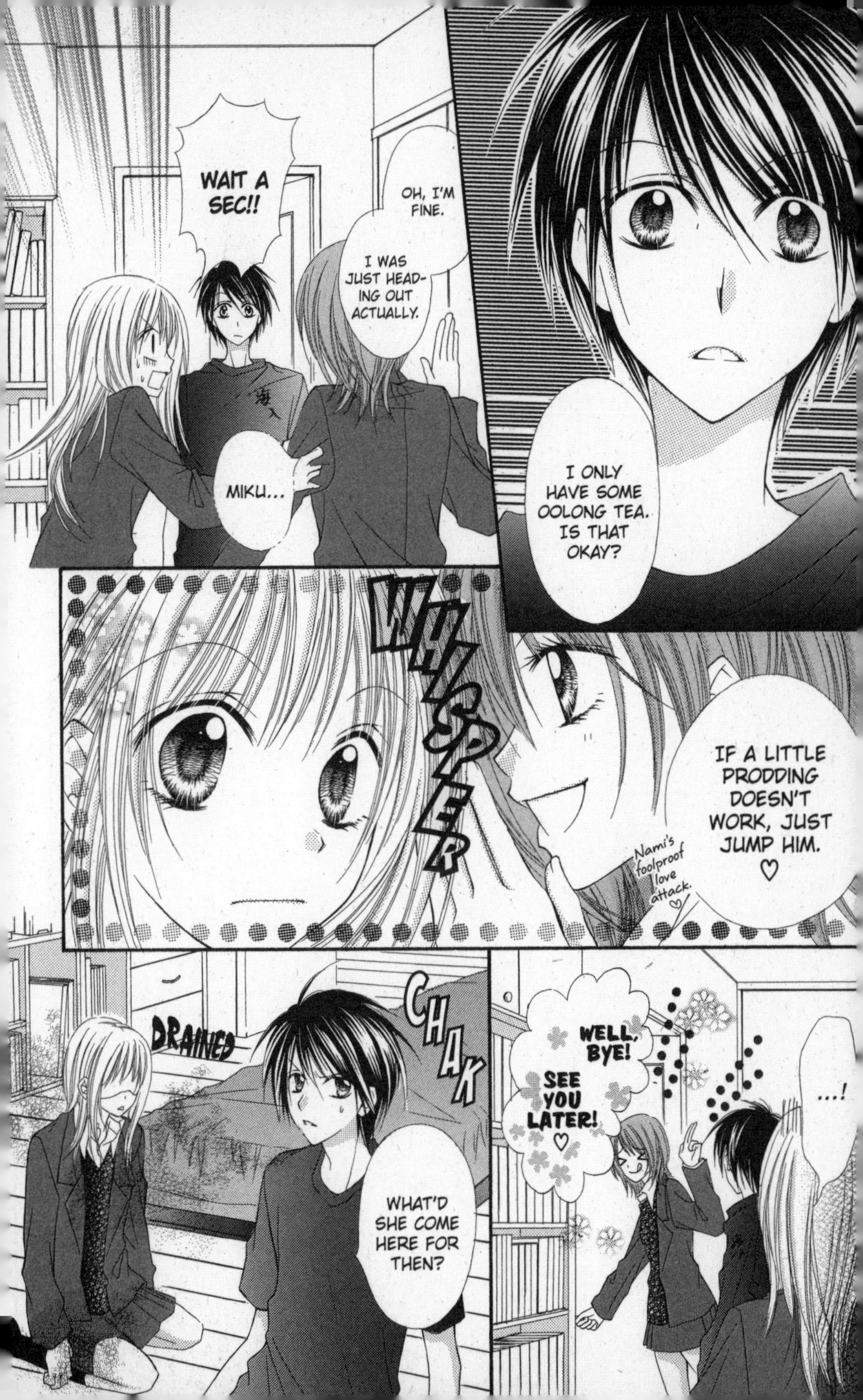
I ONLY HAVE SOME OOLONG TEA. IS THAT OKAY?
OH, I'M FINE.
I WAS JUST HEADING OUT ACTUALLY.
WAIT A SEC!!
MIKU...
WHISPER
IF A LITTLE PRODDING DOESN'T WORK, JUST JUMP HIM. ♡
Nami's foolproof love attack. ♡
...!
WELL, BYE!
SEE YOU LATER! ♡
CHAK
DRAINED
WHAT'D SHE COME HERE FOR THEN?

7

Back in volume 1, I told you a little about my real-life friend Miku-tsun (the one who kindly gave me permission to use her name for my character) in one of these author columns. This past August, I had a chance to hang out with her. It was the first time we'd hung out since graduation. The real Miku-tsun had changed so much! She had color contacts in and everything. I was so surprised! And the surprises kept on coming:

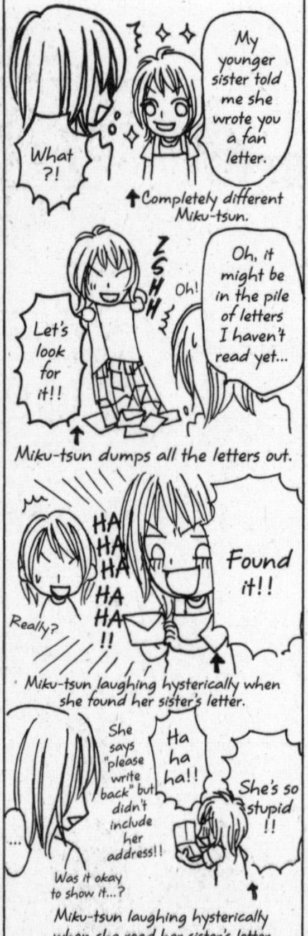
My younger sister told me she wrote you a fan letter.
What?!
Completely different Miku-tsun.
Oh, it might be in the pile of letters I haven't read yet...
Oh!
ZSHH
Let's look for it!!
Miku-tsun dumps all the letters out.
Found it!!
HA HA HA HA HA!!
Really?
Miku-tsun laughing hysterically when she found her sister's letter.
She's so stupid!!
Ha ha ha!!
She says "please write back" but didn't include her address!!
...
Was it okay to show it...?
Miku-tsun laughing hysterically when she read her sister's letter.

Thank you, Miku-tsun's sister S-chan! ✧

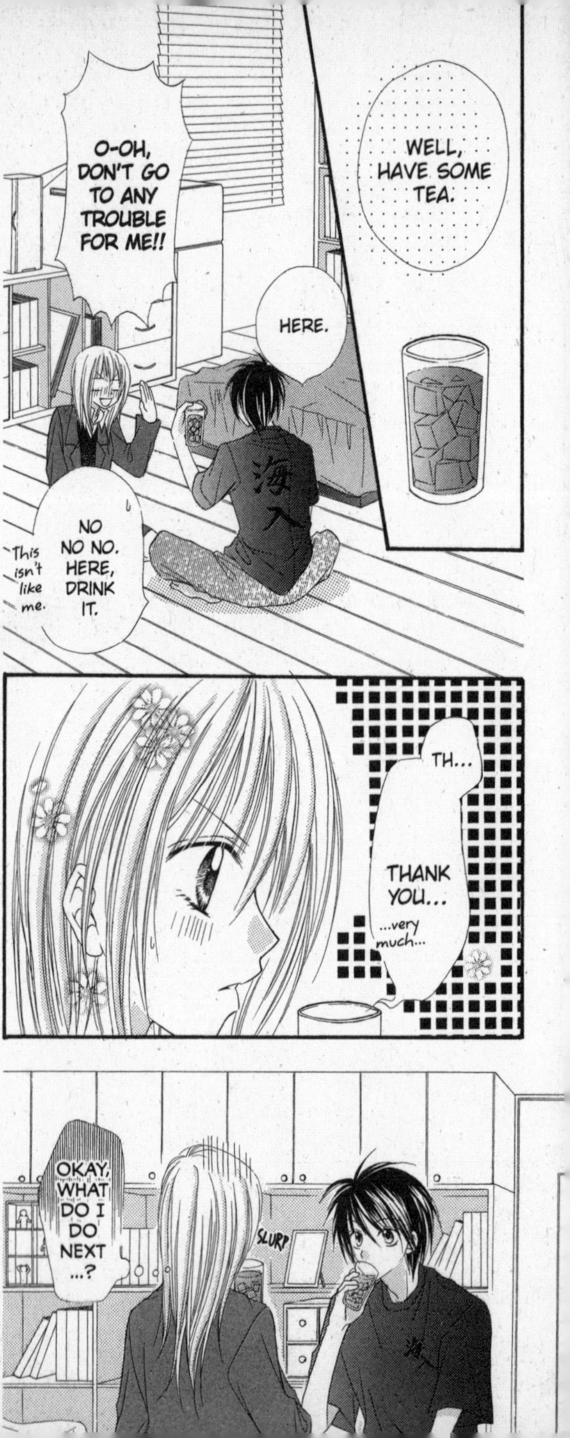
WELL, HAVE SOME TEA.
O-OH, DON'T GO TO ANY TROUBLE FOR ME!!
HERE.
NO NO NO. HERE, DRINK IT.
This isn't like me.
TH...
THANK YOU...
...very much...
OKAY, WHAT DO I DO NEXT...?
SLURP

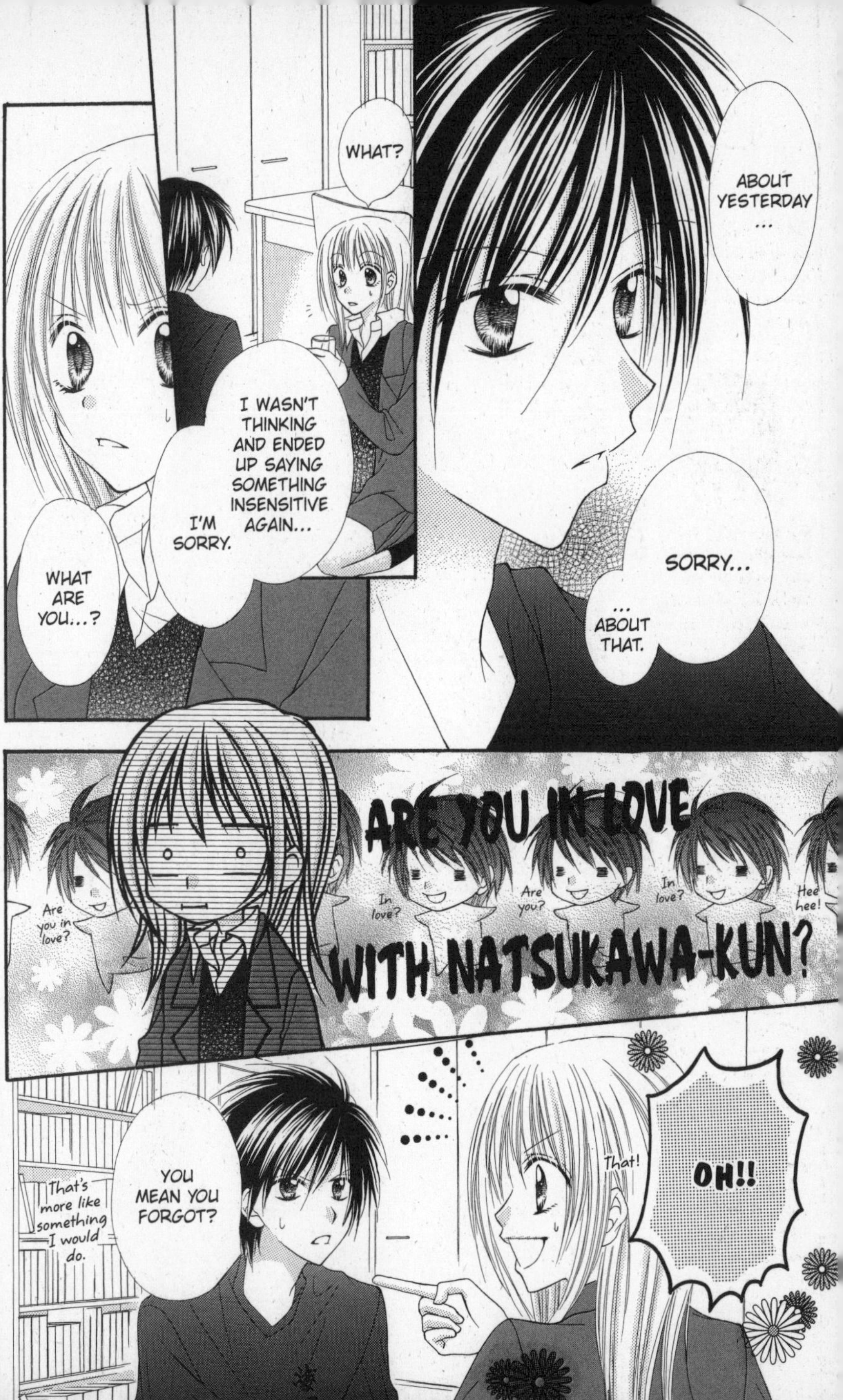
ABOUT YESTERDAY ...
SORRY...
... ABOUT THAT.
WHAT?
I WASN'T THINKING AND ENDED UP SAYING SOMETHING INSENSITIVE AGAIN...
I'M SORRY.
WHAT ARE YOU...?
ARE YOU IN LOVE WITH NATSUKAWA-KUN?
Hee hee!
In love?
Are you?
In love?
Are you in love?
OH!!
That!
YOU MEAN YOU FORGOT?
That's more like something I would do.

8

When I used Miku-tsun's name for a character, I had an unusual friend who actually said, "Use my name too!" So I did.

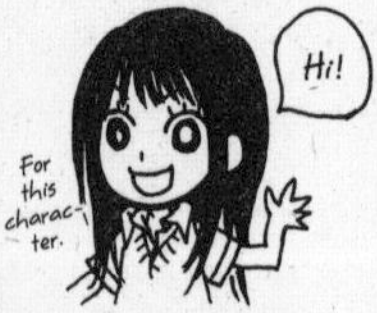
Hi!
For this charac-ter.

She's a totally minor character, but I did use your name, Saki-tii! Where are you these days...? (Super personal message.)

On the other hand, there was also someone who told me to never use his name. So to annoy him, I snuck it in somewhere. (Hey, hey!) It seems he hasn't noticed it yet though. So what do you think now, Chakoyan? (Another super personal message. Sorry.)

Once in a while, I get requests from readers that say, "Please use my name!" So maybe next time, I'll end up using one of those. It's not because I'm too lazy to think up names, you know. Hee hee. Whoops, I'm writing sloppy again. What happened to my resolution from column 1?

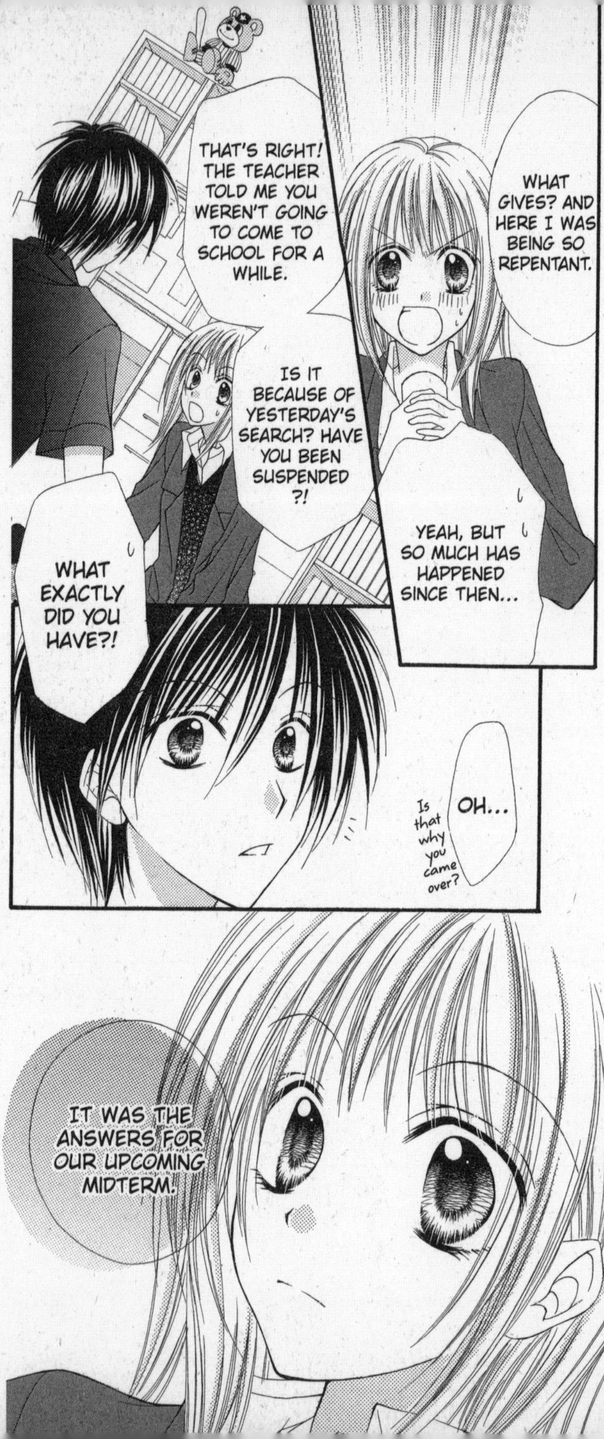
WHAT GIVES? AND HERE I WAS BEING SO REPENTANT.
YEAH, BUT SO MUCH HAS HAPPENED SINCE THEN...
THAT'S RIGHT! THE TEACHER TOLD ME YOU WEREN'T GOING TO COME TO SCHOOL FOR A WHILE.
IS IT BECAUSE OF YESTERDAY'S SEARCH? HAVE YOU BEEN SUSPENDED ?!
WHAT EXACTLY DID YOU HAVE?!
OH...
Is that why you came over?
IT WAS THE ANSWERS FOR OUR UPCOMING MIDTERM.

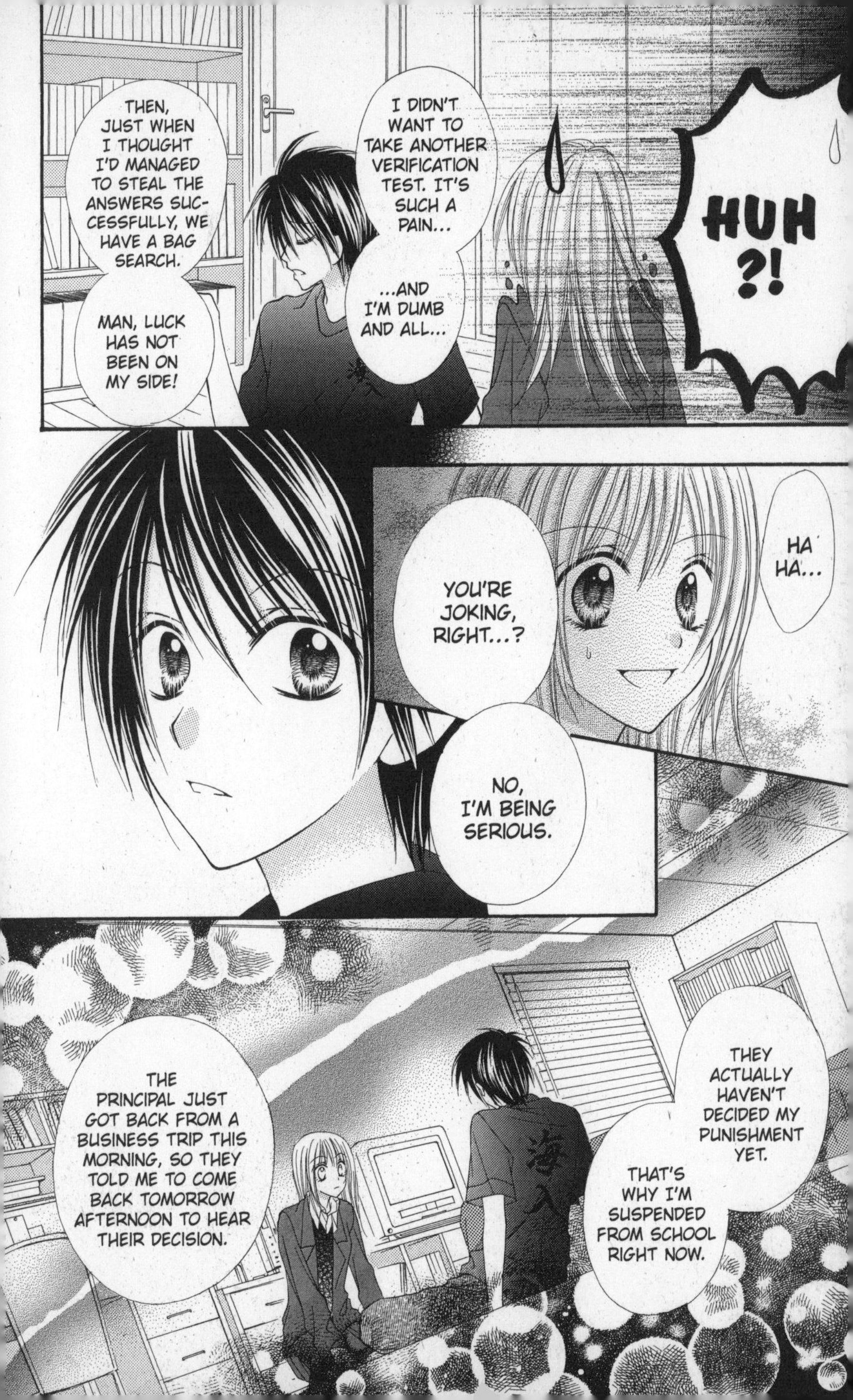
HUH ?!
I DIDN'T WANT TO TAKE ANOTHER VERIFICATION TEST. IT'S SUCH A PAIN...
...AND I'M DUMB AND ALL...
THEN, JUST WHEN I THOUGHT I'D MANAGED TO STEAL THE ANSWERS SUCCESSFULLY, WE HAVE A BAG SEARCH.
MAN, LUCK HAS NOT BEEN ON MY SIDE!
HA HA...
YOU'RE JOKING, RIGHT...?
NO, I'M BEING SERIOUS.
THEY ACTUALLY HAVEN'T DECIDED MY PUNISHMENT YET.
THAT'S WHY I'M SUSPENDED FROM SCHOOL RIGHT NOW.
THE PRINCIPAL JUST GOT BACK FROM A BUSINESS TRIP THIS MORNING, SO THEY TOLD ME TO COME BACK TOMORROW AFTERNOON TO HEAR THEIR DECISION.

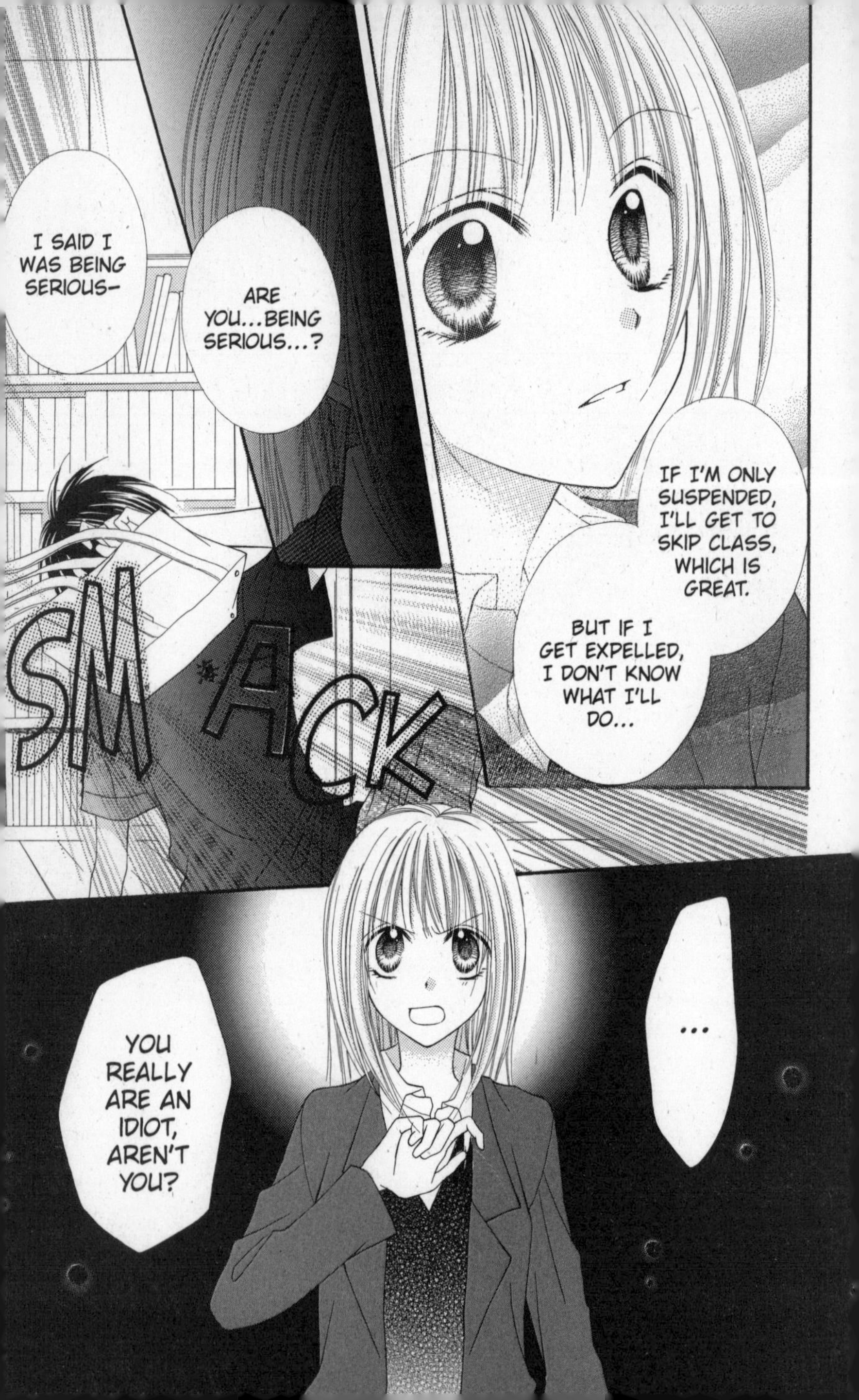
IF I'M ONLY SUSPENDED, I'LL GET TO SKIP CLASS, WHICH IS GREAT.
BUT IF I GET EXPELLED, I DON'T KNOW WHAT I'LL DO...
ARE YOU...BEING SERIOUS...?
I SAID I WAS BEING SERIOUS-
SMACK
...
YOU REALLY ARE AN IDIOT, AREN'T YOU?

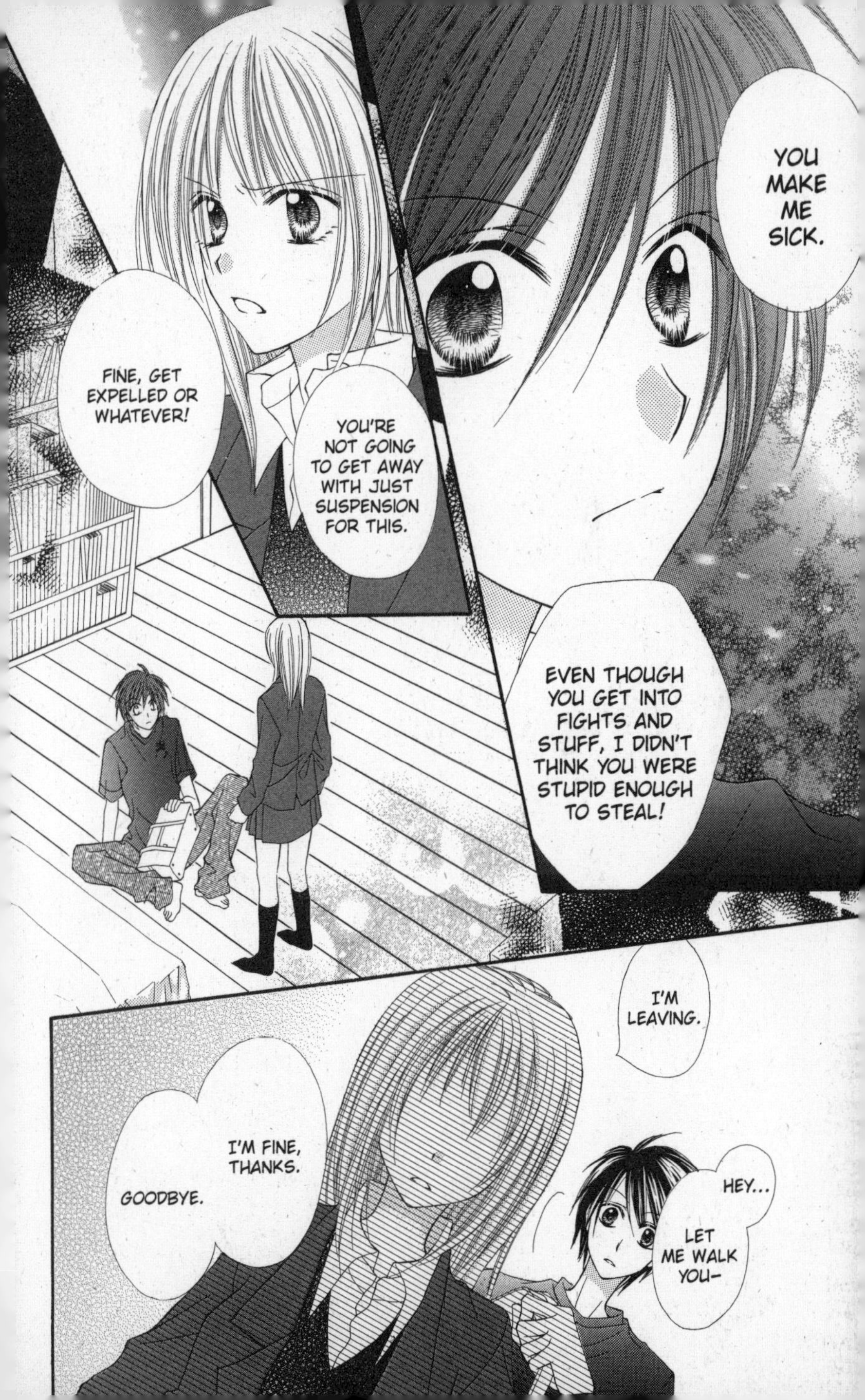
YOU MAKE ME SICK.
EVEN THOUGH YOU GET INTO FIGHTS AND STUFF, I DIDN'T THINK YOU WERE STUPID ENOUGH TO STEAL!
YOU'RE NOT GOING TO GET AWAY WITH JUST SUSPENSION FOR THIS.
FINE, GET EXPELLED OR WHATEVER!
I'M LEAVING.
HEY... LET ME WALK YOU-
I'M FINE, THANKS.
GOODBYE.

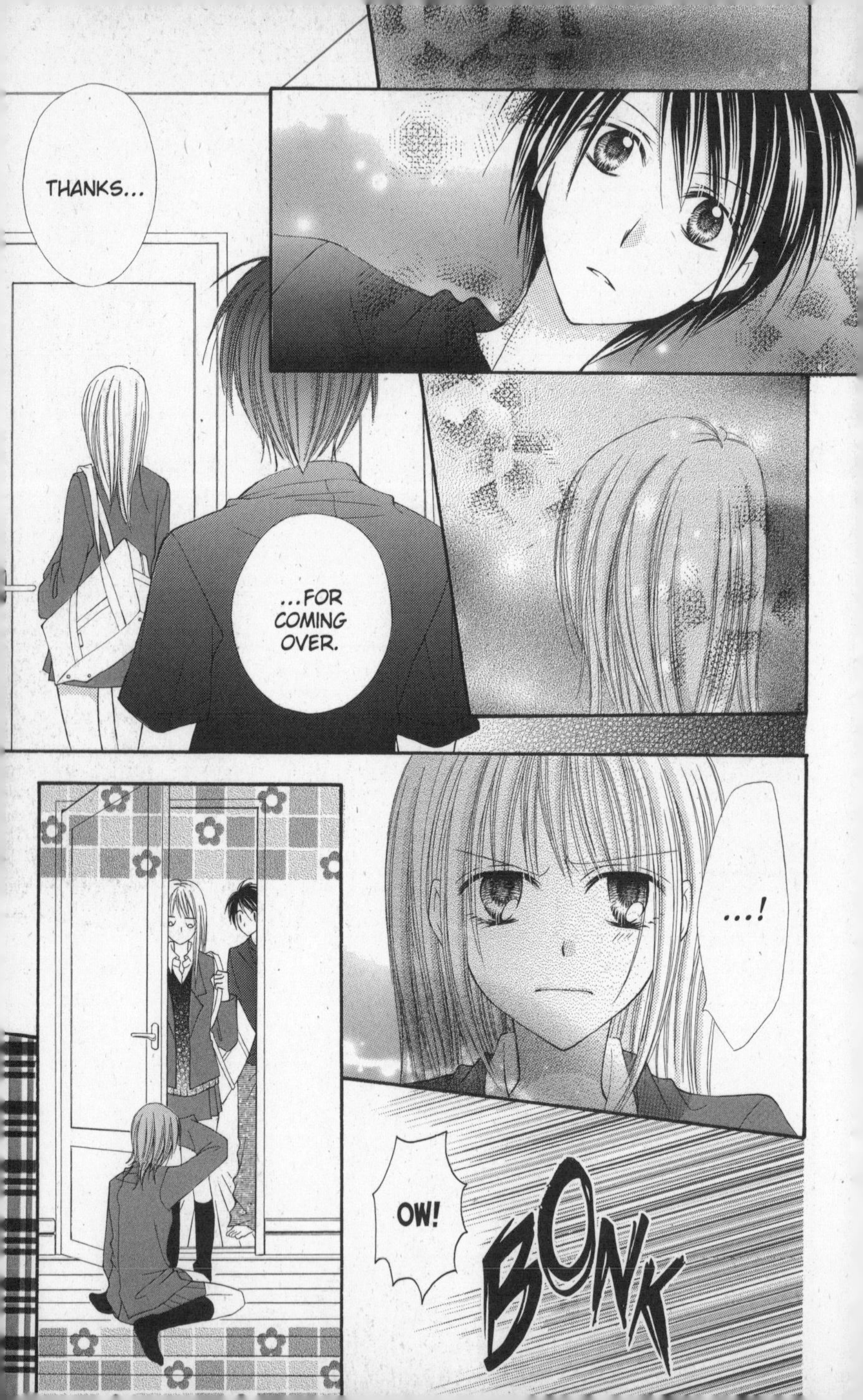
THANKS...
...FOR COMING OVER.
...!
OW!
BONK

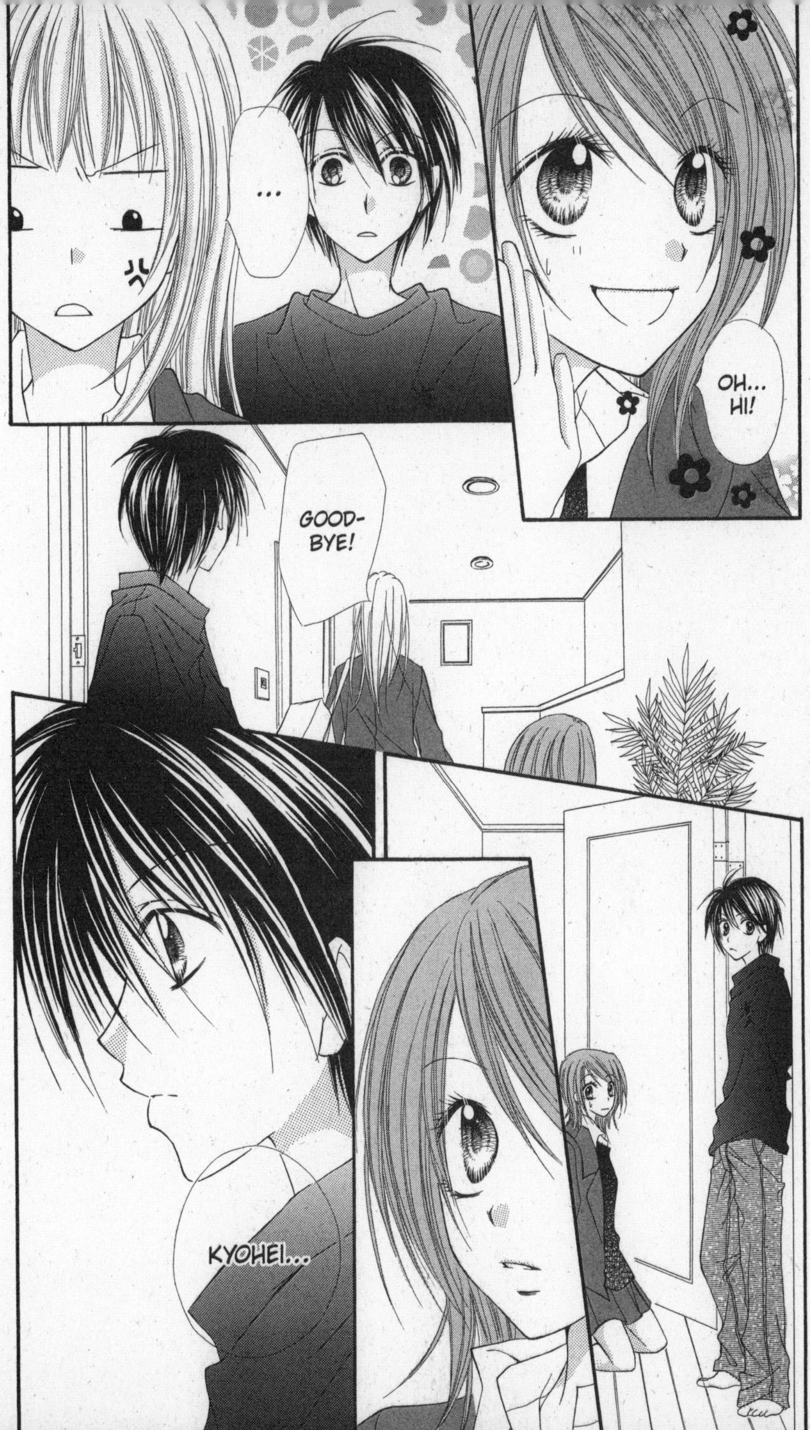
OH... HI!
...
GOOD-BYE!
KYOHEI...

9

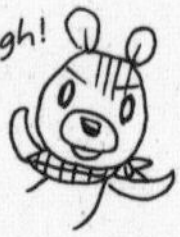
Agh!

TIME'S UP.

Sorry for not completing this, but this is going to be my last author's column for this volume. I'm really sorry! There're still some bonus notes (though I don't know if you can call them that) at the end of the book, so please forgive me! I'm going to cut out my Small Talk space too... I'm really sorry!

I SHOULD BE MORE ORGANIZED IN MY WORK. OH, THE LOOMING END-OF-YEAR WORK IS SCARING ME. I STILL HAVEN'T DRAWN THE COVER ART EITHER.

Nana Haruta

See you later!!

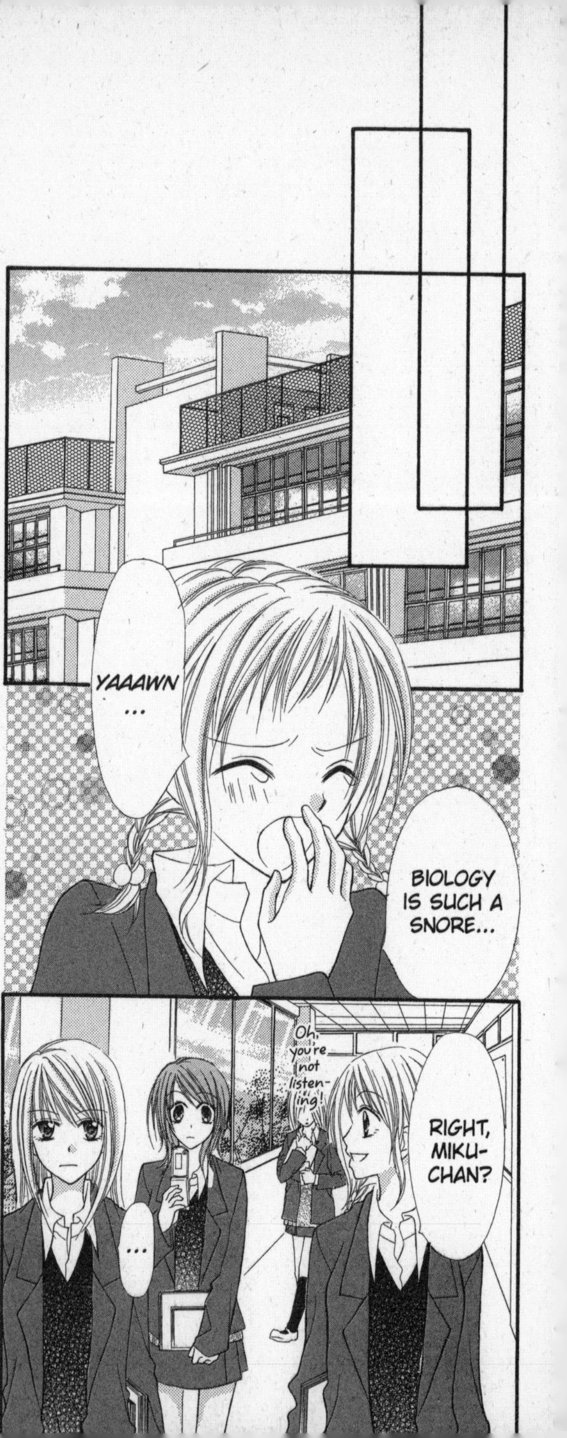
YAAAWN...
BIOLOGY IS SUCH A SNORE...
RIGHT, MIKU-CHAN?
Oh, you're not listening!
...

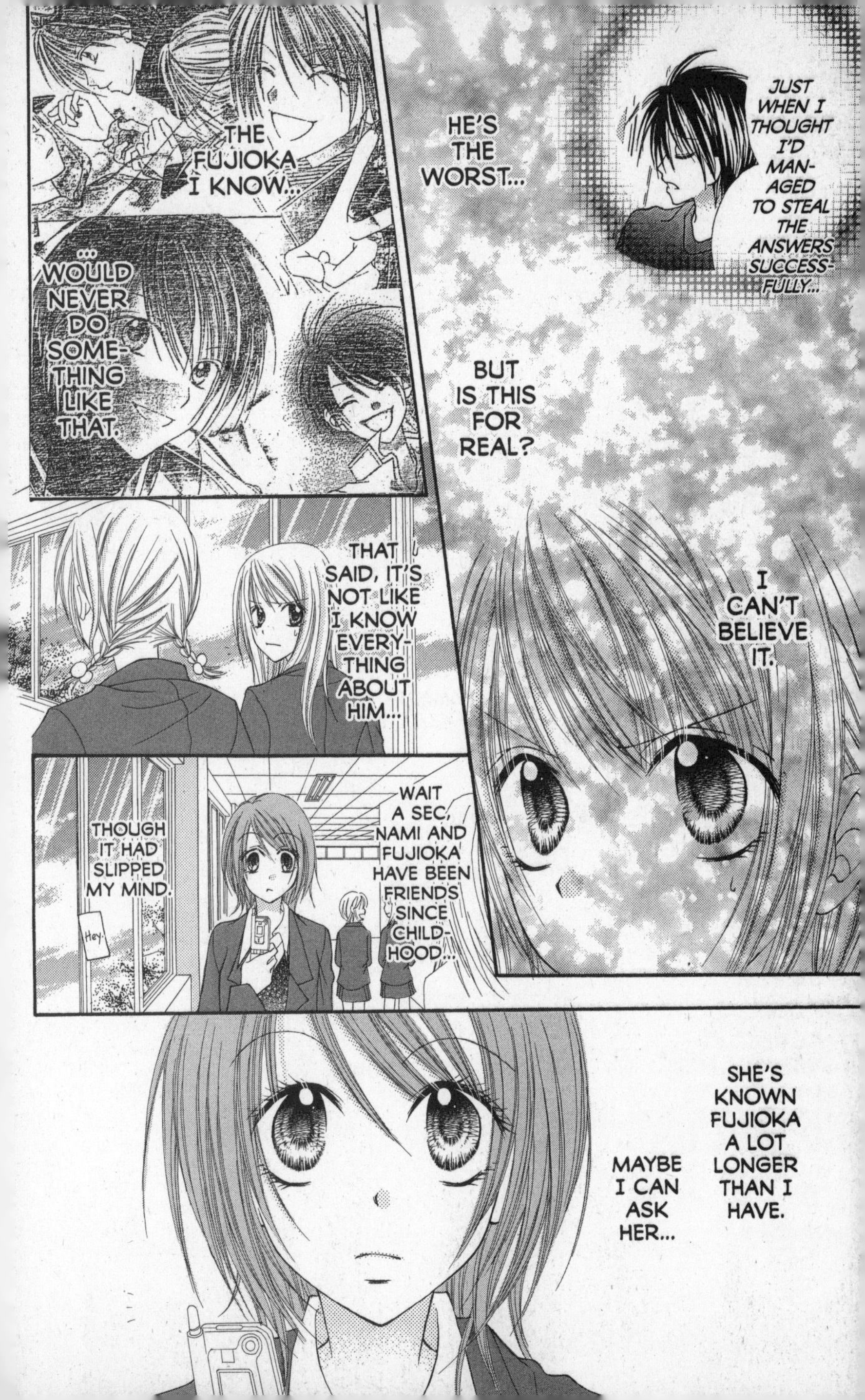
JUST WHEN I THOUGHT I'D MAN-AGED TO STEAL THE ANSWERS SUCCESS-FULLY...
HE'S THE WORST...
BUT IS THIS FOR REAL?
THE FUJIOKA I KNOW...
...WOULD NEVER DO SOME-THING LIKE THAT.
I CAN'T BELIEVE IT.
THAT SAID, IT'S NOT LIKE I KNOW EVERY-THING ABOUT HIM...
WAIT A SEC, NAMI AND FUJIOKA HAVE BEEN FRIENDS SINCE CHILD-HOOD...
THOUGH IT HAD SLIPPED MY MIND.
Hey.
SHE'S KNOWN FUJIOKA A LOT LONGER THAN I HAVE.
MAYBE I CAN ASK HER...

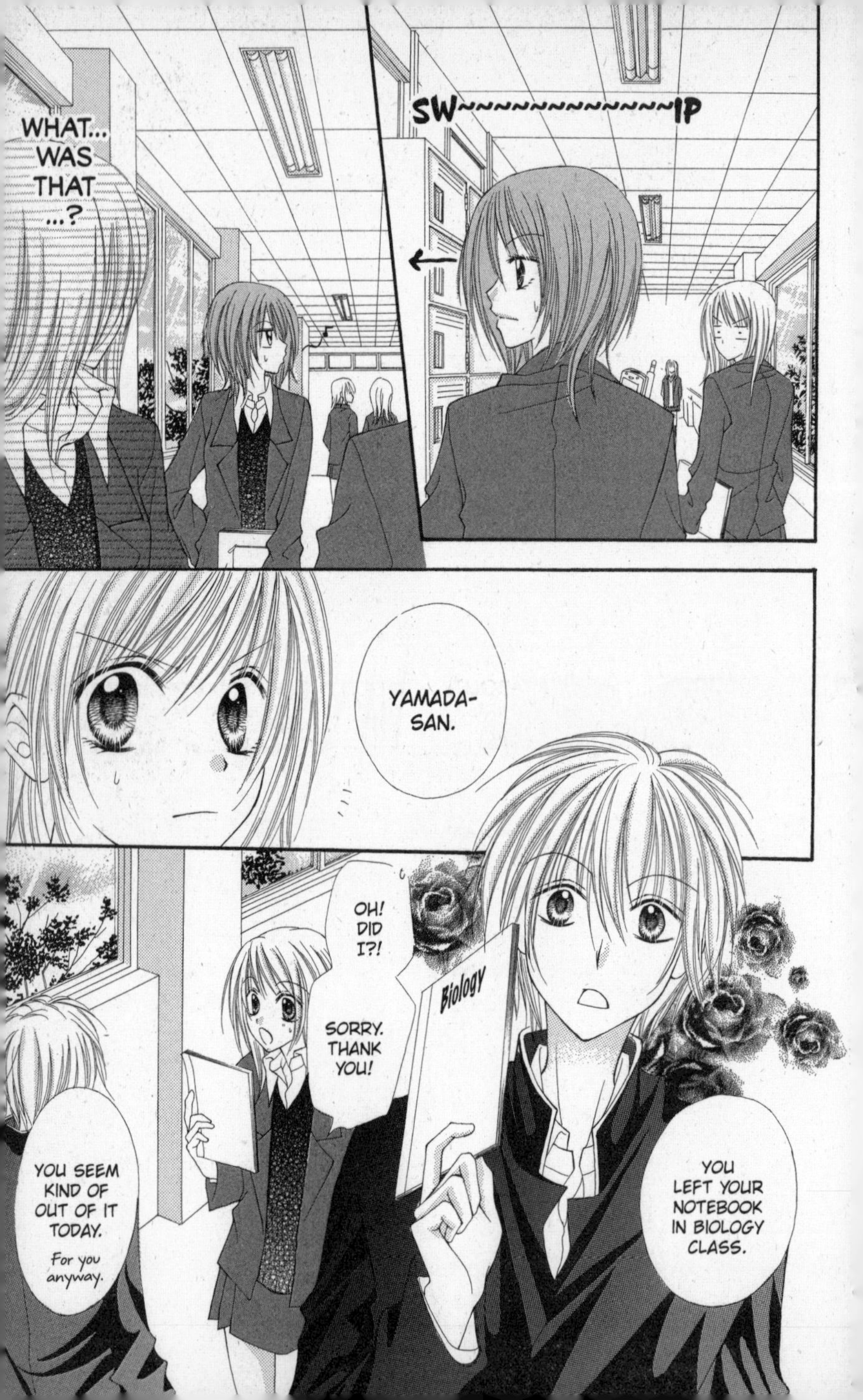
SW~~~~~~~~~~~~IP
WHAT... WAS THAT ...?
YAMADA-SAN.
YOU LEFT YOUR NOTEBOOK IN BIOLOGY CLASS.
Biology
OH! DID I?!
SORRY. THANK YOU!
YOU SEEM KIND OF OUT OF IT TODAY.
For you anyway.

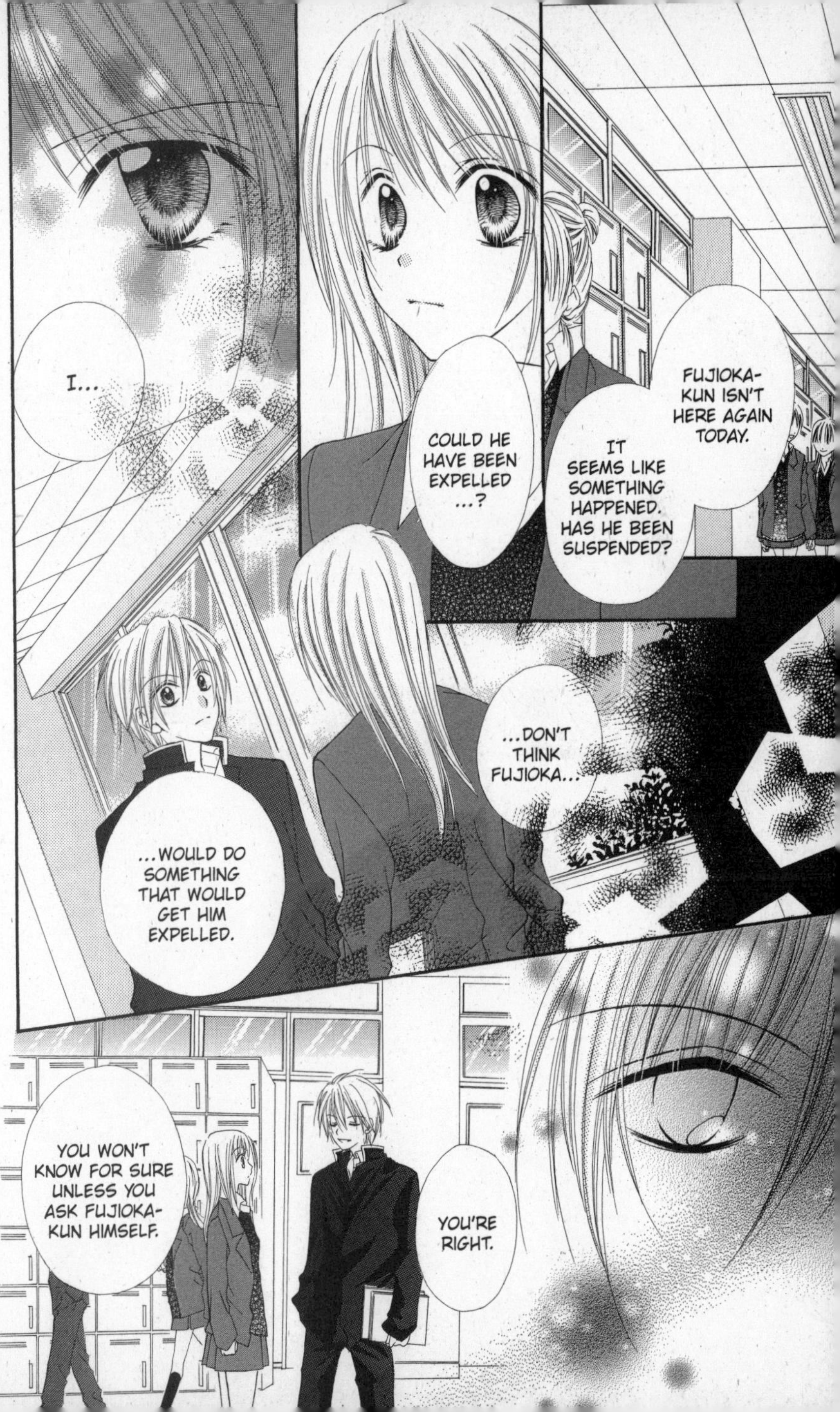
FUJIOKA-KUN ISN'T HERE AGAIN TODAY.
IT SEEMS LIKE SOMETHING HAPPENED. HAS HE BEEN SUSPENDED?
COULD HE HAVE BEEN EXPELLED ...?
I...
...DON'T THINK FUJIOKA...
...WOULD DO SOMETHING THAT WOULD GET HIM EXPELLED.
YOU WON'T KNOW FOR SURE UNLESS YOU ASK FUJIOKA-KUN HIMSELF.
YOU'RE RIGHT.

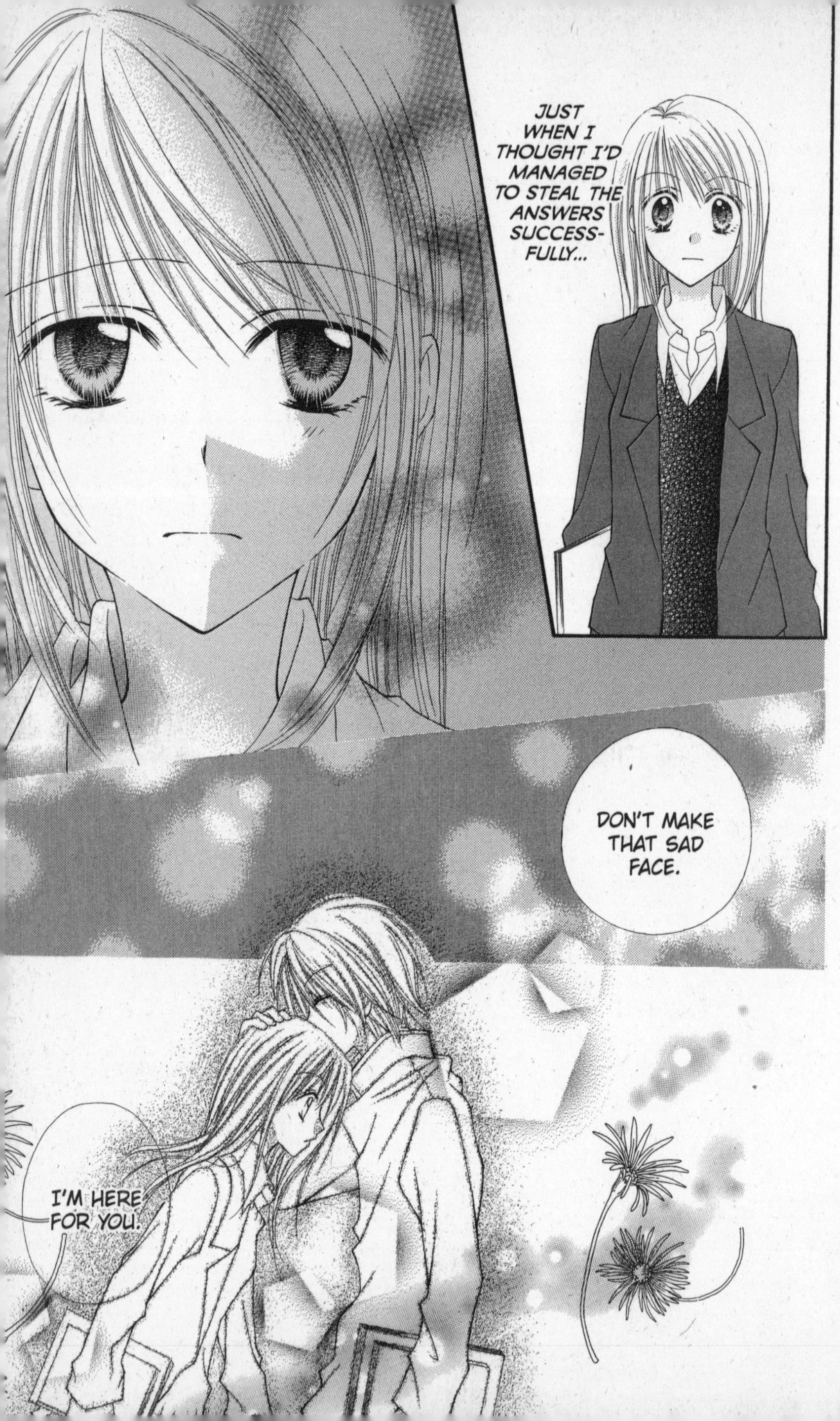
JUST WHEN I THOUGHT I'D MANAGED TO STEAL THE ANSWERS SUCCESS-FULLY...
DON'T MAKE THAT SAD FACE.
I'M HERE FOR YOU.

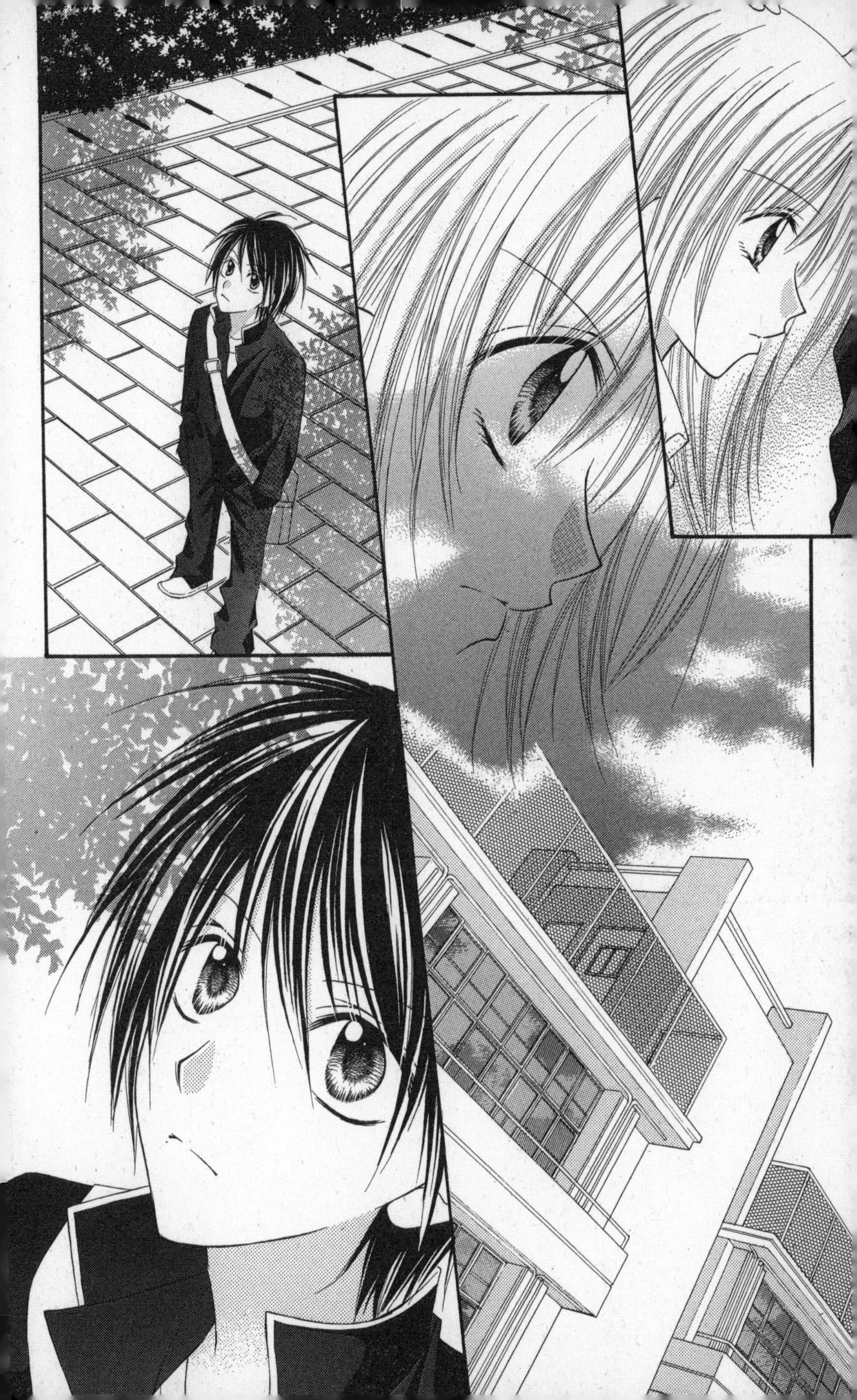

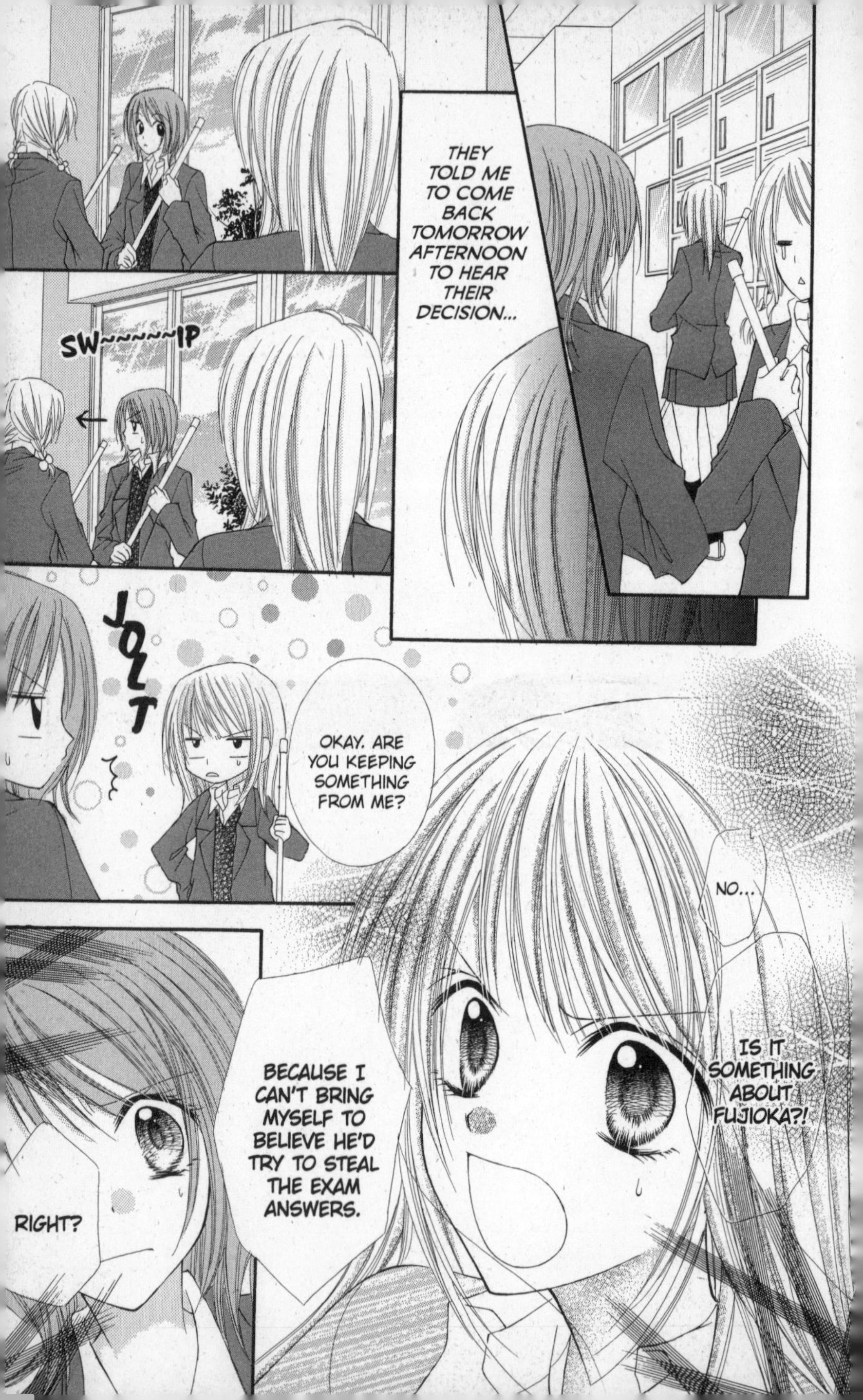
THEY TOLD ME TO COME BACK TOMORROW AFTERNOON TO HEAR THEIR DECISION...
SW~~~~~IP
JOLT
OKAY. ARE YOU KEEPING SOMETHING FROM ME?
NO...
IS IT SOMETHING ABOUT FUJIOKA?!
BECAUSE I CAN'T BRING MYSELF TO BELIEVE HE'D TRY TO STEAL THE EXAM ANSWERS.
RIGHT?

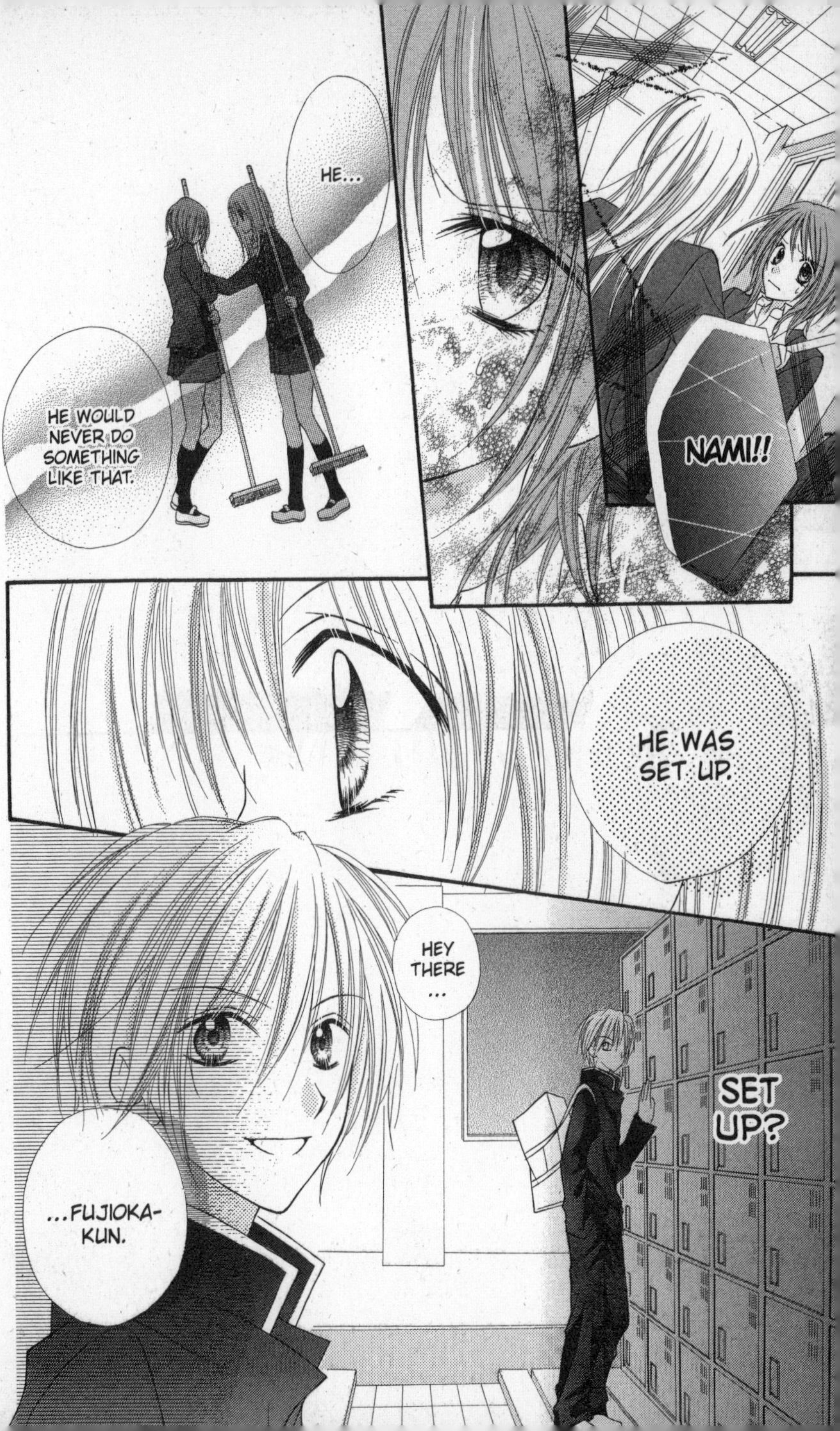
NAMI!!
HE...
HE WOULD NEVER DO SOMETHING LIKE THAT.
HE WAS SET UP.
SET UP?
HEY THERE ...
...FUJIOKA-KUN.

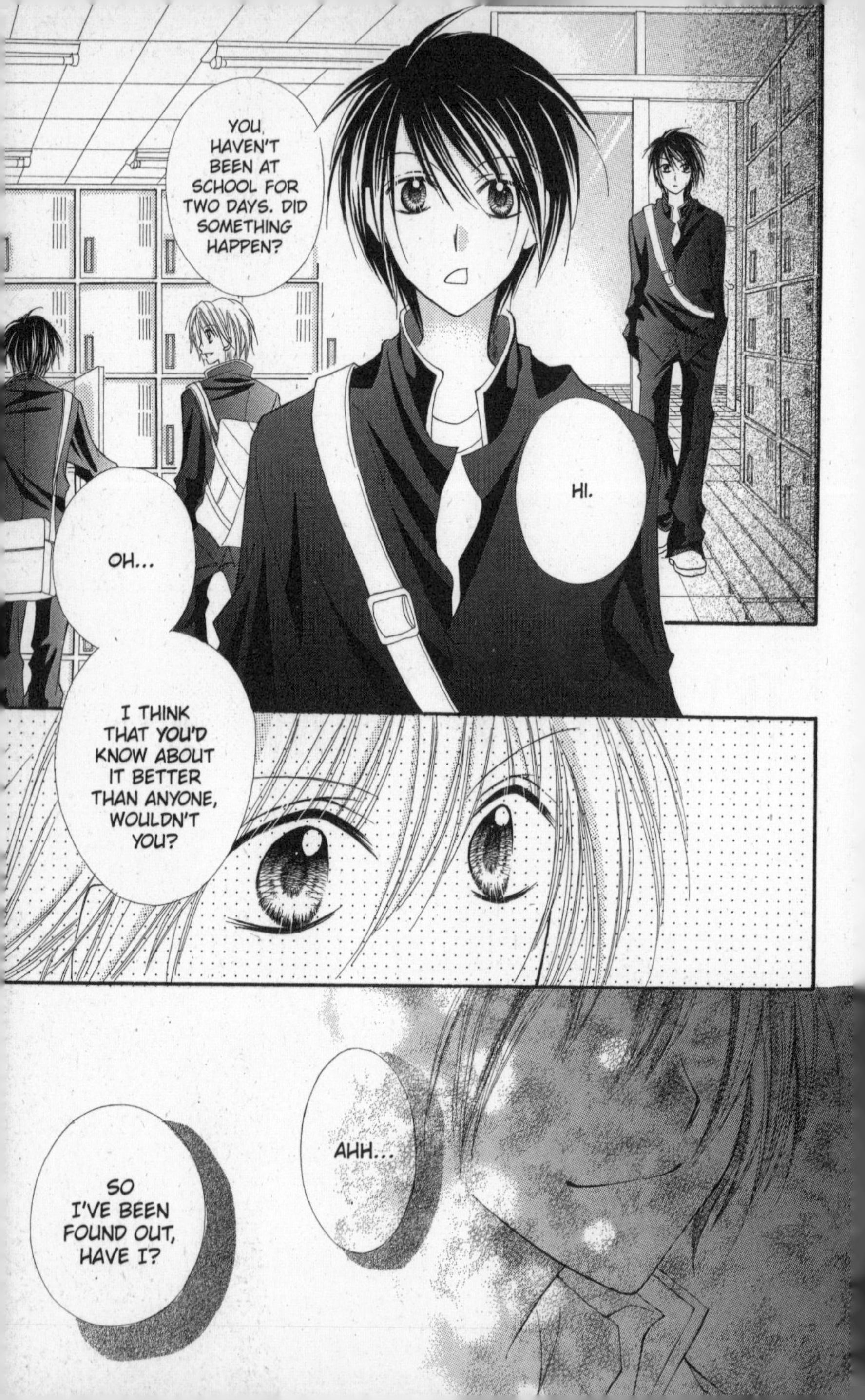
HI.
YOU, HAVEN'T BEEN AT SCHOOL FOR TWO DAYS. DID SOMETHING HAPPEN?
OH...
I THINK THAT YOU'D KNOW ABOUT IT BETTER THAN ANYONE, WOULDN'T YOU?
AHH...
SO I'VE BEEN FOUND OUT, HAVE I?

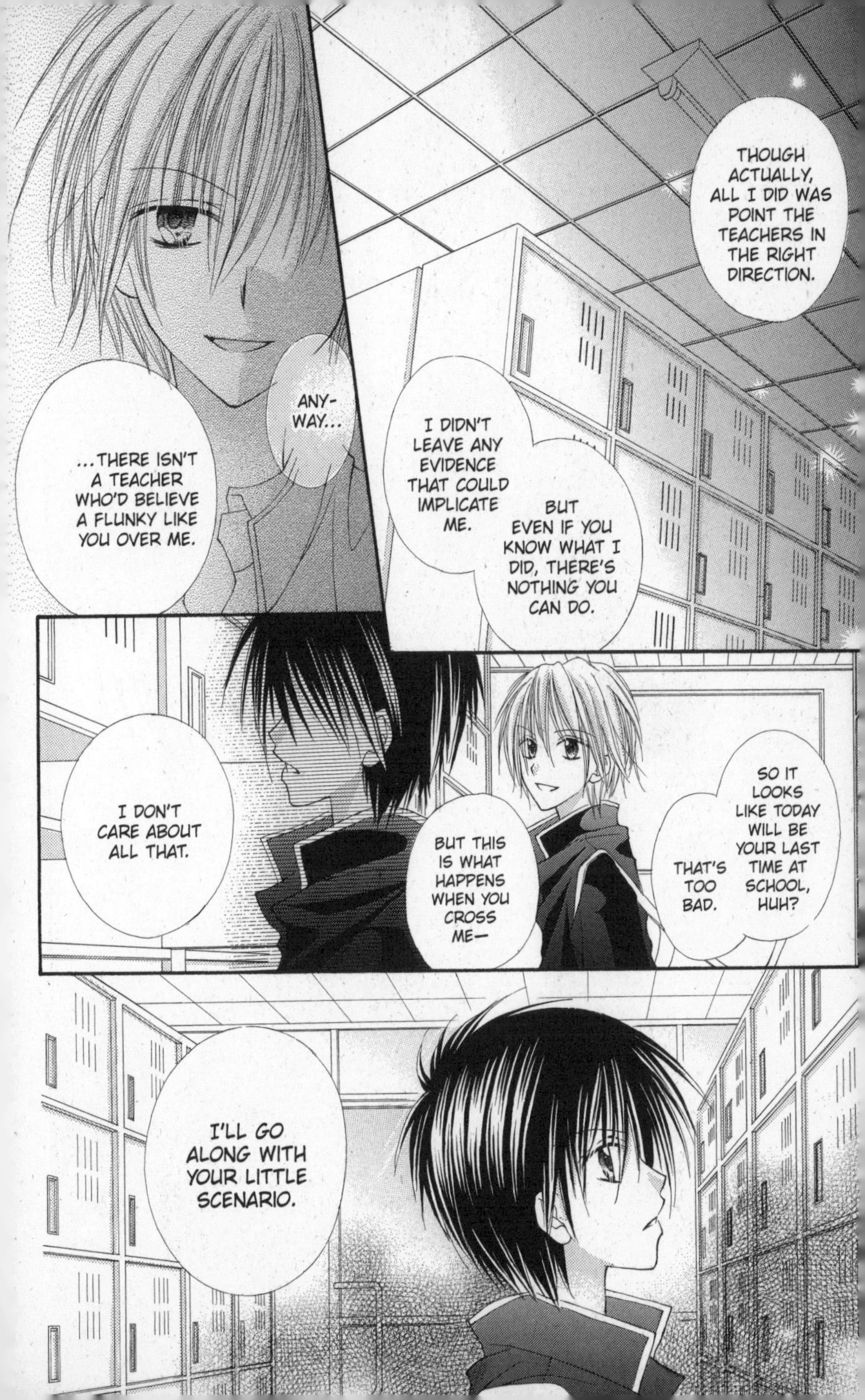
THOUGH ACTUALLY, ALL I DID WAS POINT THE TEACHERS IN THE RIGHT DIRECTION.
I DIDN'T LEAVE ANY EVIDENCE THAT COULD IMPLICATE ME.
BUT EVEN IF YOU KNOW WHAT I DID, THERE'S NOTHING YOU CAN DO.
ANY-WAY...
...THERE ISN'T A TEACHER WHO'D BELIEVE A FLUNKY LIKE YOU OVER ME.
SO IT LOOKS LIKE TODAY WILL BE YOUR LAST TIME AT SCHOOL, HUH?
THAT'S TOO BAD.
BUT THIS IS WHAT HAPPENS WHEN YOU CROSS ME—
I DON'T CARE ABOUT ALL THAT.
I'LL GO ALONG WITH YOUR LITTLE SCENARIO.

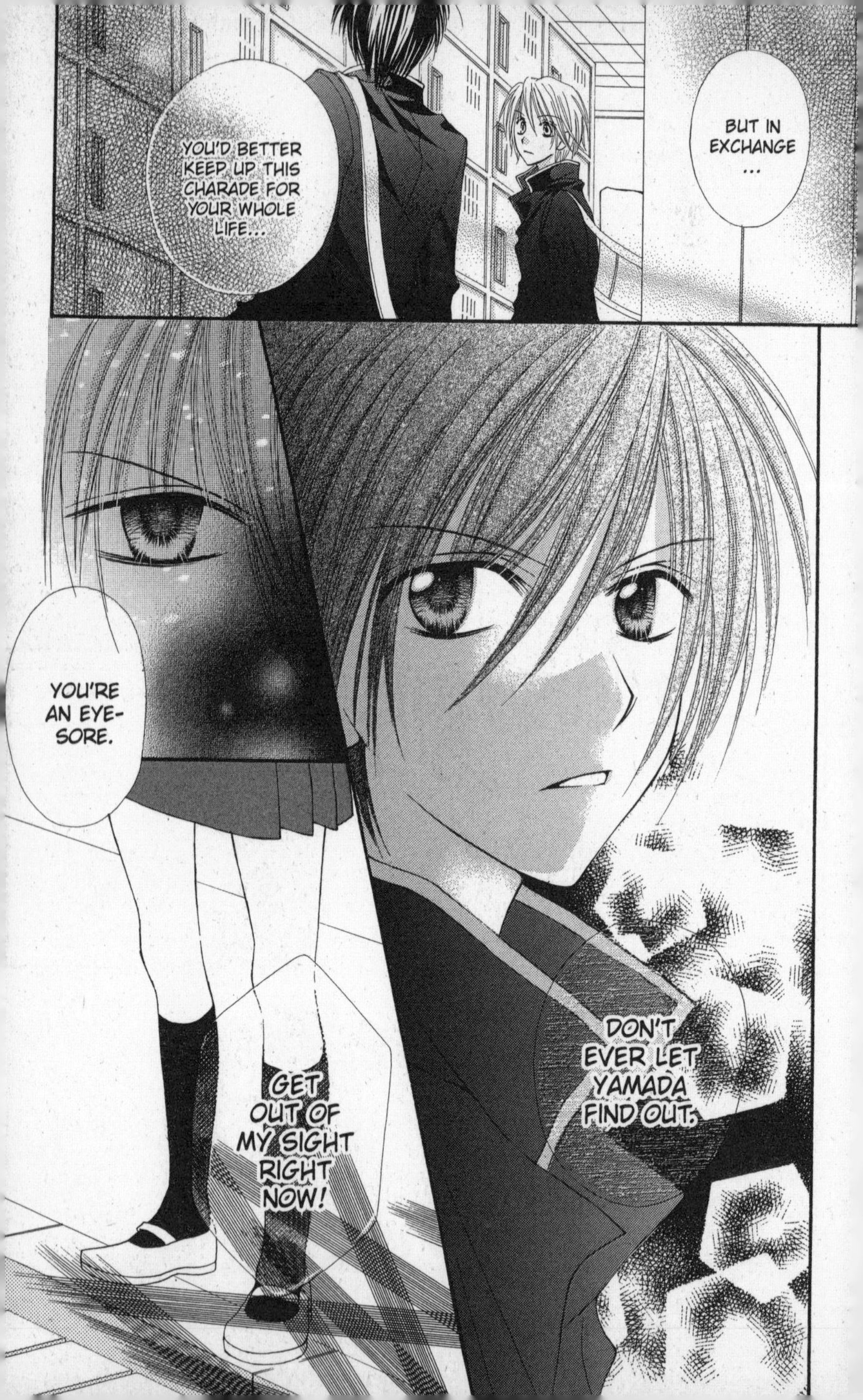
BUT IN EXCHANGE ...
YOU'D BETTER KEEP UP THIS CHARADE FOR YOUR WHOLE LIFE...
DON'T EVER LET YAMADA FIND OUT.
YOU'RE AN EYE-SORE.
GET OUT OF MY SIGHT RIGHT NOW!

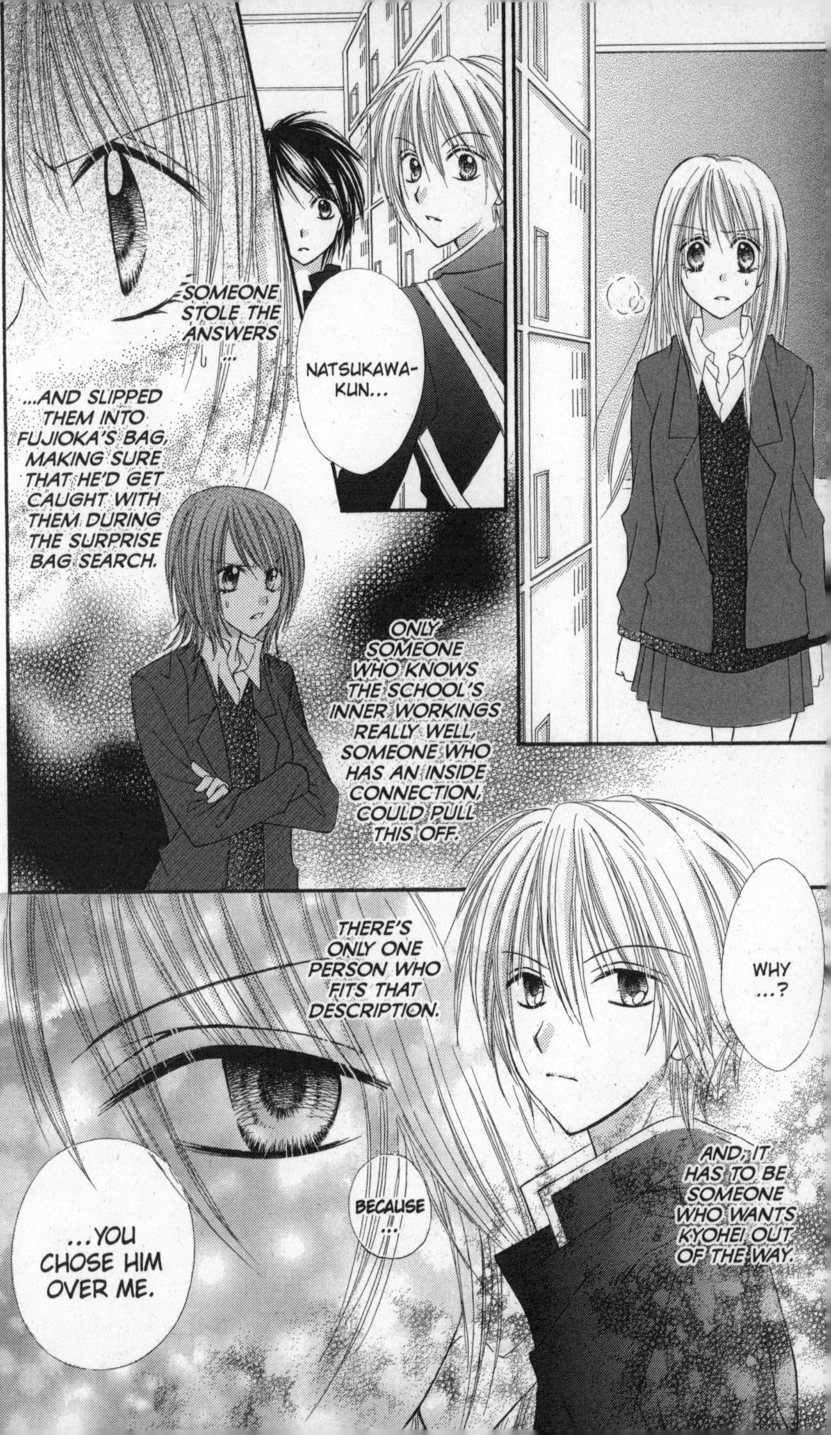
NATSUKAWA-KUN...
SOMEONE STOLE THE ANSWERS...
...AND SLIPPED THEM INTO FUJIOKA'S BAG, MAKING SURE THAT HE'D GET CAUGHT WITH THEM DURING THE SURPRISE BAG SEARCH.
ONLY SOMEONE WHO KNOWS THE SCHOOL'S INNER WORKINGS REALLY WELL, SOMEONE WHO HAS AN INSIDE CONNECTION, COULD PULL THIS OFF.
THERE'S ONLY ONE PERSON WHO FITS THAT DESCRIPTION.
AND, IT HAS TO BE SOMEONE WHO WANTS KYOHEI OUT OF THE WAY.
WHY...?
BECAUSE...
...YOU CHOSE HIM OVER ME.

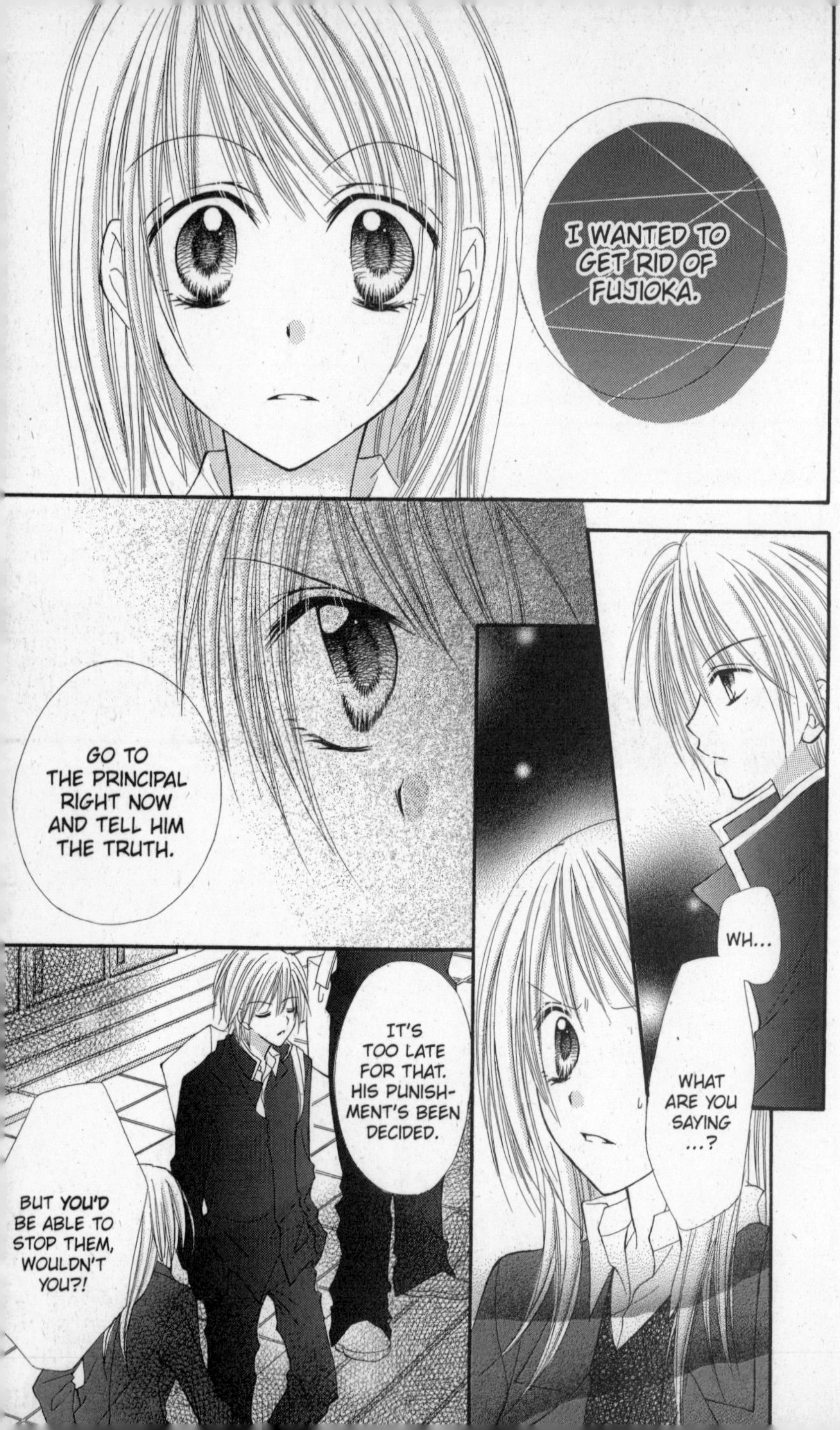
I WANTED TO GET RID OF FUJIOKA.
WH...
WHAT ARE YOU SAYING ...?
GO TO THE PRINCIPAL RIGHT NOW AND TELL HIM THE TRUTH.
IT'S TOO LATE FOR THAT. HIS PUNISHMENT'S BEEN DECIDED.
BUT YOU'D BE ABLE TO STOP THEM, WOULDN'T YOU?!

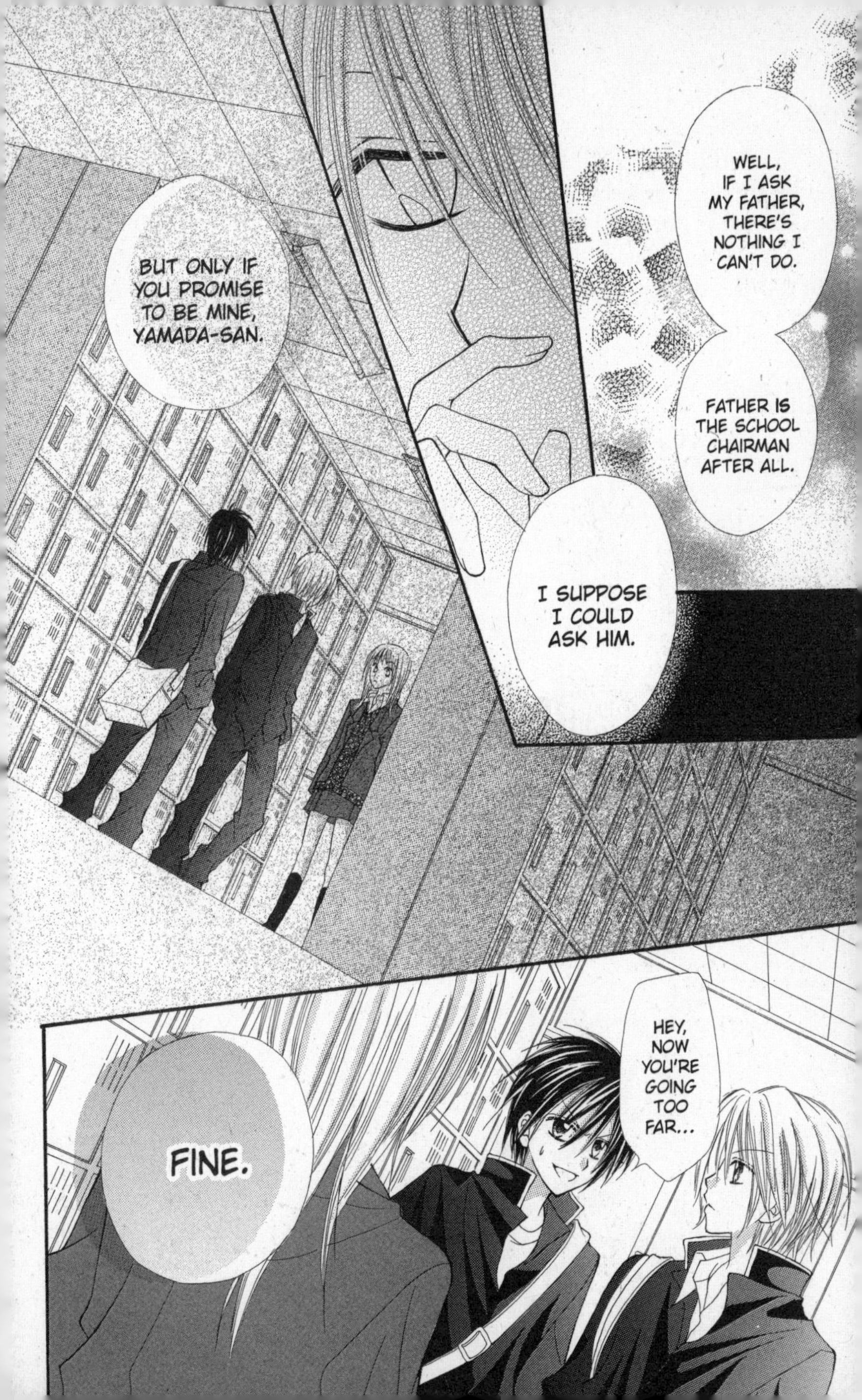
WELL, IF I ASK MY FATHER, THERE'S NOTHING I CAN'T DO.
FATHER IS THE SCHOOL CHAIRMAN AFTER ALL.
I SUPPOSE I COULD ASK HIM.
BUT ONLY IF YOU PROMISE TO BE MINE, YAMADA-SAN.
HEY, NOW YOU'RE GOING TOO FAR...
FINE.

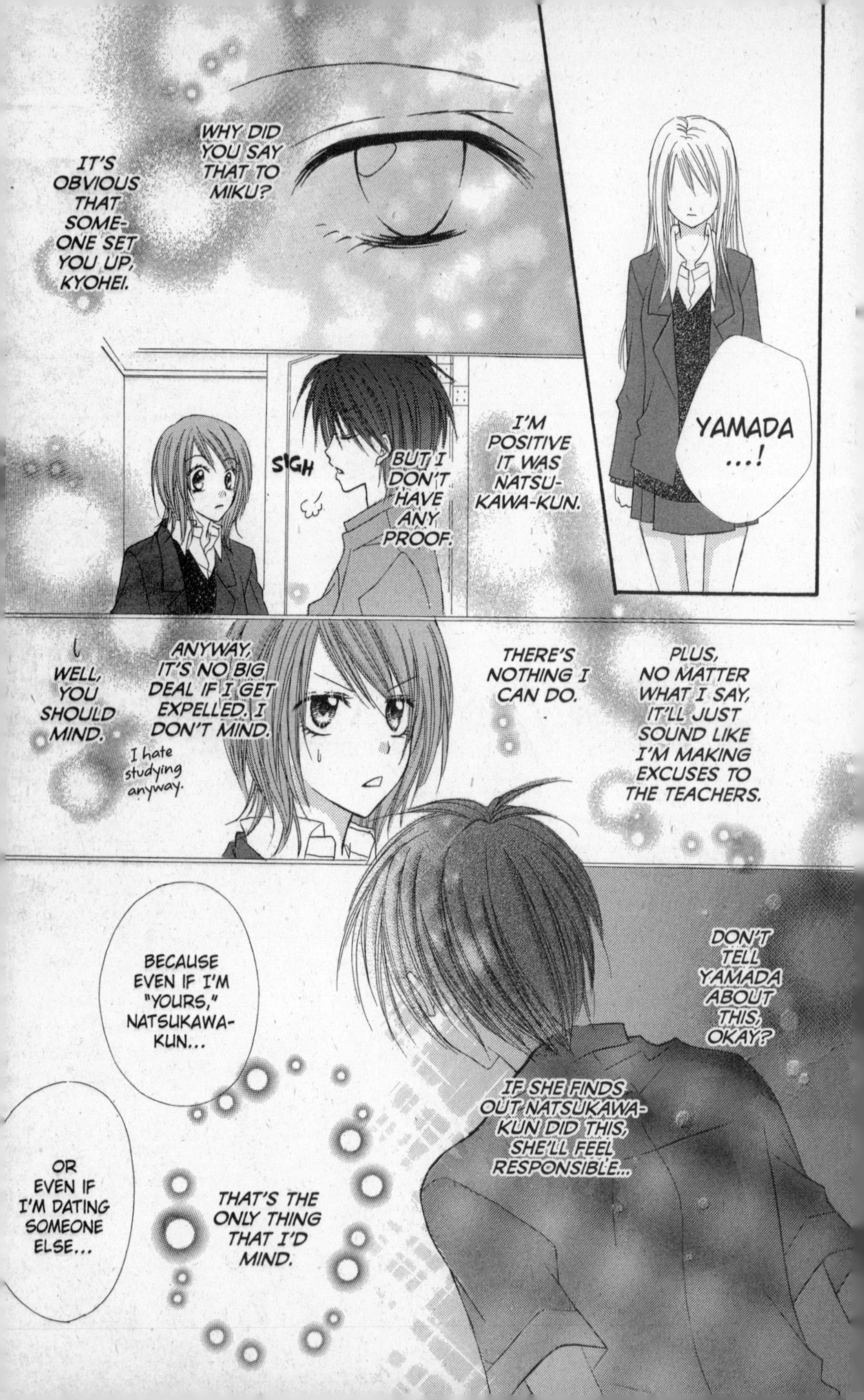
YAMADA ...!
WHY DID YOU SAY THAT TO MIKU?
IT'S OBVIOUS THAT SOME-ONE SET YOU UP, KYOHEI.
I'M POSITIVE IT WAS NATSU-KAWA-KUN.
SIGH
BUT I DON'T HAVE ANY PROOF.
PLUS, NO MATTER WHAT I SAY, IT'LL JUST SOUND LIKE I'M MAKING EXCUSES TO THE TEACHERS.
THERE'S NOTHING I CAN DO.
ANYWAY, IT'S NO BIG DEAL IF I GET EXPELLED. I DON'T MIND.
I hate studying anyway.
WELL, YOU SHOULD MIND.
DON'T TELL YAMADA ABOUT THIS, OKAY?
IF SHE FINDS OUT NATSUKAWA-KUN DID THIS, SHE'LL FEEL RESPONSIBLE...
BECAUSE EVEN IF I'M "YOURS," NATSUKAWA-KUN...
OR EVEN IF I'M DATING SOMEONE ELSE...
THAT'S THE ONLY THING THAT I'D MIND.

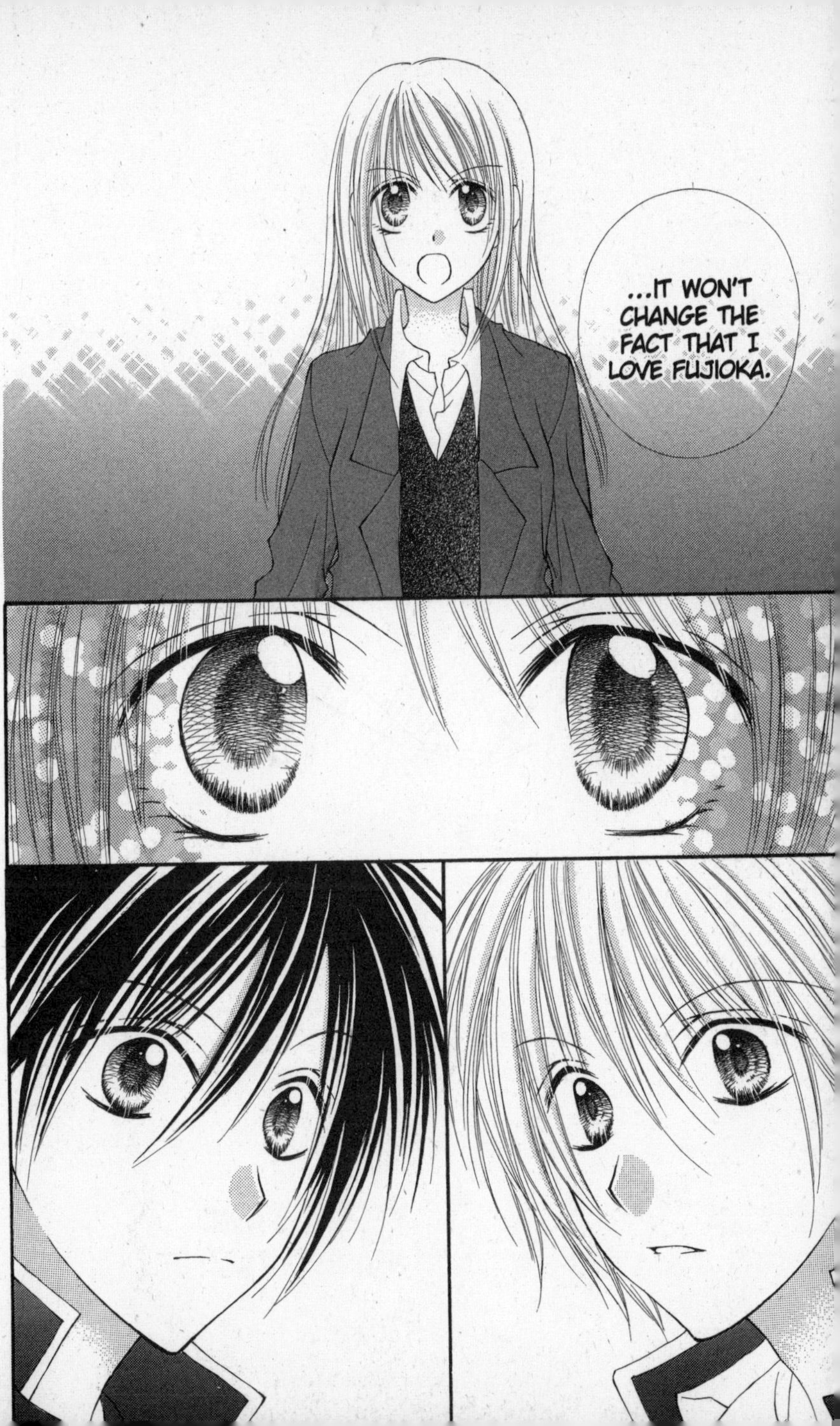
...IT WON'T CHANGE THE FACT THAT I LOVE FUJIOKA.

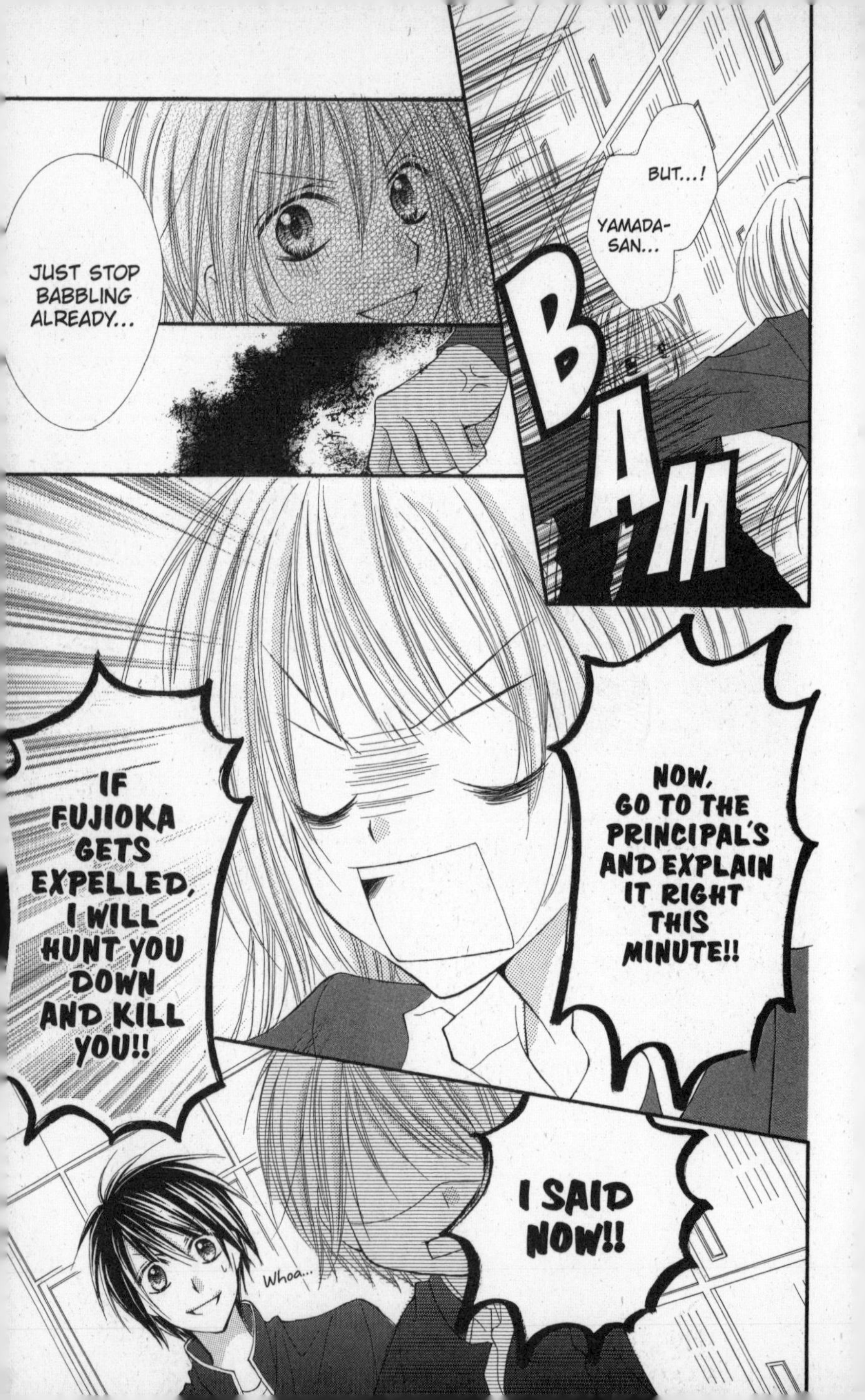
BUT...!
YAMADA-SAN...
BAM
JUST STOP BABBLING ALREADY...
NOW, GO TO THE PRINCIPAL'S AND EXPLAIN IT RIGHT THIS MINUTE!!
IF FUJIOKA GETS EXPELLED, I WILL HUNT YOU DOWN AND KILL YOU!!
I SAID NOW!!
Whoa...

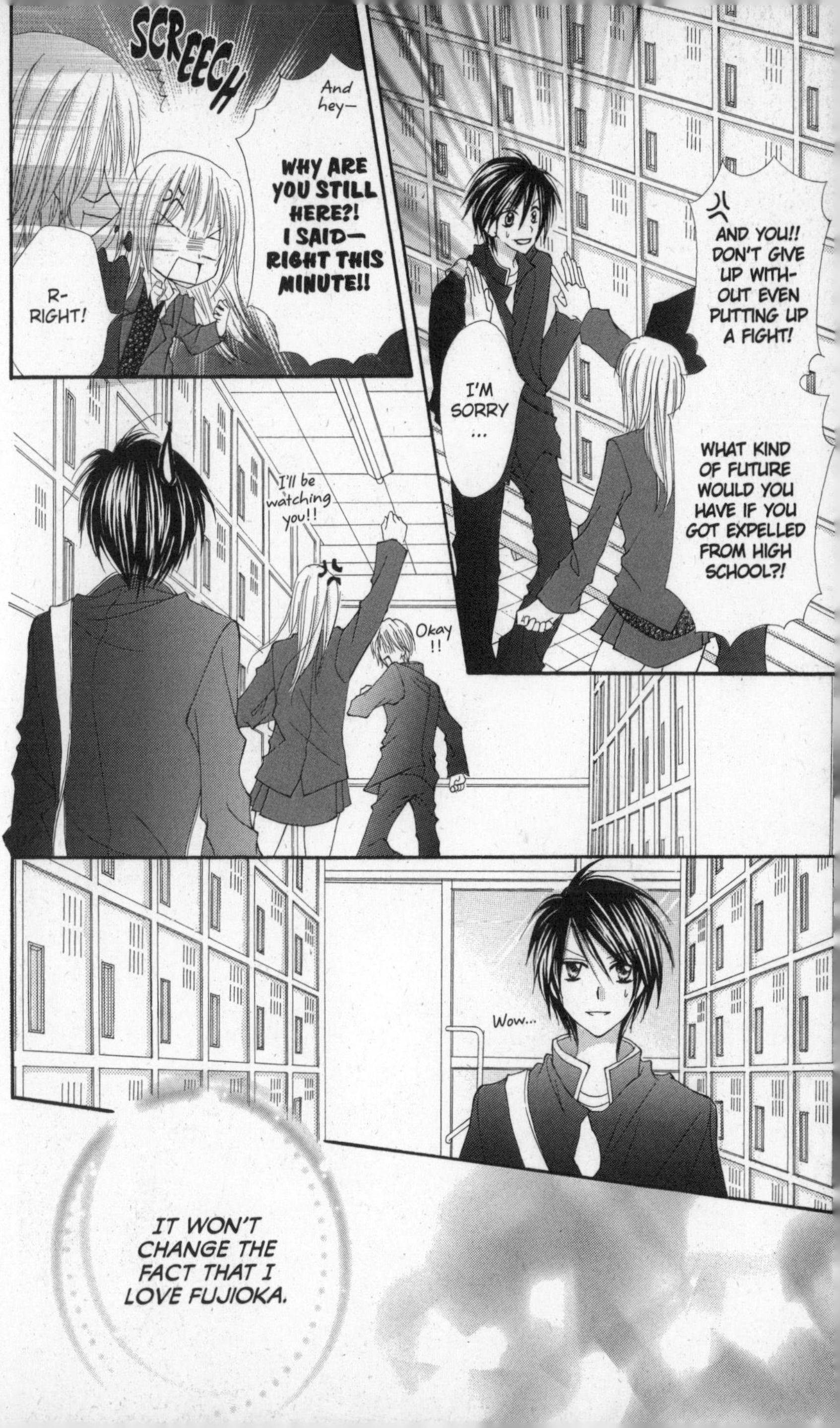
AND YOU!! DON'T GIVE UP WITH-OUT EVEN PUTTING UP A FIGHT!
I'M SORRY ...
WHAT KIND OF FUTURE WOULD YOU HAVE IF YOU GOT EXPELLED FROM HIGH SCHOOL?!
SCREECH
And hey—
WHY ARE YOU STILL HERE?! I SAID— RIGHT THIS MINUTE!!
R- RIGHT!
I'll be watching you!!
Okay !!
Wow...
IT WON'T CHANGE THE FACT THAT I LOVE FUJIOKA.

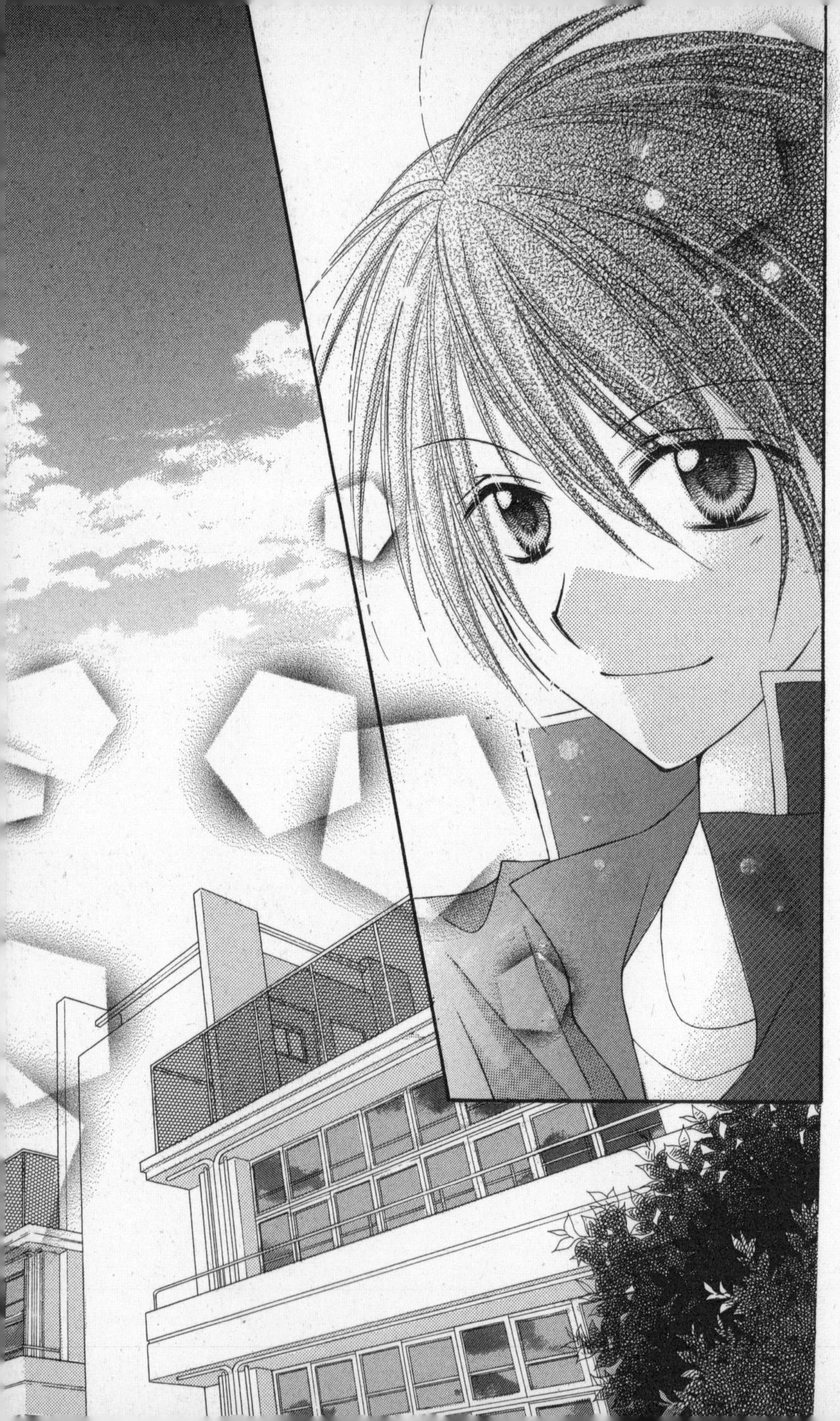

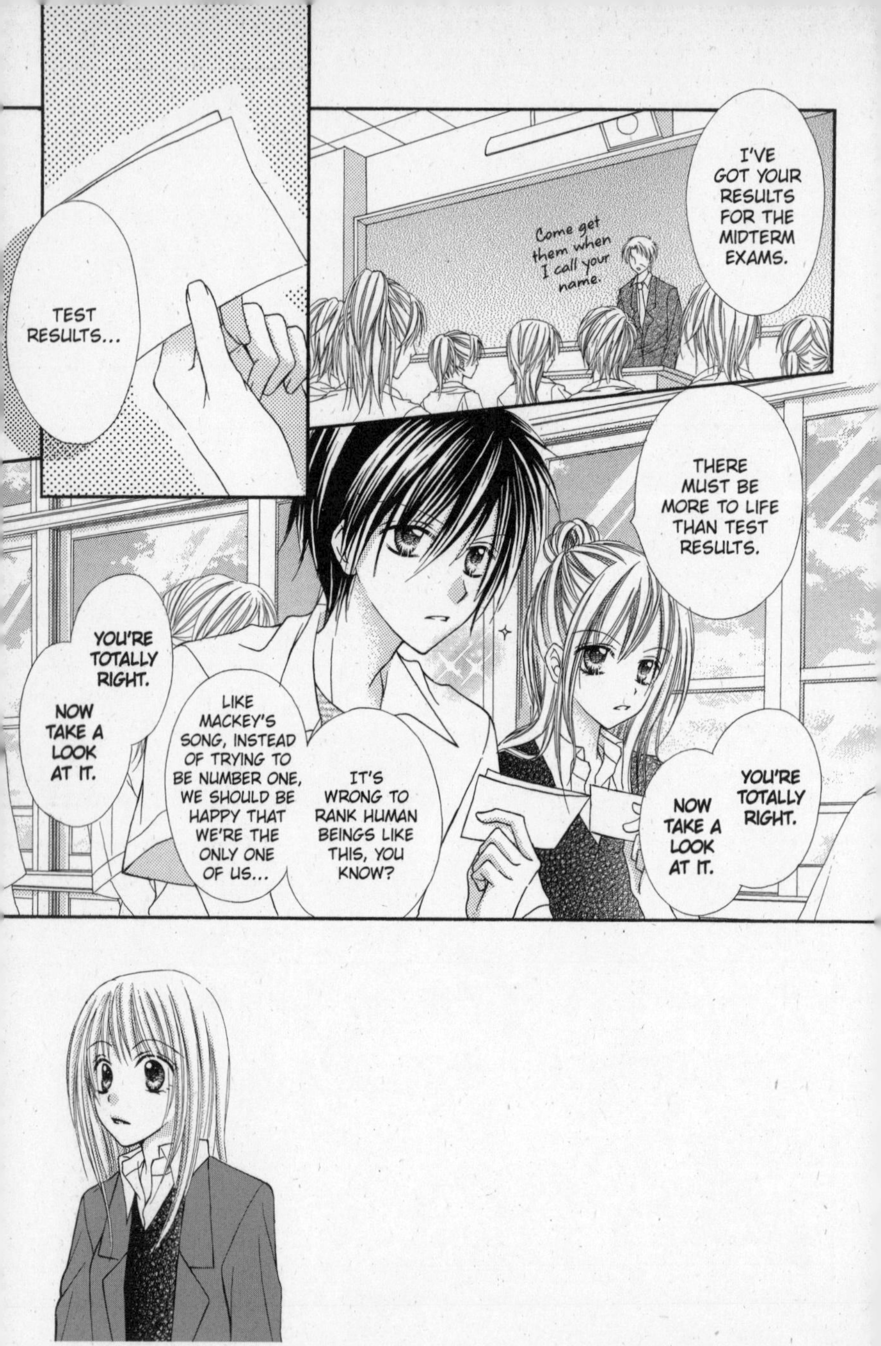
I'VE GOT YOUR RESULTS FOR THE MIDTERM EXAMS.
Come get them when I call your name.
TEST RESULTS...
THERE MUST BE MORE TO LIFE THAN TEST RESULTS.
YOU'RE TOTALLY RIGHT.
NOW TAKE A LOOK AT IT.
IT'S WRONG TO RANK HUMAN BEINGS LIKE THIS, YOU KNOW?
LIKE MACKEY'S SONG, INSTEAD OF TRYING TO BE NUMBER ONE, WE SHOULD BE HAPPY THAT WE'RE THE ONLY ONE OF US...
YOU'RE TOTALLY RIGHT.
NOW TAKE A LOOK AT IT.

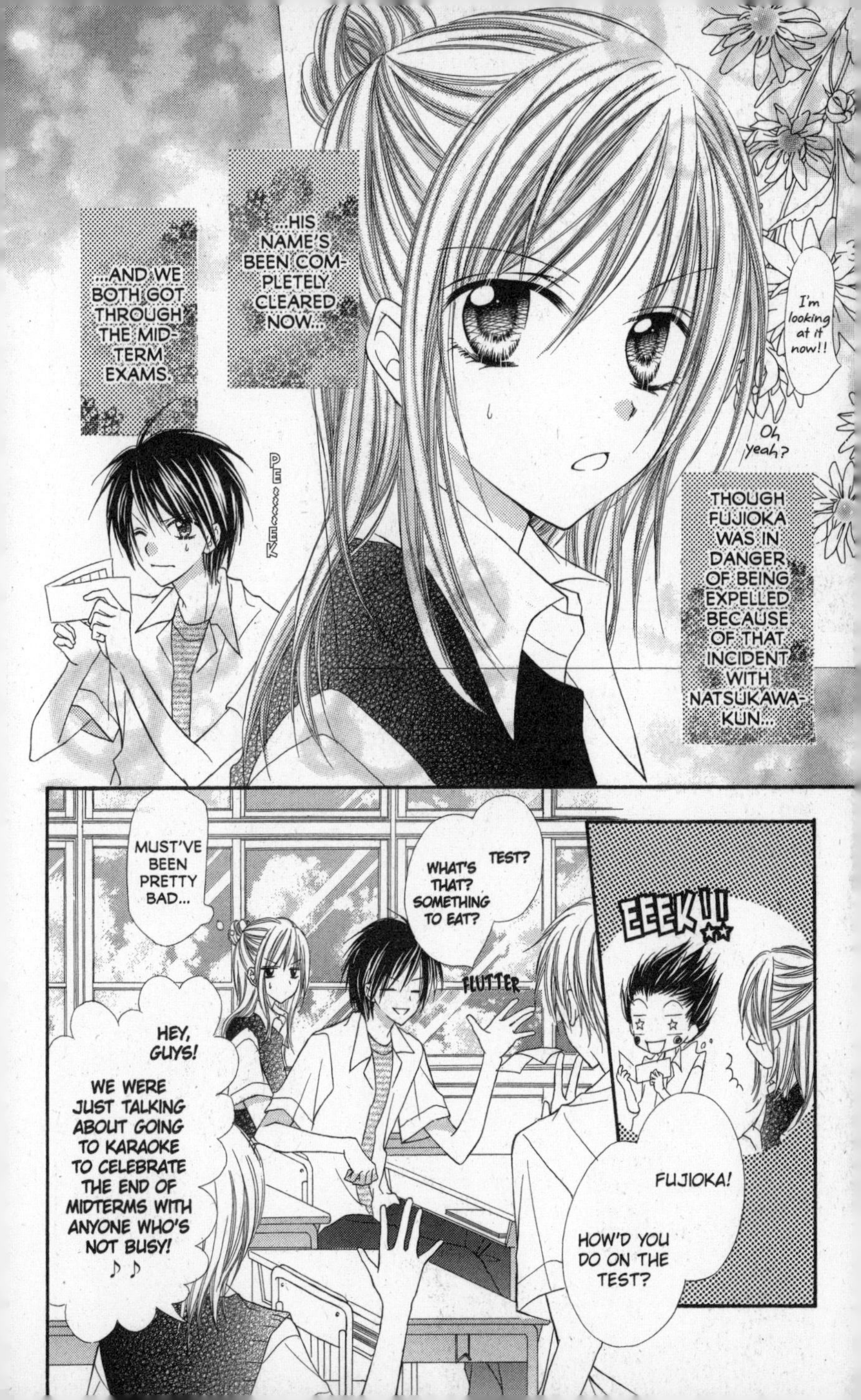
I'm looking at it now!!
Oh yeah?
THOUGH FUJIOKA WAS IN DANGER OF BEING EXPELLED BECAUSE OF THAT INCIDENT WITH NATSUKAWA-KUN...
...HIS NAME'S BEEN COMPLETELY CLEARED NOW...
...AND WE BOTH GOT THROUGH THE MIDTERM EXAMS.
PEEEEK
EEEK!!
FUJIOKA! HOW'D YOU DO ON THE TEST?
TEST? WHAT'S THAT? SOMETHING TO EAT?
FLUTTER
MUST'VE BEEN PRETTY BAD...
HEY, GUYS! WE WERE JUST TALKING ABOUT GOING TO KARAOKE TO CELEBRATE THE END OF MIDTERMS WITH ANYONE WHO'S NOT BUSY! ♪♪

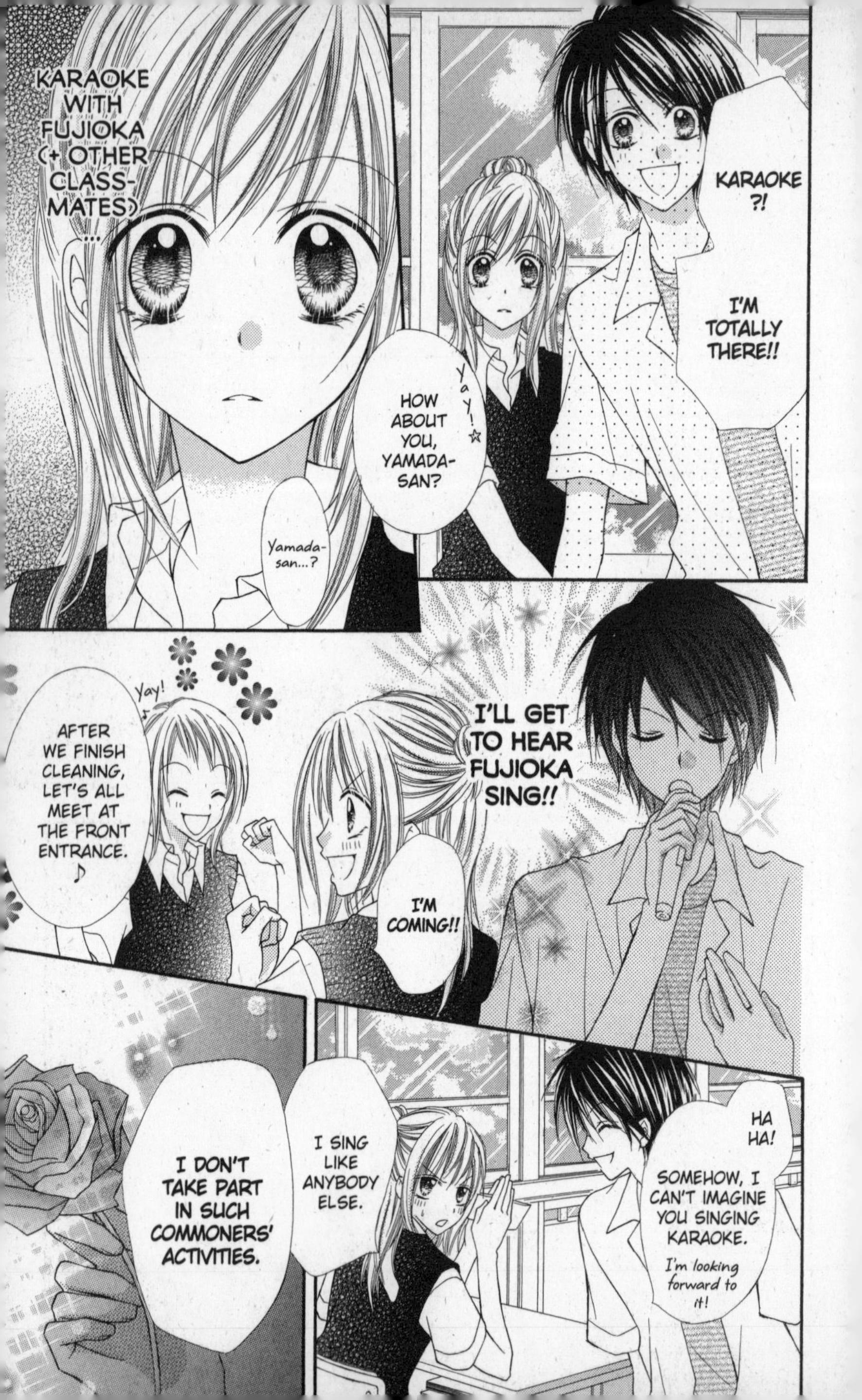
KARAOKE ?!
I'M TOTALLY THERE!!
Yay!☆
HOW ABOUT YOU, YAMADA-SAN?
KARAOKE WITH FUJIOKA (+ OTHER CLASSMATES)...
Yamada-san...?
I'LL GET TO HEAR FUJIOKA SING!!
I'M COMING!!
Yay! ♪
AFTER WE FINISH CLEANING, LET'S ALL MEET AT THE FRONT ENTRANCE. ♪
HA HA!
SOMEHOW, I CAN'T IMAGINE YOU SINGING KARAOKE.
I'm looking forward to it!
I SING LIKE ANYBODY ELSE.
I DON'T TAKE PART IN SUCH COMMONERS' ACTIVITIES.

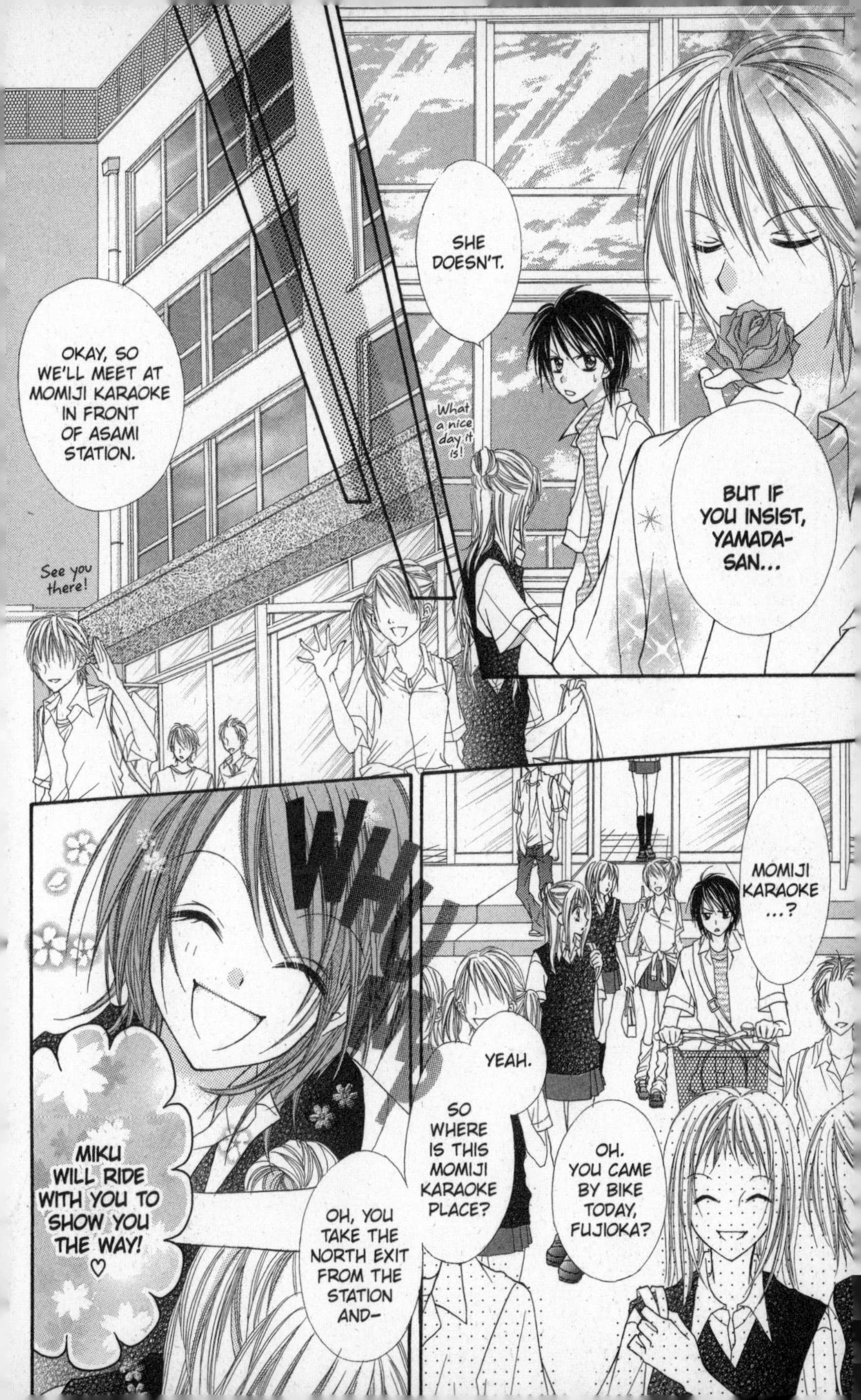
SHE DOESN'T.
What a nice day it is!
BUT IF YOU INSIST, YAMADA-SAN...
OKAY, SO WE'LL MEET AT MOMIJI KARAOKE IN FRONT OF ASAMI STATION.
See you there!
MOMIJI KARAOKE ...?
OH. YOU CAME BY BIKE TODAY, FUJIOKA?
YEAH.
SO WHERE IS THIS MOMIJI KARAOKE PLACE?
OH, YOU TAKE THE NORTH EXIT FROM THE STATION AND-
MIKU WILL RIDE WITH YOU TO SHOW YOU THE WAY! ♡

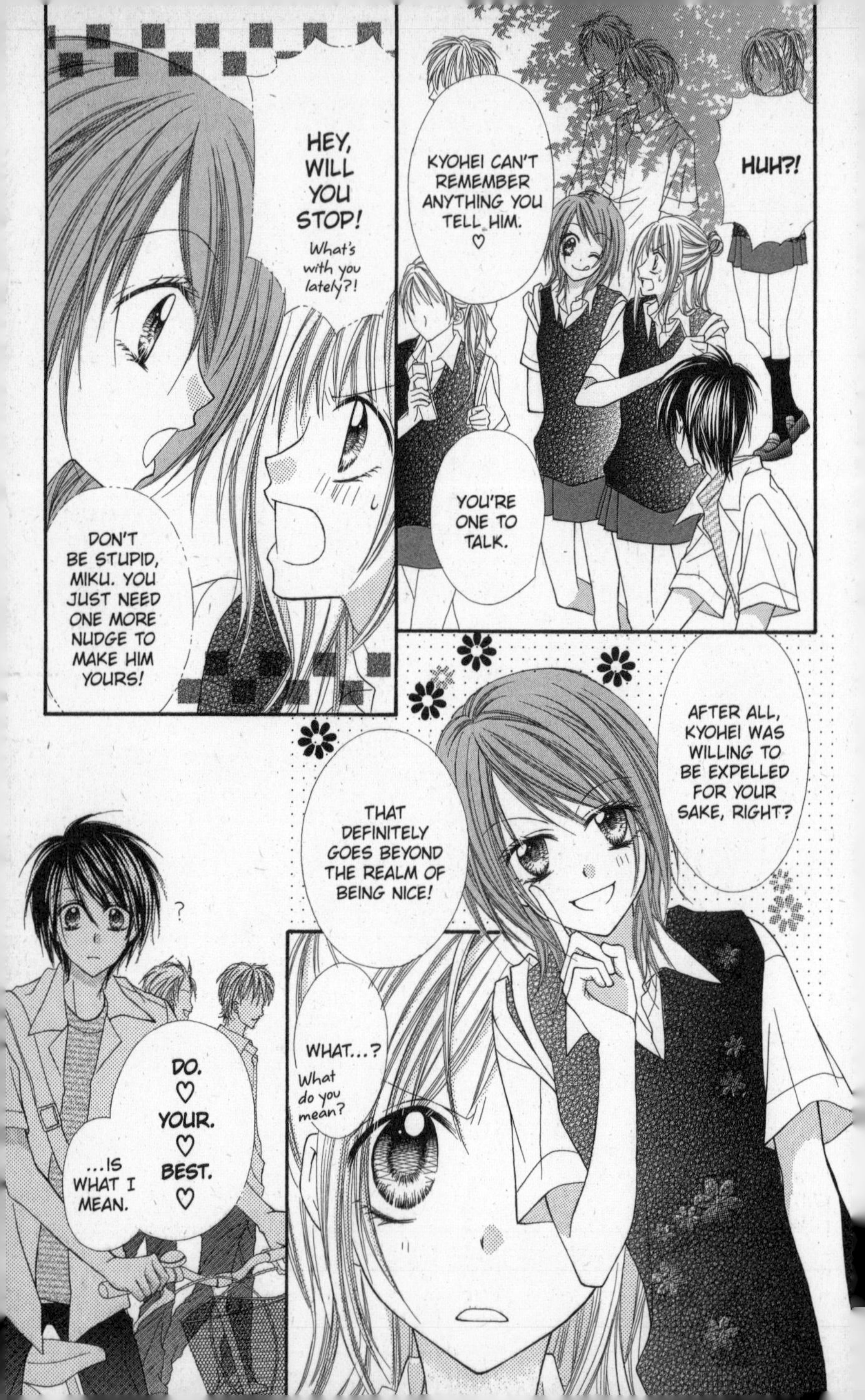
KYOHEI CAN'T REMEMBER ANYTHING YOU TELL HIM. ♡
HUH?!
YOU'RE ONE TO TALK.
HEY, WILL YOU STOP!
What's with you lately?!
DON'T BE STUPID, MIKU. YOU JUST NEED ONE MORE NUDGE TO MAKE HIM YOURS!
AFTER ALL, KYOHEI WAS WILLING TO BE EXPELLED FOR YOUR SAKE, RIGHT?
THAT DEFINITELY GOES BEYOND THE REALM OF BEING NICE!
WHAT...?
What do you mean?
?
DO. ♡ YOUR. ♡ BEST. ♡
...IS WHAT I MEAN.

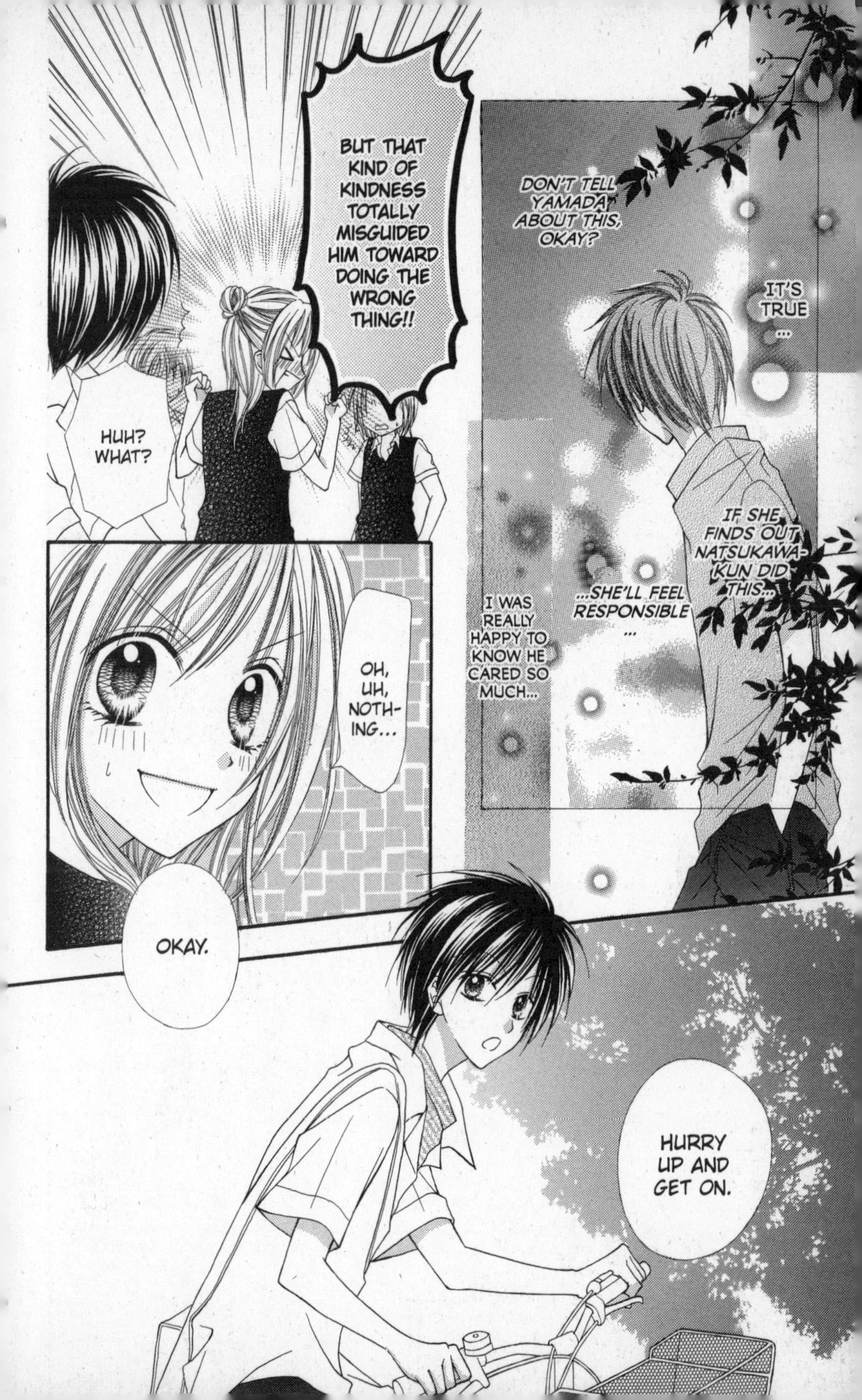
BUT THAT KIND OF KINDNESS TOTALLY MISGUIDED HIM TOWARD DOING THE WRONG THING!!
HUH? WHAT?
DON'T TELL YAMADA ABOUT THIS, OKAY?
IT'S TRUE ...
IF SHE FINDS OUT NATSUKAWA-KUN DID THIS...
...SHE'LL FEEL RESPONSIBLE ...
I WAS REALLY HAPPY TO KNOW HE CARED SO MUCH...
OH, UH, NOTHING...
OKAY.
HURRY UP AND GET ON.

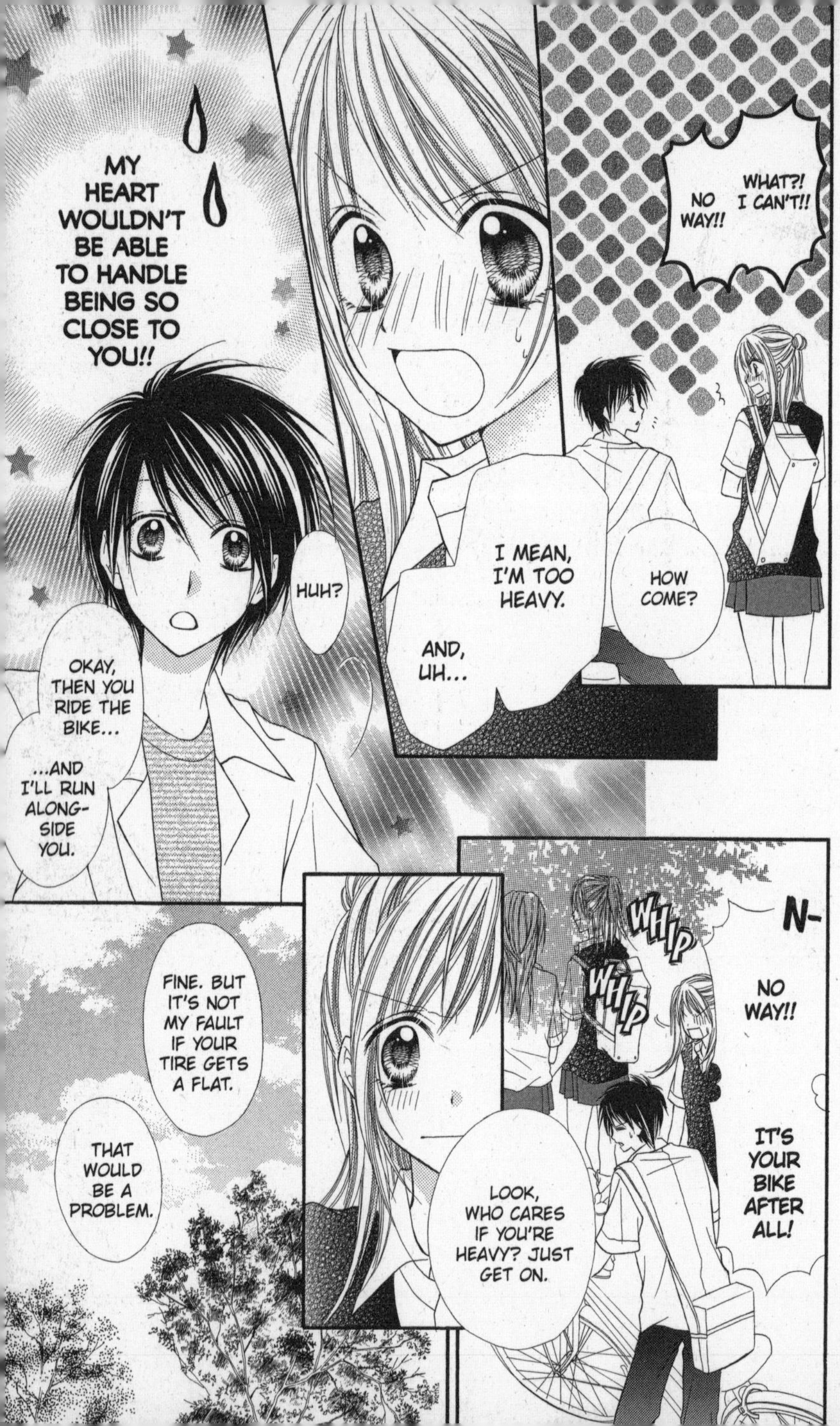
WHAT?! I CAN'T!!
NO WAY!!
HOW COME?
I MEAN, I'M TOO HEAVY.
AND, UH...
MY HEART WOULDN'T BE ABLE TO HANDLE BEING SO CLOSE TO YOU!!
HUH?
OKAY, THEN YOU RIDE THE BIKE...
...AND I'LL RUN ALONG-SIDE YOU.
N-
NO WAY!!
IT'S YOUR BIKE AFTER ALL!
WHIP
WHIP
LOOK, WHO CARES IF YOU'RE HEAVY? JUST GET ON.
FINE. BUT IT'S NOT MY FAULT IF YOUR TIRE GETS A FLAT.
THAT WOULD BE A PROBLEM.

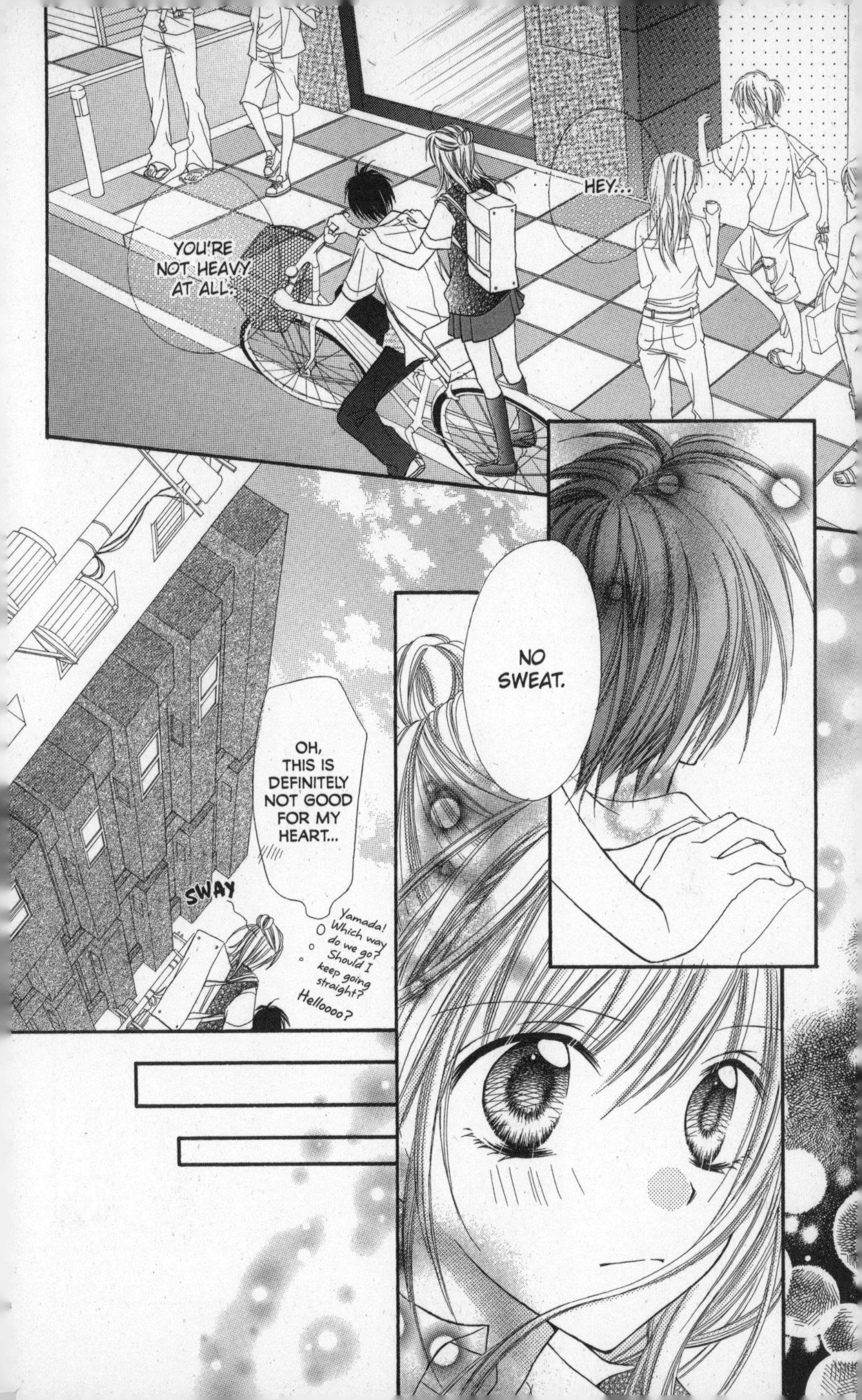
HEY...
YOU'RE NOT HEAVY AT ALL.
NO SWEAT.
OH, THIS IS DEFINITELY NOT GOOD FOR MY HEART...
SWAY
Yamada! Which way do we go? Should I keep going straight?
Helloooo?

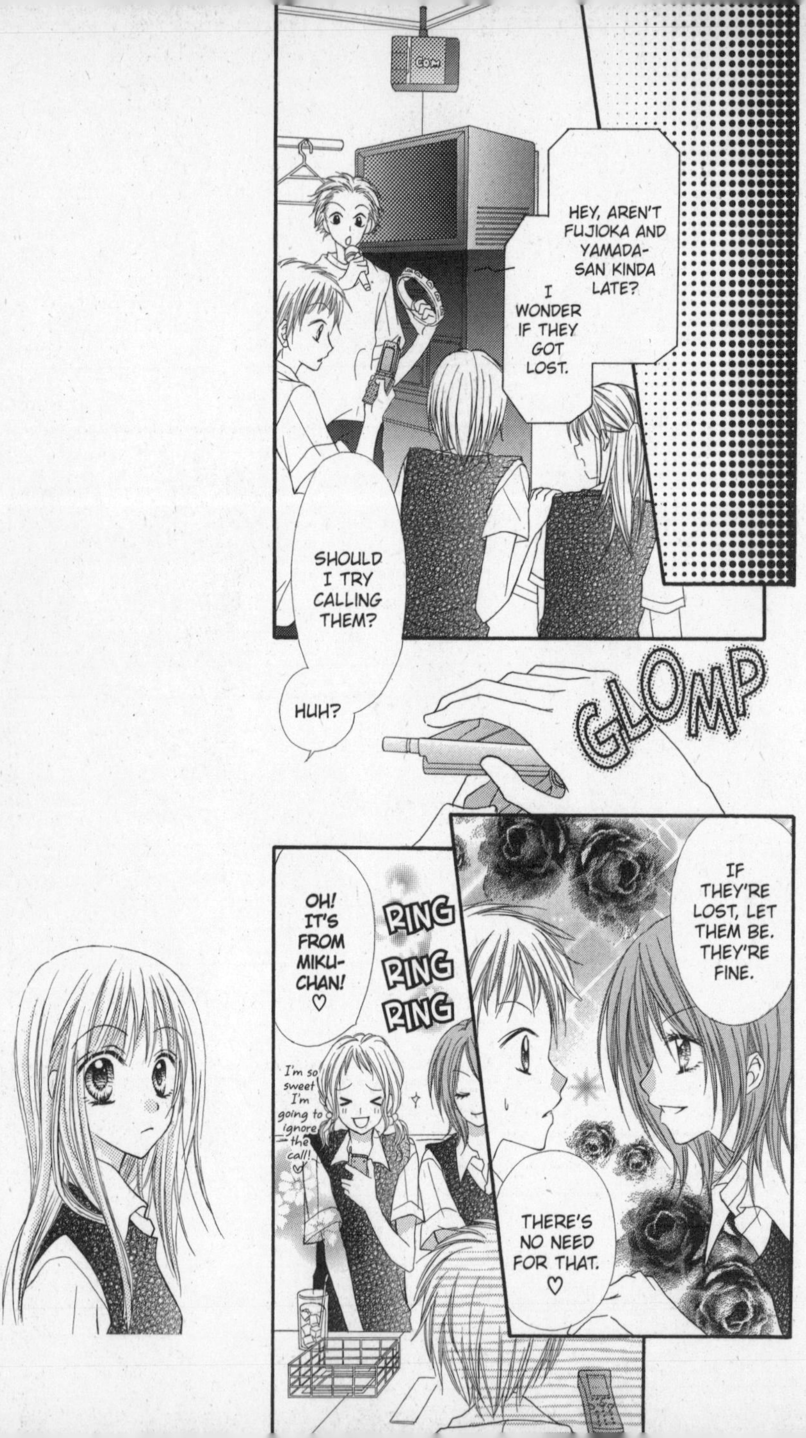
HEY, AREN'T FUJIOKA AND YAMADA-SAN KINDA LATE?
I WONDER IF THEY GOT LOST.
SHOULD I TRY CALLING THEM?
HUH?
GLOMP
IF THEY'RE LOST, LET THEM BE. THEY'RE FINE.
THERE'S NO NEED FOR THAT. ♡
RING RING RING
OH! IT'S FROM MIKU-CHAN! ♡
I'm so sweet I'm going to ignore the call! ♡

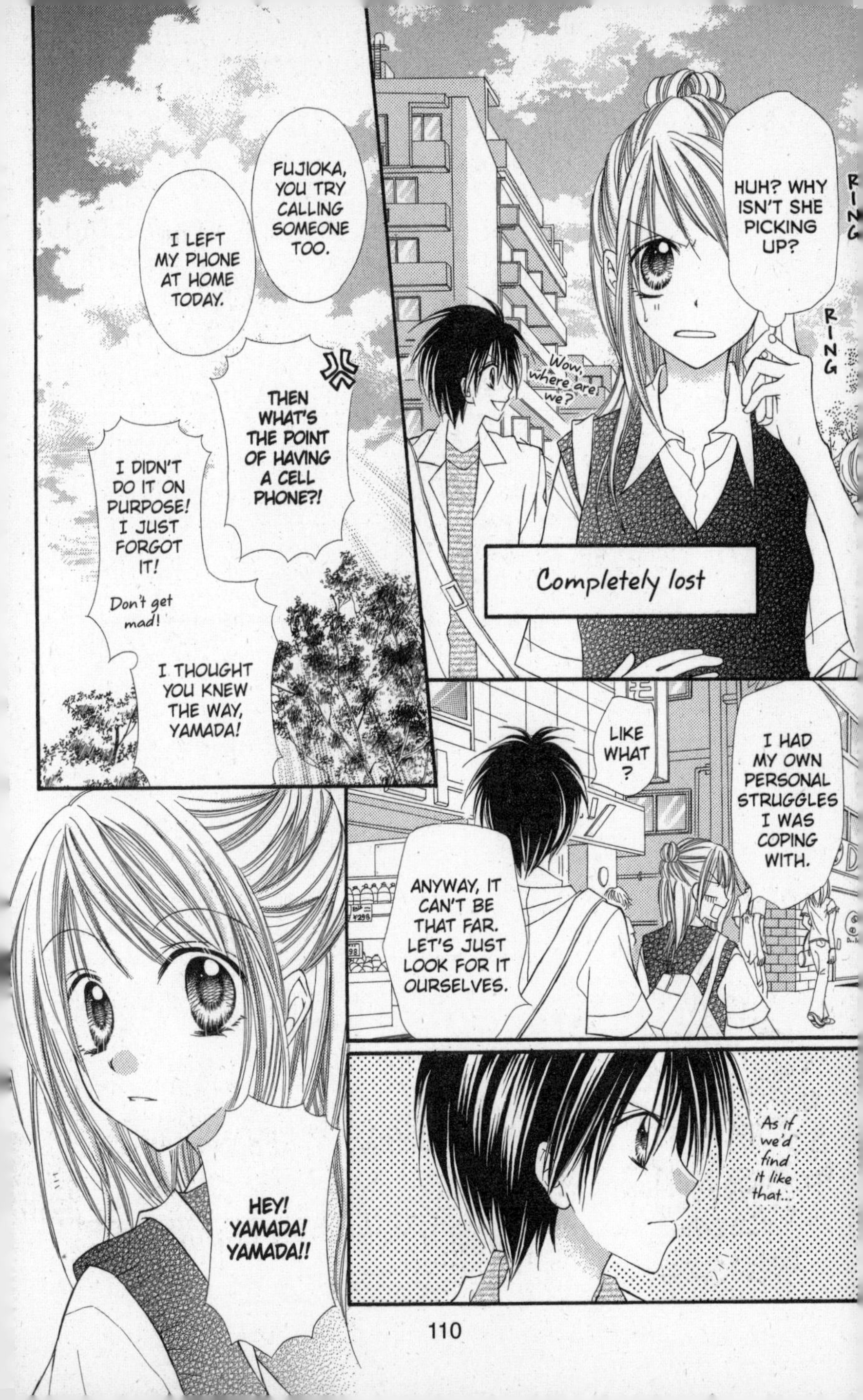
HUH? WHY ISN'T SHE PICKING UP?
RING RING
Wow, where are we?
Completely lost
FUJIOKA, YOU TRY CALLING SOMEONE TOO.
I LEFT MY PHONE AT HOME TODAY.
THEN WHAT'S THE POINT OF HAVING A CELL PHONE?!
I DIDN'T DO IT ON PURPOSE! I JUST FORGOT IT!
Don't get mad!
I THOUGHT YOU KNEW THE WAY, YAMADA!
I HAD MY OWN PERSONAL STRUGGLES I WAS COPING WITH.
LIKE WHAT?
ANYWAY, IT CAN'T BE THAT FAR. LET'S JUST LOOK FOR IT OURSELVES.
As if we'd find it like that...
HEY! YAMADA! YAMADA!!

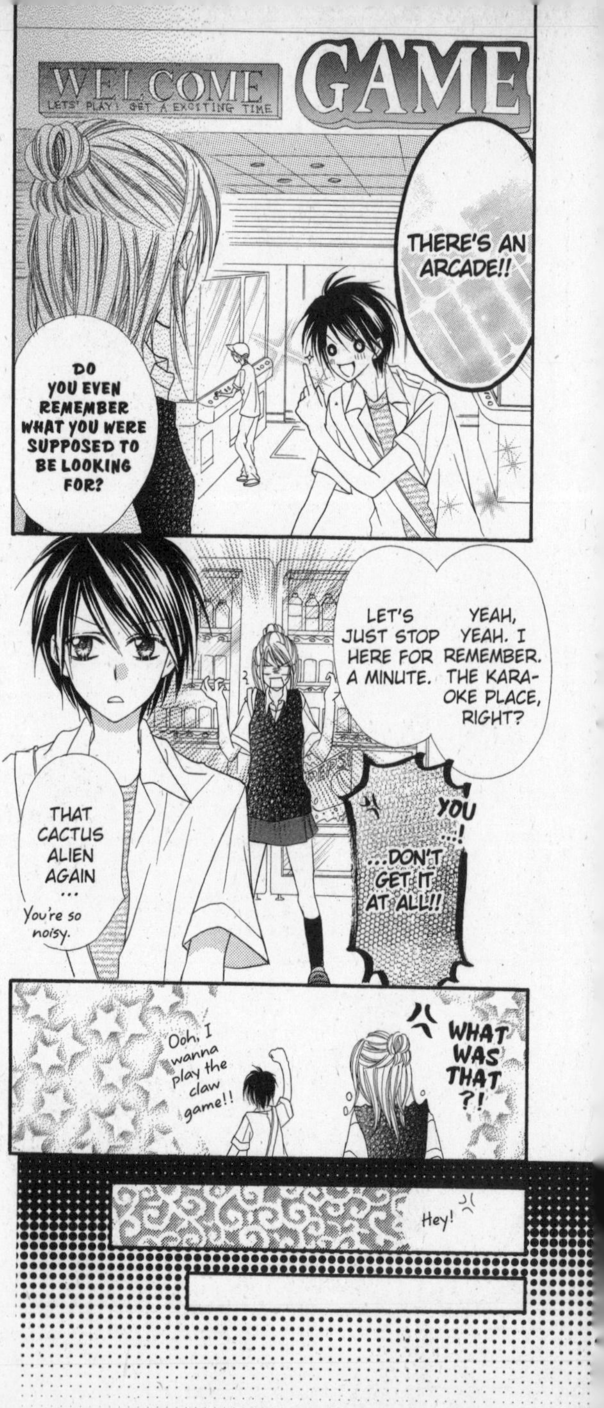
WELCOME
LET'S PLAY! GET A EXCITING TIME
GAME
THERE'S AN ARCADE!!
DO YOU EVEN REMEMBER WHAT YOU WERE SUPPOSED TO BE LOOKING FOR?
YEAH, YEAH. I REMEMBER. THE KARAOKE PLACE, RIGHT?
LET'S JUST STOP HERE FOR A MINUTE.
YOU...! ...DON'T GET IT AT ALL!!
THAT CACTUS ALIEN AGAIN...
You're so noisy.
WHAT WAS THAT?!
Ooh, I wanna play the claw game!!
Hey!

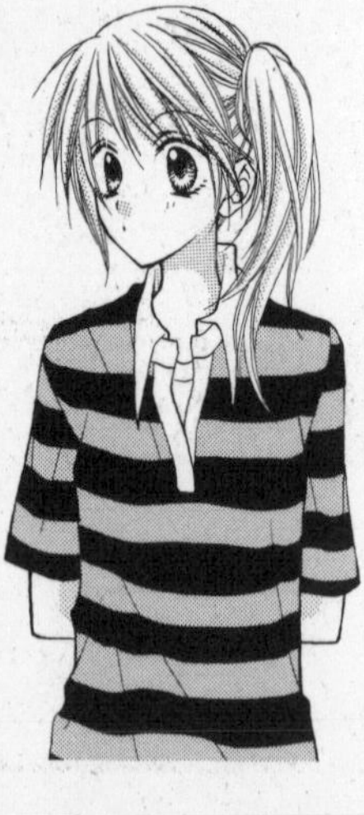

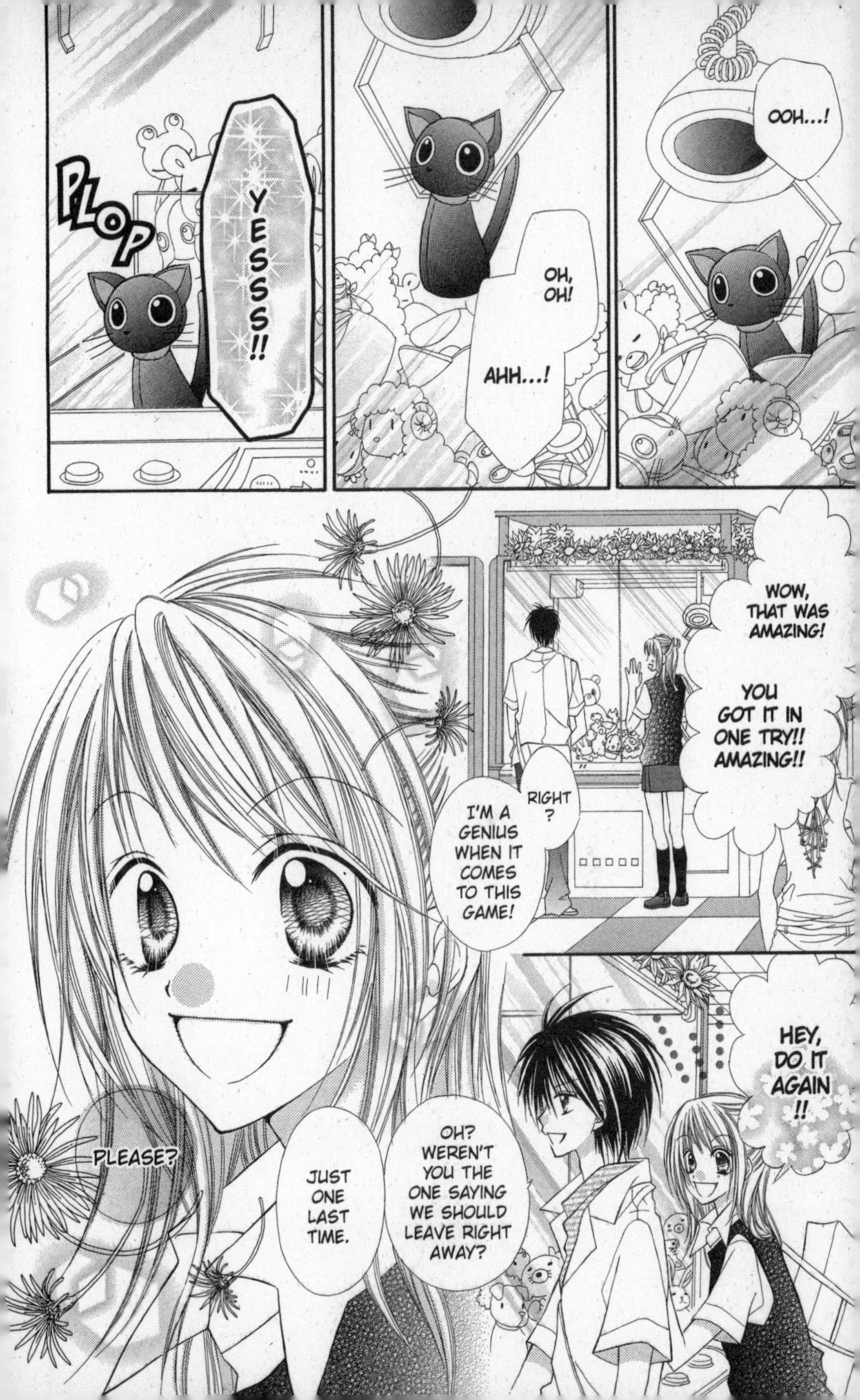
OOH...!
OH, OH!
AHH...!
PLOP
YESSS!!
WOW, THAT WAS AMAZING!
YOU GOT IT IN ONE TRY!! AMAZING!!
RIGHT?
I'M A GENIUS WHEN IT COMES TO THIS GAME!
HEY, DO IT AGAIN!!
OH? WEREN'T YOU THE ONE SAYING WE SHOULD LEAVE RIGHT AWAY?
JUST ONE LAST TIME.
PLEASE?

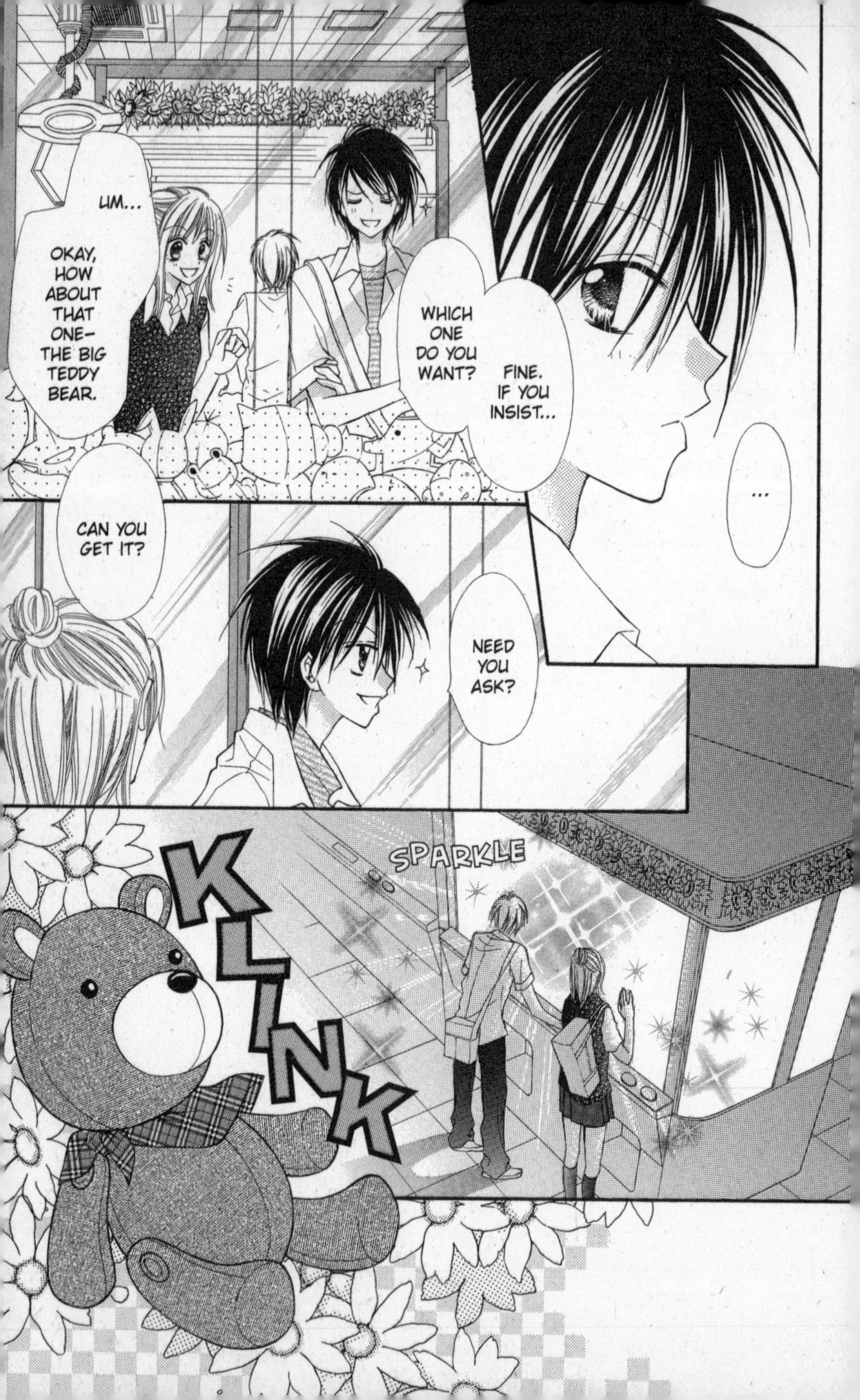
FINE. IF YOU INSIST...
...
WHICH ONE DO YOU WANT?
UM...
OKAY, HOW ABOUT THAT ONE— THE BIG TEDDY BEAR.
CAN YOU GET IT?
NEED YOU ASK?
SPARKLE
KLINK

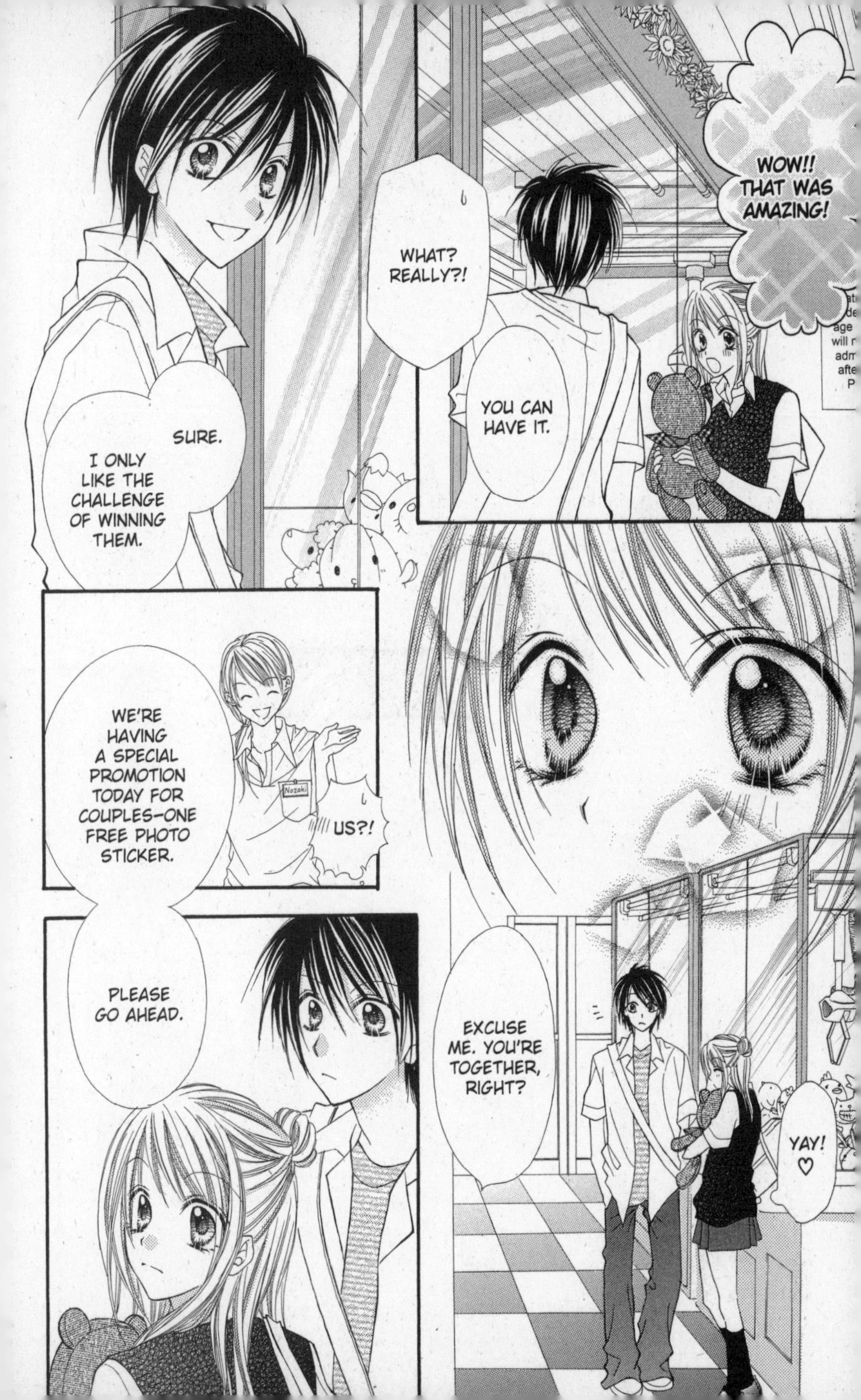
WOW!! THAT WAS AMAZING!
YOU CAN HAVE IT.
WHAT? REALLY?!
SURE.
I ONLY LIKE THE CHALLENGE OF WINNING THEM.
YAY! ♡
EXCUSE ME. YOU'RE TOGETHER, RIGHT?
WE'RE HAVING A SPECIAL PROMOTION TODAY FOR COUPLES—ONE FREE PHOTO STICKER.
US?!
PLEASE GO AHEAD.

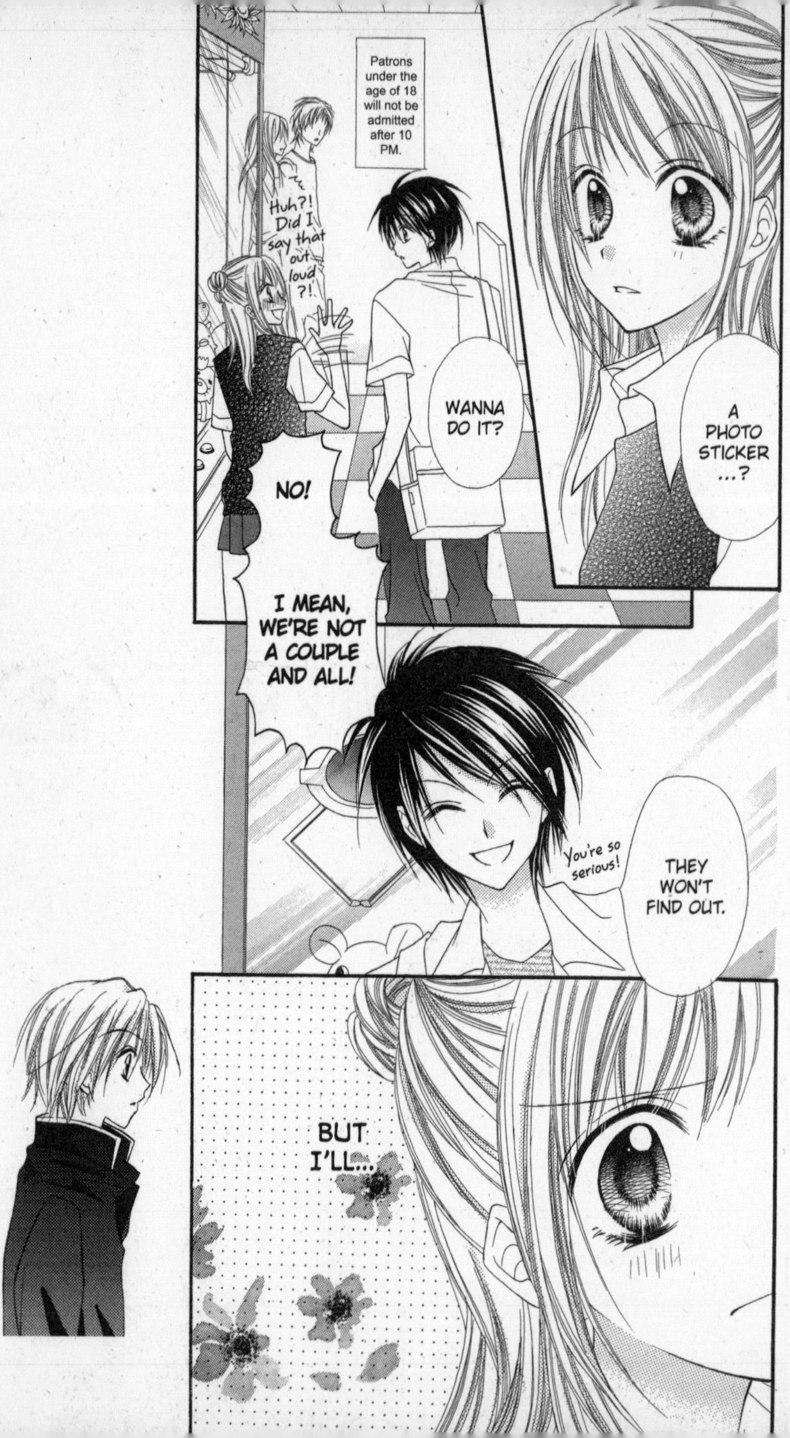
A PHOTO STICKER ...?
Patrons under the age of 18 will not be admitted after 10 PM.
WANNA DO IT?
NO!
Huh?! Did I say that out loud ?!
I MEAN, WE'RE NOT A COUPLE AND ALL!
THEY WON'T FIND OUT.
You're so serious!
BUT I'LL...

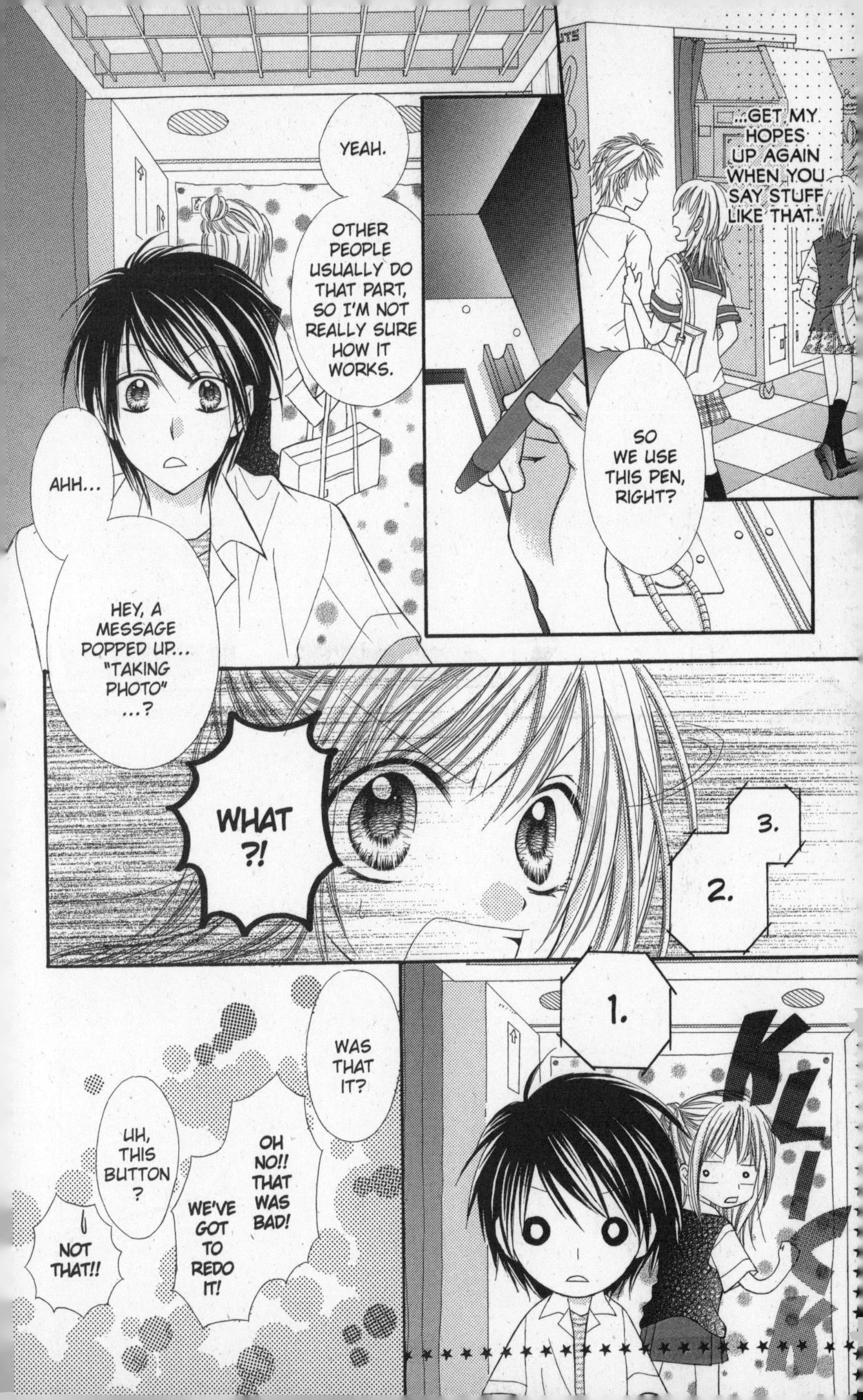
...GET MY HOPES UP AGAIN WHEN YOU SAY STUFF LIKE THAT...
SO WE USE THIS PEN, RIGHT?
YEAH.
OTHER PEOPLE USUALLY DO THAT PART, SO I'M NOT REALLY SURE HOW IT WORKS.
AHH...
HEY, A MESSAGE POPPED UP... "TAKING PHOTO" ...?
3.
2.
WHAT ?!
1.
WAS THAT IT?
UH, THIS BUTTON ?
OH NO!! THAT WAS BAD!
WE'VE GOT TO REDO IT!
NOT THAT!!

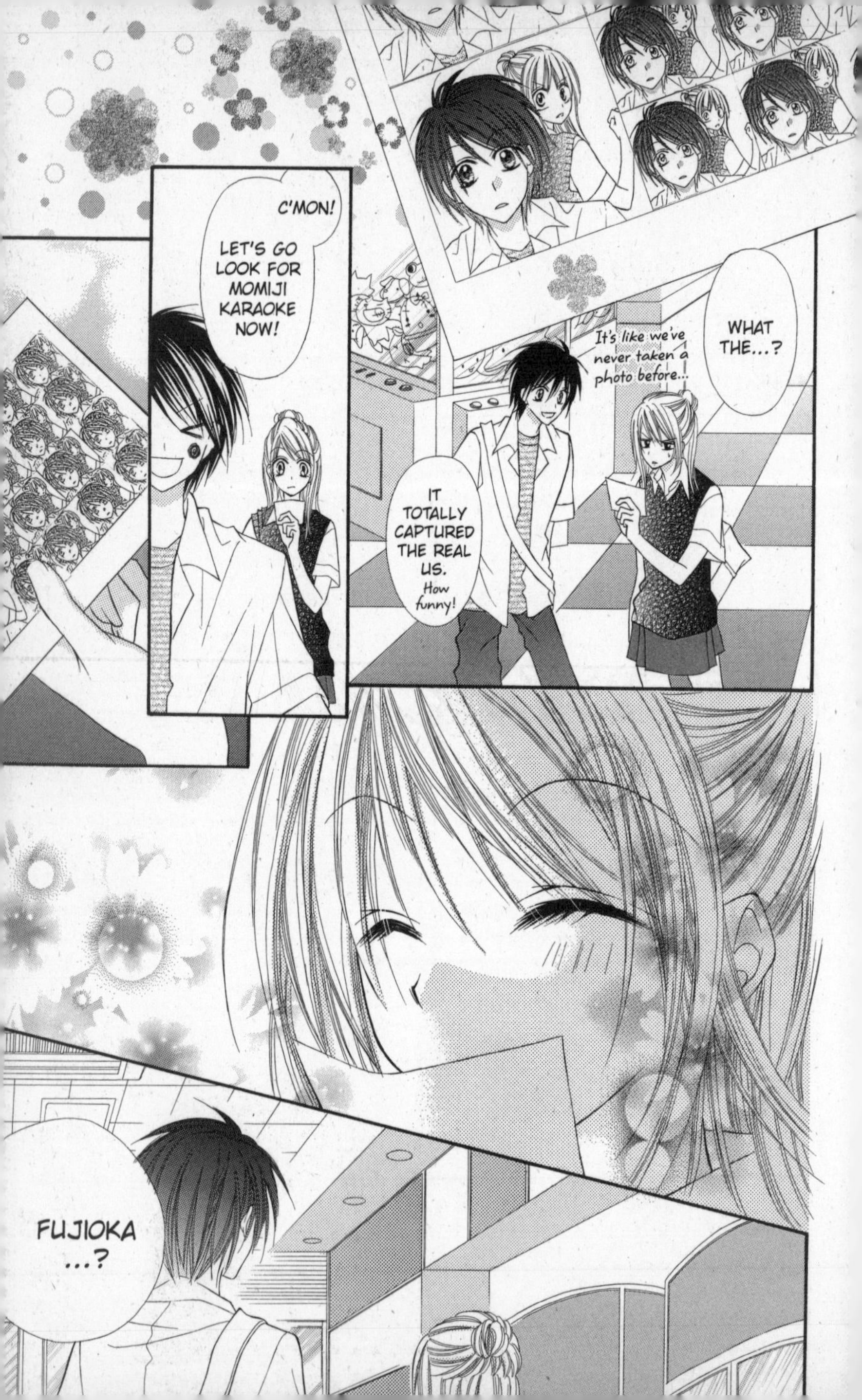
WHAT THE...?
It's like we've never taken a photo before...
IT TOTALLY CAPTURED THE REAL US. How funny!
C'MON!
LET'S GO LOOK FOR MOMIJI KARAOKE NOW!
FUJIOKA ...?

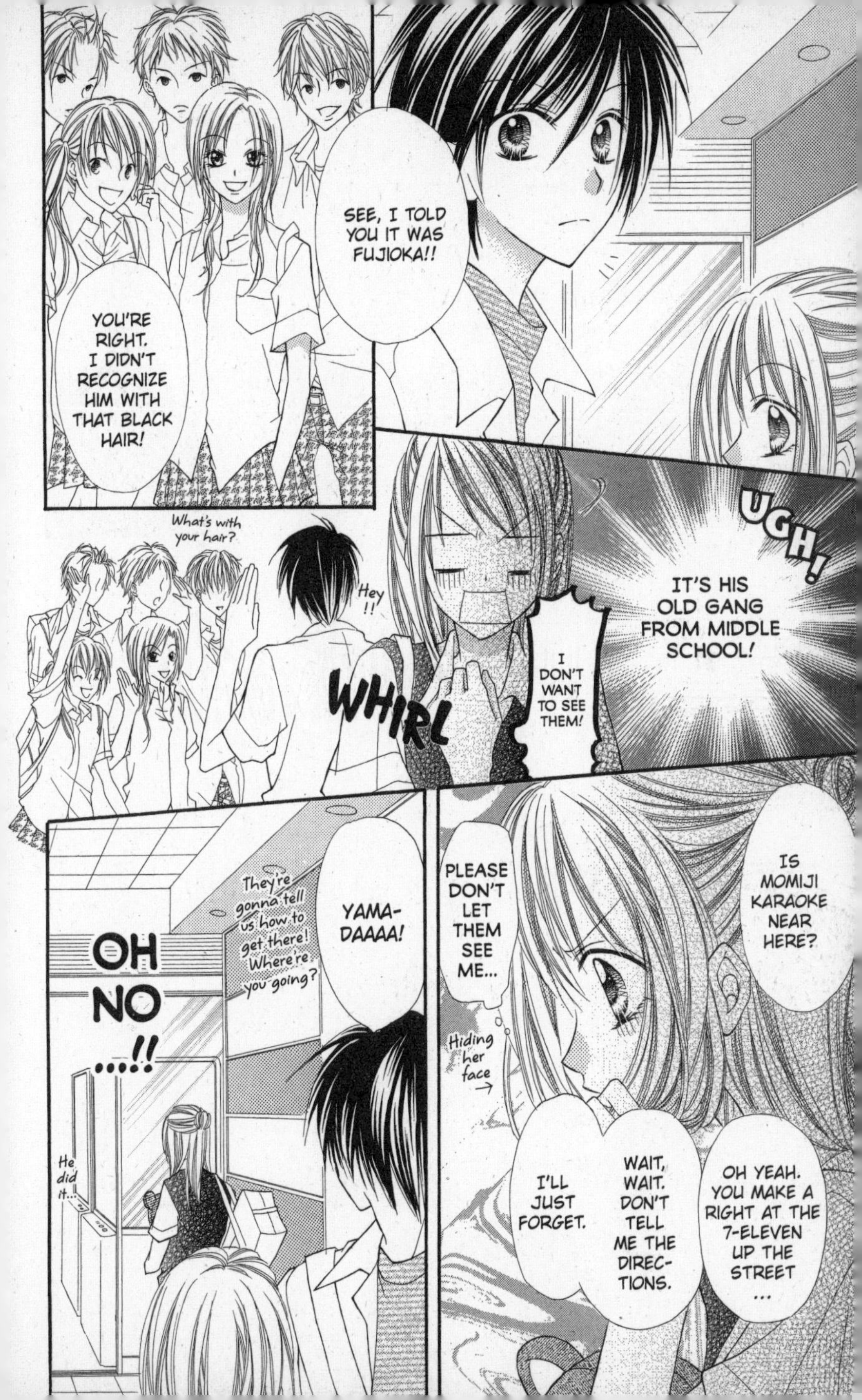
SEE, I TOLD YOU IT WAS FUJIOKA!!
YOU'RE RIGHT. I DIDN'T RECOGNIZE HIM WITH THAT BLACK HAIR!
UGH!
IT'S HIS OLD GANG FROM MIDDLE SCHOOL!
I DON'T WANT TO SEE THEM!
What's with your hair?
Hey!!
WHIRL
IS MOMIJI KARAOKE NEAR HERE?
OH YEAH. YOU MAKE A RIGHT AT THE 7-ELEVEN UP THE STREET ...
WAIT, WAIT. DON'T TELL ME THE DIRECTIONS.
I'LL JUST FORGET.
PLEASE DON'T LET THEM SEE ME...
Hiding her face →
YAMA-DAAAA!
They're gonna tell us how to get there! Where're you going?
OH NO ...!!
He did it...

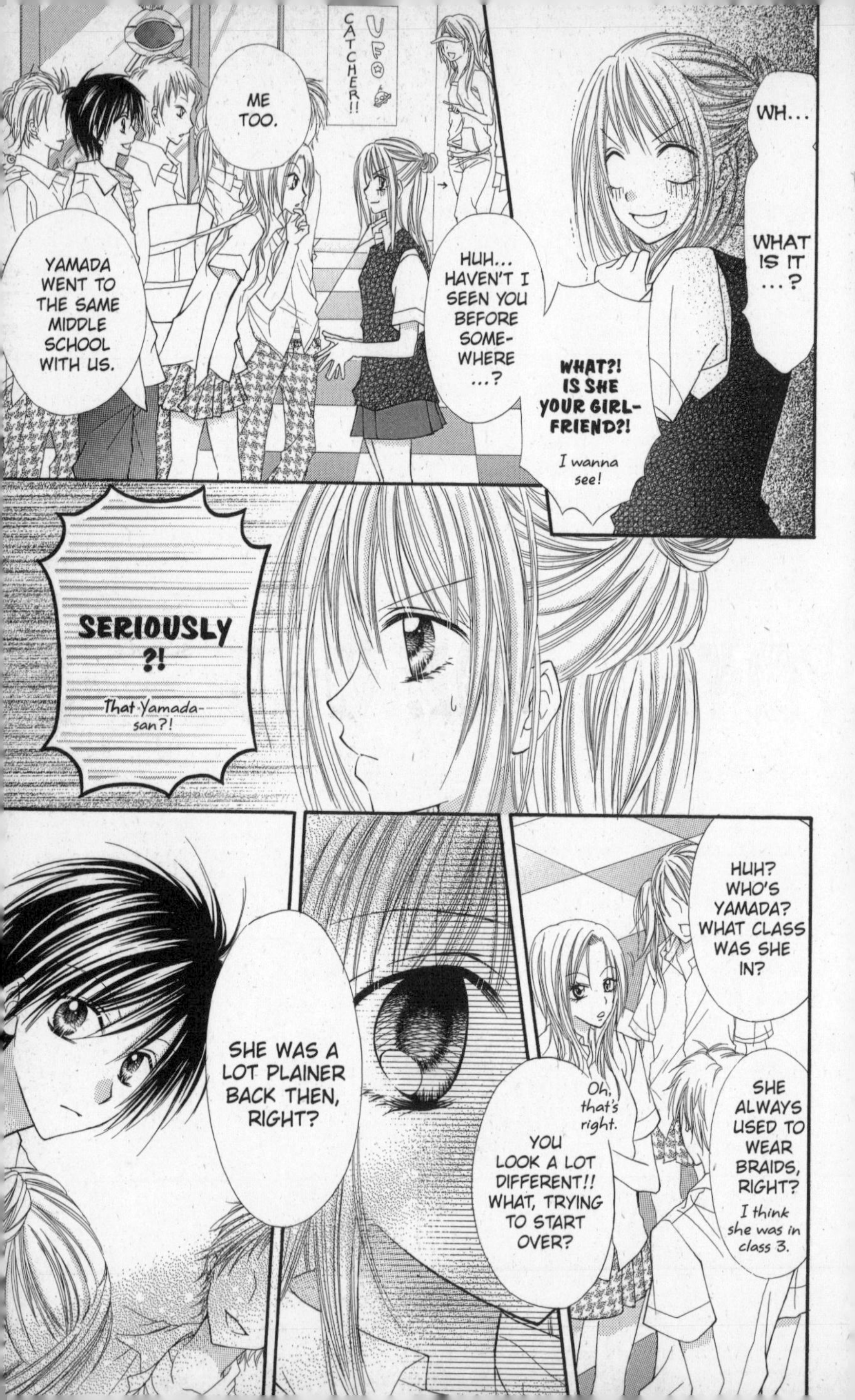
WH...
WHAT IS IT ...?
WHAT?! IS SHE YOUR GIRL-FRIEND?!
I wanna see!
HUH... HAVEN'T I SEEN YOU BEFORE SOME-WHERE ...?
UFO CATCHER!!
ME TOO.
YAMADA WENT TO THE SAME MIDDLE SCHOOL WITH US.
SERIOUSLY ?!
That Yamada-san?!
HUH? WHO'S YAMADA? WHAT CLASS WAS SHE IN?
SHE ALWAYS USED TO WEAR BRAIDS, RIGHT?
I think she was in class 3.
Oh, that's right.
YOU LOOK A LOT DIFFERENT!! WHAT, TRYING TO START OVER?
SHE WAS A LOT PLAINER BACK THEN, RIGHT?

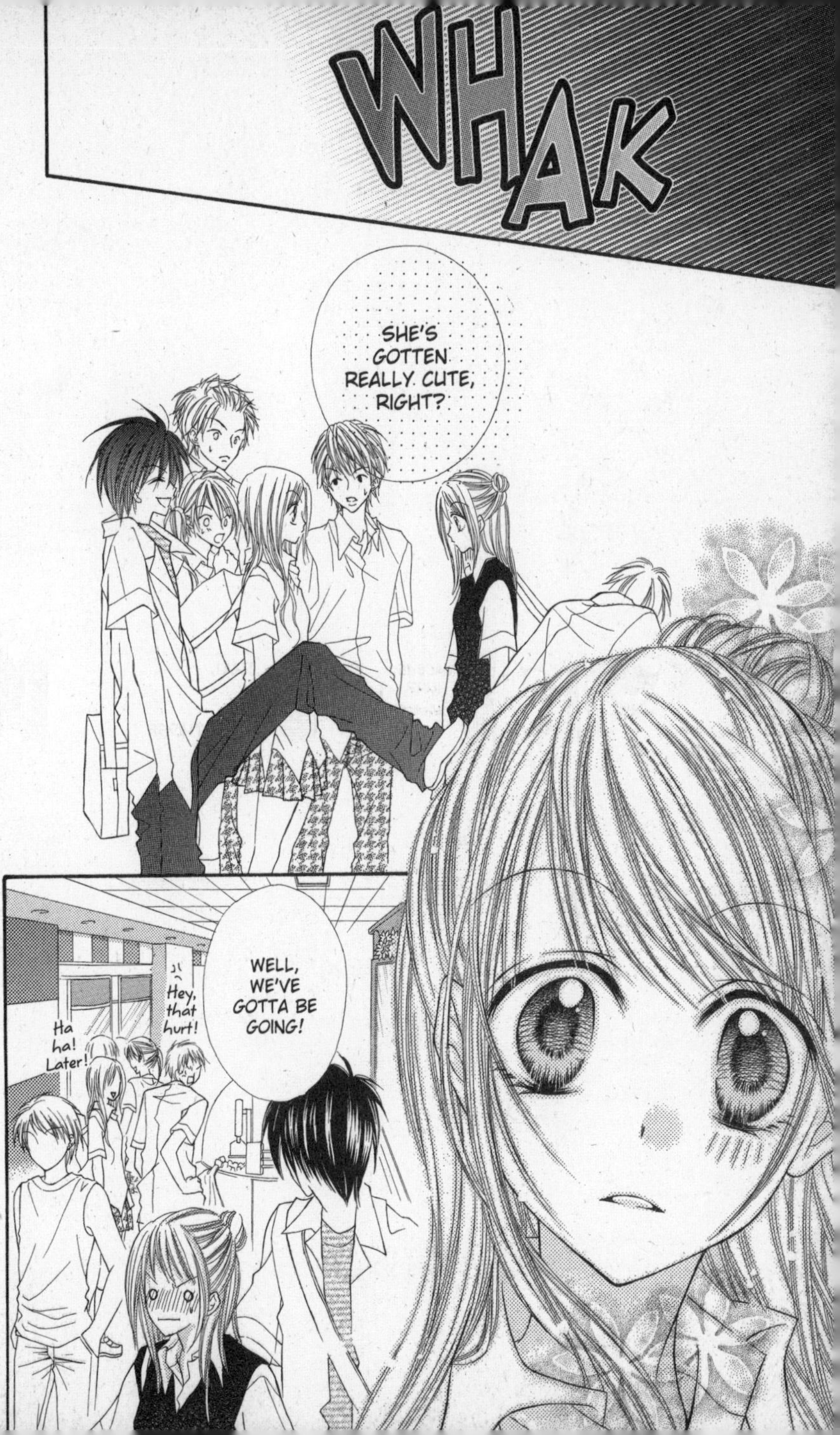
WHAK
SHE'S GOTTEN REALLY CUTE, RIGHT?
WELL, WE'VE GOTTA BE GOING!
Hey, that hurt!
Ha ha! Later!

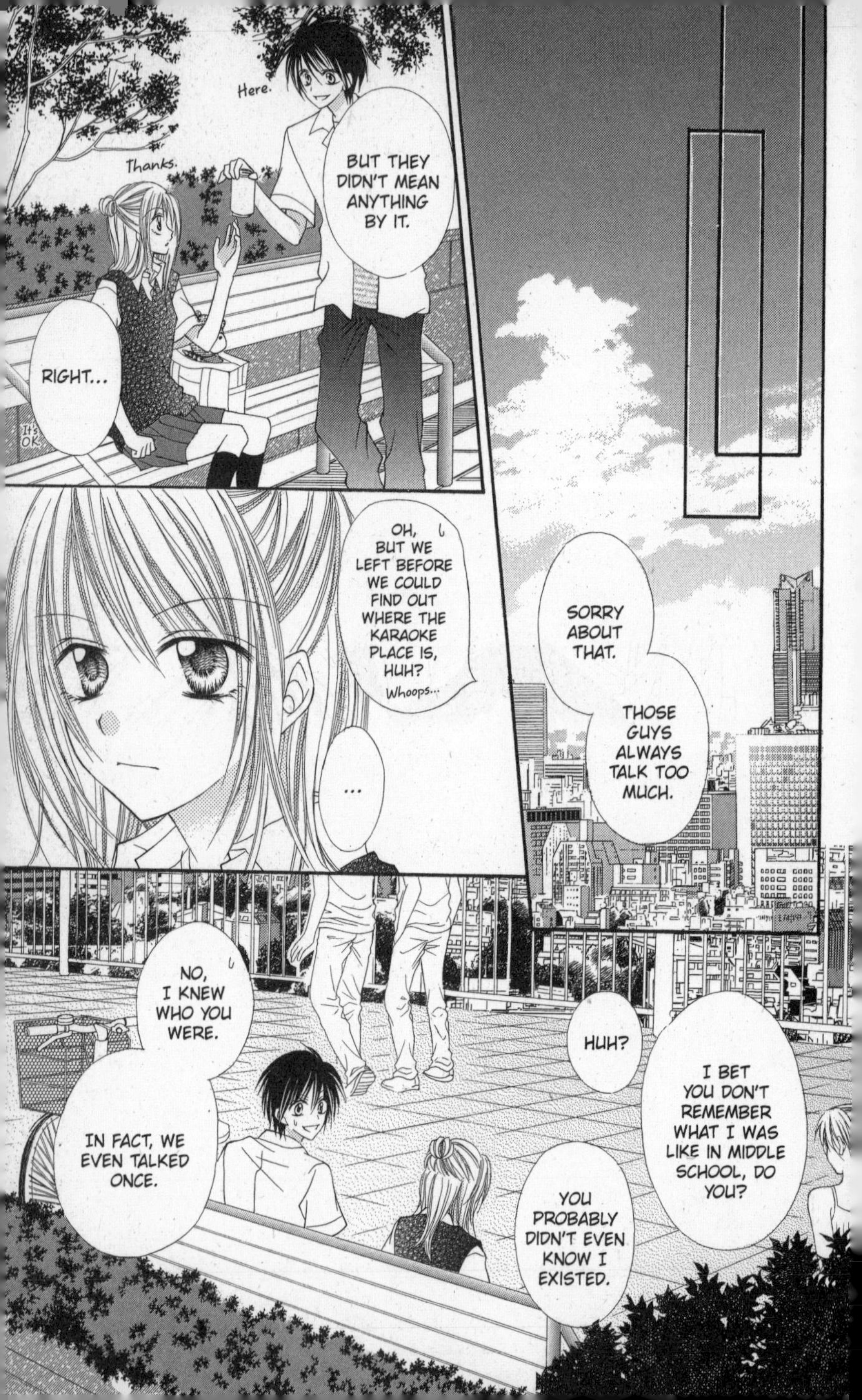
SORRY ABOUT THAT.
THOSE GUYS ALWAYS TALK TOO MUCH.
Here.
BUT THEY DIDN'T MEAN ANYTHING BY IT.
Thanks.
RIGHT...
It's OK
OH, BUT WE LEFT BEFORE WE COULD FIND OUT WHERE THE KARAOKE PLACE IS, HUH?
Whoops...
...
I BET YOU DON'T REMEMBER WHAT I WAS LIKE IN MIDDLE SCHOOL, DO YOU?
HUH?
YOU PROBABLY DIDN'T EVEN KNOW I EXISTED.
NO, I KNEW WHO YOU WERE.
IN FACT, WE EVEN TALKED ONCE.

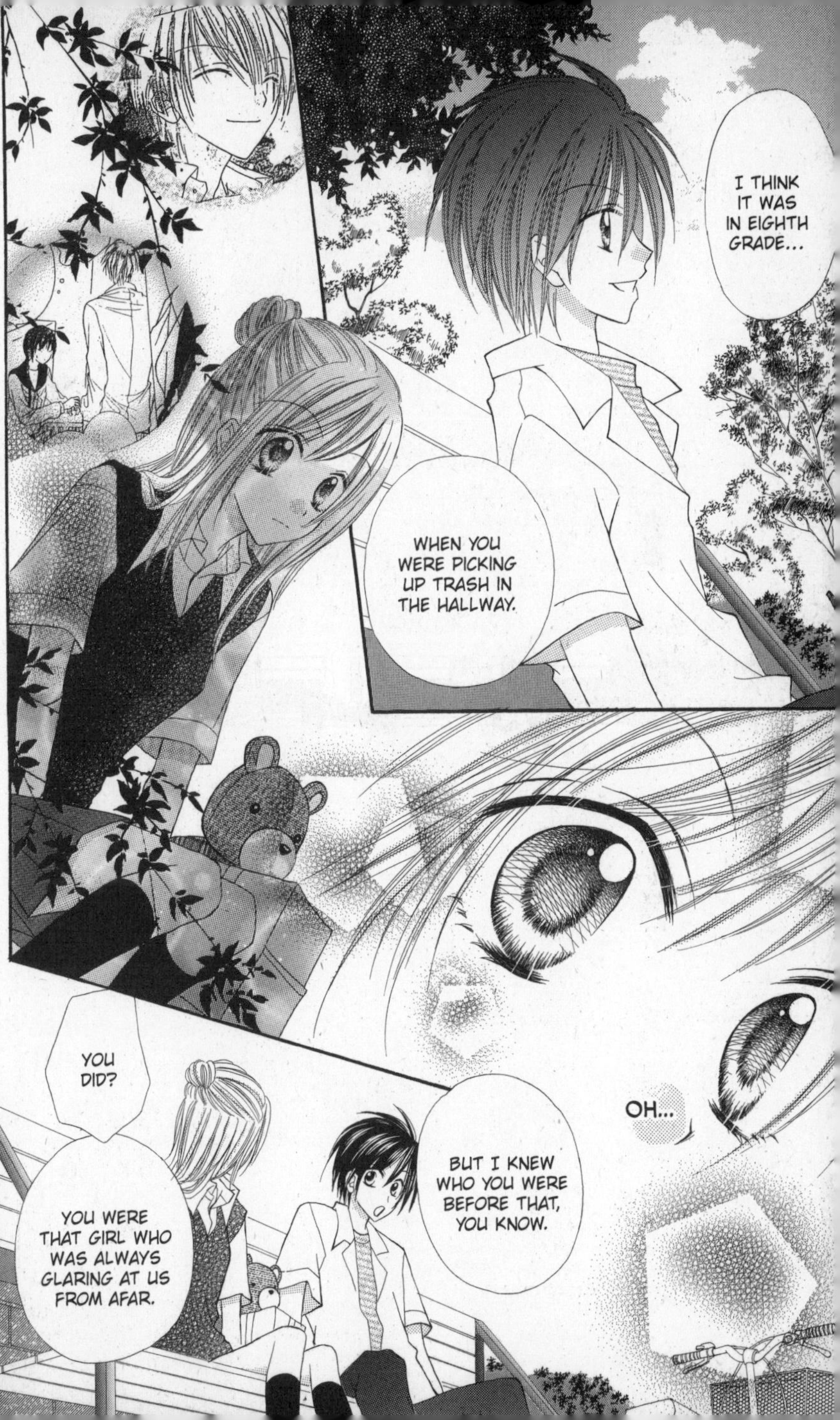
I THINK IT WAS IN EIGHTH GRADE...
WHEN YOU WERE PICKING UP TRASH IN THE HALLWAY.
OH...
BUT I KNEW WHO YOU WERE BEFORE THAT, YOU KNOW.
YOU DID?
YOU WERE THAT GIRL WHO WAS ALWAYS GLARING AT US FROM AFAR.

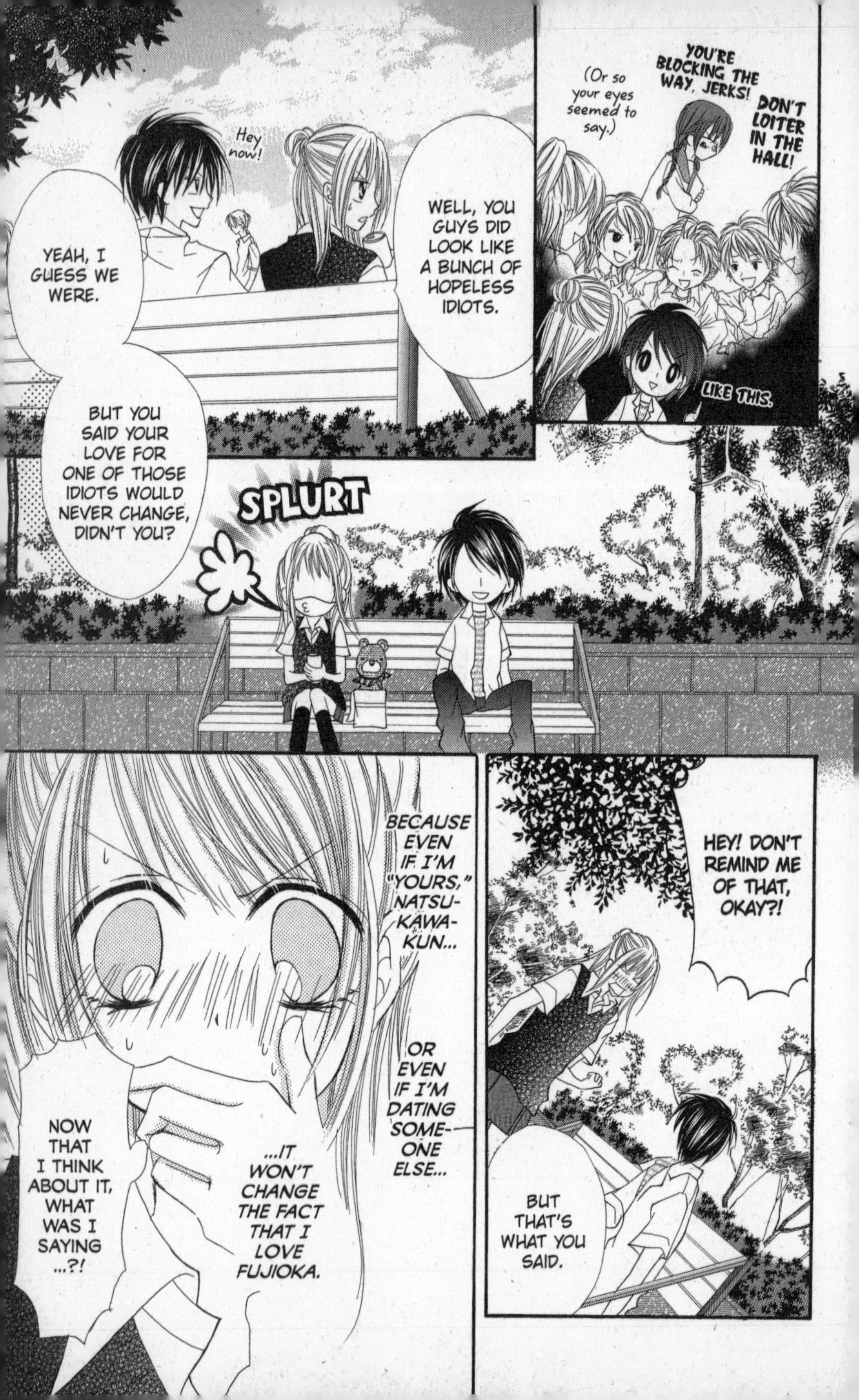

(Or so your eyes seemed to say.)
YOU'RE BLOCKING THE WAY, JERKS!
DON'T LOITER IN THE HALL!
LIKE THIS.
WELL, YOU GUYS DID LOOK LIKE A BUNCH OF HOPELESS IDIOTS.
Hey now!
YEAH, I GUESS WE WERE.
BUT YOU SAID YOUR LOVE FOR ONE OF THOSE IDIOTS WOULD NEVER CHANGE, DIDN'T YOU?
SPLURT
HEY! DON'T REMIND ME OF THAT, OKAY?!
BUT THAT'S WHAT YOU SAID.
BECAUSE EVEN IF I'M "YOURS," NATSU-KAWA-KUN...
OR EVEN IF I'M DATING SOME-ONE ELSE...
...IT WON'T CHANGE THE FACT THAT I LOVE FUJIOKA.
NOW THAT I THINK ABOUT IT, WHAT WAS I SAYING ...?!

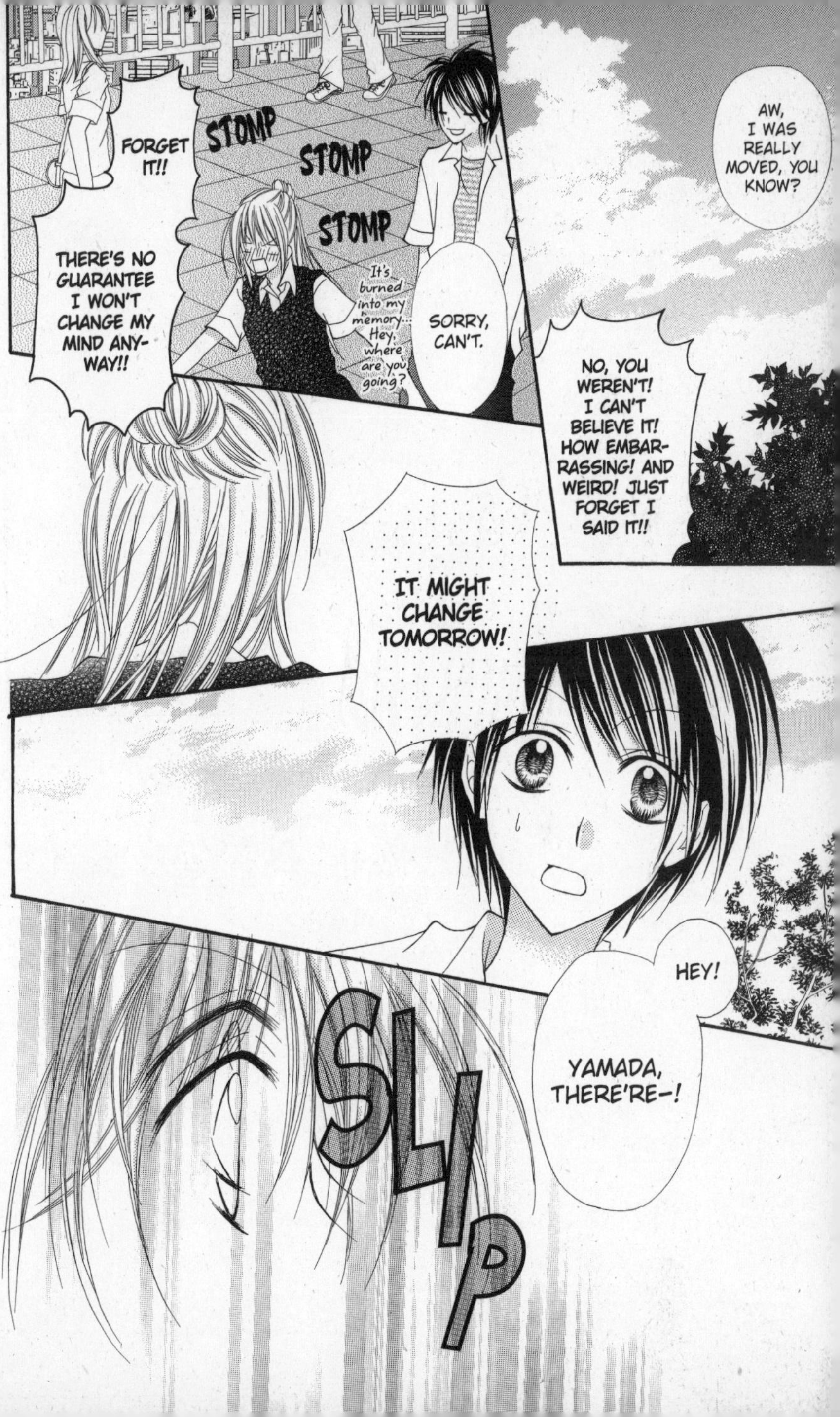
AW, I WAS REALLY MOVED, YOU KNOW?
NO, YOU WEREN'T! I CAN'T BELIEVE IT! HOW EMBAR-RASSING! AND WEIRD! JUST FORGET I SAID IT!!
SORRY, CAN'T.
It's burned into my memory... Hey, where are you going?
STOMP
STOMP
STOMP
FORGET IT!!
THERE'S NO GUARANTEE I WON'T CHANGE MY MIND ANY-WAY!!
IT MIGHT CHANGE TOMORROW!
HEY!
YAMADA, THERE'RE—!
SLIP

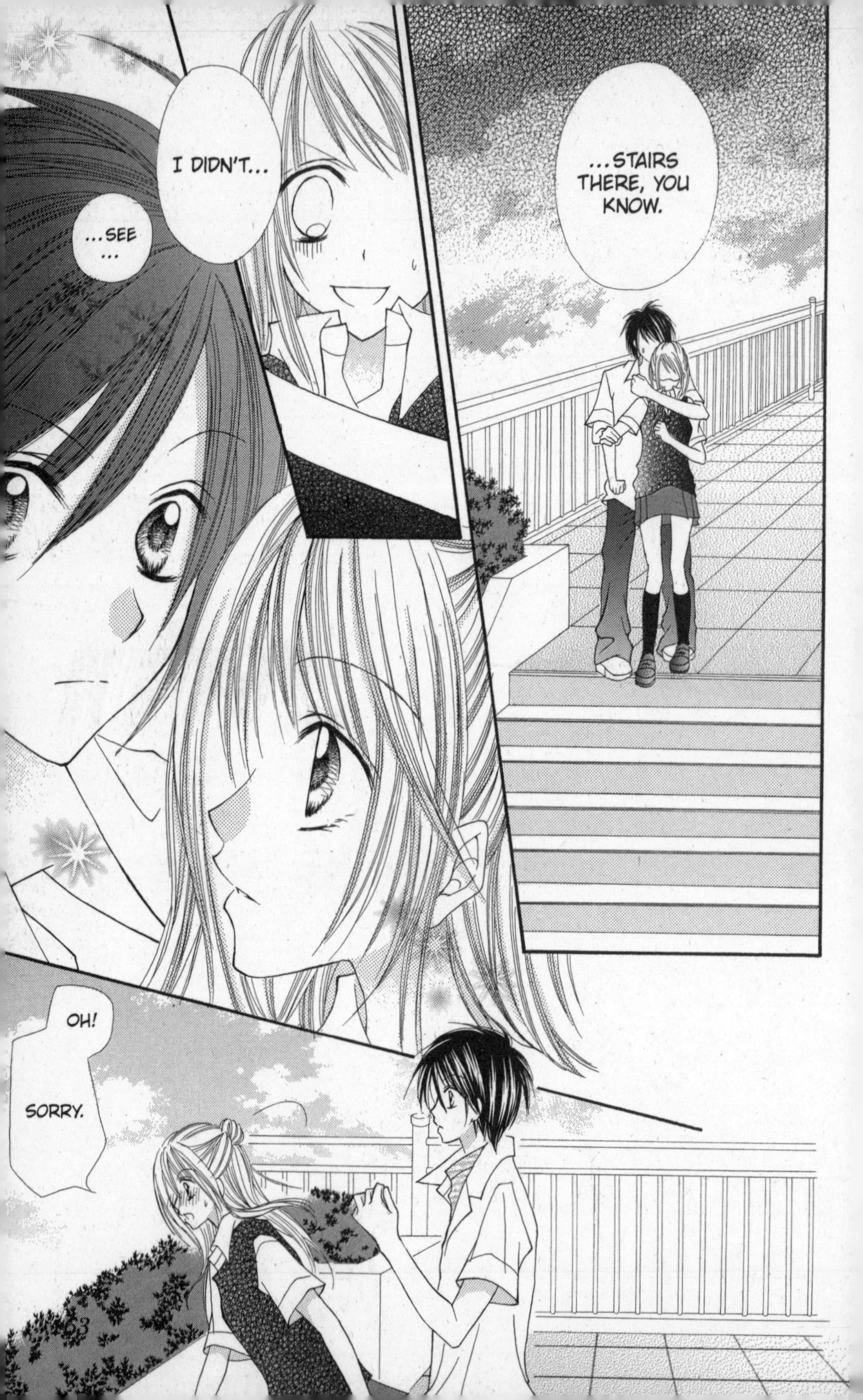
...STAIRS THERE, YOU KNOW.
I DIDN'T...
...SEE...
OH!
SORRY.

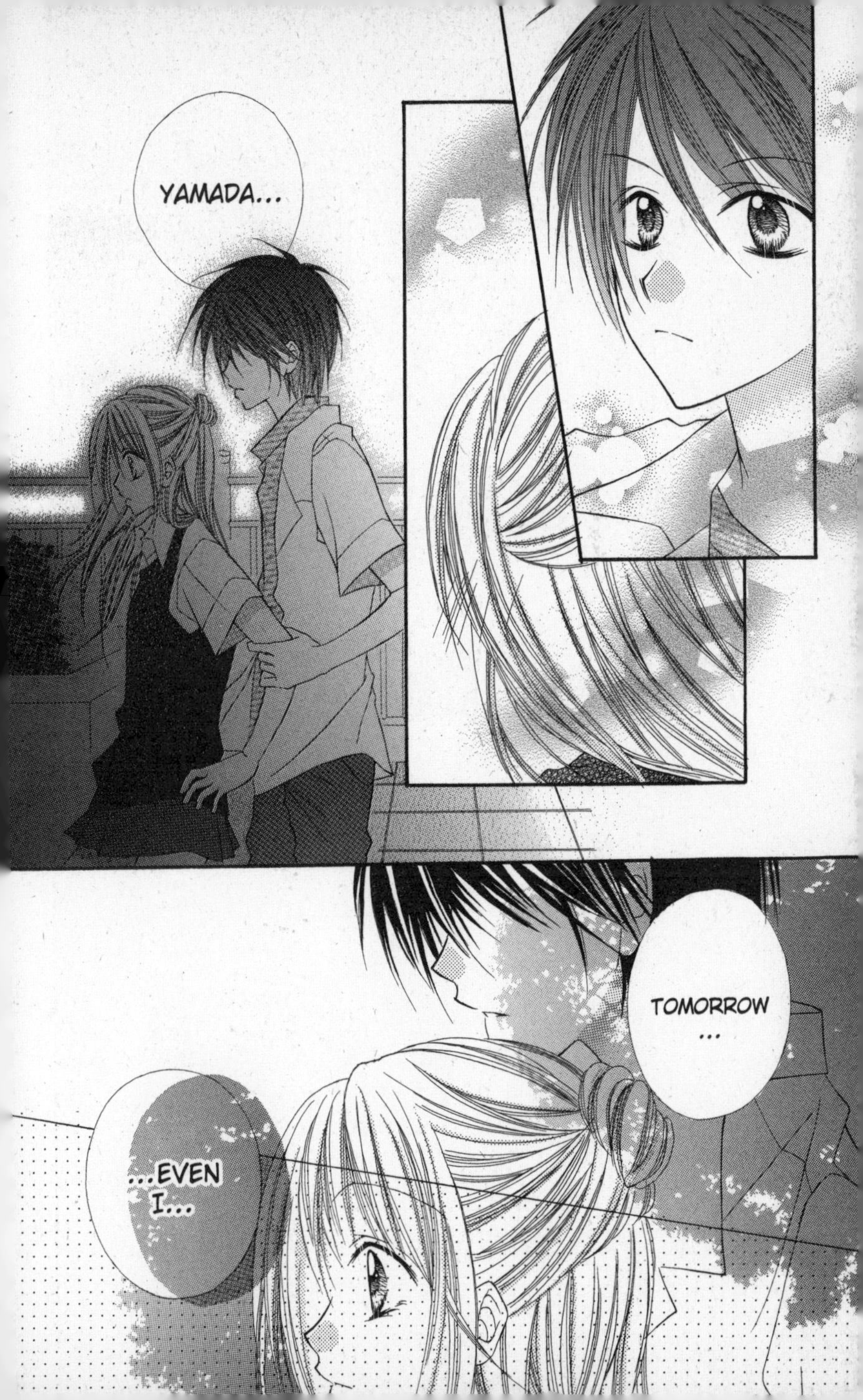
YAMADA...
TOMORROW ...
...EVEN I...

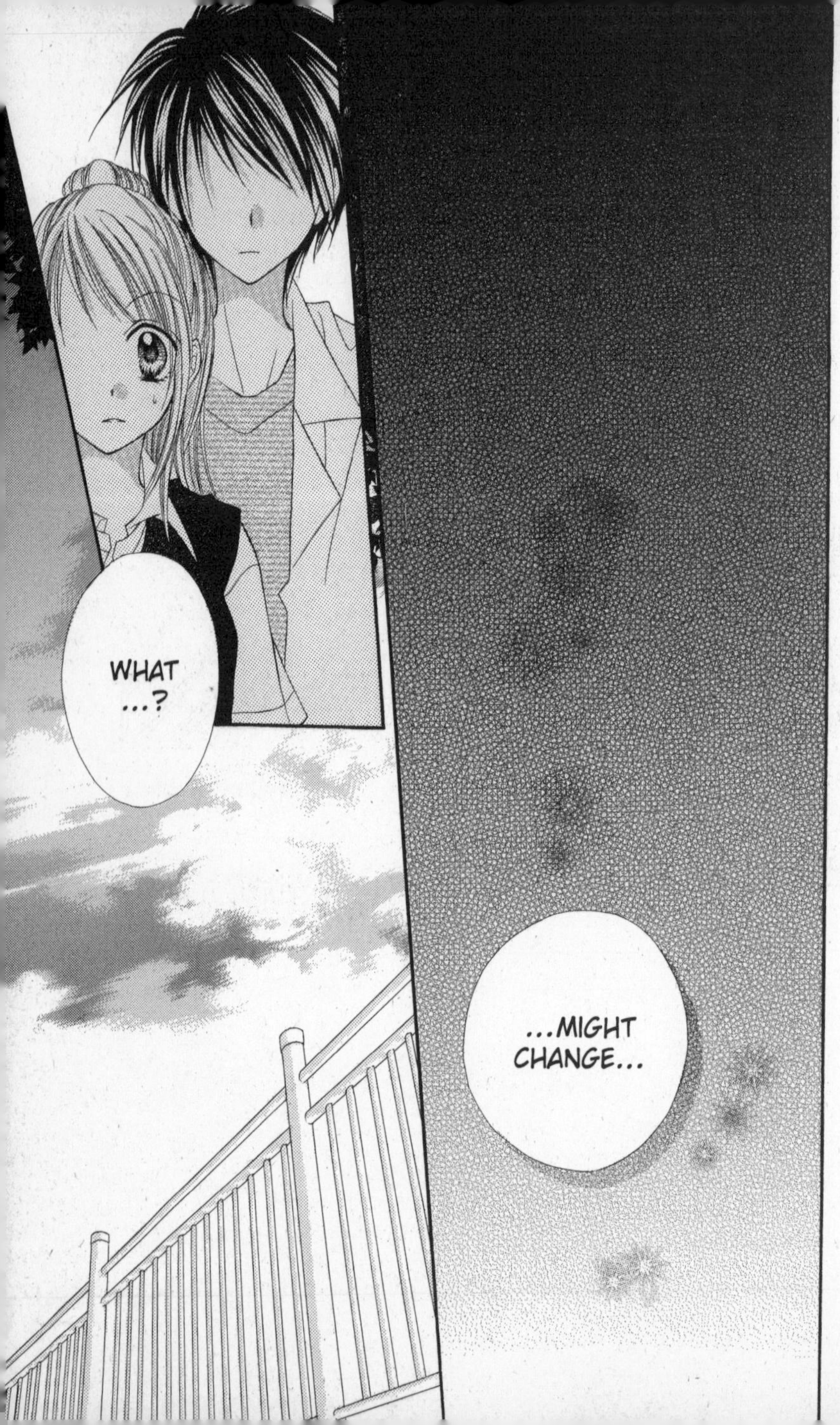
...MIGHT CHANGE...
WHAT ...?

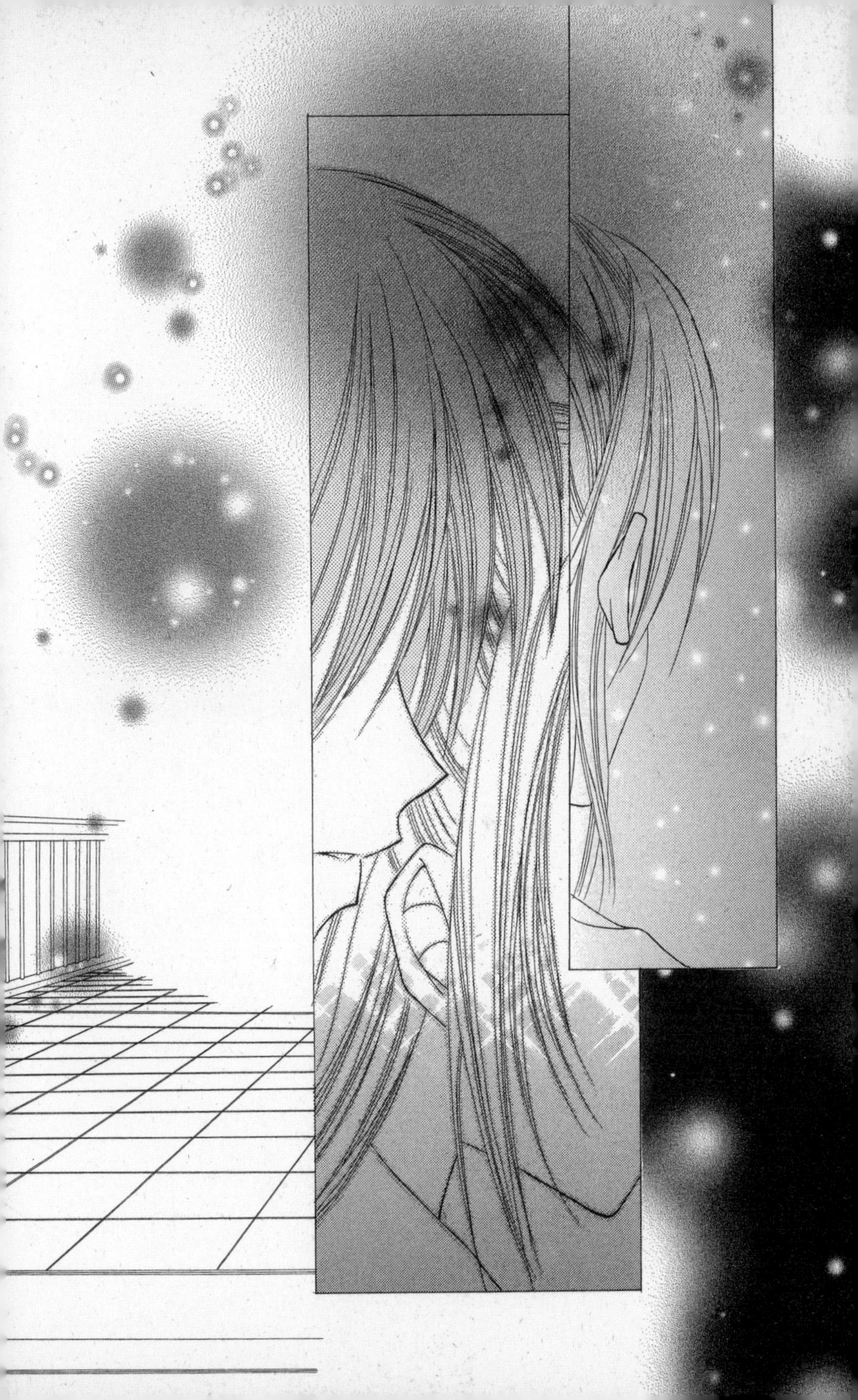

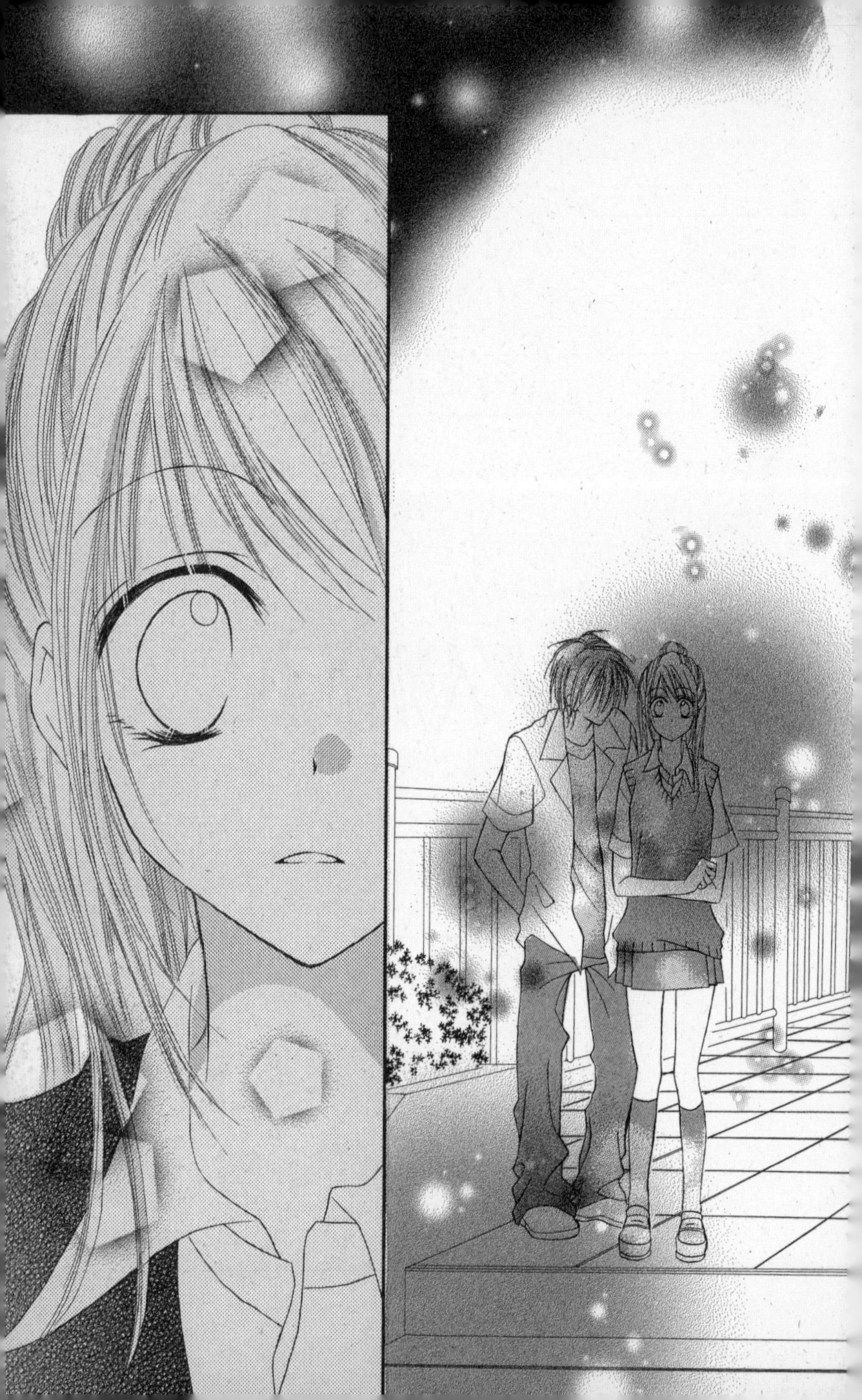

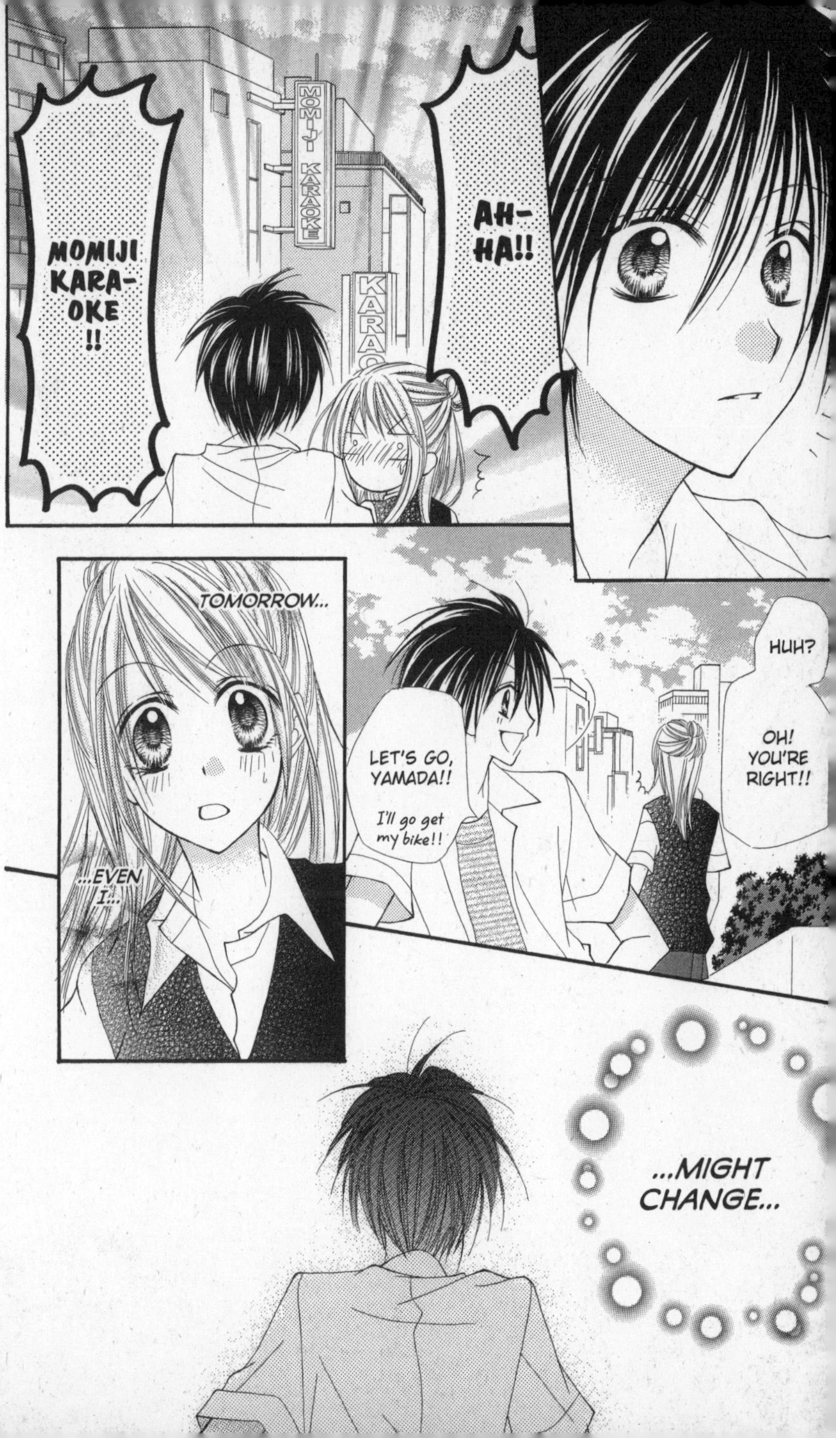
AH-HA!!
MOMIJI KARAOKE
MOMIJI KARA-OKE!!
HUH?
OH! YOU'RE RIGHT!!
LET'S GO, YAMADA!!
I'll go get my bike!!
TOMORROW...
...EVEN I...
...MIGHT CHANGE...

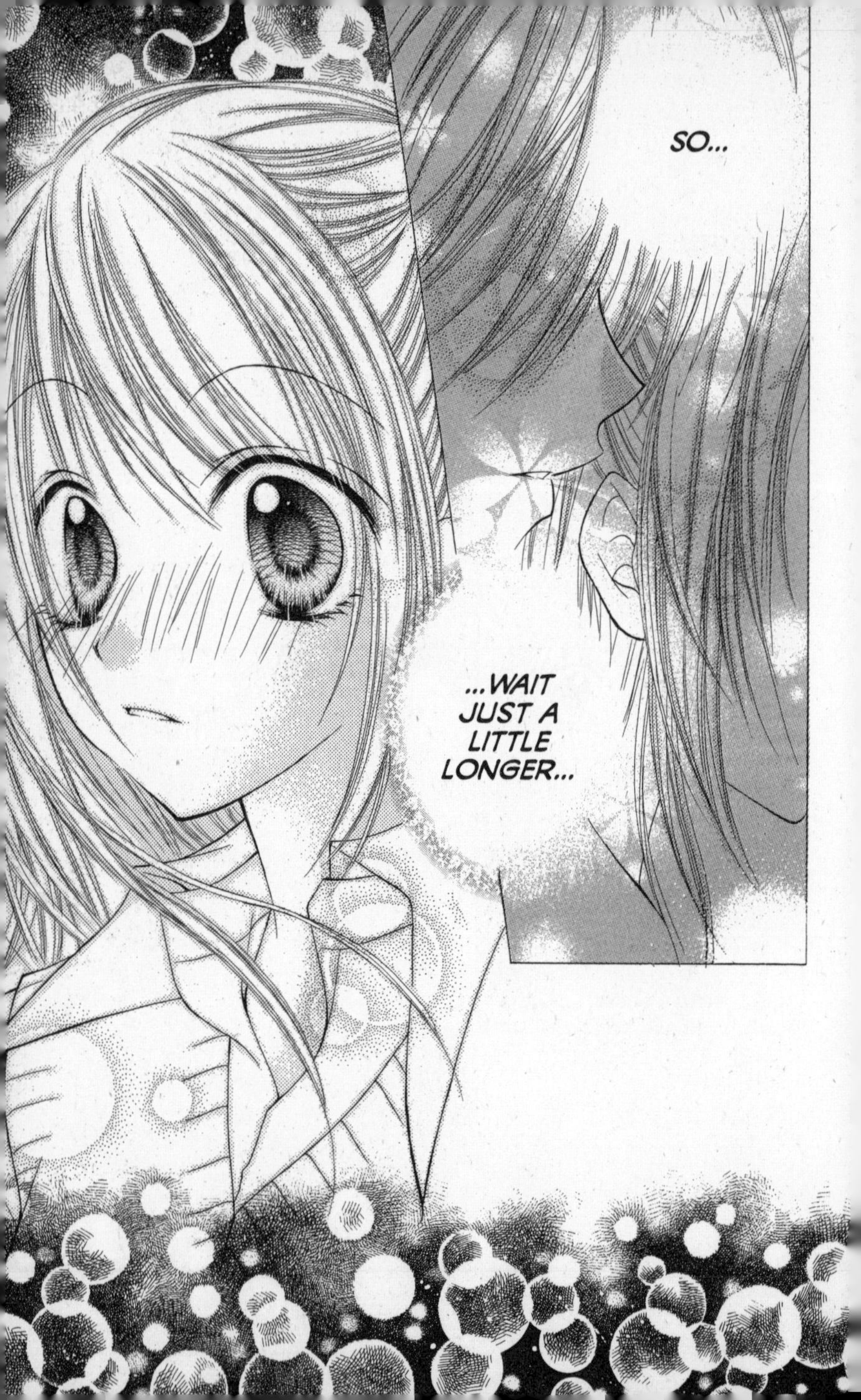
SO...
...WAIT JUST A LITTLE LONGER...

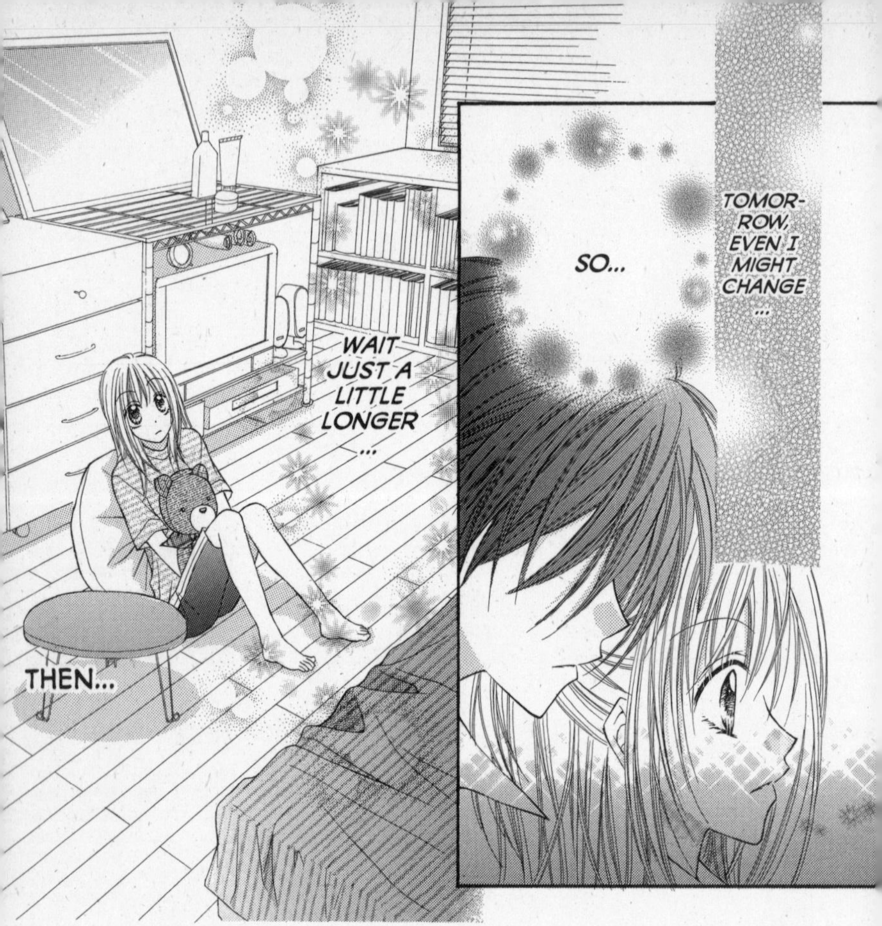
SO...
TOMORROW, EVEN I MIGHT CHANGE...
WAIT JUST A LITTLE LONGER...
THEN...

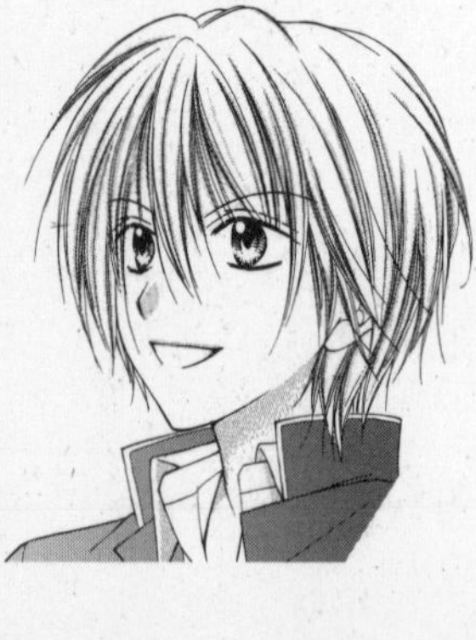

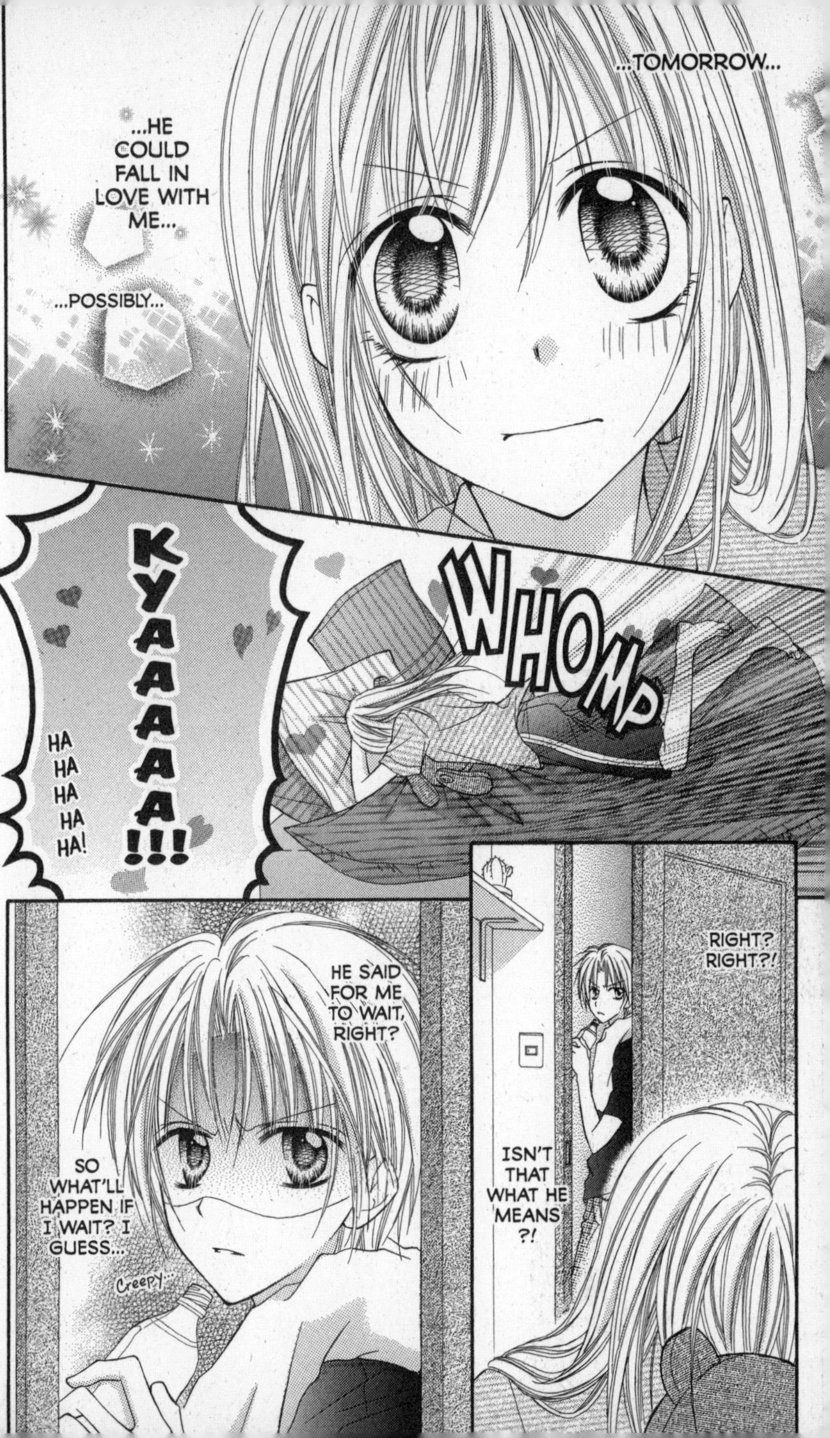
...TOMORROW...
...HE COULD FALL IN LOVE WITH ME...
...POSSIBLY...
WHOMP
KYAAAAAA!!!
HA HA HA HA HA!
RIGHT? RIGHT?!
ISN'T THAT WHAT HE MEANS?!
HE SAID FOR ME TO WAIT, RIGHT?
SO WHAT'LL HAPPEN IF I WAIT? I GUESS...
Creepy...

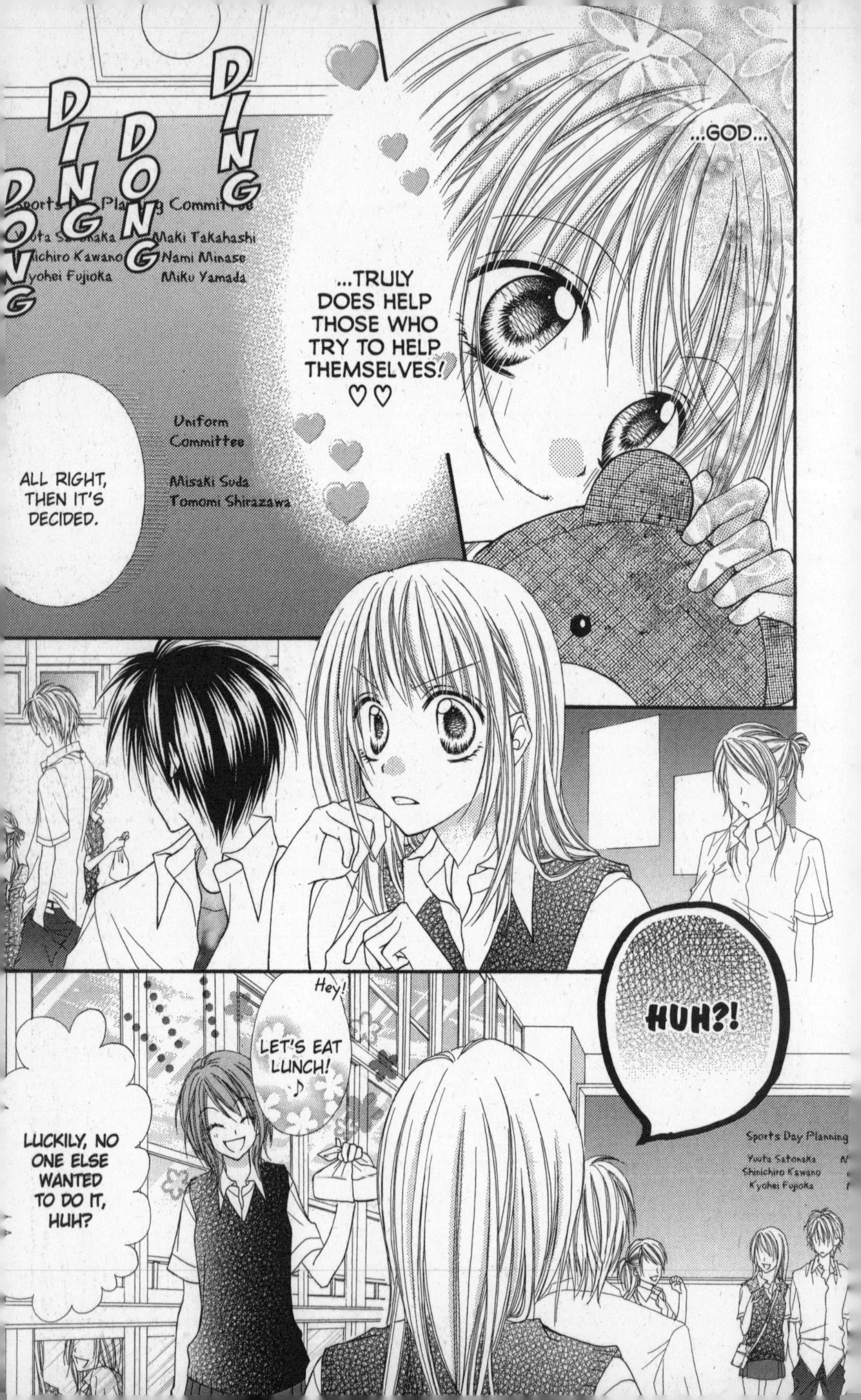
...GOD...
...TRULY DOES HELP THOSE WHO TRY TO HELP THEMSELVES! ♡♡
DING DONG DING DONG
Maki Takahashi
Nami Minase
Miku Yamada
Uniform Committee
Misaki Suda
Tomomi Shirazawa
ALL RIGHT, THEN IT'S DECIDED.
HUH?!
Hey!
LET'S EAT LUNCH! ♪
Sports Day Planning
Yuuta Satonaka
Shinichiro Kawano
Kyohei Fujioka
LUCKILY, NO ONE ELSE WANTED TO DO IT, HUH?

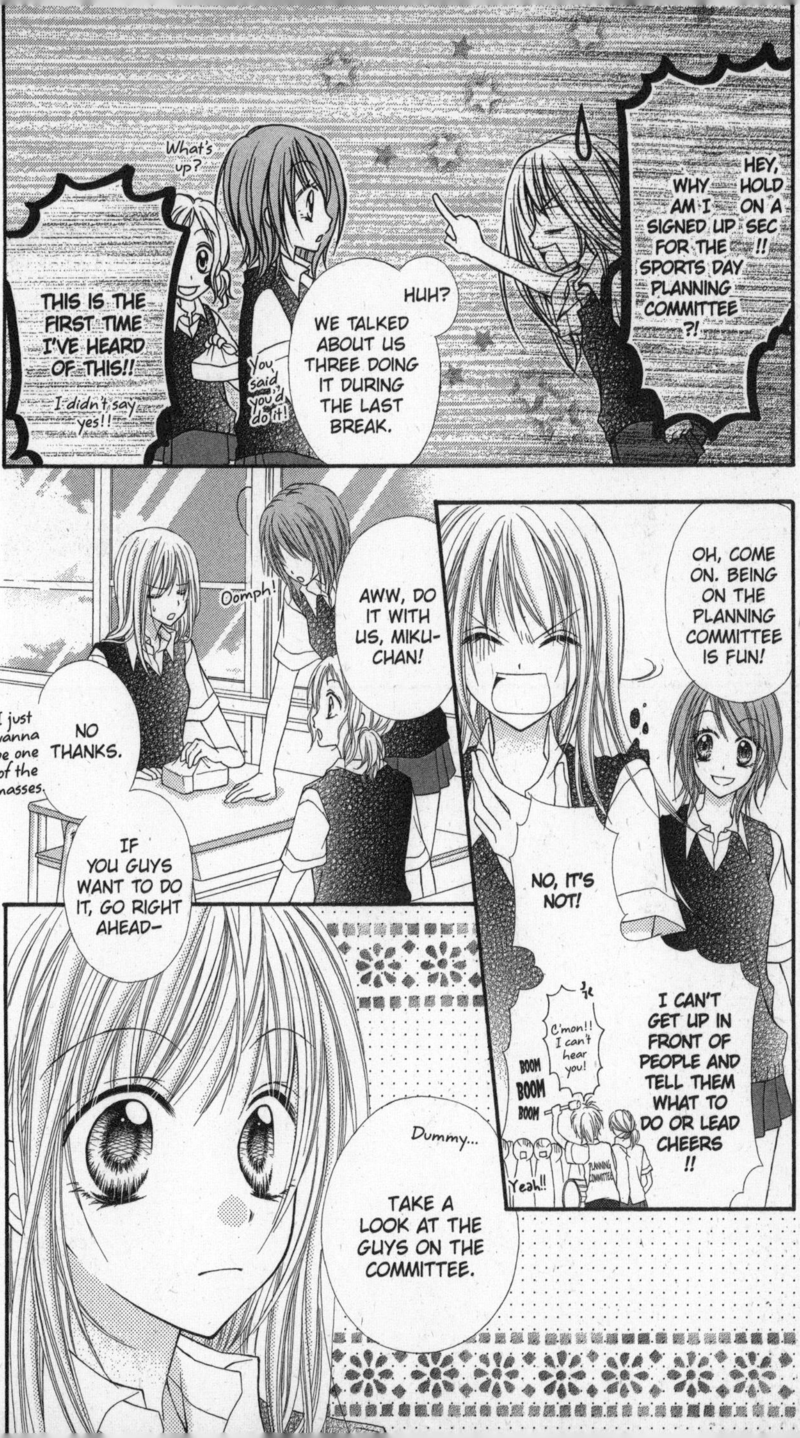
HEY, HOLD ON A SEC!!
WHY AM I SIGNED UP FOR THE SPORTS DAY PLANNING COMMITTEE?!
HUH?
WE TALKED ABOUT US THREE DOING IT DURING THE LAST BREAK.
You said you'd do it!
What's up?
THIS IS THE FIRST TIME I'VE HEARD OF THIS!!
I didn't say yes!!
AWW, DO IT WITH US, MIKU-CHAN!
Oomph!
NO THANKS.
I just wanna be one of the masses.
OH, COME ON. BEING ON THE PLANNING COMMITTEE IS FUN!
NO, IT'S NOT!
I CAN'T GET UP IN FRONT OF PEOPLE AND TELL THEM WHAT TO DO OR LEAD CHEERS!!
C'mon!! I can't hear you!
BOOM BOOM BOOM
PLANNING COMMITTEE
Yeah!!
IF YOU GUYS WANT TO DO IT, GO RIGHT AHEAD—
Dummy...
TAKE A LOOK AT THE GUYS ON THE COMMITTEE.

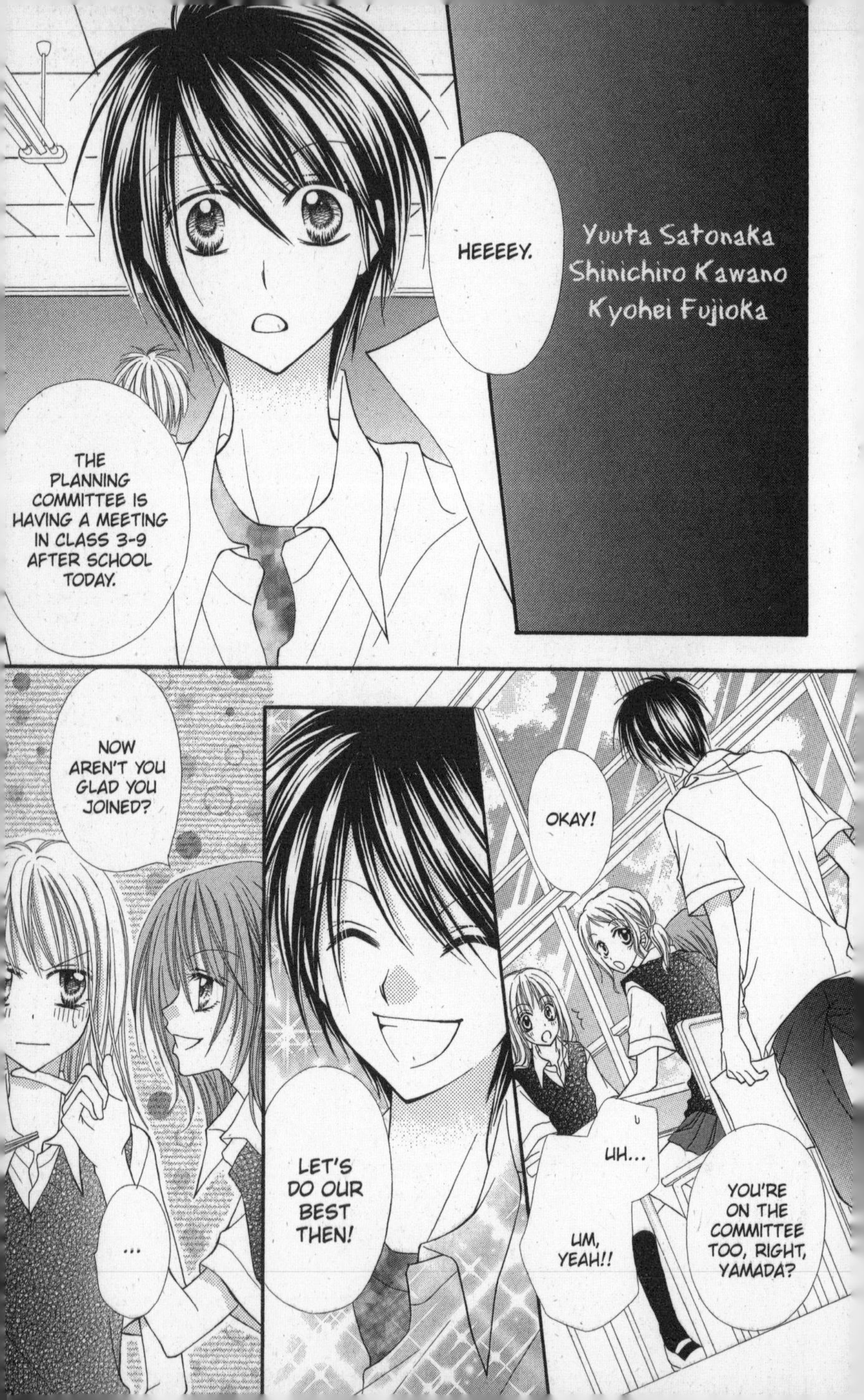
Yuuta Satonaka
Shinichiro Kawano
Kyohei Fujioka
HEEEEY.
THE PLANNING COMMITTEE IS HAVING A MEETING IN CLASS 3-9 AFTER SCHOOL TODAY.
YOU'RE ON THE COMMITTEE TOO, RIGHT, YAMADA?
UH...
UM, YEAH!!
OKAY!
LET'S DO OUR BEST THEN!
NOW AREN'T YOU GLAD YOU JOINED?
...

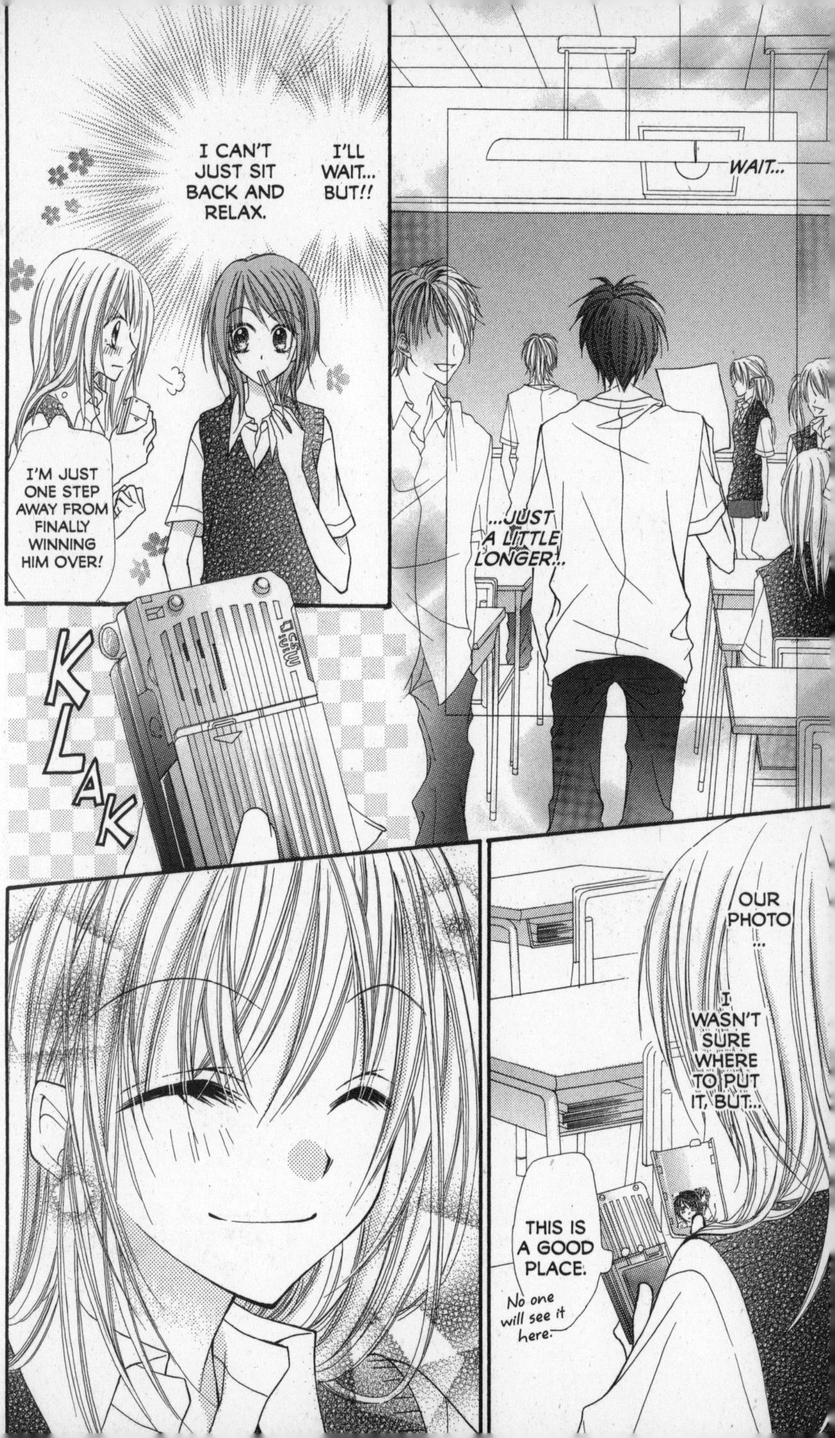
WAIT...
...JUST A LITTLE LONGER...
I'LL WAIT... BUT!!
I CAN'T JUST SIT BACK AND RELAX.
I'M JUST ONE STEP AWAY FROM FINALLY WINNING HIM OVER!
KLAK
OUR PHOTO...
I WASN'T SURE WHERE TO PUT IT, BUT...
THIS IS A GOOD PLACE.
No one will see it here.

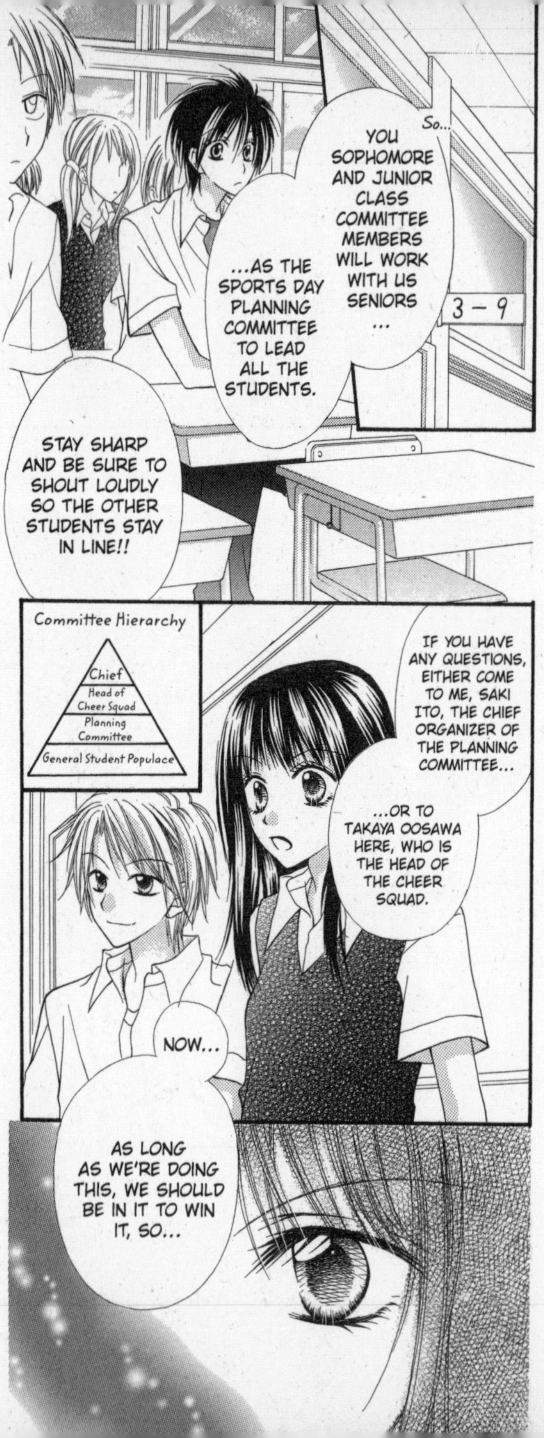
So...
YOU SOPHOMORE AND JUNIOR CLASS COMMITTEE MEMBERS WILL WORK WITH US SENIORS ...
...AS THE SPORTS DAY PLANNING COMMITTEE TO LEAD ALL THE STUDENTS.
3-9
STAY SHARP AND BE SURE TO SHOUT LOUDLY SO THE OTHER STUDENTS STAY IN LINE!!
IF YOU HAVE ANY QUESTIONS, EITHER COME TO ME, SAKI ITO, THE CHIEF ORGANIZER OF THE PLANNING COMMITTEE...
...OR TO TAKAYA OOSAWA HERE, WHO IS THE HEAD OF THE CHEER SQUAD.
Committee Hierarchy
Chief
Head of Cheer Squad
Planning Committee
General Student Populace
NOW...
AS LONG AS WE'RE DOING THIS, WE SHOULD BE IN IT TO WIN IT, SO...

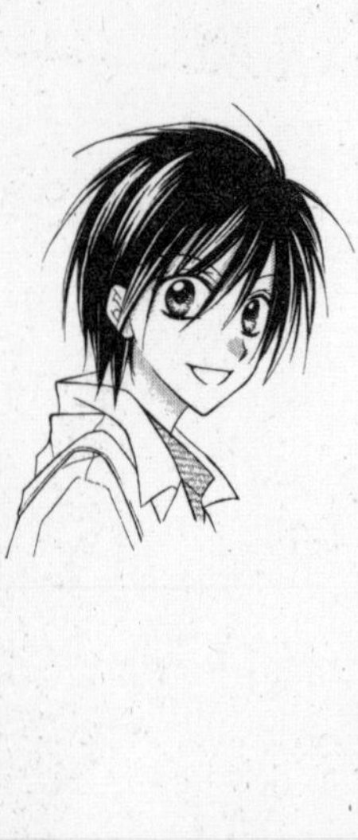

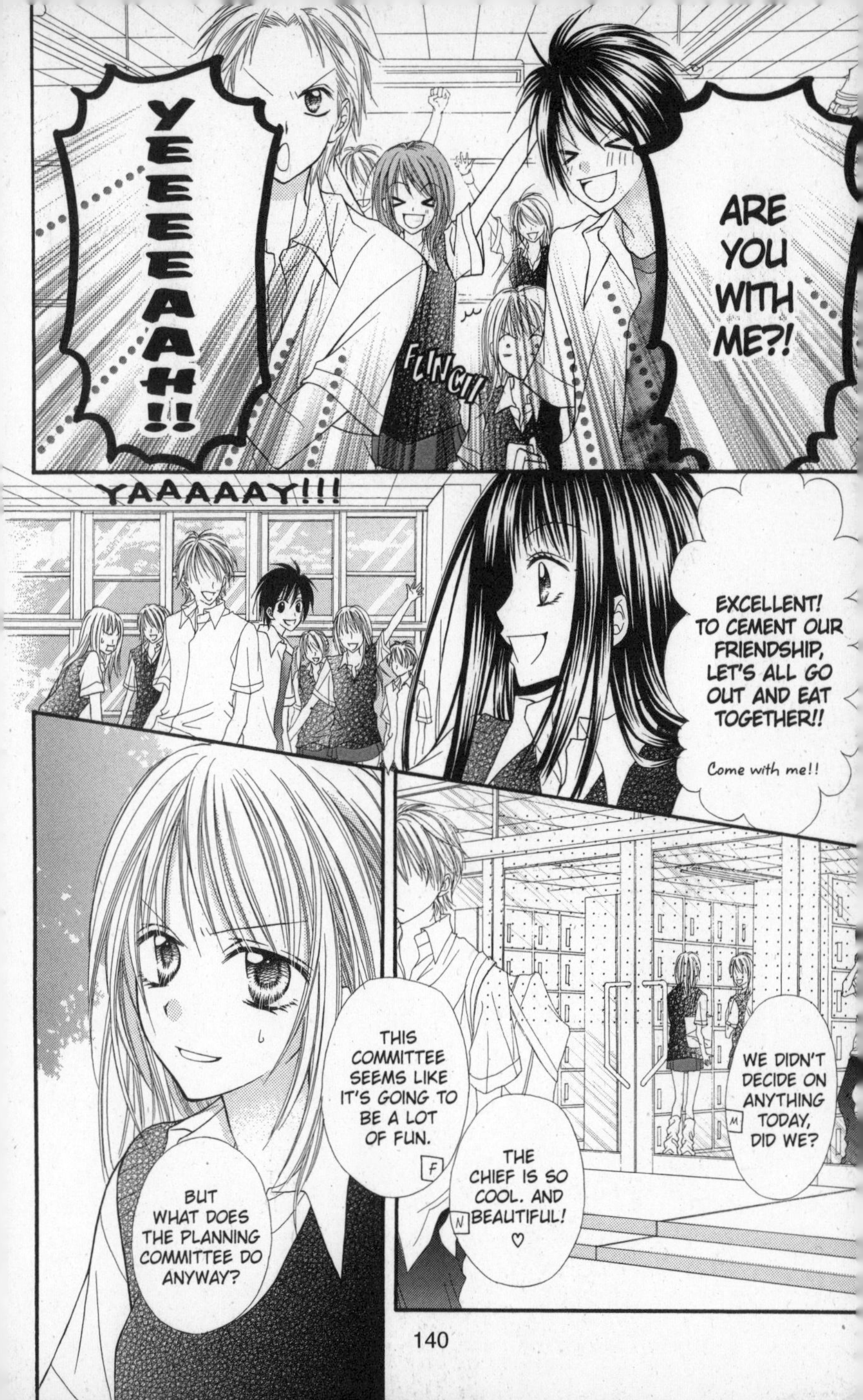
ARE YOU WITH ME?!
YEEEEAAAH!!
FLINCH
EXCELLENT! TO CEMENT OUR FRIENDSHIP, LET'S ALL GO OUT AND EAT TOGETHER!!
Come with me!!
YAAAAAY!!!
WE DIDN'T DECIDE ON ANYTHING TODAY, DID WE?
THE CHIEF IS SO COOL. AND BEAUTIFUL! ♥
THIS COMMITTEE SEEMS LIKE IT'S GOING TO BE A LOT OF FUN.
BUT WHAT DOES THE PLANNING COMMITTEE DO ANYWAY?

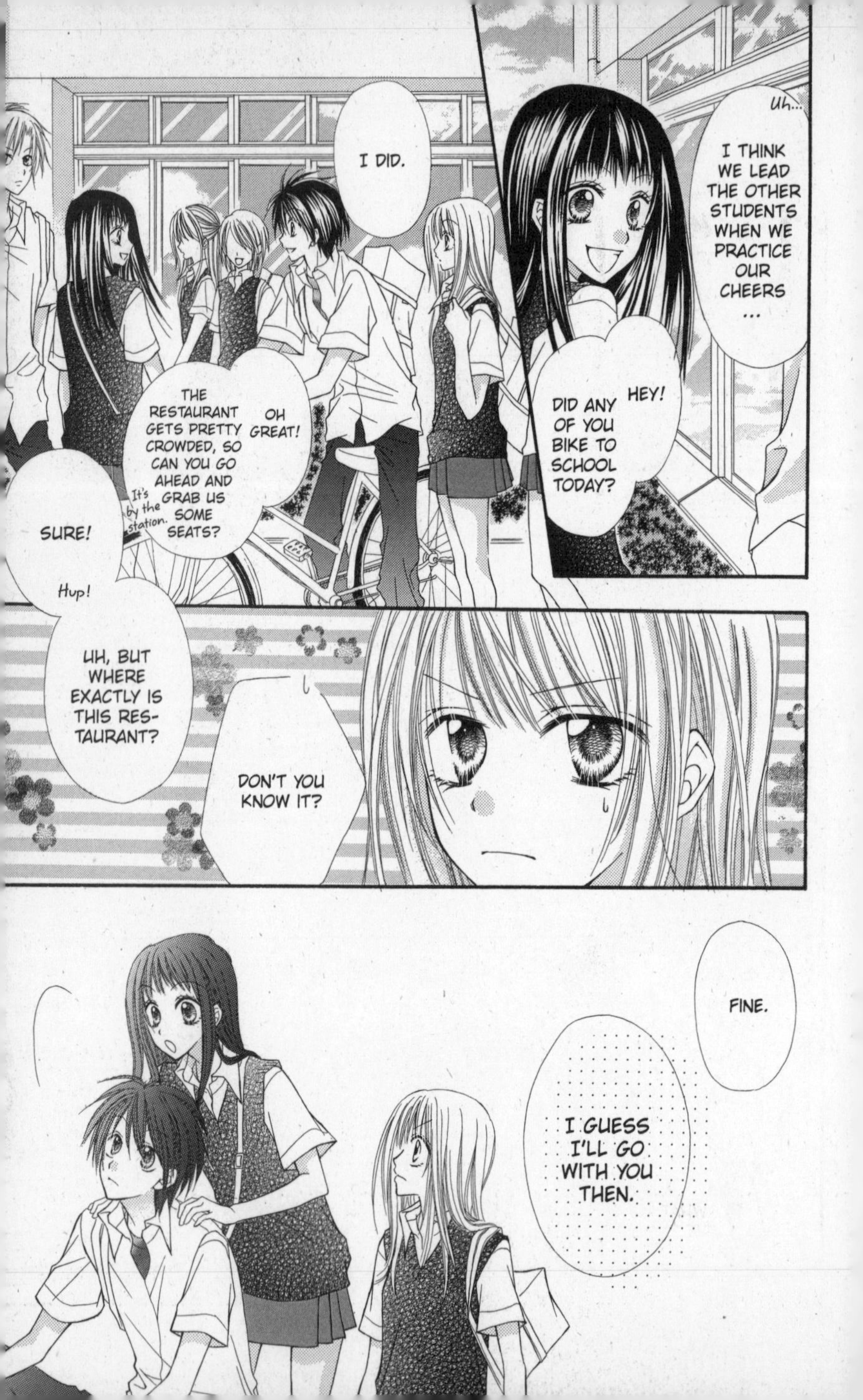
Uh...
I THINK WE LEAD THE OTHER STUDENTS WHEN WE PRACTICE OUR CHEERS ...
HEY!
DID ANY OF YOU BIKE TO SCHOOL TODAY?
I DID.
OH GREAT!
THE RESTAURANT GETS PRETTY CROWDED, SO CAN YOU GO AHEAD AND GRAB US SOME SEATS?
It's by the station.
SURE!
Hup!
UH, BUT WHERE EXACTLY IS THIS RES-TAURANT?
DON'T YOU KNOW IT?
FINE.
I GUESS I'LL GO WITH YOU THEN.

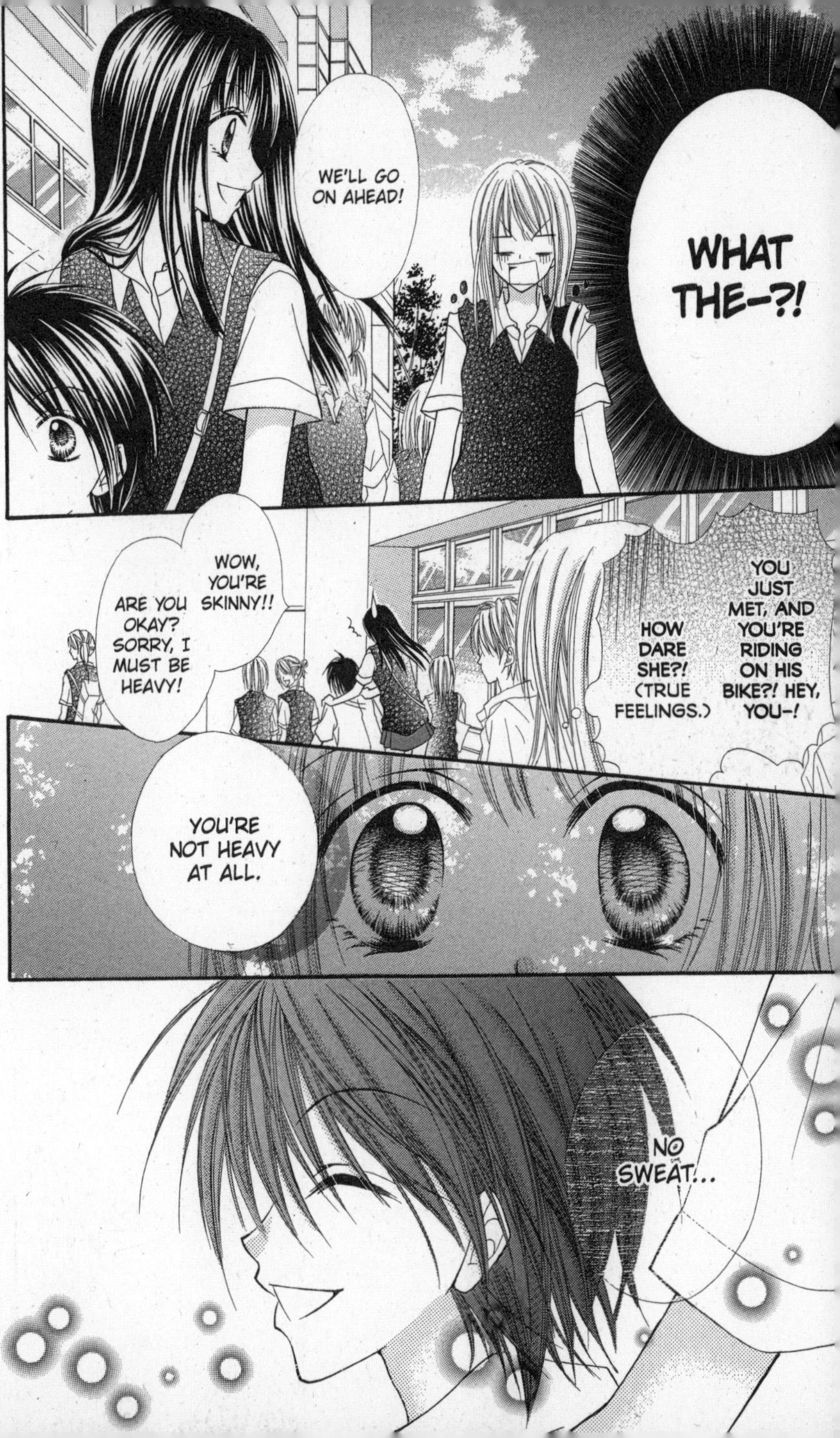
WHAT THE-?!
WE'LL GO ON AHEAD!
YOU JUST MET, AND YOU'RE RIDING ON HIS BIKE?! HEY, YOU-!
HOW DARE SHE?! (TRUE FEELINGS.)
WOW, YOU'RE SKINNY!!
ARE YOU OKAY? SORRY, I MUST BE HEAVY!
YOU'RE NOT HEAVY AT ALL.
NO SWEAT...

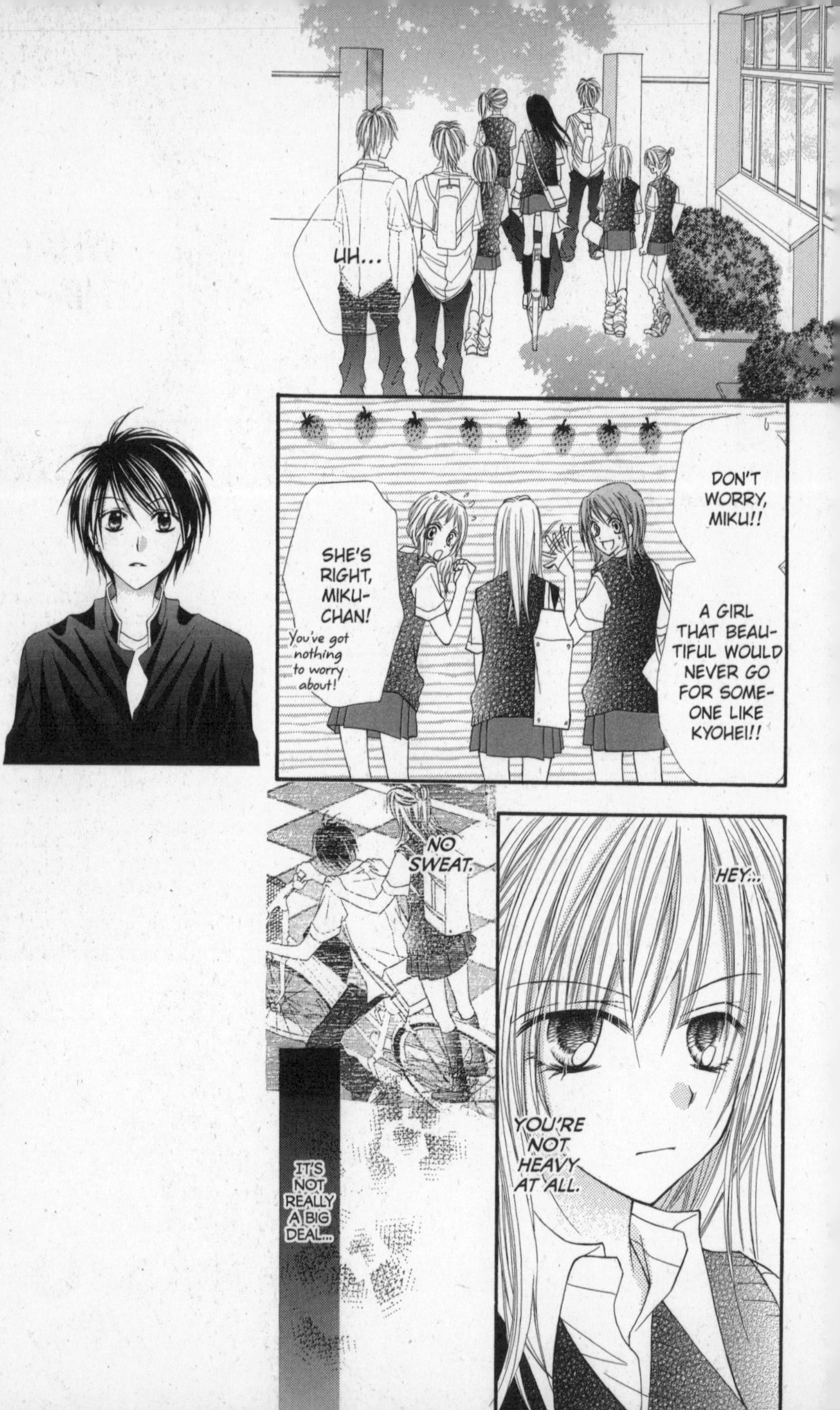
UH...
DON'T WORRY, MIKU!!
A GIRL THAT BEAUTIFUL WOULD NEVER GO FOR SOMEONE LIKE KYOHEI!!
SHE'S RIGHT, MIKU-CHAN!
You've got nothing to worry about!
HEY...
YOU'RE NOT HEAVY AT ALL.
NO SWEAT.
IT'S NOT REALLY A BIG DEAL...

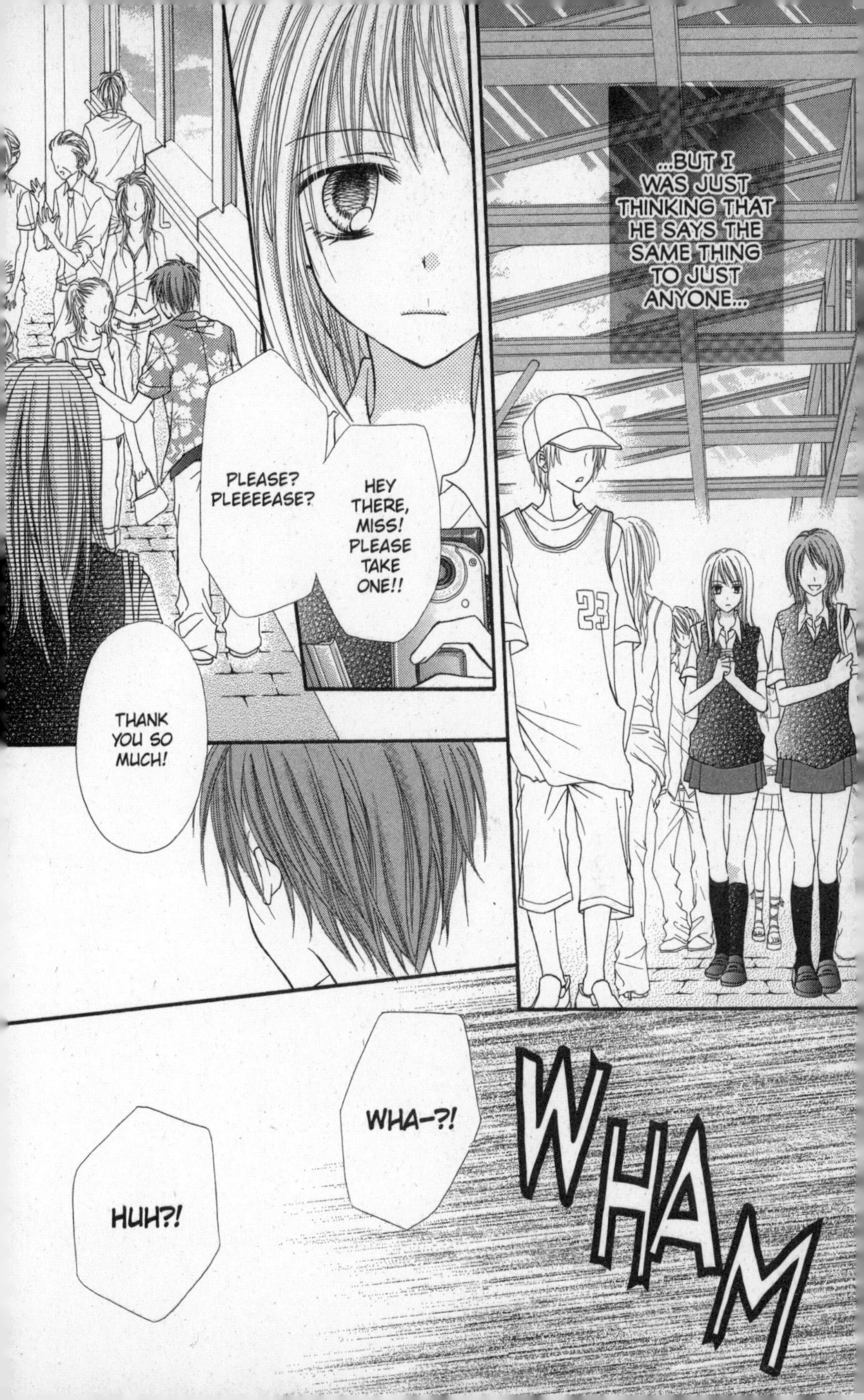
...BUT I WAS JUST THINKING THAT HE SAYS THE SAME THING TO JUST ANYONE...
HEY THERE, MISS! PLEASE TAKE ONE!!
PLEASE? PLEEEEASE?
THANK YOU SO MUCH!
WHAM
WHA-?!
HUH?!

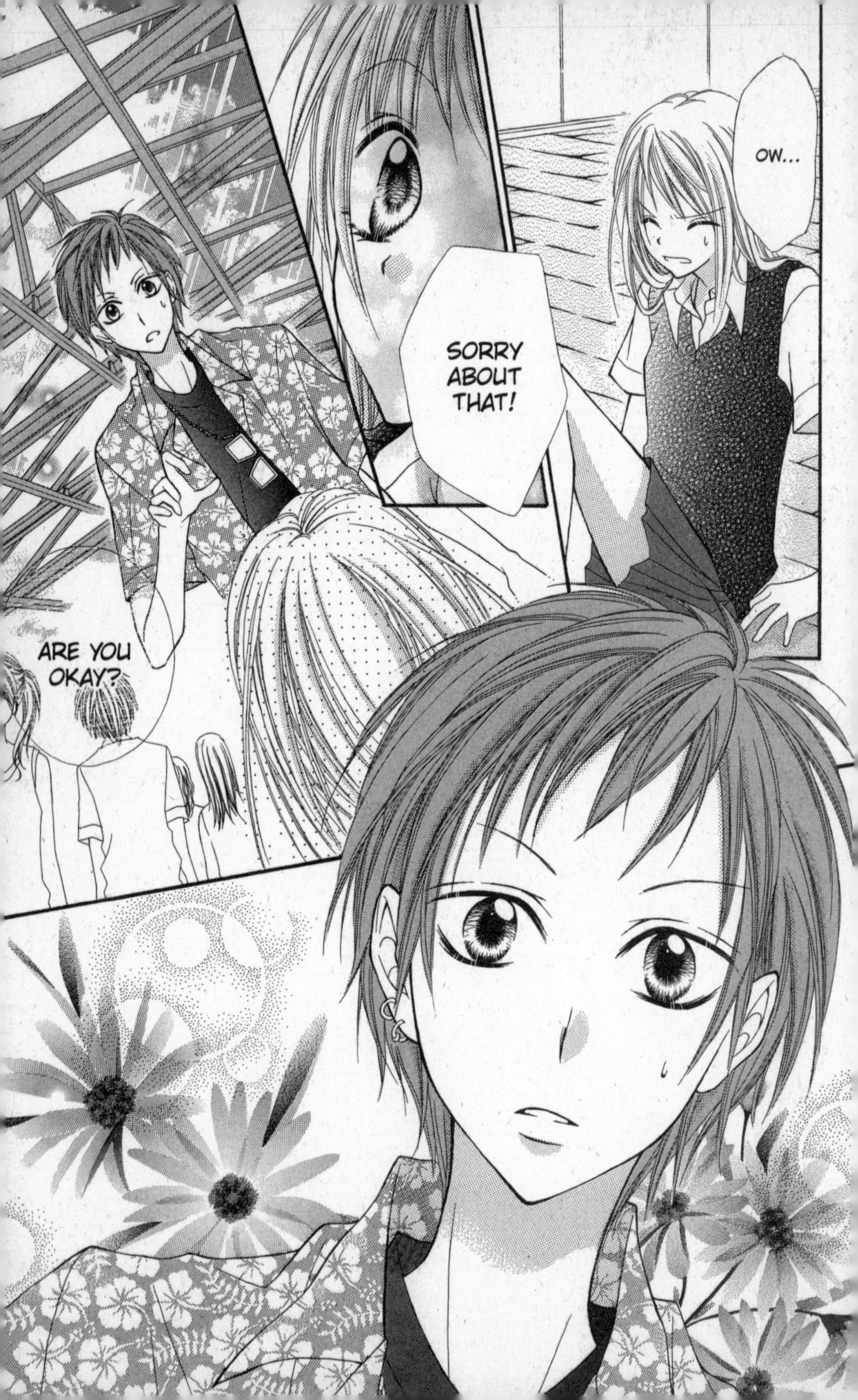
OW...
SORRY ABOUT THAT!
ARE YOU OKAY?

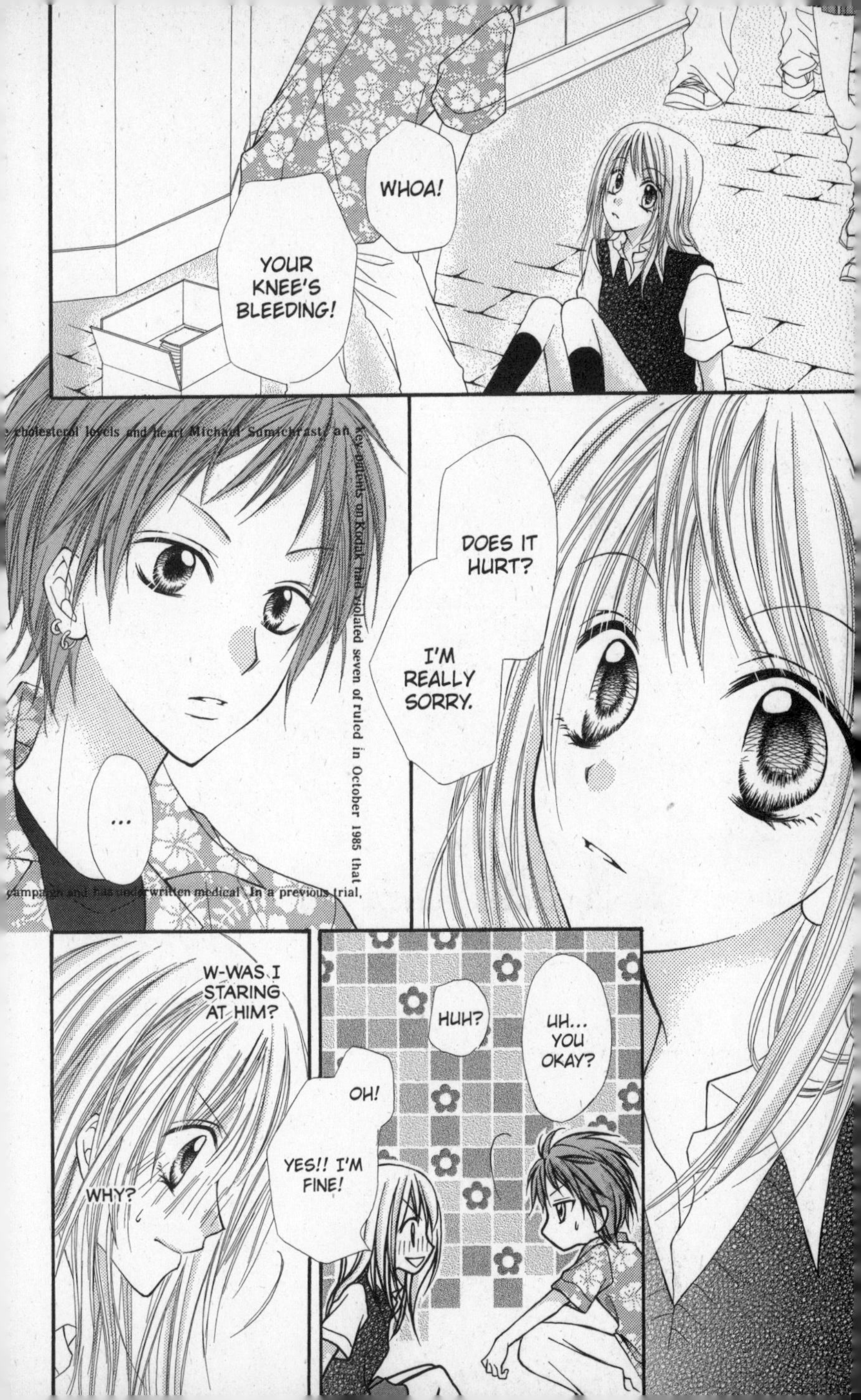
WHOA!
YOUR KNEE'S BLEEDING!
DOES IT HURT?
I'M REALLY SORRY.
...
UH... YOU OKAY?
HUH?
OH!
YES!! I'M FINE!
W-WAS I STARING AT HIM?
WHY?

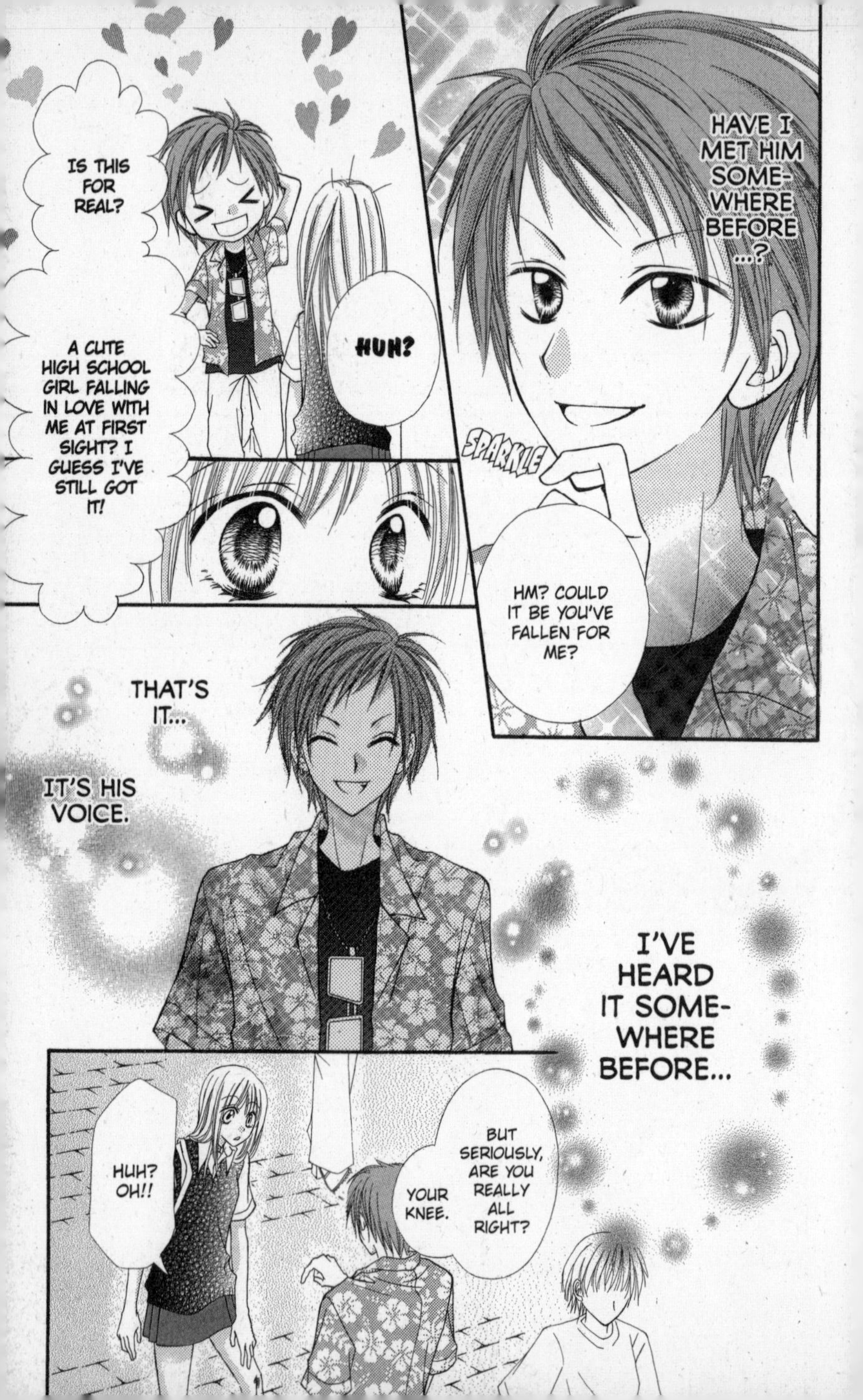
HAVE I MET HIM SOME-WHERE BEFORE ...?
SPARKLE
HM? COULD IT BE YOU'VE FALLEN FOR ME?
HUH?
IS THIS FOR REAL?
A CUTE HIGH SCHOOL GIRL FALLING IN LOVE WITH ME AT FIRST SIGHT? I GUESS I'VE STILL GOT IT!
THAT'S IT...
IT'S HIS VOICE.
I'VE HEARD IT SOME-WHERE BEFORE...
BUT SERIOUSLY, ARE YOU REALLY ALL RIGHT?
YOUR KNEE.
HUH? OH!!

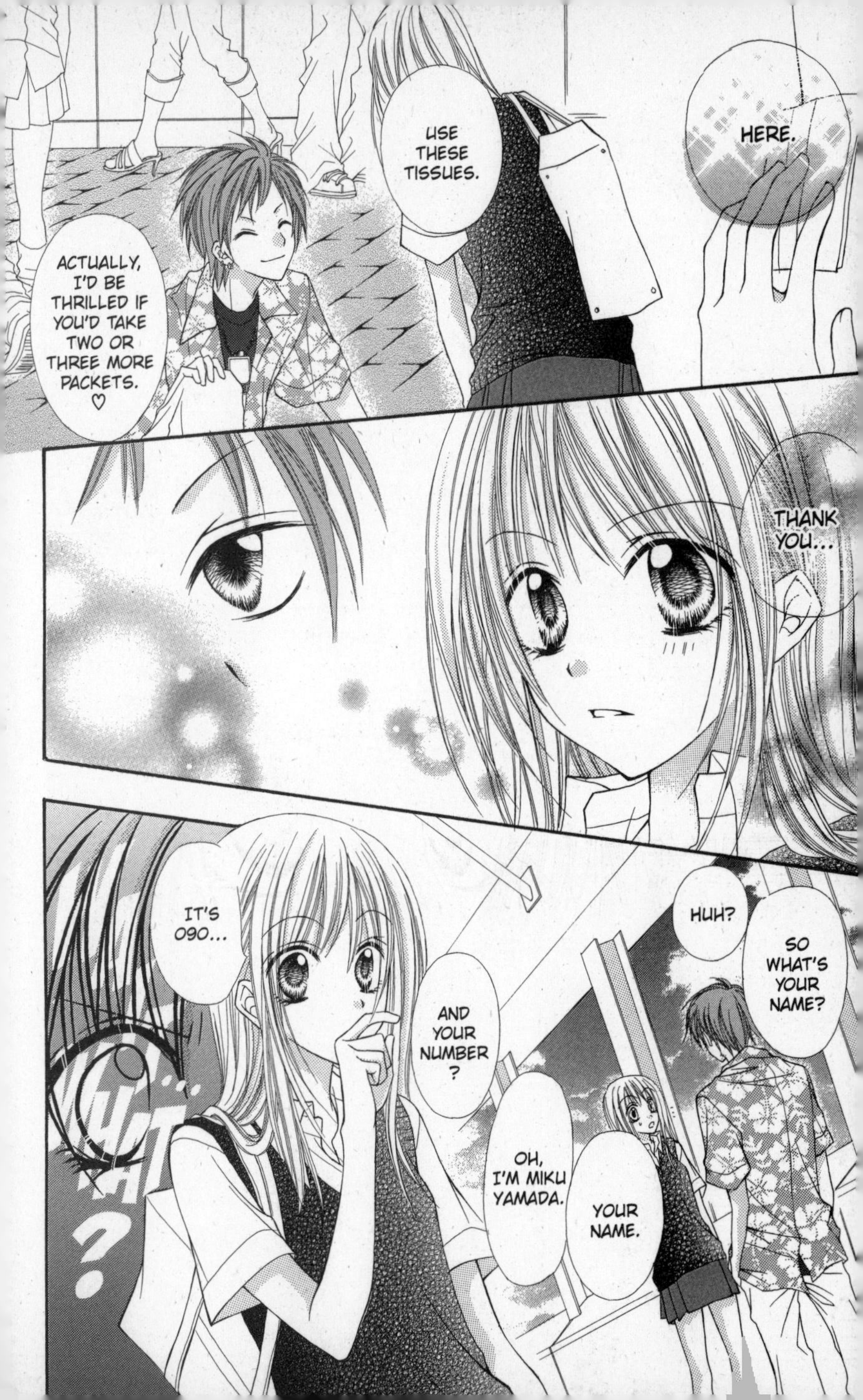
HERE.
USE THESE TISSUES.
ACTUALLY, I'D BE THRILLED IF YOU'D TAKE TWO OR THREE MORE PACKETS. ♡
THANK YOU...
SO WHAT'S YOUR NAME?
HUH?
YOUR NAME.
OH, I'M MIKU YAMADA.
AND YOUR NUMBER?
IT'S 090...

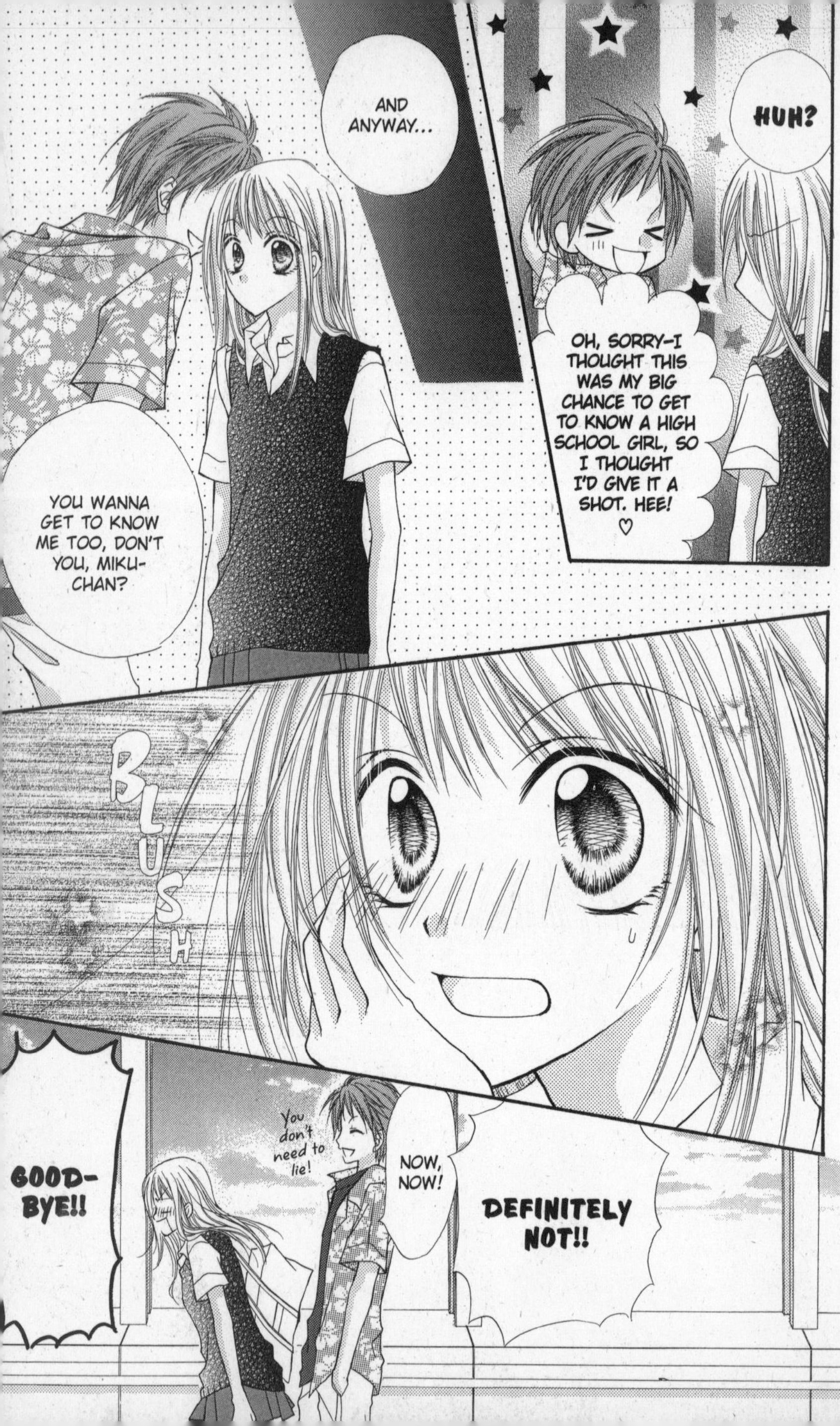
HUH?
OH, SORRY—I THOUGHT THIS WAS MY BIG CHANCE TO GET TO KNOW A HIGH SCHOOL GIRL, SO I THOUGHT I'D GIVE IT A SHOT. HEE! ♡
AND ANYWAY...
YOU WANNA GET TO KNOW ME TOO, DON'T YOU, MIKU-CHAN?
BLUSH
DEFINITELY NOT!!
NOW, NOW!
You don't need to lie!
GOOD-BYE!!

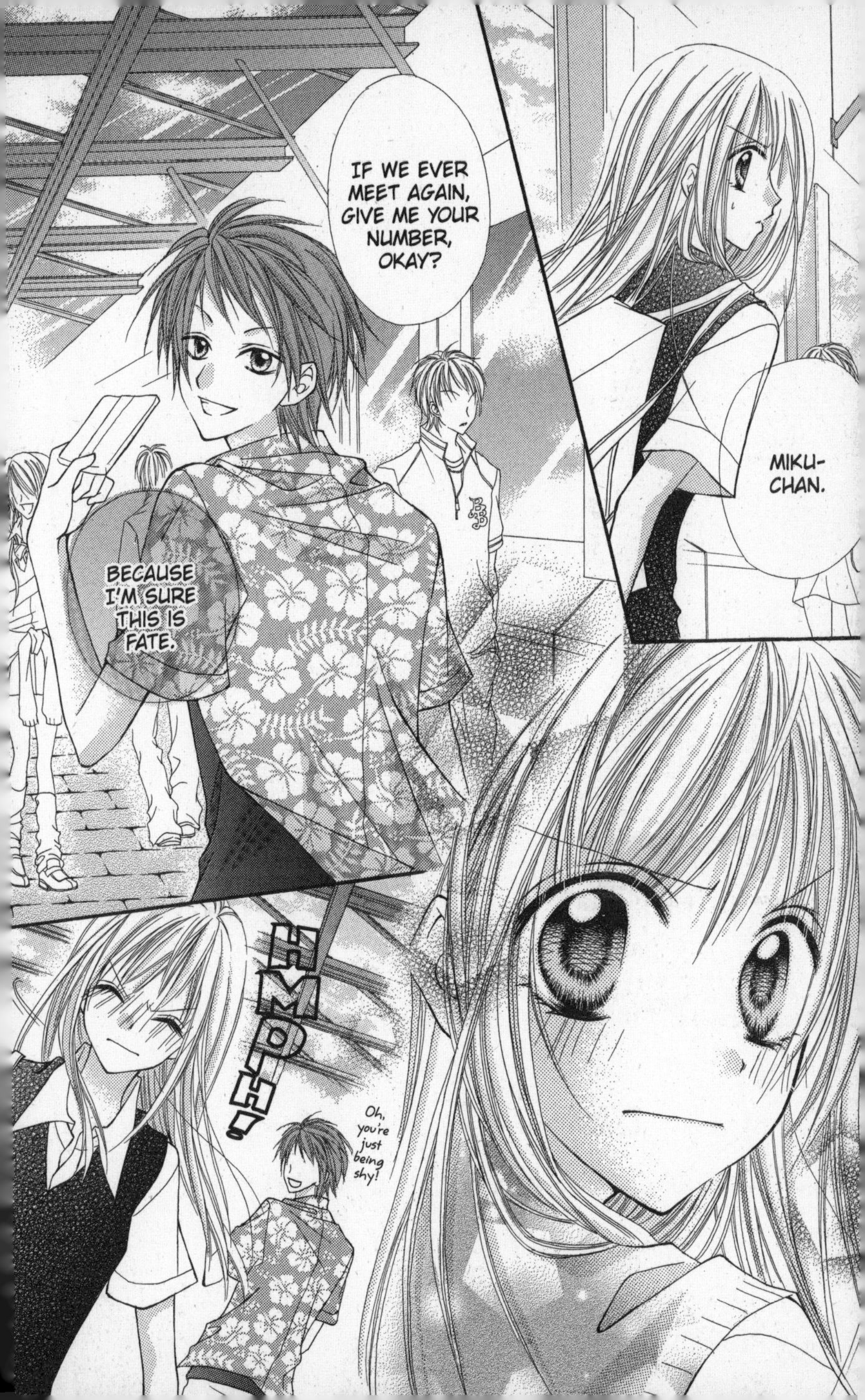
MIKU-CHAN.
IF WE EVER MEET AGAIN, GIVE ME YOUR NUMBER, OKAY?
BECAUSE I'M SURE THIS IS FATE.
HMPH!
Oh, you're just being shy!

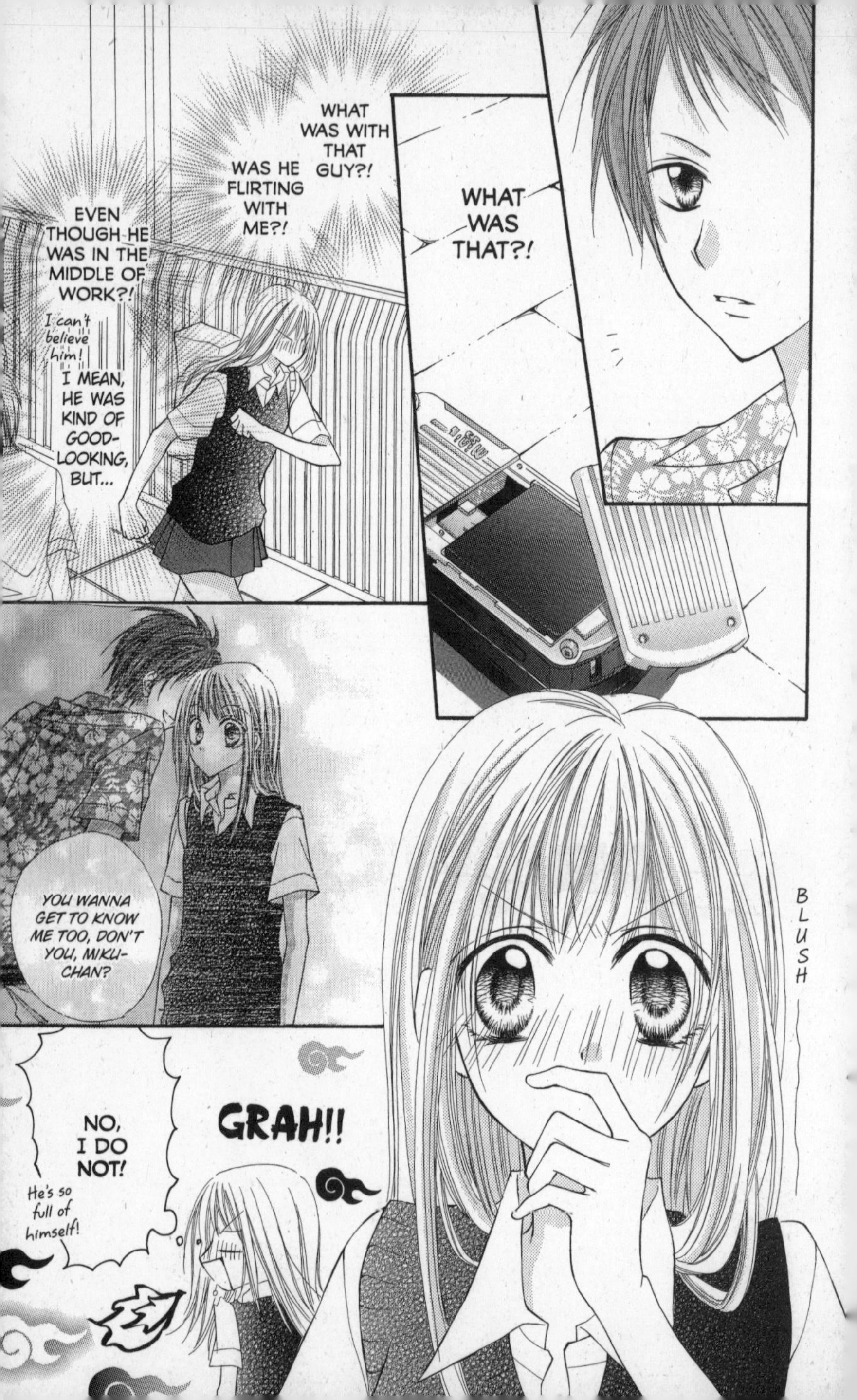
WHAT WAS THAT?!
WHAT WAS WITH THAT GUY?!
WAS HE FLIRTING WITH ME?!
EVEN THOUGH HE WAS IN THE MIDDLE OF WORK?!
I can't believe him!
I MEAN, HE WAS KIND OF GOOD-LOOKING, BUT...
BLUSH
YOU WANNA GET TO KNOW ME TOO, DON'T YOU, MIKU-CHAN?
GRAH!!
NO, I DO NOT!
He's so full of himself!

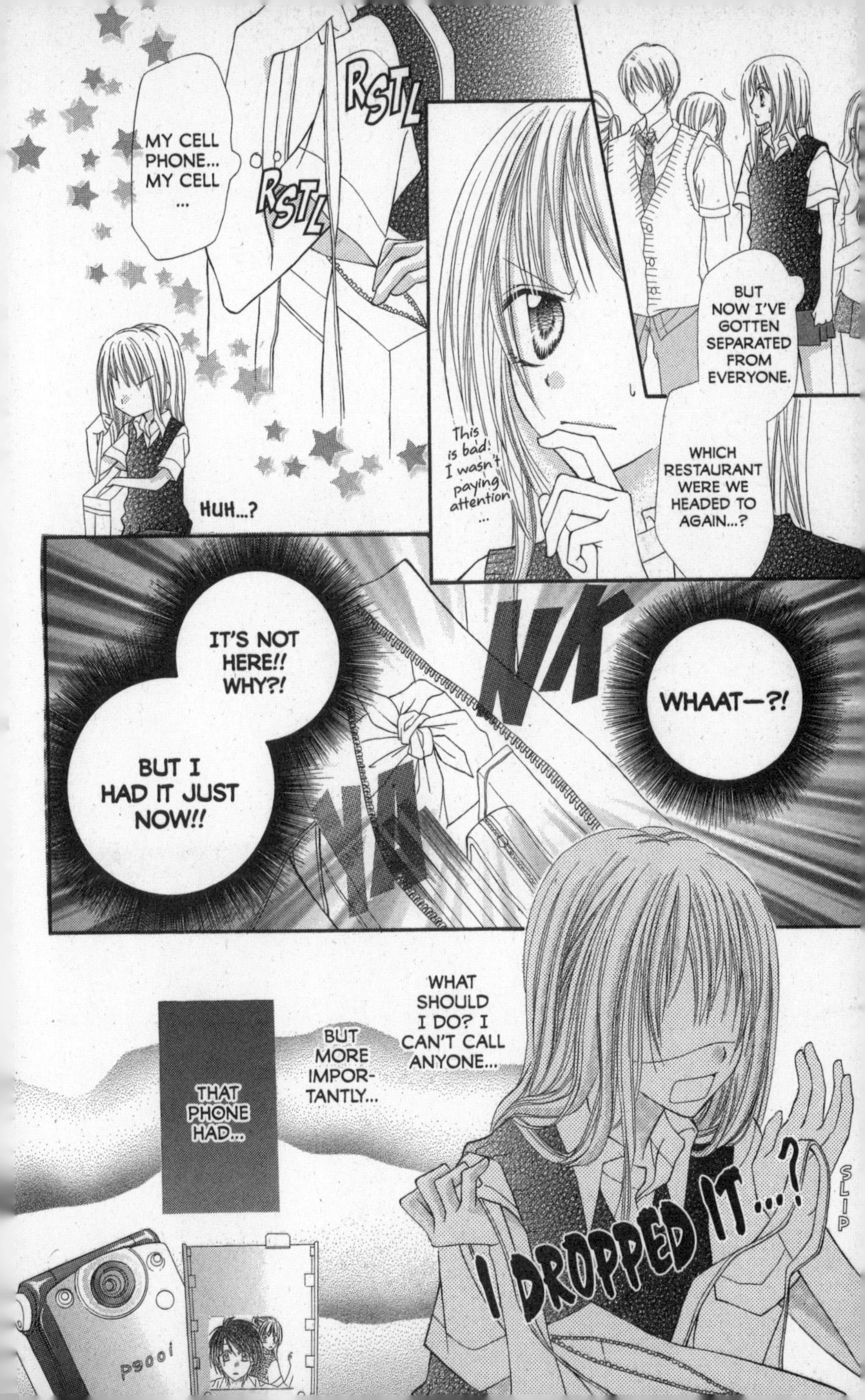
BUT NOW I'VE GOTTEN SEPARATED FROM EVERYONE.
WHICH RESTAURANT WERE WE HEADED TO AGAIN...?
This is bad! I wasn't paying attention ...
RSTL
RSTL
MY CELL PHONE... MY CELL ...
HUH...?
WHAAT—?!
NK
NA
IT'S NOT HERE!! WHY?!
BUT I HAD IT JUST NOW!!
SLIP
I DROPPED IT...?
WHAT SHOULD I DO? I CAN'T CALL ANYONE...
BUT MORE IMPOR-TANTLY...
THAT PHONE HAD...

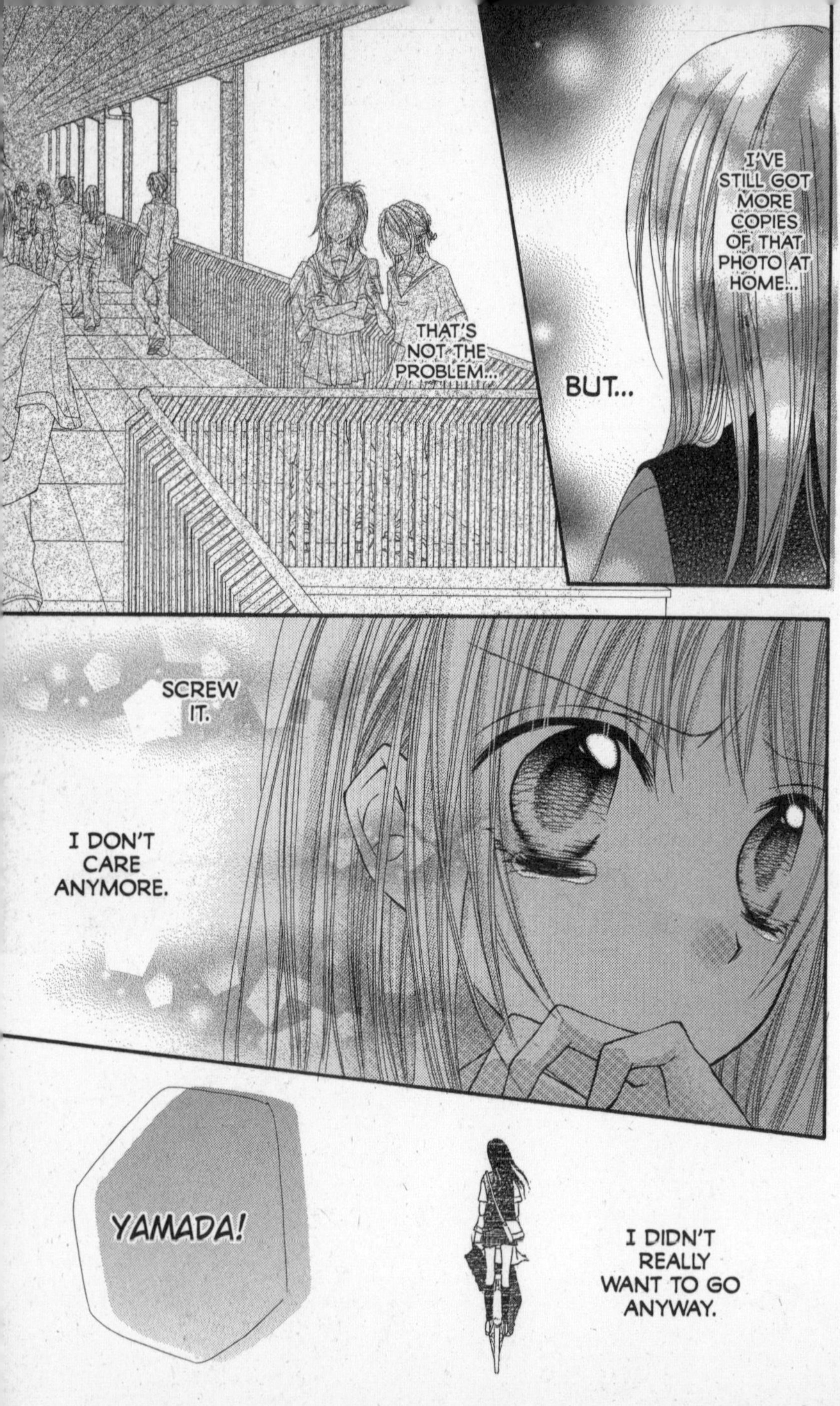

I'VE STILL GOT MORE COPIES OF THAT PHOTO AT HOME...
BUT...
THAT'S NOT THE PROBLEM...
SCREW IT.
I DON'T CARE ANYMORE.
I DIDN'T REALLY WANT TO GO ANYWAY.
YAMADA!

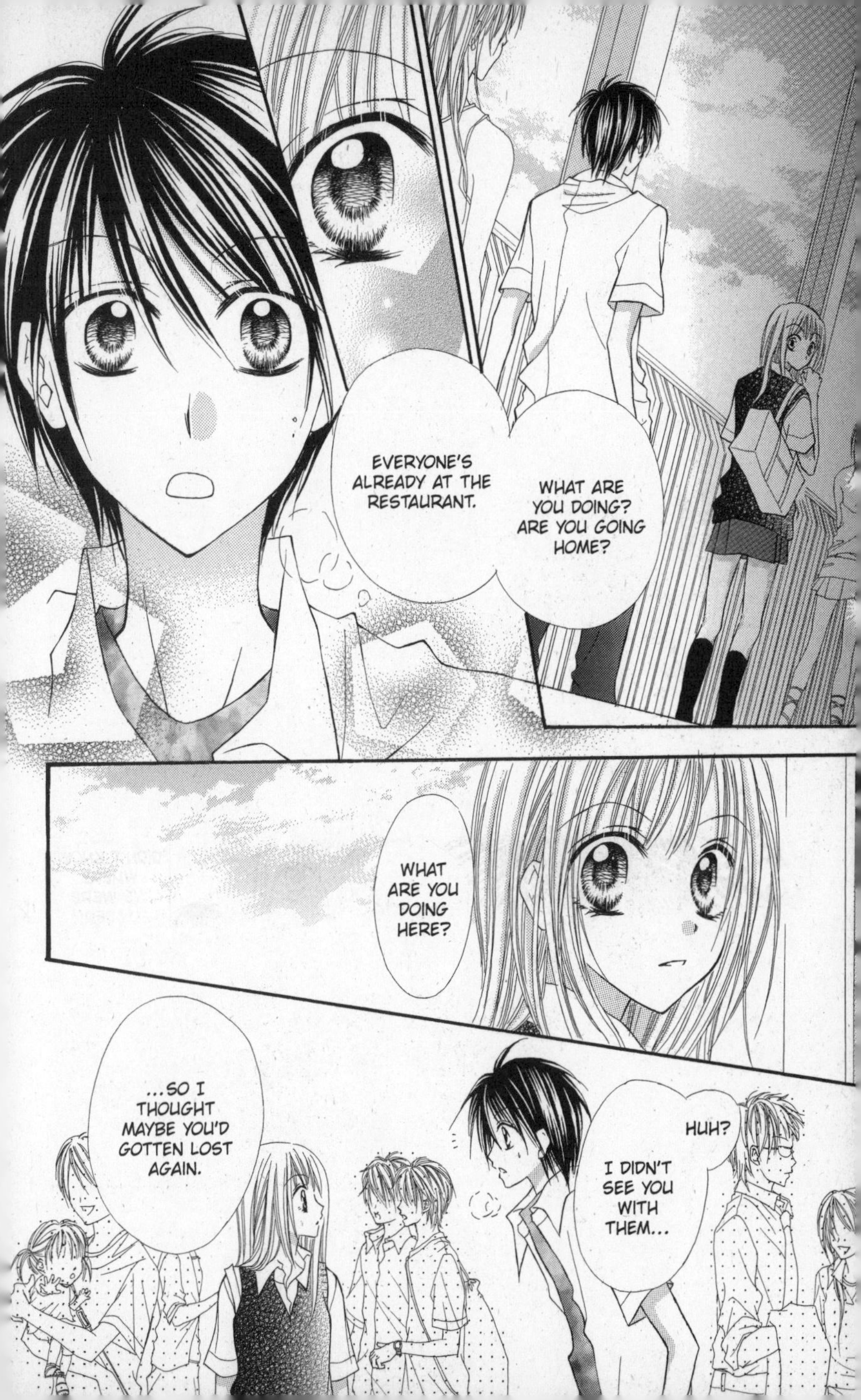
WHAT ARE YOU DOING? ARE YOU GOING HOME?
EVERYONE'S ALREADY AT THE RESTAURANT.
WHAT ARE YOU DOING HERE?
HUH?
I DIDN'T SEE YOU WITH THEM...
...SO I THOUGHT MAYBE YOU'D GOTTEN LOST AGAIN.

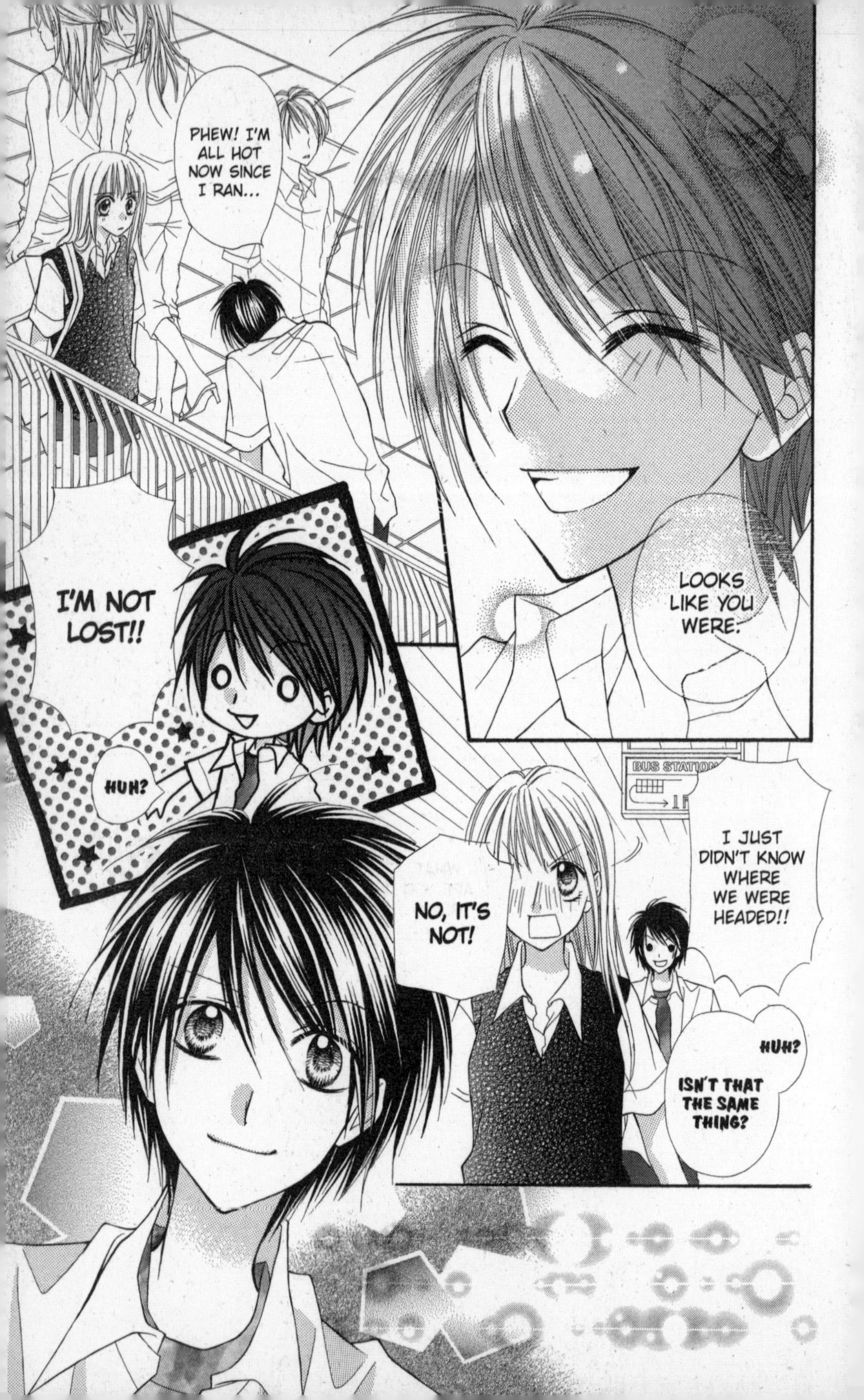
PHEW! I'M ALL HOT NOW SINCE I RAN...
LOOKS LIKE YOU WERE.
I'M NOT LOST!!
HUH?
BUS STATION
I JUST DIDN'T KNOW WHERE WE WERE HEADED!!
HUH?
ISN'T THAT THE SAME THING?
NO, IT'S NOT!

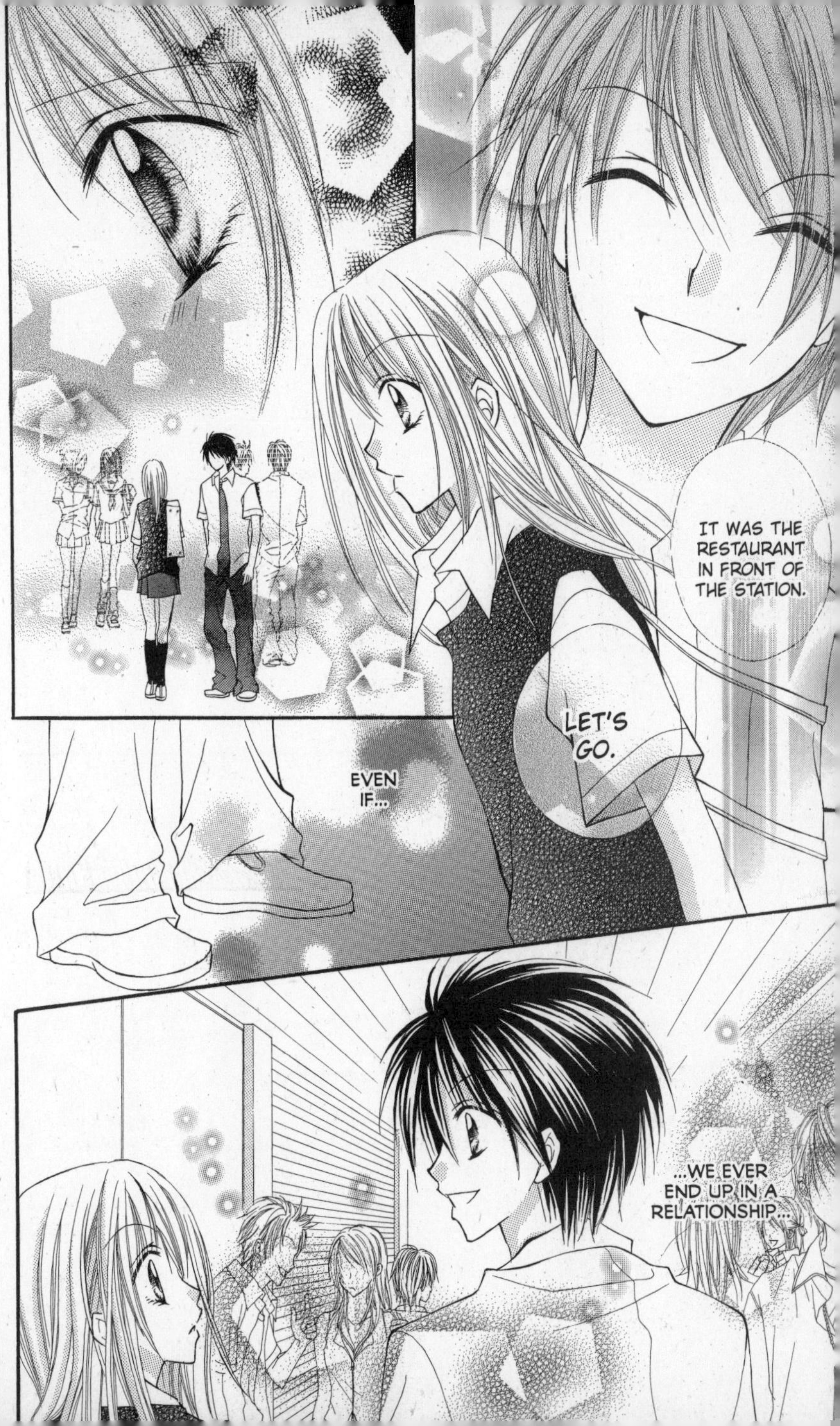
IT WAS THE RESTAURANT IN FRONT OF THE STATION.
LET'S GO.
EVEN IF...
...WE EVER END UP IN A RELATIONSHIP...

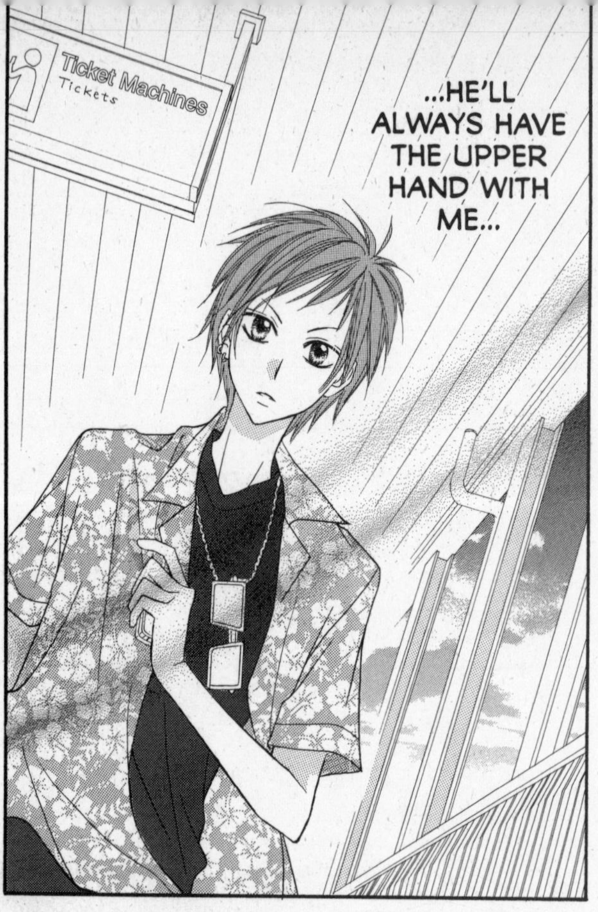
Ticket Machines
Tickets
...HE'LL ALWAYS HAVE THE UPPER HAND WITH ME...

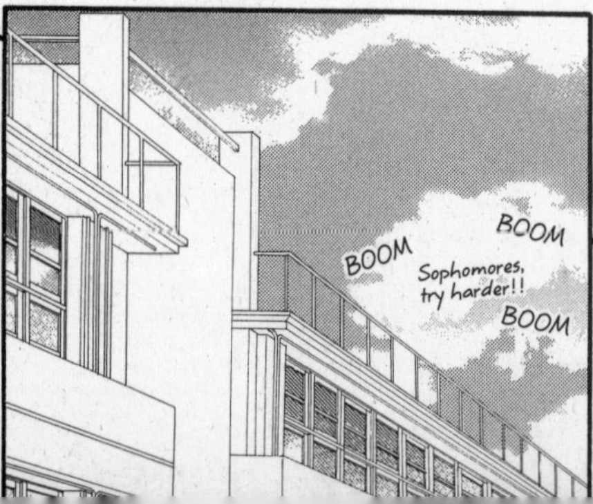
BOOM
BOOM
Sophomores, try harder!!
BOOM

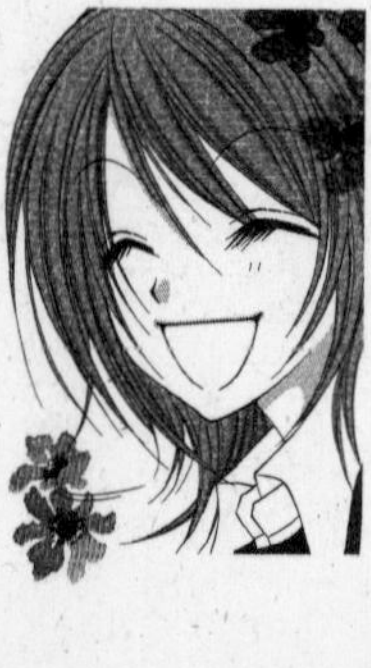

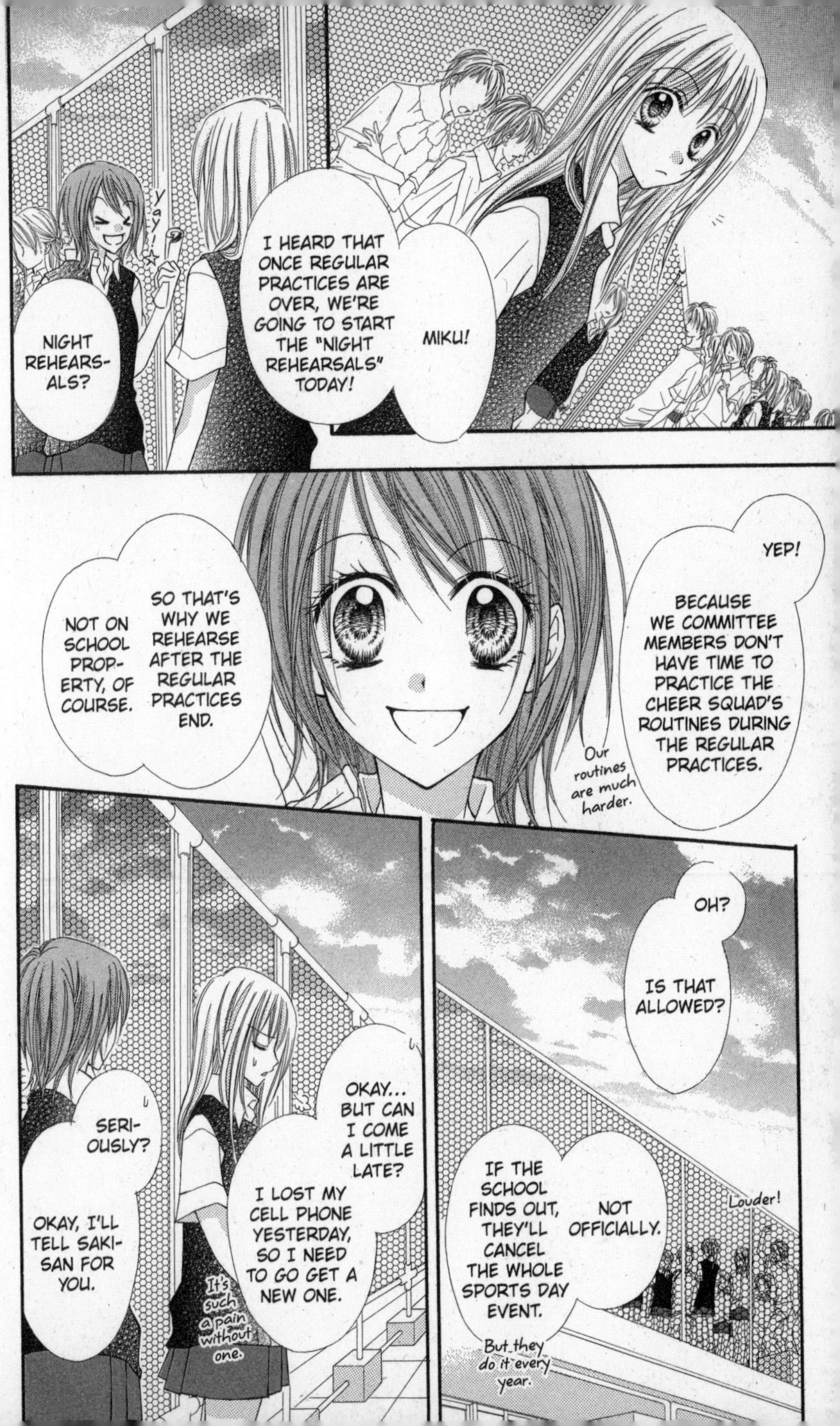
MIKU!
I HEARD THAT ONCE REGULAR PRACTICES ARE OVER, WE'RE GOING TO START THE "NIGHT REHEARSALS" TODAY!
yay!☆
NIGHT REHEARS-ALS?
YEP!
BECAUSE WE COMMITTEE MEMBERS DON'T HAVE TIME TO PRACTICE THE CHEER SQUAD'S ROUTINES DURING THE REGULAR PRACTICES.
Our routines are much harder.
SO THAT'S WHY WE REHEARSE AFTER THE REGULAR PRACTICES END.
NOT ON SCHOOL PROP-ERTY, OF COURSE.
OH?
IS THAT ALLOWED?
NOT OFFICIALLY.
IF THE SCHOOL FINDS OUT, THEY'LL CANCEL THE WHOLE SPORTS DAY EVENT.
But they do it every year.
Louder!
OKAY... BUT CAN I COME A LITTLE LATE?
I LOST MY CELL PHONE YESTERDAY, SO I NEED TO GO GET A NEW ONE.
It's such a pain without one.
SERI-OUSLY?
OKAY, I'LL TELL SAKI-SAN FOR YOU.

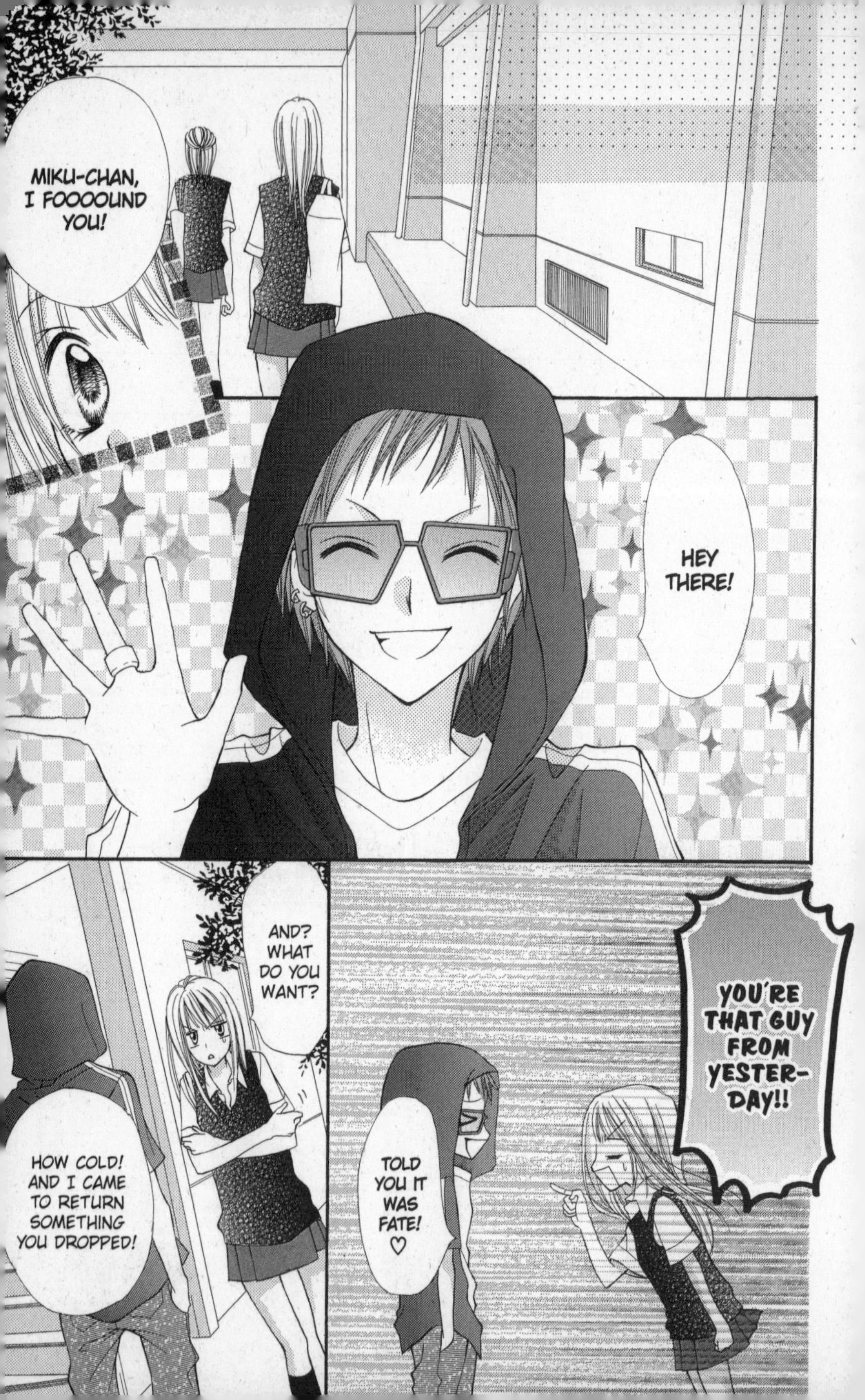
MIKU-CHAN, I FOOOOUND YOU!
HEY THERE!
YOU'RE THAT GUY FROM YESTER-DAY!!
TOLD YOU IT WAS FATE! ♡
AND? WHAT DO YOU WANT?
HOW COLD! AND I CAME TO RETURN SOMETHING YOU DROPPED!

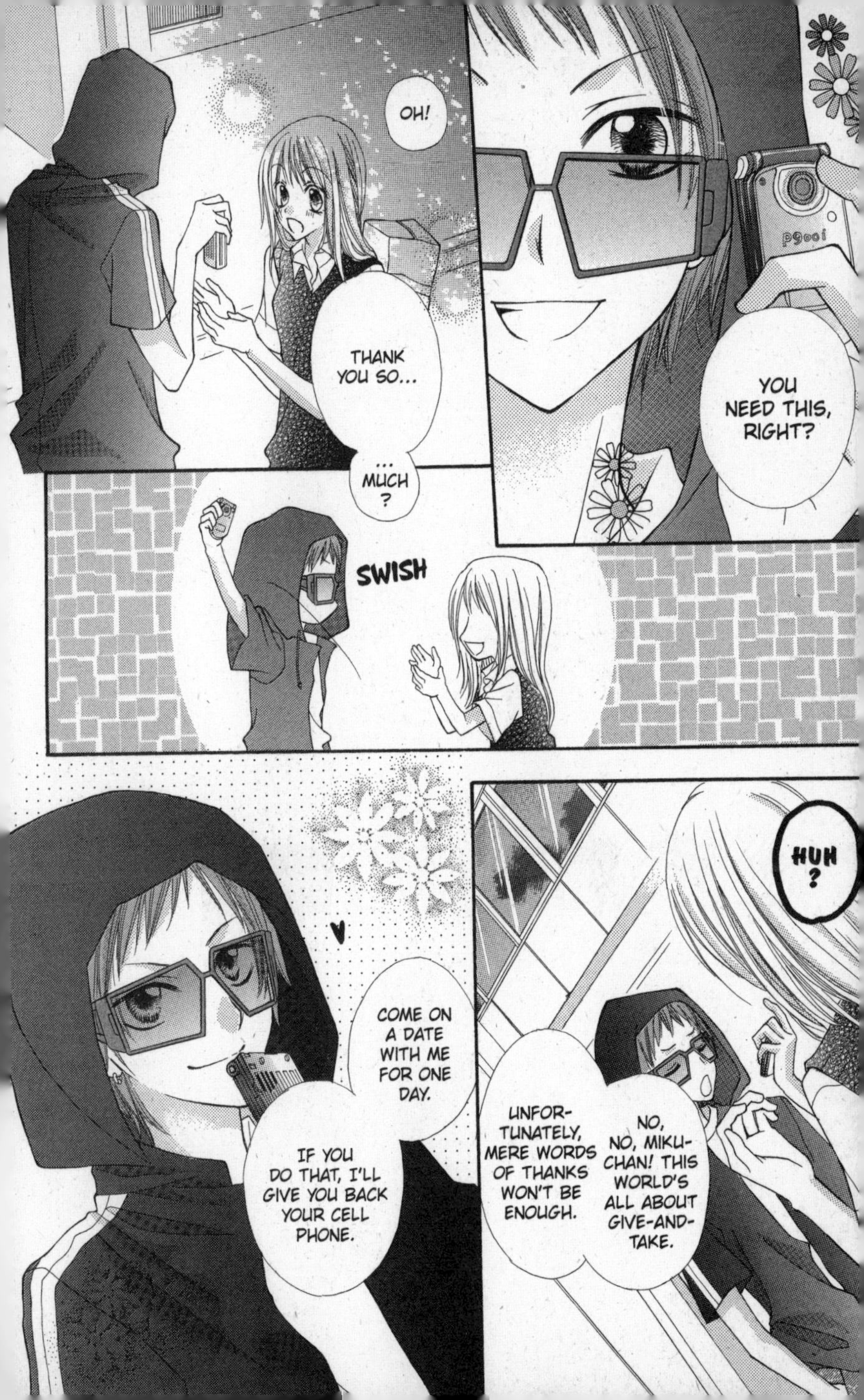
YOU NEED THIS, RIGHT?
OH!
THANK YOU SO...
...MUCH?
SWISH
HUH?
NO, NO, MIKU-CHAN! THIS WORLD'S ALL ABOUT GIVE-AND-TAKE.
UNFORTUNATELY, MERE WORDS OF THANKS WON'T BE ENOUGH.
COME ON A DATE WITH ME FOR ONE DAY.
IF YOU DO THAT, I'LL GIVE YOU BACK YOUR CELL PHONE.

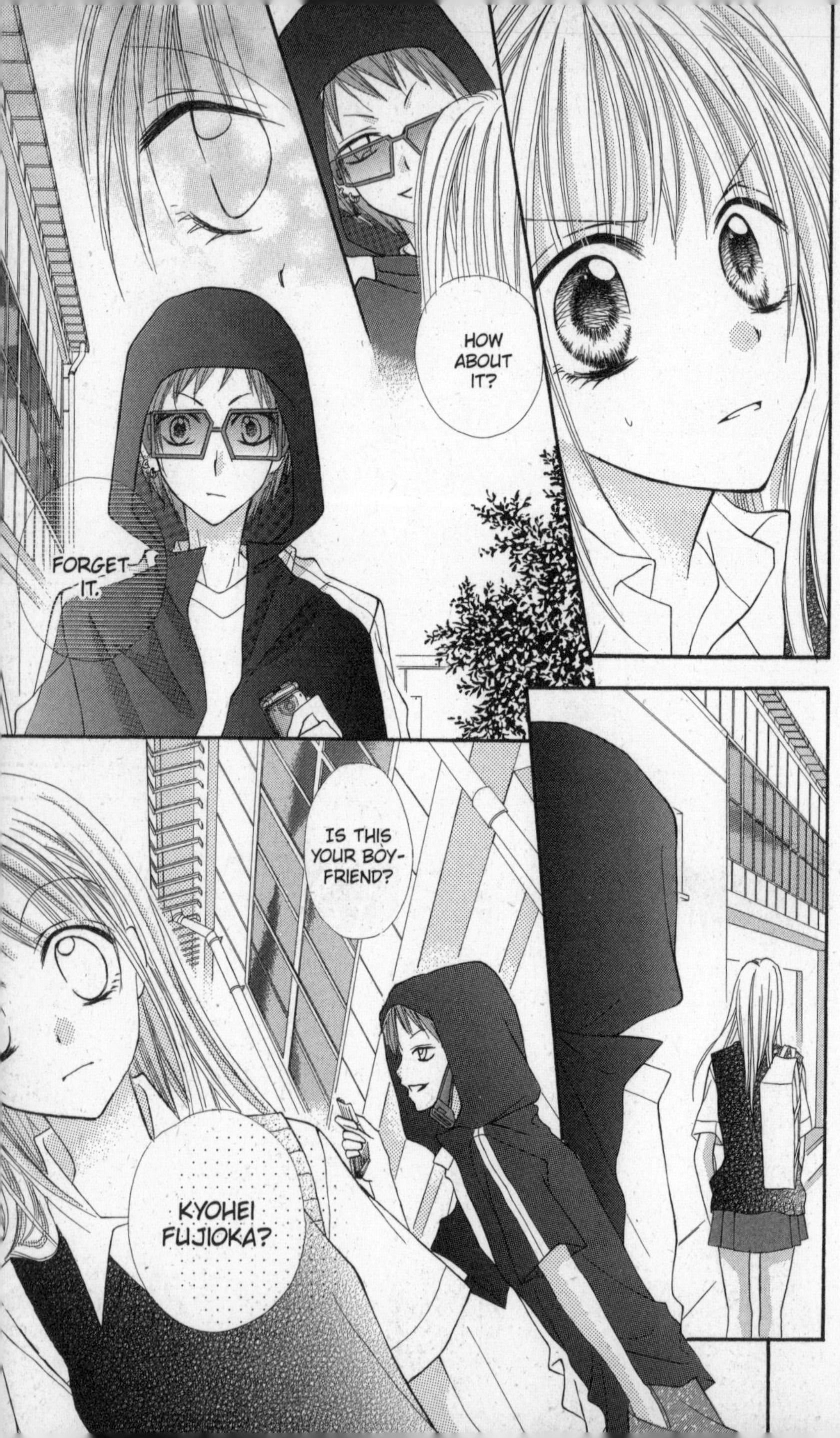
HOW ABOUT IT?
FORGET IT.
IS THIS YOUR BOY-FRIEND?
KYOHEI FUJIOKA?

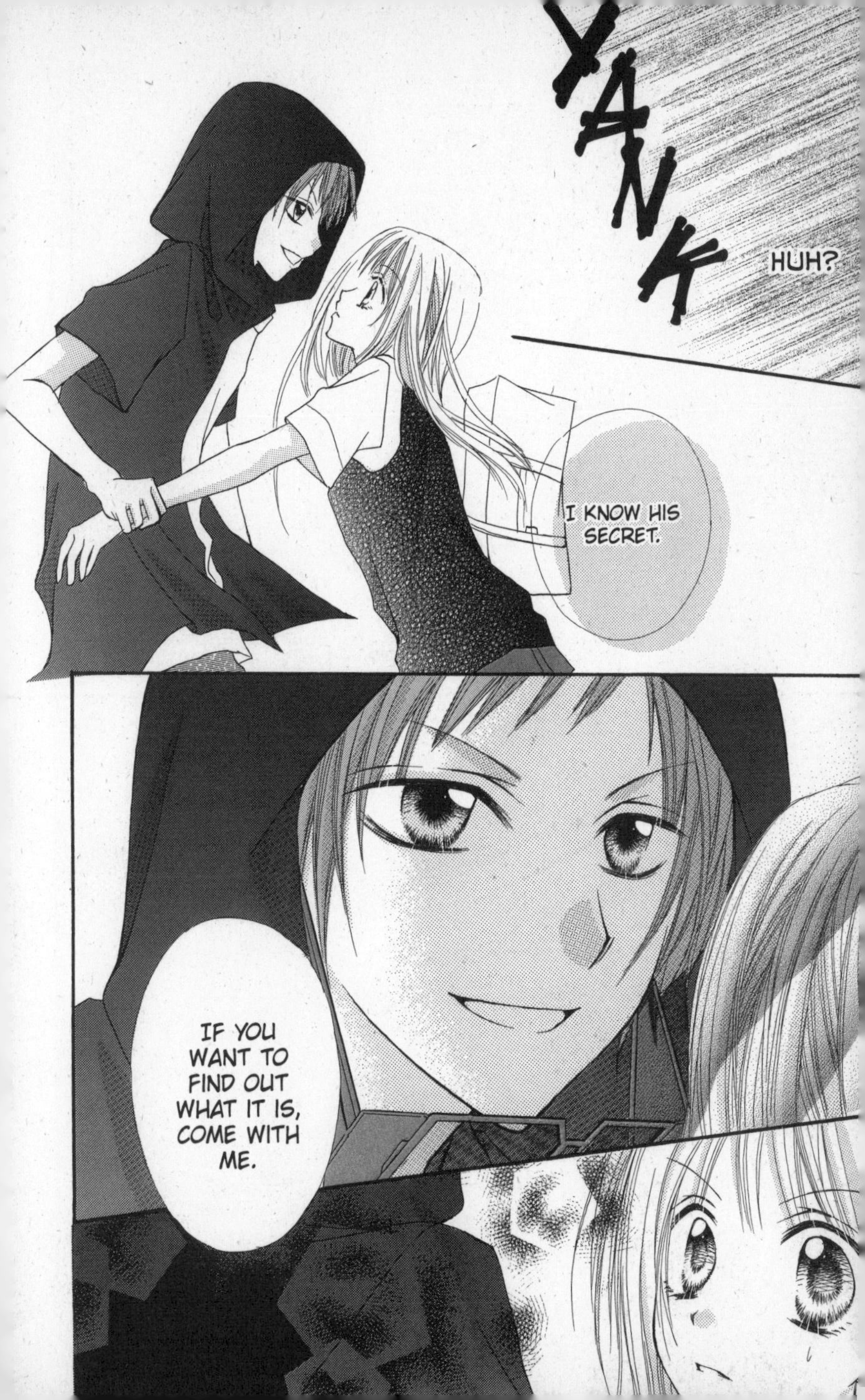
YANK
HUH?
I KNOW HIS SECRET.
IF YOU WANT TO FIND OUT WHAT IT IS, COME WITH ME.

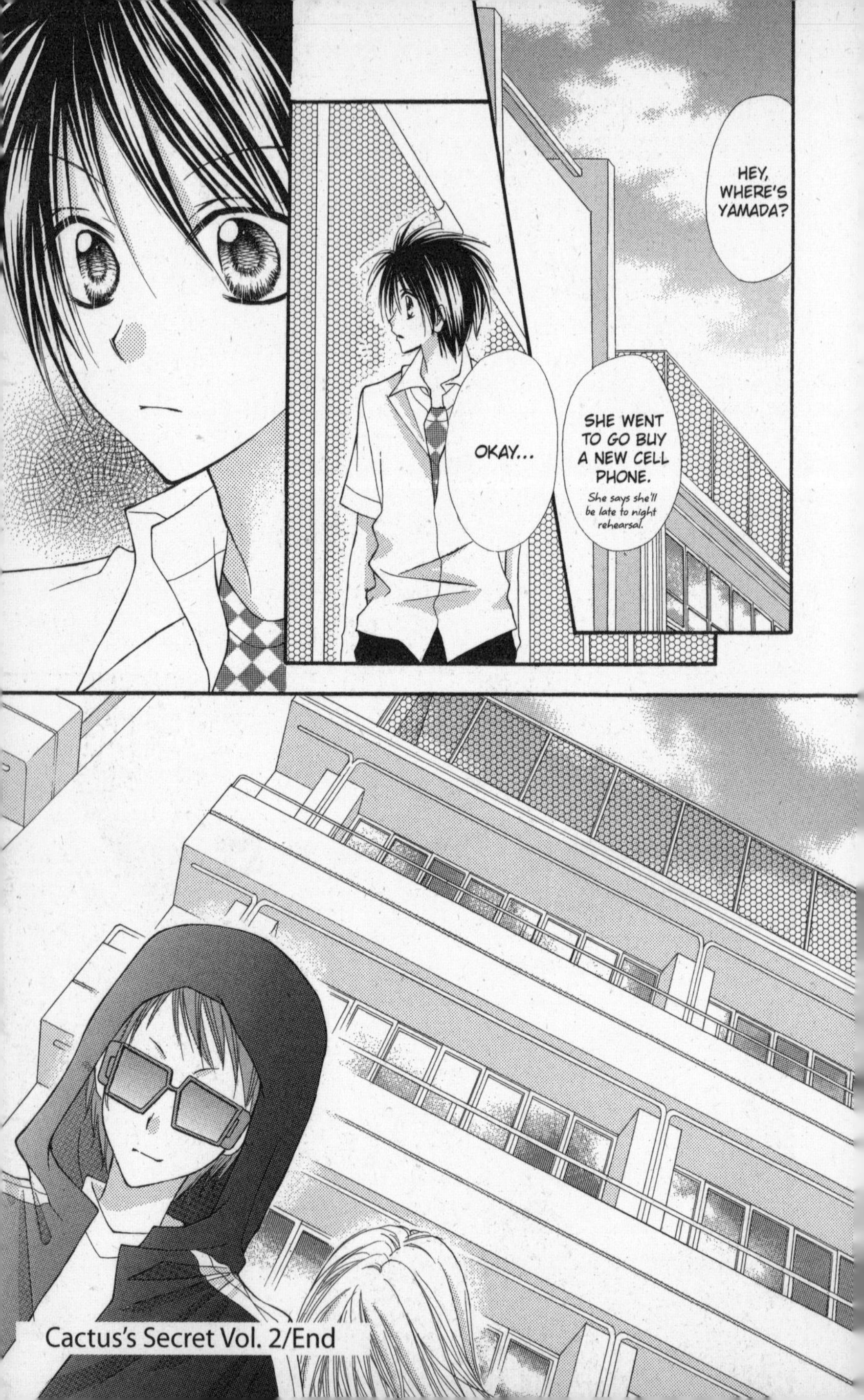
HEY, WHERE'S YAMADA?
SHE WENT TO GO BUY A NEW CELL PHONE.
She says she'll be late to night rehearsal.
OKAY...

Cactus's Secret Vol. 2/End

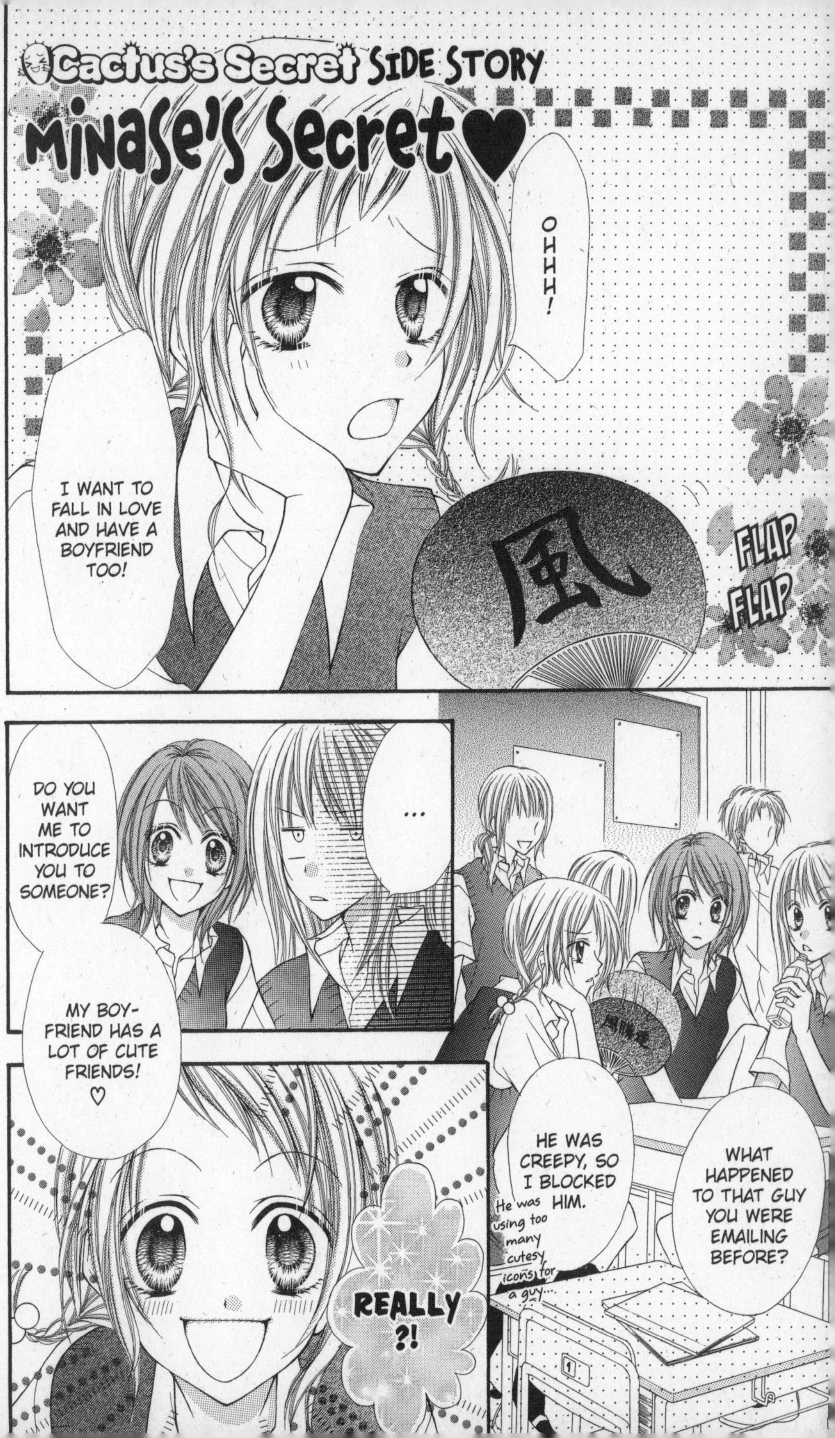
Cactus's Secret SIDE STORY
Minase's Secret ♥
OHHH!
FLAP FLAP
I WANT TO FALL IN LOVE AND HAVE A BOYFRIEND TOO!
WHAT HAPPENED TO THAT GUY YOU WERE EMAILING BEFORE?
HE WAS CREEPY, SO I BLOCKED HIM.
He was using too many cutesy icons for a guy...
...
DO YOU WANT ME TO INTRODUCE YOU TO SOMEONE?
MY BOY-FRIEND HAS A LOT OF CUTE FRIENDS! ♡
REALLY ?!

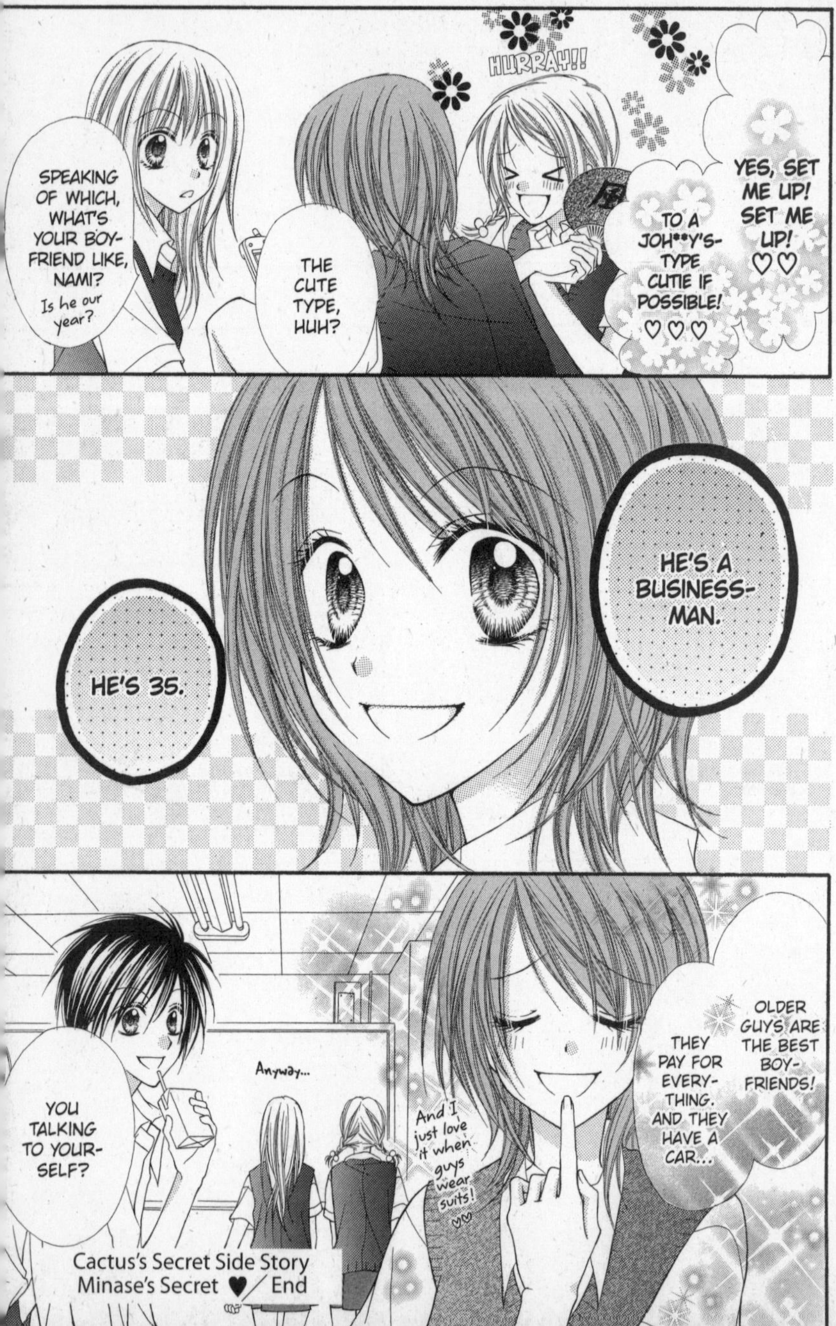
HURRAY!!
YES, SET ME UP! SET ME UP! ♡♡
TO A JOH**Y'S-TYPE CUTIE IF POSSIBLE! ♡♡♡
THE CUTE TYPE, HUH?
SPEAKING OF WHICH, WHAT'S YOUR BOY-FRIEND LIKE, NAMI?
Is he our year?
HE'S A BUSINESS-MAN.
HE'S 35.
OLDER GUYS ARE THE BEST BOY-FRIENDS!
THEY PAY FOR EVERY-THING. AND THEY HAVE A CAR...
And I just love it when guys wear suits! ♡
Anyway...
YOU TALKING TO YOUR-SELF?
Cactus's Secret Side Story
Minase's Secret ♥ / End

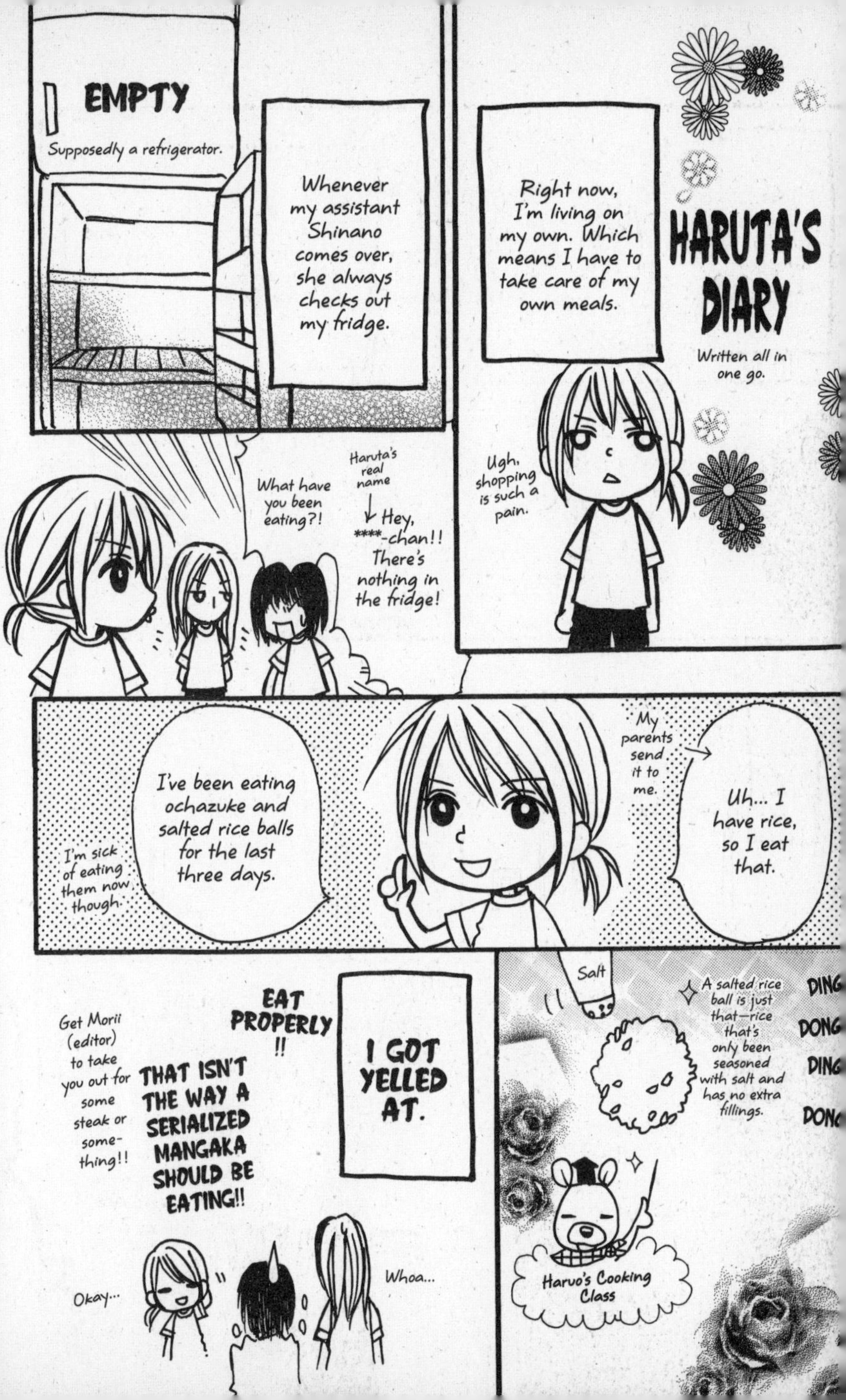
HARUTA'S DIARY
Written all in one go.
Right now, I'm living on my own. Which means I have to take care of my own meals.
Ugh, shopping is such a pain.
Whenever my assistant Shinano comes over, she always checks out my fridge.
EMPTY
Supposedly a refrigerator.
Hey, ****-chan!! There's nothing in the fridge!
Haruta's real name
What have you been eating?!
Uh... I have rice, so I eat that.
My parents send it to me.
I've been eating ochazuke and salted rice balls for the last three days.
I'm sick of eating them now though.
Salt
A salted rice ball is just that—rice that's only been seasoned with salt and has no extra fillings.
DING
DONG
DING
DONG
Haruo's Cooking Class
I GOT YELLED AT.
EAT PROPERLY!!
THAT ISN'T THE WAY A SERIALIZED MANGAKA SHOULD BE EATING!!
Get Morii (editor) to take you out for some steak or some-thing!!
Whoa...
Okay...

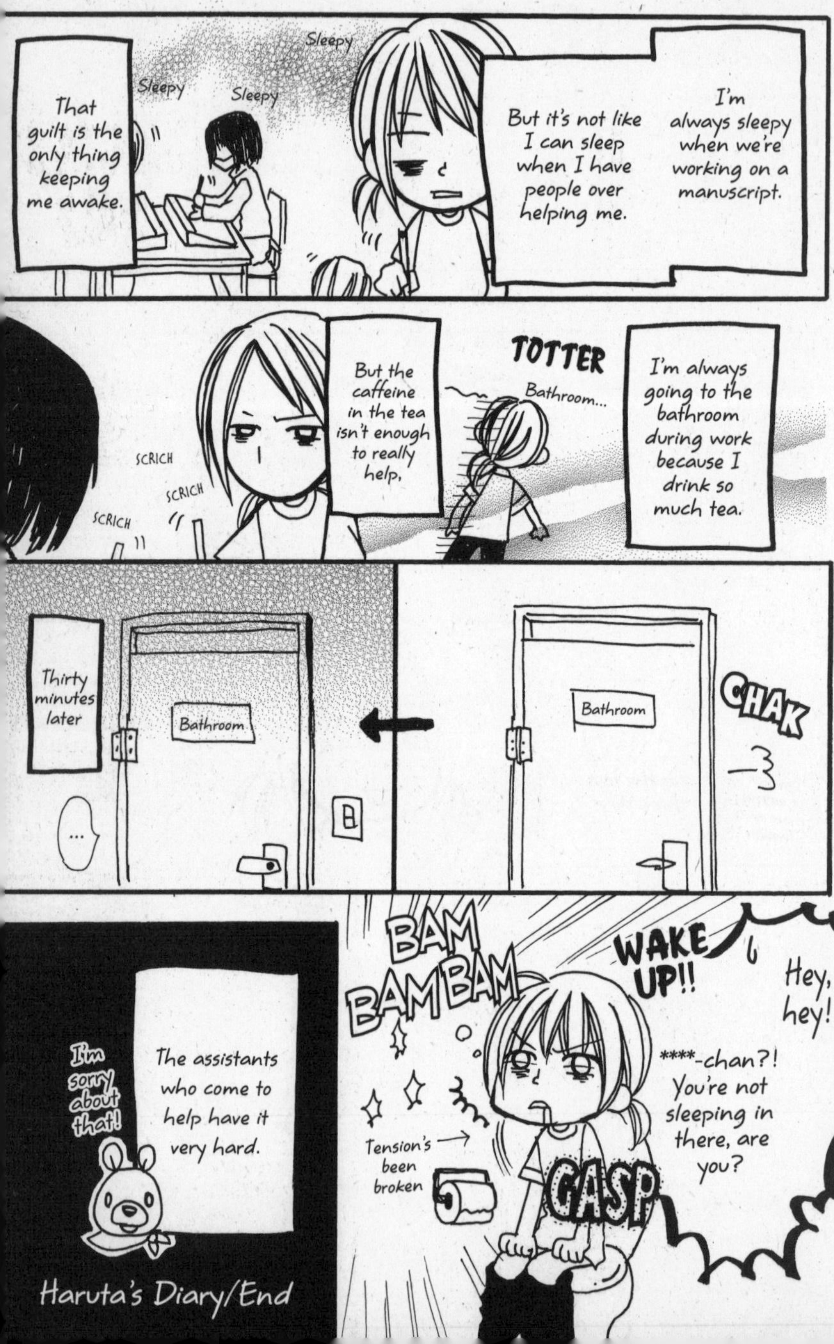
I'm always sleepy when we're working on a manuscript.
But it's not like I can sleep when I have people over helping me.
Sleepy
Sleepy
Sleepy
That guilt is the only thing keeping me awake.
I'm always going to the bathroom during work because I drink so much tea.
TOTTER
Bathroom...
But the caffeine in the tea isn't enough to really help.
SCRICH
SCRICH
SCRICH
Bathroom
CHAK
Thirty minutes later
Bathroom
...
Hey, hey!
****-chan?! You're not sleeping in there, are you?
WAKE UP!!
BAM BAM BAM
GASP
Tension's been broken
The assistants who come to help have it very hard.
I'm sorry about that!
Haruta's Diary/End

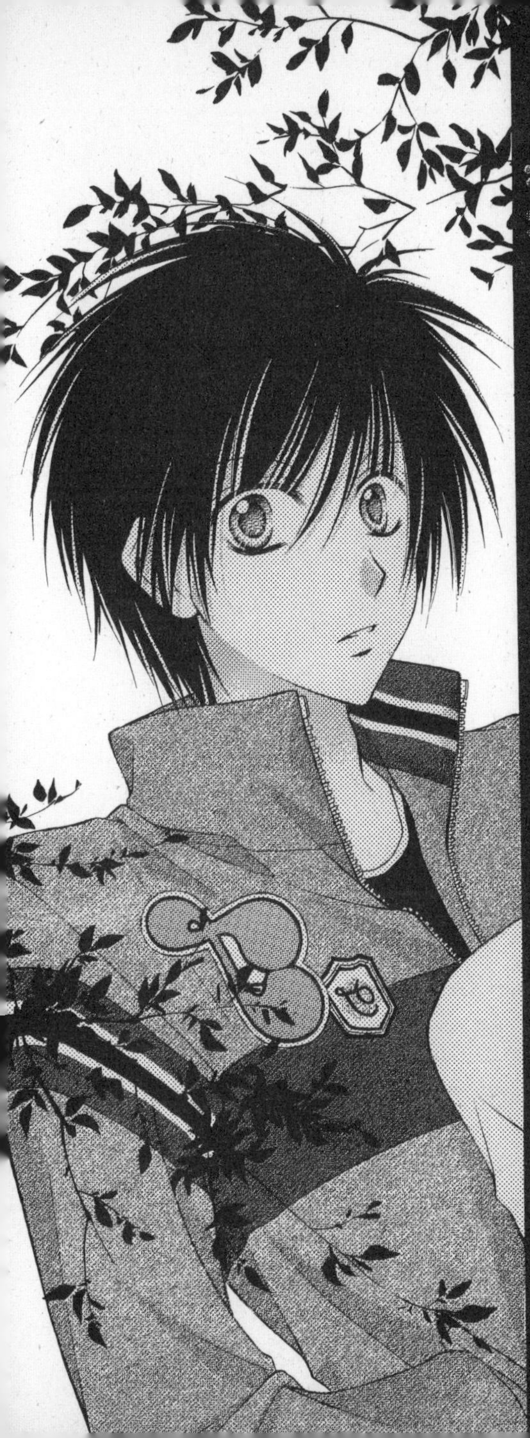

Special Thanks

M. Shinaho
M. Umezawa
A. Ryui
S. Nakano
R. Sawatari
R. Hayase

H. Kyono
H. Moriwake

and You!

Thank you
for reading.

2004.11
NaNa. Haruta

Notes

Honorifics
In Japan, people are usually addressed by their name plus
a suffix. The suffix shows familiarity or respect, depending
on the relationship.

MALE (familiar): first or last name + kun

FEMALE (familiar): first or last name + chan

ADULT (polite): last name + san

UPPERCLASSMAN (polite): last name + senpai

TEACHER or PROFESSIONAL: last name + sensei

CLOSE FRIENDS or LOVERS: first name only, no suffix

Terms
w-inds is a boy band known for their dancing skills.

On Octobter 23, 2004, a magnitude 6.8 earthquake rocked Niigata,
a prefecture to the northeast of Tokyo.

Tirol chocolates are tiny, square-shaped chocolates that cost about
10–20 cents each.

Some strict schools have random bag searches to make sure students
don't bring inappropriate things (i.e. video games, comics, etc.).

Noriyuki "Mackey" Makihara wrote the lyrics to "Sekai ni hitotsu dake
no hana" (The Only Flower of Its Kind in the World).

Joh**y's Entertainment is a talent agency known for its cute boys.

Ochazuke is a simple meal where tea (hot or cold) is poured over rice.
Toppings (pickled plum, salmon, seaweed, etc.) can be added to taste.

Even though I tried to be extra careful, I still ended up making 5-6 errors anyway when this was first printed in the magazine. I am such an idiot. Even readers in elementary school pointed out my mistakes. I really am an idiot. Well anyway, thank you very much for reading this manga that was written by such an idiot!

　-NANA HARUTA

Nana Haruta debuted in 2000 with *Ai no* ♥ *Ai no Shirushi* (Love's ♥, Love's Symbol) in *Ribon Original* magazine. She was born in Niigata Prefecture and likes reading manga and taking baths. Her other works include *Love Berrish!* and *Chocolate Cosmos*. Her current series, *Stardust ★ Wink*, is serialized in *Ribon* magazine.

Cactus's Secret
VOL. 2
Shojo Beat Edition

Story and Art by
Nana Haruta

TRANSLATION & ADAPTATION Su Mon Han
TOUCH-UP ART & LETTERING Deron Bennett
DESIGN Courtney Utt
EDITOR Nancy Thistlethwaite and Yuki Murashige

VP, PRODUCTION Alvin Lu
VP, SALES & PRODUCT MARKETING Gonzalo Ferreyra
VP, CREATIVE Linda Espinosa
PUBLISHER Hyoe Narita

SABOTEN NO HIMITSU © 2003 by Nana Haruta. All rights
reserved. First published in Japan in 2003 by SHUEISHA Inc.,
Tokyo. English translation rights arranged by SHUEISHA Inc.

Printed in Canada

Published by VIZ Media, LLC
P.O. Box 77010
San Francisco, CA 94107

10 9 8 7 6 5 4 3 2 1
First printing, June 2010

www.shojobeat.com

www.viz.com

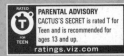

MANGA from the HEART

OTOMEN

STORY AND ART BY
AYA KANNO

VAMPIRE KNIGHT

STORY AND ART BY
MATSURI HINO

Natsume's BOOK of FRIENDS

STORY AND ART BY
YUKI MIDORIKAWA

Want to see more of what you're looking for?

Let your voice be heard!

shojobeat.com/mangasurvey

Help us give you more manga from the heart!